British Business in Asia since 1860

British Business in Asia since 1860

Edited by
R. P. T. DAVENPORT-HINES
and
GEOFFREY JONES

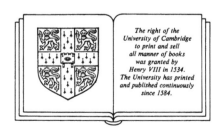

Cambridge University Press
Cambridge
New York   New Rochelle   Melbourne   Sydney

PUBLISHED BY THE PRESS SYNDICATE OF THE UNIVERSITY OF CAMBRIDGE
The Pitt Building, Trumpington Street, Cambridge, United Kingdom

CAMBRIDGE UNIVERSITY PRESS
The Edinburgh Building, Cambridge CB2 2RU, UK
40 West 20th Street, New York NY 10011–4211, USA
477 Williamstown Road, Port Melbourne, VIC 3207, Australia
Ruiz de Alarcón 13, 28014 Madrid, Spain
Dock House, The Waterfront, Cape Town 8001, South Africa

http://www.cambridge.org

© Cambridge University Press 1989

This book is in copyright. Subject to statutory exception
and to the provisions of relevant collective licensing agreements,
no reproduction of any part may take place without
the written permission of Cambridge University Press.

First published 1989
First paperback edition 2002

A catalogue record for this book is available from the British Library

Library of Congress cataloguing in publication data
British business in Asia since 1860/edited by
R. P. T. Davenport-Hines and Geoffrey Jones.
    p.   cm.
Includes index.
1. Investments, British – Asia – Case studies.
I. Davenport-Hines, R. P. T. (Richard Peter Treadwell), 1953–
II. Jones, Geoffrey.
HG5702.B75 1988
332.6 7341105–pc19   88-10212 CIP

ISBN 0 521 335272 hardback
ISBN 0 521 53058X paperback

Contents

List of illustrations	*page* viii
List of maps	x
List of tables	xi
List of contributors	xii
Preface	xv

1 British business in Asia since 1860 1
R. P. T. Davenport-Hines and Geoffrey Jones

1.1 Britain and Asia: enterprise, capital and trade	1
1.2 Structures and strategies of British business	9
1.3 British business performance in Asia	20
1.4 British business and the British government	22
1.5 Impact and response	25
1.6 The Asian impact on Britain	28

2 British business in Iran, 1860s–1970s 31
Frances Bostock and Geoffrey Jones

2.1 The business of imperialism	31
2.2 British business under the Qajars, 1860–1925	33
2.3 Conflict and contraction, 1925–54	45
2.4 The flawed miracle, 1954–78	58
2.5 The impact of British business	62
2.6 Conclusion	66

3 British business in Russian Asia since the 1860s: an 68
opportunity lost?
Christine White

3.1 Introduction	68
3.2 Hostage to Fortune: the British foreign direct investor in pre-war Russia	71
3.3 A new chance: the Soviet Russian market	79

vi *Contents*

| | 3.4 The eldorado revisited: British technical trade agreements and the development of modern Soviet industry | 88 |
| | 3.5 Conclusion | 89 |

4 British business in India, 1860–1970   92
B. R. Tomlinson

	4.1 Introduction	92
	4.2 Expatriate firms and managing agency houses	96
	4.3 Multinational enterprise	101
	4.4 State and enterprise in a colonial context	106
	4.5 Conclusion	112
	Appendix	114

5 Early British business in Thailand   117
Malcolm Falkus

	5.1 Political, economic and social context of Siam	117
	5.2 The phases of British enterprise in Siam	126
	5.3 British business from 1855 to the 1880s	128
	5.4 Teak and British enterprise	133
	5.5 Tin and British enterprise	146
	5.6 British business in Siam before 1940	155

6 British business in Malaysia and Singapore since the 1870s   157
Jean-Jacques van Helten and Geoffrey Jones

	6.1 A British success story	157
	6.2 The growth of Singapore	160
	6.3 British business and Malayan tin	161
	6.4 Rubber and the agency houses	171
	6.5 British banks in Malaya	175
	6.6 British business since 1945: diversification and *Bumiputra*	179
	6.7 Conclusion	187

7 British business in China, 1860s–1950s   189
Jürgen Osterhammel

	7.1 Introduction	189
	7.2 The nineteenth century: the age of trade	190
	7.3 Completing the system, 1895 to 1914	193
	7.4 Holding the line, 1914 to 1937	200
	7.5 A small rise and a deep fall, 1937 to 1957	210
	7.6 Conclusion	214

Contents vii

8 British business in Japan since 1868   217
R. P. T. Davenport-Hines and Geoffrey Jones

8.1 Diseases and miracles   217
8.2 British business and Meiji Japan   218
8.3 The inter-war years: British influence in decline   229
8.4 British business and the economic miracle   234
8.5 Conclusion   243

Notes   245
Index   295

Illustrations

1.1	Hong Kong harbour in the 1930s (courtesy of Hongkong Bank Group).	*page* 12
1.2	Des Voeux Road entrance to Hongkong and Shanghai Bank headquarters in Hong Kong, built in 1935 (courtesy of Hongkong Bank Group).	14
1.3	A Chinese rickshaw boy bearing a European burden in inter-war Queens Road, Hong Kong (courtesy of Hongkong Bank Group).	17
1.4	The new Hong Kong head office of the Hongkong Bank, erected in 1985 (courtesy of Hongkong Bank Group).	29
2.1	An oil strike at Masjed-e Soleyman, s.w. Iran, in 1909 (courtesy of British Petroleum).	37
2.2	Imperial Bank of Persia banknote (courtesy of Hongkong Bank Group).	43
2.3	One of two large span bridges across the Ab-e Cesar River, and one of the seven tunnels through rock, constructed by Costains in its eleven-mile section of the Trans-Iranian railway (courtesy of Richard Costain Ltd).	52
3.1	Bibi-Eibat oilfields, Baku (author's collection).	73
3.2	Plots at Grozny belonging to Spies Petroleum Company (author's collection)	74
3.3	Share certificate of Russo-Asiatic Consolidated Ltd (courtesy of Michael Viessid & Company).	76
3.4	J. Leslie Urquhart (1874–1933) (courtesy of BBC Hulton Picture Library).	81
4.1	The Chartered Mercantile Bank of India, London and China's Bombay office in 1854 (courtesy of Hongkong Bank Group).	95
4.2	The Bhandup works in Bombay of GKN's subsidiary Guest, Keen, Williams Ltd which made pressings under Sankey patents (courtesy of GKN plc).	103
4.3	The Bombay office of the Mercantile Bank of India in 1950 (courtesy of Hongkong Bank Group).	110

List of illustrations ix

5.1 Siam Forest Company's teak logs on the River Me Wang, c. 1905 (courtesy of Inchcape Group: Borneo Company Archives). 132

5.2 Siam Forest Company elephants at work in Muang Ngow district (courtesy of Inchcape Group: Borneo Company Archives). 135

5.3 European forest managers with their forresters in Chieng Mai, 1893 (courtesy of Mrs Brocklehurst). 137

5.4 Siam Forest Company office at Bangkok, c. 1910 (courtesy of Inchcape Group). 139

5.5 The first tin mining dredge in Siam at Phuket, c. 1907 (author's collection). 151

6.1 Sir Frank Swettenham (1850–1946) (courtesy of BBC Hulton Picture Library). 162

6.2 Ten-dollar note issued by Chartered Mercantile Bank of India, London and China at Penang, 1886 (courtesy of Hongkong Bank Group). 175

6.3 The Penang office of the Hongkong and Shanghai Bank in the late nineteenth century (courtesy of Hongkong Bank Group. 177

6.4 The Kuala Trengganu agency of the Mercantile Bank of India, 1940 (courtesy of Hongkong Bank Group). 178

6.5 Sime Darby meets *Bumiputra*, 1976 (Cartoon courtesy of *Far Eastern Economic Review*). 185

7.1 A. G. Stephen, Shanghai manager of the Hongkong Bank, and his *compradore*, c. 1910 (courtesy of Hongkong Bank Group). 194

7.2 A sampling crew and advertising placard bearers for British American Tobacco's Swallow brand at Kirin, central Manchuria (courtesy of BAT Industries). 196

7.3 BAT's private railway carriage with sleeping and living accommodation for its peregrinatory sales force (courtesy of BAT Industries). 205

7.4 Advertising hoardings on the building site of Shanghai's most luxurious department store, Whiteaway Laidlaw (courtesy of BAT Industries). 207

8.1 The Master of Sempill who headed mission to reorganise Japanese aviation during the 1920s (courtesy of BBC Hulton Picture Library). 220

8.2 Sir David Low depicts the British view of Japanese competition, 1934. 231

Maps

2.1	Iran before 1914	*page* 32
3.1	USSR in Asia, 1984	69
5.1	Modern Thailand	118
6.1	Modern Malaysia and Singapore	158

Tables

1.1	Foreign direct investment in Asia in 1975 by country of origin (book value in countries of origin, excluding oil, banking and insurance) in US$ at end of 1974	*page* 8
4.1	British subsidiary companies in India (1975) with assets of over Rs 100 million	102
4.2	Total British long-term private business investment in India, excluding banking and insurance, 1921–60	116
5.1	Composition of Siam's exports (% of value), 1890–1938	122
5.2	Tin output in Siam and British share, 1907–37	122
5.3	Foreign long-term capital investment in Siam, 1880–1938	123
5.4	Number of foreign vessels entering Bangkok, 1848–73	130
5.5	Nationality of ships arriving in Bangkok, 1861–82	131
5.6	Annual teak output sent to Bangkok, c. 1902	143
5.7	Share of British and Australian companies in Siam's tin production, 1910–18	153
6.1	Tin and rubber production in British Malaya and world market share, 1890–1960	163
8.1	British imports as a percentage of total Japanese imports, 1875–1965	218
8.2	Foreign banks in Japan, 1860–1914	223
8.3	Geographical sources of technology supplies to Japan, 1950–64	235
8.4	British foreign direct investment in Japan, April 1982	236

Contributors

Frances Bostock has been on the staff of the London School of Economics since 1982. Between then and 1985 she worked with Geoffrey Jones on his history of the British Bank of the Middle East. Subsequently she wrote, jointly with Geoffrey Jones, a biography of the Iranian central banker and economic planner, Abol Hassan Ebtehaj, *Planning and Power in Iran* (1988).

R. P. T. Davenport-Hines completed a doctorate on the history of the armaments industry (1918–36) at Cambridge in 1979, and worked at the London School of Economics during the years 1982–6. He edited the quarterly journal *Business History* in 1984–8, together with three collections of historical essays: *Speculators and Patriots* (1986), *Markets and Bagmen* (1986), and *Business in the Age of Reason* (1987). His biography *Dudley Docker* (1984) won the Wolfson Literary prize for 1985 and the Wadsworth Prize for business history in 1986. He has completed a history of the Glaxo pharmaceutical group and an account of the historical perspectives of human immuno-deficiency virus.

Malcolm Falkus is Professor of Economic History at the University of New England, Armidale, Australia. He taught for twenty-five years at the London School of Economics and has held visiting teaching posts in several countries including Australia, Japan, Uganda and Papua New Guinea. He has written extensively on international economic history, is author of *The Industrialization of Russia, 1700–1914* (1972), and is general editor for Macmillan of the series Studies in the Contemporary Japanese Economy. His current research interests include the economic history of Southeast Asia.

Geoffrey Jones is Reader in Business History in the Economics Department of Reading University. He took his degrees of MA and PhD from Cambridge University, and was Lecturer in Economic History at the London School of Economics between 1981 and 1988. He has been successively book review editor (1985–8) and co-editor since 1988 of

Business History. He is the author of *The State and the Emergence of the British Oil Industry* (1981), *Banking and Empire in Iran* (1986), *Banking and Oil* (1987) and (with Frances Bostock) *Planning and Power in Iran* (1988). He has also edited several books, including *British Multinationals: Origins, Management and Performance* (1986) and (with Peter Hertner) *Multinationals: Theory and History* (1986), and has translated and edited (with Grigori Gerenstein) P.V. Ol', *Foreign Capital in Russia* (English edition, 1983).

Jürgen Osterhammel teaches political science at the University of Freiburg im Breisgau, West Germany. He is author of *Britischer Imperialismus im Fernen Osten* (1983) and editor (with Wolfgang J. Mommsen) of *Imperialism and After: Continuities and Discontinuities* (1986) and *Max Weber and his Contemporaries* (1987). After completing a series of articles on the work of Joseph A. Schumpeter he is now preparing a study on the anthropological foundations of European political theory in the eighteenth century.

B. R. Tomlinson is a Senior Lecturer in the Department of Economic and Social History, University of Birmingham. He is author of *The Indian National Congress and the Raj, 1929–1942* (1976), *The Political Economy of the Raj 1914–1947: the Economics of Decolonization in India* (1979), and of articles on modern Indian and imperial history. His current research interest lies in developing comparative perspectives on the history of economic growth and development in modern India, China and Japan.

Jean-Jacques van Helten was formerly on the staff of the Institute of Commonwealth Studies and Visitor at the London School of Economics. After working as a lecturer at La Trobe University, the Polytechnic of North London and the University of London, he joined the public service in Canberra as an economist at the Office of National Assessments. He now works as an international banker in Melbourne.

Christine White left a career in broadcast engineering and editing in the USA to pursue research at Sidney Sussex College, Cambridge. Her doctoral thesis dealt with British and American economic and commercial relations with Soviet Russia during the period after 1917, and her current work is primarily concerned with Western business in the USSR. She is now Assistant Professor in History at Penn State University.

Preface

This book is a study of British business in Asia since the 1860s. The focus is on business enterprise, rather than on trade or investment flows, and the perspective is therefore that of business history rather than macro-economic investment or trade theory. We asked each author to write a survey essay, incorporating the latest research, because our concern in this volume is to offer an overview of long-term trends. Authors were not constricted by editorial controls, however, and the essays in this collection show a variety of methodologies and conclusions as well as chronological periods. Such variety is deliberate: this book seeks to provoke research and debate rather than to enforce *ex cathedra* judgments on any subject. In line with this policy the introductory chapter puts the individual essays in a wider context and identifies some of the more important issues, but does not pretend to offer a comprehensive synthesis.

We hope that this book will attract a wide range of readers: business historians wanting to know how British business performed overseas; Third World specialists concerned with foreign enterprises in their local economies; economists and political scientists interested in multinationals and their antecedents; even – ideally – contemporary Western business people seeking a long-term perspective on current situations in Asian markets. As a result we have felt obliged, especially in chapter 1, to discuss matters and make statements which specialists will regard as elementary if not trite. Our excuse is a belief that most British business historians know little if anything about Asia; most Third World historians know little about current preoccupations in Western business history; and few economists or entrepreneurs have any historical knowledge at all.

The volume is organised on a country by country basis. The diversity of Asian countries justifies this approach, although our selection of particular countries will probably be regarded as idiosyncratic. We believe that the inclusion of Russian Asia and Iran – both of which are geographically part of the Asian continent – is valuable in widening the focus of the volume, and in challenging occasionally narrow Western conventions about what comprises 'Asia'.

xvi *Preface*

Preliminary versions of the essays contained in this collection were pre-circulated and discussed at a conference at the London School of Economics in September 1986. The meeting was attended by all the contributors except one, together with others who commented on individual papers and general themes. We are grateful to these commentators: Ian Brown, Gill Burke, Clive Dewey and Ian Nish. The footnotes to individual chapters contain more specific acknowledgements by contributors.

Davenport-Hines received a grant of £2,970 from the Nuffield Foundation which eased the preparation of this collection. As a result of this grant, Charlie Wilkinson undertook research at the Public Record Office, the School of Oriental and African Studies and elsewhere which enhanced chapters 1, 2, 6 and particularly 8. Jonathan Smith rendered the disordered holographs of chapters 1 and 8 into typescript acceptable to the printers. Their humour and insight sustained the preparation of this book, and were a joyous discovery amidst the dreary exigencies of academic life. We also thank Susan Crawshaw, Helen Denore and Rosemary Hudson for typing other sections of the volume.

We are grateful to the Hongkong Bank for permission to cite material from their archives in chapters 2, 6 and 8, and also for providing several photographs used in this book. Two of the Bank's officers, Margaret Lee in Hong Kong and S. W. Muirhead in London, have been particularly helpful. Other illustrations were provided by the kindness of R. Glyn Davies of BAT Industries.

We would like to thank the peoples of Asia, especially those of China, Hong Kong, Japan, Malaysia, Singapore and Thailand, for their cultures, hospitality and cuisines, which have done so much to inspire our burgeoning interest in the region.

1 British business in Asia since 1860

R. P. T. Davenport-Hines and Geoffrey Jones

1.1 Britain and Asia: enterprise, capital and trade

The purpose of this book is to provide a long-term historical perspective on British business in Asia. Its growth, impact and decline since the mid-nineteenth century are scrutinised in Iran, Russian Asia, India, Thailand, Malaya, China and Japan. The focus is on business enterprise: that is, on British-owned and managed organisations which had manufacturing, distributive, extractive or financial operations in Asia. In the 1980s most such ventures are multinational corporations or international banks. A hundred years ago, however, the diversity of British enterprises in Asia was so wide as to seem almost illimitable: they were crucial to the first stages of modern economic growth in that continent.

Most research on the economic relationships between the West and Asia has concentrated on flows of capital and trade,[1] but the significance of British business in Asia transcends such flows. British companies, for example, often invested capital in Asian subsidiaries, but also mobilised local savings to support their operations, or ploughed back profits. As well as capital they transferred skills, technologies, management structures and cultural attitudes across boundaries. In the nineteenth century, in particular, British capital exports to Asia often took the form of portfolio investment – the acquisition of foreign securities by British individuals or institutions without control over the management of such funds – and was unrelated to British business activity in Asia. Again, although British trading companies often marketed British goods in Asia, and British overseas banks financed this trade, when British manufacturing companies established plants in Asian countries they substituted for British imports.

'Asia' is a concept invented by European geographers rather than a description of political, economic or cultural unity: since the second half of the nineteenth century the countries or regions treated in this volume have shown marked diversity. Some had fallen under the control of the great imperial powers of Europe. In 1858 the anachronistic rule of the East India Company over a large area of the Indian sub-continent was

2   *R. P. T. Davenport-Hines and Geoffrey Jones*

replaced by the direct rule of the British Crown. Over the next fifty years India was the proverbial jewel of the British Empire. The gradual annexation of Burma, begun in 1826, was concluded sixty years later when, under Lord Dufferin's viceroyalty, the Alaungpaya dynasty was dethroned and its territories consolidated into British India. Further east, from the late eighteenth century, the British had established themselves in the 'Straits Settlement' of Penang, Malacca and Singapore. Over a period of four decades after 1874 a series of treaties with states on the Malay Peninsula brought them under British control. Most of Siberia had been incorporated in Tsarist Russia since the mid-seventeenth century, although in the late nineteenth century the region experienced a wave of emigration from European Russia which paralleled the development of the American West. The boundaries of the southern empire also moved southwards into the Caucasus during the nineteenth century, incorporating much territory previously ruled by Persia or independent Islamic states. The other four countries – Persia (known increasingly as Iran after 1927, and formally so from 1935), China, Japan and Siam (renamed Thailand in 1939) – remained independent, although subject to varying degrees of interference from Western powers.

The continent's political diversity has persisted in the twentieth century. Russian Asia became part of the world's first socialist state following the Bolshevik Revolution of 1917. In 1949, after a bitter civil war, the People's Republic of China was born, and embarked, at least for a time, on a similar course of socialist development. During the first half of the century Japan emerged as an imperialist power in its own right. By 1942 Japan controlled, albeit briefly, large areas of Asia. Total defeat in 1945 was followed by Japan's rehabilitation as a democratic ally of the United States. In South Asia the retreat of the British Empire led to the creation of the independent states of India, Pakistan, Ceylon (called Sri Lanka since 1972) and Burma in 1947–8, followed in 1957 by Malaya (renamed Malaysia after 1963), from which Singapore seceded in 1965. By the mid-1980s Hong Kong was the only British colony left in Asia. Thailand and Iran followed pro-American policies during and after the Cold War of the 1950s, but the exile of the Shah of Iran in 1978 followed by the creation of an Islamic republic led to a major political reorientation in that country.

The arrangement of this volume as country case-studies is an acknowledgement of Asian diversity, and of the need to study the experience of British business within each unique national market. Before examining the nature of British business in Asia, however, the remainder of this section will sketch the changing patterns in trade and investment between Britain and Asia.

The economic predominance which Britain acquired in nineteenth-

British business in Asia since 1860   3

century Asia was, in part, the result of the world pre-eminence which it had secured in cotton textile manufacture and shipbuilding as a result of the Industrial Revolution. British penetration of Asian markets was assisted by the political control which the East India Company enjoyed over large areas of India from the second half of the eighteenth century, and by the British possession of Singapore and Hong Kong. Singapore was taken by Sir Stamford Raffles for a reluctant East India Company in 1819, and was formally ceded by the Dutch in 1824. Hong Kong's cession to Britain by China in 1841 was one of the chief results of the First Opium War. Both islands developed as flourishing entrepôts through which British goods and capital flowed into Asia. The termination of the East India Company's stranglehold on British trade with Asia – in 1813 the company's monopoly of Indian trade was abolished, and in 1834 it also lost its monopoly of China trade – opened floodgates through which British business and trade poured into the continent.

By the second half of the nineteenth century the trade between Britain and Asia was mutually important. In 1860 33% of British exports by value went to Asia (excluding Russian Asia and Iran). The bulk of these – 13% of total British exports – went to India, and the next largest amount – 3% – to China. By 1880 the Asian share had fallen to 21%, and it remained around this level until the First World War. In 1913 24% of British exports went to Asia, with 14% going to India, 3% each to China and Japan, and 1% to Malaya.[2] In 1913 India was the largest single market for British exports. Asia, especially India and China, was particularly important to British cotton textile exporters. In 1850 Asia took 24% of British cotton textile exports by value: India took 18% and China 4%. By 1913 Asia took 47% of British cotton textile exports: India took 28% and China 10%. India ranked as the largest single market for British cotton goods between 1843 and 1939, while China ranked second only to India between 1869 and 1926.[3] Exports of manufactured goods to Asia – and to India in particular – enabled Britain to pay off its deficits with continental Europe and the United States from which foodstuffs and manufactured goods were bought.[4]

From an Asian perspective, Britain was the major supplier of cotton goods for most Asian countries, as well as a major market for the primary commodities which formed the great proportion of Asian exports before 1914. Britain provided over 80% of Indian imports in 1870 and over 60% in 1913.[5] The other Asian countries treated in this volume had a similar trading relationship with Britain before 1914, although in some countries, notably China and Japan, Britain's significance as a trading partner began declining in the late nineteenth century. Until the mid-1880s Britain was the leading exporter to Japan, but thereafter its importance receded as Japan imported relatively fewer finished manufactured goods and more

4   *R. P. T. Davenport-Hines and Geoffrey Jones*

raw materials and semi-manufactured goods. By 1914 Britain provided under 20% of Japanese imports. The British proportion of Chinese foreign trade also declined over the period. Its share of Chinese exports appears to have fallen from 62% in 1868 to 4% in 1913, a fall partly associated with the shifting British consumer preference for Indian tea, while the British share of imports into China seems to have declined from 33% to 17% over the same period.[6]

Asia was also important to Britain before the First World War as a recipient of capital exports. Britain was the world's largest capital exporting economy before 1914. Estimates of the size and direction of this capital outflow present a confusing array, partly because of data inadequacies, and partly because writers have been concerned with different measurements, such as capital transfers or new issues on the London Stock Exchange.[7] We cannot in this chapter join the debate on the size of British capital exports, but there is general agreement that although Asia was never the largest recipient of British capital during the period 1860–1914, the sums invested there, especially in India, were large. According to the estimate of British holdings of overseas capital by Sir George Paish, 10% of British investment in 1913 was invested in the Indian empire and a further 1.2% was invested in China. British investment in other Asian countries was tiny.

Such estimates are unfortunately concerned with *total* British investment, rather than *private* business investment. The bulk of British foreign investment in India before 1914 was in government stock and railways, while as much as 80% of British investment in China in the same period was probably in railways. Figures for capital inflows into Indian railways or public debt bonds, however, are scarcely relevant to the operations of British firms or businesses in Asia. It is almost impossible to disaggregate the public and private capital figures for the period before 1939. At best the available foreign investment statistics serve as proxies indicating the scale of British business enterprise in particular countries.

From the Asian perspective, Britain was the largest single supplier of foreign capital to the region before 1914, although there was substantial French investment in Russian Asia, while Russian investment was larger than British in Iran before 1914. Again, however, it is impossible to give figures for the British percentage of overall private capital formation, and even estimates of inward foreign investment are open to objections.[8] Many Government of India securities, for example, were bought in India itself.[9] It was common for the designation 'British' to refer to the British Empire rather than the United Kingdom: thus Australian capital in Siam was often described as 'British'. Some Chinese entrepreneurs in Asia were British nationals whose enterprises were occasionally designated as British. Nevertheless generalisations about total British foreign invest-

British business in Asia since 1860   5

ment are possible. India derived almost all its foreign investment from the United Kingdom before 1914, while Britain was the largest single source of foreign capital for China. Even Japan was a substantial borrower between 1899 and 1914 – her government raising about £200 million during that period – and Britain again was the largest single source of these funds. The bulk of this investment was in government and railway stocks.

During the inter-war years trading and financial links between Britain and Asia diminished. Asia's significance as a market for British low-quality goods declined, partly because of the growth of import-substitution in Asian countries and the decreasing competitiveness of British goods, and partly because of changes in Britain's domestic industrial structure, whereby traditional export-oriented staple industries were superseded by 'new' industries, which either sold to the home market or to other advanced economies. During the 1920s Britain continued to enjoy an overall surplus on its trade with the Asian economies, although this surplus was a much smaller percentage of her deficit with the Dollar Area than it was before 1914. During the 1930s, however, Britain's trade with India, China and Japan entered deficit, ending the era when her surplus with Asia met her trading deficits with the United States and continental Europe. The biggest single factor in this changing pattern was the decline of British exports of cotton piece goods to India from 2,507 million square yards in 1913 to 356 million in 1937, the main cause of which was the development of the Indian domestic cotton industry under tariff protection.[10] India remained, however, the largest single market for British exports of cotton piece goods.

Britain remained significant as a market and as a supplier of imports to Asia in the inter-war years, but there were notable changes in relations. Britain was the leading supplier of Indian imports and the leading destination for Indian exports throughout the period. However, while Britain's share of Indian exports rose from 25% to 33% between 1918 and 1938, its role as a supplier of Indian imports fell from 54% to 29.9%, a trend associated with increasing Japanese textile imports and supplies of petroleum and machinery from the United States.[11] Britain's share of Chinese exports stagnated around 9% between 1919 and 1936, while her share of Chinese imports rose slightly from 9% to 12%. Britain remained a significant trading partner of the other Asian countries. It ranked second after the United States as a purchaser of Malayan exports (mainly rubber, tin, coconuts and palm oil), and was Malaya's main supplier of cotton textiles in the 1920s before being overtaken by Japan in the 1930s. Britain was also the main supplier of imports to Siam in the 1920s, but was supplanted in this role by Japan in the following decade.[12] Britain was the main supplier of imports to Iran from the First World War until the 1930s,

6   *R. P. T. Davenport-Hines and Geoffrey Jones*

and the main recipient of Iran's exports (including oil) from 1920 until 1950.

During the inter-war years the United States replaced Britain as the world's major international lender, but the latter remained the leading creditor in Asia, although during the 1930s the overall level of British investment declined. There was a rise in the relative importance of Asia, and especially India, as a recipient of British investment, and a corresponding decline in the importance of other regions, notably the United States. Britain remained Asia's most important source of capital in the inter-war years.[13] By 1938 Britain was by far the most important source of foreign capital for India, the largest foreign investor in Siam and Malaya, and the second largest investor (after Japan) in China.

The forty years after 1945 saw a decline in every aspect of Anglo-Asian economic relations. The collapse of British staple exports to Asian markets was completed. The post-war years saw a restructuring of British exports away from low-technology products to more sophisticated goods, notably chemicals, electrical engineering products and – until the 1970s – motor cars. This change in the composition of British exports led to a decline in trade with the less developed world, including Asia. In the 1950s British trade with developing countries in the Sterling Area remained substantial, but the principal growth in exports, especially after 1960, was located in Western Europe. There was a similar shift in the structure of British imports at the expense of foodstuffs and raw materials. Between 1951 and 1981 the percentage of manufactured goods in total British imports rose from 19.7% to 62.5%. Before 1960 trade with Asia, and the Sterling Area generally remained important for Britain, but as manufactures have become a major component of imports, so British imports were drawn increasingly from advanced industrial countries.[14] The percentage of Britain's exports going to Western Europe and North America increased from 57% to 73% between 1964 and 1984, while the percentage of Britain's imports coming from those regions rose from 54.5% to 76% over the same period. In contrast the relative importance of most Asian countries in Britain's trade stagnated or declined. India became much less significant as a trading partner in this period: only 1.1% of Britain's exports went there in 1984 compared to 3% twenty years previously, while Britain obtained only 0.7% of her imports from India compared to 2.5% in 1964. Only Japan grew in importance in Britain's trade, its share of British imports expanding from 1.3% in 1964 to 5% in 1984.

Just as the importance of Asian trade for Britain declined after the Second World War, and especially after 1969, so the significance of British trade for Asia has fallen. At the beginning of the 1960s Britain was still an important trading partner to the successor states of its Indian

British business in Asia since 1860 7

empire and to the Malay States. Britain, for example, took 29% of Ceylon's exports, 25% of India's, 16% of Pakistan's and 11.5% of the exports of the Malay States. Britain remained a significant source of imports. In the 1960s she supplied 21% of Indian imports, 19% of Ceylon's, 18.5% of Pakistan's and 22% of the imports of the Malay States. Yet a decline in Britain's importance was evident, in line with the United Kingdom's diminishing role in the trade of the world's less developed countries.[15]

Asia, and particularly India, remained an important area for British foreign investment after 1945. Most of this took the form of direct investment (involving control over the use of the capital) rather than portfolio investment, and the improvement in statistical information enables a clearer quantification of British private business investment. British foreign direct investment after 1945 preferred the Commonwealth and the Sterling Area, initially at least because of British government exchange controls. In 1957 about 12% of total British foreign investment was in Asia. By 1962 India was the fifth most important recipient of British direct investment (measured by book values of accumulated investments, and excluding oil, banking and insurance) and Malaysia was sixth. During the 1960s, and especially after Britain joined the European Economic Community in 1972, British investment re-aligned towards the United States and Western Europe. In 1981 only Hong Kong was included (in eighth place) in a list of Britain's top ten investment territories.[16] In the late 1950s India was the recipient of around 7.5% of British direct foreign investment, but this declined to 4.5% by 1970 and later fell further.[17]

Although Asia's importance for British investors dwindled after the 1960s, Britain remained a major source of capital for certain Asian countries. An estimate of foreign direct investment in Asia in 1975 given in Table 1.1 shows the United Kingdom as third largest investor after the United States and Japan. Britain retained its position as the largest single investor in India and Malaysia, and large sums were also invested in Pakistan and two Newly Industrialised Countries (NICs), Hong Kong and Singapore. The People's Republic of China ceased to be an area for British investment from 1949 until the era of economic liberalisation in the 1980s, and Britain never regained its position as a significant source of capital for China. At the end of 1986 the three largest investors in China (in order of importance) were Hong Kong, the United States and Japan.

A peculiarity of British direct investment in Asia after 1945 was the continuing low share in manufacturing. Well under 50% of the British direct investment shown in Table 1.1 was in manufacturing, despite the exclusion of important banking and insurance investments, especially in Hong Kong and Singapore. Britain's small contribution to manufacturing in Hong Kong and Singapore after 1945 is particularly striking given the

8 R. P. T. Davenport-Hines and Geoffrey Jones

Table 1.1 *Foreign direct investment in Asia in 1975 by country of origin (book value in countries of origin, excluding oil, banking and insurance) in US$ (millions) at end of 1974*

	United States	Japan	United Kingdom	Other	Total
Hong Kong	730	190	330	270	1,520
India	290	60	640	590	1,580
Indonesia	310	650	30	690	1,680
South Korea	100	380	–	90	570
Malaysia	100	180	640	390	1,310
Pakistan	50	small	100	140	290
Philippines	530	110	10	150	800
Singapore	320	130	130	380	960
Taiwan	260	120	small	400	780
Thailand	50	150	40	140	380
TOTALS	2,740	1,970	1,920	3,240	9,870

Source: A. Edwards, *Asian International Expansion* (London, 1977), p. 43

large British involvement in those countries. A large proportion of British investment was in agricultural and forestry activities, notably in Malaysia.

Several conclusions emerge from this sketch of trade and investment relations between Britain and Asia. The relationship was intimate before 1914, remained strong despite modifications in the inter-war years, and considerably weakened thereafter. Asia has been highly significant for the British economy over a long period. Before 1914 the region's trading deficit with Britain played a key role in the latter's balance of payments. Trade relations between Asia and Britain loosened during the inter-war years, but Asia remained a major area of British investment up to the 1960s. Additionally, in terms of absolute size, and ignoring the special cases of the Hong Kong and Singapore entrepôts, trading and investment relations between Britain and India had the highest significance. China was never as important for Britain, or Britain as important for China, and after 1949 their economic relationship was all but obliterated. British trade and investment links with smaller Asian economies were always less significant for the British economy, but at least until the 1930s Britain was a leading market and a source of imports for many of them.

The rest of this chapter explores themes suggested by the case-studies in the remainder of the volume. Section 1.2 examines the structure and organisation of British business in Asia. Section 1.3 discusses the performance of British business. Section 1.4 explores the links between British business and British diplomacy. Section 1.5 looks at the impact of British business on Asia, and Section 1.6 the response of Asia.

1.2 Structures and strategies of British business

Most discussion of nineteenth-century British investment in Asia assumes that this investment was overwhelmingly portfolio in nature, outstandingly investment in government and railway stocks. However recent research indicates that as much as 40% of British overseas investment even by 1914 may have taken the form of direct investment, involving the ownership and management of a foreign business operation.[18] J. H. Dunning suggests that total foreign direct investment in Asia in 1914 amounted to US$2,950 million, or 20.9% of the world total, of which $1,100 million was in China and $450 million in India and Ceylon.[19] The correlation of these sums to those for aggregate British investment is uncertain, yet it is clear that there were many British-owned and managed enterprises operating in nineteenth-century Asia. These were the conduits for British direct investment in the region and for British trade.

Despite the diversity of structure and function, these enterprises were inter-related. At the most basic level, there were individual British nationals who established firms in Asia, usually transferring capital from the United Kingdom in the process. Such individuals do not fit the category of 'direct' investment: British entrepreneurs who established businesses in the United States in the same period are classified as emigrants. Yet in some cases they played important roles in Asian countries. Thomas Glover in Japan (see p. 225) is one example. The British concession-hunters who were active in nineteenth-century China and Iran are others. In China such individuals were usually rapacious and their concessions often negative in result, but elsewhere, for example when British concessionaires in Iran secured rights on which large British oil and banking interests grew, they facilitated the flow of full-scale foreign direct investment into Asian countries.[20]

Two regions of the United Kingdom were prominent in exporting entrepreneurs. The profusion of Scottish emigrants has often been noted: the late nineteenth century saw a considerable Scots influence in Japan.[21] In addition, the decline of Cornish tin mining from the 1850s was followed by a flow of Cornish savings and emigrants into overseas mining concerns in Malaya and elsewhere.

A more clearly recognisable form of British direct investment was the expatriate firms which spread across Asia in the nineteenth century. Such organisations have been described by Mira Wilkins, in the context of British investment in the United States, as 'free-standing firms'.[22] In Asia they took two forms. The first was of a British-registered company with a board of directors, perhaps supported by a small secretariat, which ran a Russian oil company or an Indian jute mill. These companies owned no oil

10   *R. P. T. Davenport-Hines and Geoffrey Jones*

or jute interests within Britain itself, and typically their business was conducted in only one foreign country. The other form was a locally registered company, which was established by locally resident British business interests. In practice these two types of companies are scarcely to be differentiated. Their boards of directors consisted overwhelmingly of British nationals, although some boards sat in London and others in Asia. Their senior management was almost always British. Place of registration gives no consistent guide to sources of capital, although as a general rule locally registered companies seem to have drawn at least some of their capital from locally resident Europeans and occasionally Asians.

In India expatriate firms were often managed by 'managing agents', organisations which developed in the early nineteenth century to control the management of firms in many sectors. This system spread from India westwards to Iran and eastwards to the Malayan peninsula, as British merchants expanded their activities. In Malaya the 'agency houses' emerged as diversified business groups, active in trading, plantations and (after 1945) manufacturing. Outside South and Southeast Asia, where the managing agency system did not evolve, it was common for expatriate firms, like British oil companies in Russia, to be 'allied' in groups of one kind or another, usually with interlocking directorships.

A related phenomenon was the British trading and shipping companies active in Asia. Companies such as Jardine Matheson, Butterfield & Swire, Dodwells, Gray Mackenzie, Peninsula and Orient, and the British Indian Steam Navigation Company were the agents by which British trade with Asia expanded in the nineteenth century, and they were important to the history of British overseas business. Several such companies gave their name and reputation to support subsidiary trading, manufacturing, mining or financial enterprises and became the nexus of investment groups with geographically dispersed interests. British companies were often active in several Asian countries, and were thus more 'international' businesses than the British expatriate firms. They were also, as the chapters below demonstrate, not simply marketing ventures. In late nineteenth-century Japan and China British trading companies entered manufacturing. In Thailand the teak industry was pioneered by trading companies such as the Borneo Company, which also had strong trading interests in Singapore, Borneo and Java.[23]

Another form of British enterprise in nineteenth-century Asia was the progenitor of the modern extractive multinational. Iran's small 'free-standing' British oil company in Iran developed into the giant British Petroleum group. Another of the world's largest oil companies, the Royal Dutch Shell Group, derived indirectly from Asian business, and directly from a merger in 1907 between a British company, the Shell Transport and Trading Company, and a Dutch concern, the Royal Dutch Petroleum

British business in Asia since 1860   11

Company. Shell started as a merchant firm, trading in the Far East, which in the mid-1880s began marketing Russian oil in Asia and which in 1898 discovered oil in Dutch Borneo. Royal Dutch struck oil in the Dutch East Indies in the early 1890s, and marketed it in neighbouring Asian countries. After 1907 the Group, which was 60% Dutch-owned, expanded rapidly, including the acquisition of large Russian oil interests (see p. 72). By 1914 Shell controlled almost 20% of total Russian oil production.[24] It was also the major supplier of oil to China and Japan, although its schemes to establish or buy oilfields in the Indian empire and Iran were blocked by the British and colonial Indian governments.[25]

Examples of these different forms of enterprise were to be found in other Asian countries not covered in this collection. In Burma examples of free-standing firms included Steel Brothers & Company, with a commercial empire based from 1870 on Burma's resources of rice, timber, oil and cotton, with other interests in imports, shipping agencies and insurance; the Bombay Burmah Trading Corporation founded in 1863 to develop Burmese teak forests; the Irrawaddy Flotilla and Burmese Steam Navigation Company which was registered at Glasgow in 1865 and managed locally by agents; and the nascent extractive multinational, the Burmah Oil Company, formed in 1886.[26]

Another category of British enterprise should be mentioned, although it receives little attention in the chapters of this book. From the late nineteenth century British interests were involved in exporting indentured or other labourers from Asian countries such as India or China either to other undeveloped areas of Asia or (most notoriously) to Transvaal, where the 'coolie trade' became politically controversial in 1905–6. Labour use and the organisation of work-forces by foreign business in India indeed raises a large and complex congeries of questions requiring an interdisciplinary approach: it is hoped that this book will prompt further research on the internal organisation of foreign firms, and the ways in which management and labour adapted to different Asiatic environments. Too little is known about the roles played by native staff at different levels within managerial hierarchies or about the use of contractual labour in different local cultures.[27]

A final form of British enterprise in nineteenth-century Asia was overseas banks, which appear from the second quarter of the nineteenth century. Some were predominantly concerned with banking in a given territory. In India, a number of joint stock banks, such as Agra Bank and Alliance Bank of Simla, were promoted by locally resident Europeans. A distinctive group of British overseas banks comprised the 'exchange banks', which specialised in short-term finance of international trade, by providing bill finance and overseas currencies, and often had branch networks in a number of countries. In nineteenth-century Asia the leading

1.1 Hong Kong harbour, looking towards Kowloon, in the 1930s.

British overseas banks included the Oriental Bank Corporation, which was founded in 1845 and was for several decades the most important British bank in the East, the Chartered Bank of India, Australia and China (1853), the Chartered Mercantile Bank of India, London and China (1857), and the Hongkong and Shanghai Banking Corporation (or Hongkong Bank), which was founded in 1864 and by 1914 was the most powerful bank in the East.[28]

These banks were striking examples of nineteenth-century international business. Exchange banks were distinguished by the spread of their branch networks, and by the range of their banking activities. In the early 1880s, for example, the Oriental Bank Corporation's branches spanned Africa and Australia as well as Asia. Its most important Asian branches included Bombay, Calcutta, Colombo, Foochow, Kobe, Hong Kong, Kandy, Madras, Shanghai, Singapore and Yokohama. Usually the Eastern exchange banks confined their branch networks to Asia, but they were widely spread in the region. By the 1900s the Hongkong Bank had a branch network covering every country discussed in this book except Russian Asia. At the turn of the century British banks had introduced modern banking into every one of the countries, except Russian Asia (although four British banks jointly formed the South Russian Banking Agency to finance the export of manganese ore from the Caucasus in 1919).

British business in Asia since 1860   13

The second feature of British overseas banks in Asia was the diversity of their business. In the nineteenth century they financed international trade and undertook exchange operations. They served therefore as agents in the spread of British trade. Most of the banks initially established their branches at the ports of the East, but from the late nineteenth century they began to open offices in the interiors, and became more involved in domestic banking and trade. The Chartered Bank of India, Australia and China, for example, opened its branches in Taiping and Kuala Lumpur in Malaysia in 1888, and at Amritsar in the Punjab in 1910.[29] The overseas banks also floated loans for Asian countries on the London Stock Exchange, acted as state banks, issued banknotes, and even, as chapter 2 (on Iran) discusses, became involved in infrastructural investments.

The British overseas banks were an unstable component of British business in nineteenth-century Asia. There were major crises in 1864–6 and in the early 1890s, when some banks floundered and others had to be reconstructed. A major source of instability for British banks in Asia was the depreciation of the region's silver-based currencies in terms of gold from the mid-1870s. This depreciation, which was related to large increases in world silver production, was important to the region's economic history, and influenced the pattern of British trade and investment. It was often argued by London financial interests in the late nineteenth century that British investors refrained from heavy investment because of the instability of the rupee exchange. Banks with balance sheets in sterling but whose businesses were located in silver-based currencies had exchange instability added to their problems. When such banks transferred sterling capital to support their business in Asian countries, depreciation in the silver exchange rate meant a devaluation in the sterling worth of such transferred capital. The early 1890s proved a particularly difficult period on the silver exchanges. The New Oriental Bank Corporation (successor to the Oriental Bank Corporation, which had failed in 1884) was liquidated in 1892; the Chartered Mercantile Bank of India, London and China was forced into reconstruction in 1892; and the Imperial Bank of Persia, only founded in 1889, had to write down its capital by one-third in 1894. However, poor management or bad investment decisions were more important influences in these crises than the 'silver problem'.[30] A greater hazard for British banks was their dependence on the finance of primary commodity exports, whose price fluctuations would wreak disaster. A crisis in the coffee economy of Ceylon in the early 1880s ruined the Oriental Bank Corporation.

Instability in British Eastern banking was aggravated by the difficulty of managing wide networks of branches. There were particular difficulties between London-based boards of directors, anxious to see their banks follow conventional British banking principles, and their managers in

1.2 Des Voeux Road entrance to Hongkong and Shanghai Bank headquarters in Hong Kong, built in 1935.

Asia who felt they needed to adapt – partially at least – to local conventions on, for example, security for loans. This problem was mitigated by the Hongkong Bank by retaining its headquarters in Hong Kong, where it had been founded by a group of merchants.[31]

The Hongkong Bank, however, illustrates some of the difficulties of defining 'British' business in Asia. In some senses the Bank represented an international merchant community in Hong Kong. Its founding committee included American, German, Danish and Parsee as well as British

British business in Asia since 1860 15

members, and as late as 1913 the Bank had five German directors. In contrast, the senior staff of the Bank were overwhelmingly United Kingdom nationals from the 1860s until the 1980s, although share registers were kept in both London and Hong Kong before the late 1960s. In the early 1890s about 55% of the shares were recorded in the London register, but a Hong Kong resident could own such shares, and people in Britain could own Hong Kong shares. With the closing of the London register there was a move in 'ownership' towards Hong Kong. By the 1980s over 80% of the Bank's shares were owned by people with a Hong Kong address, but it is unknown how many of these shares were owned by United Kingdom expatriates and how many by Chinese-speaking Hong Kong citizens (who are themselves British subjects). The British government has been ambivalent over the question of the Bank's nationality. From the late nineteenth century it was regarded by the Foreign Office as a major British commercial interest in Asia, and used as an instrument of diplomacy; but in 1981–2 the Hongkong Bank's attempt to buy a major domestic British bank, the Royal Bank of Scotland, was opposed by the Bank of England on the grounds that the Hongkong Bank's overseas head office might obstruct regulation by the British authorities.[32]

Similar problems arise when defining the 'Britishness' of other Hong Kong-based companies, such as Jardine Matheson, which was registered in the colony until it shifted its domicile to Bermuda in 1984. 'British', Hong Kong Chinese and other capital was often intertwined. Significantly it was not until 1987 that British businesses felt prompted to establish a British Chamber of Commerce in Hong Kong: until then, they were content to be represented in the Hong Kong general chamber.

The different types of British enterprise active in nineteenth-century Asia were often interlinked. As we have already mentioned, the Hongkong Bank was established by merchant firms active in Hong Kong. This was not unusual. Prominent among the founders of the Imperial Bank of Persia was the Bombay firm of David Sassoon & Company, which had wide trading interests in Iran, India and China.[33] There were also links between British business interests in various Asian countries. This was obviously the case for the British trading companies and overseas banks whose activities spanned the whole region, but nominally independent ventures in different countries were connected as well. Chapter 2 notes the strong links between the British parties in China and Iran, the 'poor man's China' (p. 39). Through the activities of British merchants selling Russian oil in Southeast Asia – and after 1912 the Shell Group's ownership of Russian oilfields – even Russian Asia was brought into this commercial nexus. In a real sense there was a British business community active in Asia – not just in individual countries – before 1914. British banks financed other forms of British enterprise. Companies floated in

London, and controlling factories, plantations and mines in India, often depended upon London-based exchange banks for part of their initial financial requirements and working capital.[34]

In brief, the two major trends for British business in twentieth-century Asia have been investments by British multinational corporations, and the decline of 'older' forms of British business in Asia, notably expatriate firms and managing agencies.

The arrival of British multinationals in Asia was part of a global trend noted by business historians. During the 1880s and 1890s British companies such as Dunlop or J. and P. Coats with domestic manufacturing operations began to erect overseas factories. By 1914 British multinational investment was extensive, and probably larger than that of the two other major multinational investors of the period, the United States and Germany. Britain has remained the world's largest multinational investor, after the United States, since the Second World War.[35] Several factors prompted the growth of British and other multinationals. Companies undertaking foreign direct investments had some 'advantages' over indigenous competitors, including access to cheap capital, technology and market skills, or superior management ability. Although many firms preferred to exploit these advantages in foreign markets by exporting, they were obliged to undertake local manufacturing by factors such as tariffs and other forms of government pressure, patent legislation and the behaviour of competitors.[36]

These forces stimulated British multinational investment in Asia, particularly in India between the wars. Tariffs and government pressure were significant factors leading to these investments. Yet the most striking fact is the small proportion of British multinational investment which was drawn to Asia before the Second World War. As chapter 8 shows (pp. 225–6), a few British companies established factories in Japan before 1914. In China, British American Tobacco – originally largely American-owned but British in ownership and management by 1923 – dominated cigarette production. The overwhelming majority of British multinational investments, however, went to higher per capita income markets such as the United States, Western Europe, and especially from the 1920s, 'white' Dominions like Australia and South Africa. This continued after the Second World War. During the 1960s new British multinational investment largely focussed on Western Europe and North America. By 1971 84% of British foreign direct investment was in North America, Europe, Australasia and South Africa: the remaining 16% went to the rest of the world.[37]

When British multinationals invested in Asia they often pursued joint ventures. In 1971 10% of total joint ventures established by British companies were in India, whereas only 4% of the total subsidiaries of

British business in Asia since 1860 17

1.3 A Chinese rickshaw boy bearing a European burden in inter-war Queens Road, Hong Kong.

18   R. P. T. Davenport-Hines and Geoffrey Jones

British companies were there. In Iran from the mid-1950s and in Japan practically all British companies had joint venture arrangements. In some countries, such as Iran, government pressure made such arrangements almost obligatory. In others, such as Japan and even India, the difficulties of the market were more important. According to one survey of the reasons given by British multinationals for starting joint ventures in India before 1967 (after which date the Indian government legislated to make them obligatory) the need for a local partner to provide facilities and resources was paramount.[38] Overall the preference for joint ventures illustrates the risks and difficulties British business felt that it faced in Asia after 1945.[39]

The decline of the older forms of British direct investment in Asia is harder to explain than the rise of multinationals. A preliminary point is that some traditional institutions have remained powerful. Jardine Matheson, the Swire group and other British trading companies, for example, retain important roles in many Asian economies, although several have also expanded their operations beyond Asia.

British overseas banks also remained major forces in Asian banking, albeit declining in market share because of the rise of modern indigenous banking institutions. The Hongkong Bank persisted as a leading bank in Asia in the inter-war period, and from the 1950s was transformed from a regional into an international bank heading one of the largest banking groups in the world. A substantial part of this growth was due to the rapid post-1950 economic growth of Hong Kong, where the Bank retained its headquarters, and derived the great proportion of its profits, and where it continued to be largely responsible for the colony's note issue and acted as *de facto* lender of last resort. However the Bank also grew through geographical diversification. In part this expansion came by acquisition. In 1959–60 the Bank bought two other long-established British overseas banks active in Asia. The Mercantile Bank of India had a network of branches in India, Malaysia and elsewhere in Asia. The British Bank of the Middle East was descended from the Imperial Bank of Persia and since the 1940s had created a commanding position as the leading bank in most of the Arabian Gulf and elsewhere in the Middle East, notably Lebanon. An even more momentous acquisition was the purchase in 1980 of majority control of Marine Midland Bank, then America's thirteenth largest bank.[40]

The experience of other 'older' forms of British investment, however, did not parallel that of the Hongkong Bank. British enterprises active in Russian Asia and China were nationalised after their communist revolutions in 1917 and 1949. Elsewhere the institutions established by British business frequently survived, but their ownership and control were transferred into Asian hands. The chronology of this transfer varied

British business in Asia since 1860 19

between countries. In Asia, Marwaris (an Indian business caste) and others began buying British firms in the 1920s. In Malaysia shares of many of the British agency houses drifted into local hands in the thirty years after the Second World War, while during the 1970s and early 1980s the government used a variety of devices to replace the British management of those companies with Malaysian nationals. Hong Kong followed a similar pattern without official *dirigisme*. During the 1970s and 1980s a series of 'British' companies in the colony fell to local Chinese entrepreneurs. Two milestones were the acquisition in 1979 of Hutchinson Whampoa by Li Ka-shing, originally a toy manufacturer, and the take-over of Wheelock Marden in 1985 by the shipping magnate Sir Y. K. Pao.[41]

A full explanation of these phenomena needs to include a range of political and economic influences. Relevant political factors included the rise of socialism, the decline of Western imperialism and the growth of Third World nationalism. The decline of British business in Soviet Russia and the People's Republic of China, and the troubled history and ultimate destruction between the 1920s and the early 1950s of British business in Iran, all derive from political forces. Political tension has also been an intermittent influence in Anglo-Japanese business relations since the 1920s. In India the decline of British business has often been linked to the decline of British imperialism, but as chapter 4 notes, this is an inadequate explanation which neglects structural changes occurring in the indigenous economy.[42]

The rise of modern indigenous enterprise was at least as important as political factors outside Russia and China. The reasons why indigenous Asian business was able to overtake or acquire British 'free-standing' firms lie in both the strengths of the indigenous entrepreneurs, like the Marwaris, and the weaknesses of the British ones, but the problem can be understood through the concept of 'advantage'. The advantage over local competitors held by British free-standing companies in nineteenth-century Asia lay not only in their ability to tap British capital markets, but in entrepreneurial and managerial skills which enabled them to mobilise local Asian savings and (often) to introduce superior Western technology and/or marketing methods. From the inter-war years these 'advantages' began to decline, both as portfolio investment from Britain fell in response to British government restrictions, and as indigenous enterprise (private or public sector) developed ways to mobilise local savings and gain access to modern technology. British managers often retained skills which were required and respected even after equity shareholding was firmly in national hands. However, as indigenous educated business elites developed even this advantage disappeared, and the services of British managers were dispensed with.

20   R. P. T. Davenport-Hines and Geoffrey Jones

Finally the decline of traditional British business was aggravated by changes in international trade and investment. In the inter-war years falling prices and disruption in world markets for certain primary products, combined with the growth of import substitution behind tariff barriers in the Asian countries, were disadvantageous to expatriate firms which had flourished in economies based on the export of raw materials and processed agricultural products and the import of finished consumer goods. The collapse of the world market for Indian tea and jute, for example, eroded the core of expatriate enterprise in eastern India.

1.3 British business performance in Asia

The issue of whether British business in Asia was successful and attempts to measure its performance over the last century, raise funda-mental empirical and theoretical difficulties. There is no satisfactory definition of business success or failure. Profits, or better still, rates of return, offer one measure, but collecting and comparing the profits or dividends of thousands of enterprises present problems of data and interpretation. British overseas banks, for example, all maintained large hidden reserves to which transfers were made before published profits were declared. The 'real' profits of the Imperial Bank of Persia have now been published, but the 'real' profitability of other Eastern banks remains a mystery.[43] Declared dividend rates were subject to distorting factors such as taxation policy or exchange fluctuations. Thus the high dividends issued in India by many British managing agency companies and their concerns in the early 1920s were more a response to demands for short-term profit-taking of retained earnings from the wartime period, coupled with low rates of dividend taxation in India and a highly favourable exchange rate for the rupee against sterling, than the result of spectacularly successful enterprise during 1919–21. Inter-country and inter-industry comparisons create further difficulties. There is little to be gained in understanding business 'success' or 'failure' by comparing the dividends of a British bank in Iran, a British trading company in Hong Kong and a British oil company in Russia.

There are more doubts over the role of a firm or an entrepreneur in an economy. Is a firm simply a passive agent of change, responding to the 'market' or to wider economic and social conditions? Most business historians regard such a neo-classical view as absurd; but the question of the freedom of manoeuvre of individual economic units is open to complex argument.

In historical perspective, the most satisfactory measure of success or failure is 'market share'. Using that criterion, the overall picture of declining British importance in Asian business is abundantly clear, as

British business in Asia since 1860 21

outlined in section 1.1. Subjective measures of British business 'influence' tell the same story. In the late nineteenth century British enterprise was dominant in most of the countries covered by this volume. In Iran as late as the 1920s the entire modern business sector was under British control. By the 1980s there was nowhere in Asia where British business played such a role.

One feature of the decline in British influence is its varying velocity in different countries. In Japan the decline was visible from the late nineteenth century. In Iran British business began to lose market share in the 1930s and by the early 1950s it was virtually eliminated, albeit temporarily, from the country. In Malaya the British agency houses retained leading roles in the economy until the 1970s, and even subsequently British business interests remain significant. British business in China was affected by the Slump in the 1930s, but performed well compared to its counterparts in other Asian countries and in comparison with Chinese business in China. In India the inter-war decline of the expatriate sector was compensated for to some extent by new multinational investment, but the overall significance of British business in India fell from 1929 at the latest.

It may be objected that declining market share is a poor indicator of 'failure' or at least sub-optimal performance by British businesses in Asia, because that decline was inevitable, unavoidable and desirable. It is arguable that the decline was inevitable because of the rise of other industrial powers from the mid-nineteenth century onwards. This is both true and misleading, for like the 'early start' hypothesis for poor British economic performance since the 1880s, it is a self-exculpation for inadequate competitive performance (indeed it was produced as an alibi by some British entrepreneurs or commentators as early as 1900–10). There was nothing inevitable, for example, in the fact that Britain's share of imports into Hong Kong and Singapore fell between 1960 and 1980 from 11.3% to 4.9% and from 8.9% to 3.0%, while Japan's share of imports into those two economies rose from 16.1% to 23% and from 7.3% to 18.8%.[44] Japanese business provided what those two fast-growing economies required; British business did not.

Another argument is that the decline of British business was unavoidable given adverse exogenous circumstances, including the spread of nationalism and the end of the British Empire. This view is more persuasive for some countries than for others. British business was almost powerless to cope with governments in Russia and China which were fundamentally hostile to Western foreign investment (even if they were sometimes willing to offer 'concessions' to Westerners). Elsewhere, however, the story is less straightforward. Frances Bostock and Geoffrey Jones argue, for example, in chapter 2 that the hostility of the Iranian government to British business from the 1920s until the 1950s was, in part at least, in response to the behaviour of that business in Iran: in particular its close links with the British Foreign Office, racialist employment practices, and enclavism. B. R. Tomlinson, in chapter 4, suggests, however, that the correlation attributed to Indian independence and the decline of British business has been exaggerated. There are suggestions in our chapter 8 that British entrepreneurs preferred to avoid involvement in Japan because of distaste for its social and political systems.

A third contention is that the decline of British business in Asia has been desirable. Certainly the fall in traditional British textile exports to Asia after 1918 was part of a process of restructuring of the British economy towards 'newer' industries with higher value added, which sold in more prosperous markets (including Britain) than Asia offered. Equally, if foreign direct investment in Western Europe and North America offered higher returns than in Asia, it was rational that British investment was redirected to these economies. However several writers in this volume suggest that commercial opportunities were lost or ignored by British business underestimating market opportunities (as in Japan), by their exaggeration of market possibilities (as in Russian Asia), or by poor management (as in India or Iran). American, German or Japanese business has often performed more keenly than British. However, the essays in this volume cannot be used to explain the wasting of the British economy in the twentieth century: each market presented peculiarities which would render such an attempt futile.

1.4 British business and the British government

The relationship between the British government and its overseas business interests has been much discussed by historians and economists. Diplomatic historians of the late nineteenth and early twentieth centuries have described the growing association between British diplomats and business in areas of international diplomatic rivalry such as China and Iran in 1890–1914, and China in the inter-war years.[45] The issue re-emerges in discussions about the impact of multinationals on Third World countries, and is reflected in debate about relations between British-owned commercial interests and British colonial governments.[46] In 'strategic' countries such as Iran or China British business and diplomacy drew together from the 1890s. This was often an uneasy relationship. Entrepreneurs resented diplomatic considerations overriding commercial criteria, yet usually found Foreign Office support was indispensable. In turn officials often distrusted private bankers, traders and concessionaires, although the support of both the German and

Russian governments for their business interests forced Whitehall to acknowledge the tie between commercial and diplomatic influence.[47]

In chapter 2 Frances Bostock and Geoffrey Jones suggest that, in Iran at least, relations between diplomats and entrepreneurs were uneasy, with deterioration, or at least greater complications, after 1918. Some elements at the Foreign Office foresaw political convulsions in Iran – before the British bank and oil company – after Reza Shah Pahlavi was proclaimed Shah in 1925, and were reluctant to support British commercial interests as strongly as the companies wished. Conversely the pressure of the new nationalist government in the country made British interests more eager for diplomatic support than before 1914.

The long controversy as to whether the Foreign Office gave British business sufficient support in overseas markets is not clearly resolved by these essays. The counter-arguments are familiar. 'English merchants accuse the Foreign Office of lack of initiative, but they are often ignorant and bigoted', one widely travelled Asian expert, Lord Curzon, told Lord Mersey in 1899; 'they must learn if they wish to succeed.' Another Viceroy of India, Lord Wavell, noted after meeting a delegation in 1947 (in a comment applicable at different times to Iran, China and Malaya), 'British businessmen in India have not moved with the times; their chief plea was that they should still have, after the transfer of power, their own settlements, their own clubs, and should in fact keep to themselves.' The contrary case was forcibly advanced against British diplomats in Asia, typified by a comment of Sir William Ramsay in 1910: 'Two things are certain, (1) the English Ambassador does not care a — what happens to any English enterprise, so long as he can get his shooting and his golf, and avoid being pestered with … business; (2) the German Ambassador is watchful, active, always on the outlook to be hospitable … and as full of experience and knowledge as the English one is ignorant of facts and men.'[48] Wherein lies the truth?

The British government does not emerge as a dynamic champion of British business in Japan after 1945. Commercial opportunities in occupied Japan were lost, as a result, in the period to 1952. In the 1950s, and subsequently, British officialdom failed to reduce Japanese discrimination against foreign business. Conversely in post-1945 Iran the British government pushed reluctant British companies to seek business opportunities. However the fact that Iran was a large holder of sterling, and thus an important element in Whitehall's increasingly futile defence of the international role of the British currency, made the country a special case. There is some evidence that although senior diplomats, such as Sir Victor Wellesley, responsible for Far Eastern policy as framed in London were conscious of the importance of economics and business, the diplomats *en poste* in marginal markets such as Thailand were likely to be complacent

24   R. P. T. Davenport-Hines and Geoffrey Jones

idlers unfit for responsibility elsewhere at least as late as the 1960s.[49] There is little evidence in this volume that British officials were a vigorous force behind British business expansion in Asia or elsewhere in the world. As in the domestic British economy, some British politicians and civil servants, weaned on liberal economic policies, were content to observe British business floundering at home and abroad as the century wore on with the comforting view that the 'market' knew best, while others agonised at the decline but seemed as enervated and fatalistic as Sir Victor Wellesley, who lamented 'the position is hopeless, and we are helpless'.[50]

The massive literature on the relationship between multinationals, host governments and home governments has few, if any, references to the experience of British multinationals in Asia. The role of American companies in Latin America has received most attention: the International Telephone & Telegraph Corporation (ITT), for example, has become notorious for its cooperation during the early 1970s with the United States government in overthrowing the democratic government of Chile in favour of a reactionary military dictatorship. The involvement of the British multinational Lonrho in African politics, as well as the role of the British oil companies BP and Shell in maintaining oil supplies between 1965 and 1978 to the rebel regime in Rhodesia (called Zimbabwe since 1980), have also been publicised.[51] However the essays in this collection identify only one major abuse of sovereignty: the overthrow in 1953 of the Iranian government which had nationalised the British oil company there in 1951, and in this case Anglo-Iranian Oil was not directly involved in the intrigues against Mohammed Mossadeq's government.

British colonial governments were not intimately concerned with British business. It is true that to some extent British business interests were able to participate in the economic institutional structure of the colonial government. The most obvious gainers in India were the defence stores suppliers and railway contractors, and the shipping lines that secured mail contracts. In these cases British administrators discriminated against Indian-owned firms. In Malaya the British rubber interests were clear gainers from the policies pursued by the colonial government between the 1890s and the mid-1950s, but these policies were not adopted at the direct instigation of British business interests. For the most part the links between British business and colonial governments were weak. When Sir David Yule, arguably the most important British merchant in Calcutta or even in India, attended the Durbar celebrations of 1911, he was scarcely known by sight to any official, and mistook the Viceroy of India for King George V's private detective.[52] Whatever favouritism occurred, its effect was not strong enough to withstand the long-term challenge of both domestic and foreign rivals.[53]

1.5 Impact and response

Any study of the impact of British business on Asia would ideally be set in the context of the great dramas of development and under-development played out in that continent. Unfortunately the extreme diversity of British business activities and of the Asian economies prevent such an approach. However it is clear that the importance of British business for all Asian economies was probably greater before 1914 than thereafter, even though the absolute size of capital invested and trade associated with British enterprise grew. Before 1914 British business was pioneering: overall it brought new products and industries into Asian economies. After 1918 there were increasing numbers of indigenous or other foreign-owned businesses active in Asian economies, and these became more prominent in innovation and in launching new products

It is easier to assess the impact of British business on the smaller Asian economies, such as those of Iran, Thailand and Malaya, than on the larger, more complex economies of India and China. In Iran before 1914 the modern business sector consisted of a narrow range of activities, dominated by a handful of British enterprises. There might be controversy over the impact of British business in Iran, but at least the debate can be sustained with a controllable amount of information. India and China were always large economies: the manufacturing output of both countries exceeded Britain's even in the mid-nineteenth century. Discussing the impact of the whole of British business on the whole of India or China would involve generalisations so bold as to be valueless.

Moreover, there is no evidence that British business or foreign business was the sole crucial factor in the long-run economic development of any Asian economy, except perhaps in Iran where the oil industry developed by a British company had a decisive influence on the country's development. It seems untenable to correlate India's very slow growth rate – a 1.4% annual growth in real gross national product per capita between 1960 and 1980 – with the fact that the country received the largest amount of British direct investment in Asia in much of that period. Nor would it be plausible to relate Thailand's fast growth rate of 4.7% annually over the same period to the small amount of British foreign direct investment which it received. This is not the place to enter the debate about the dependency critique of foreign investment, which would necessitate a discussion of public as well as private foreign investment, together with analysis of matters such as dividends, royalties and redemption payments. But it does seem that divergences in growth rates derive from factors within the societies themselves.[54]

Nevertheless there were areas in which British businesses had an impact on Asia. For example they transferred capital into Asian economies. This was never crucial, however, even though the classic picture of a developing economy is of capital shortage. Apart from the sums invested in India and China, British foreign direct investment was small by any criterion, and in the two largest economies it was small in per capita terms. By the late nineteenth century most 'British' enterprise in India was financed by ploughing back profits. The same was true in Iran after 1914. Significantly, Asia's fastest-growing economies have also been those with very high domestic saving ratios. This also applied to Japan during the last hundred years, and has been true of the four Asian NICs (Taiwan, South Korea, Hong Kong and Singapore) since the 1960s.[55]

British banks did play a role, especially before 1914, in mobilising local savings. These banks disliked transferring capital from Britain to the countries in which they operated, and preferred to finance operations from locally generated resources. In Iran, the Imperial Bank of Persia controlled almost all bank deposits in the modern banking sector before 1928. In India, the exchange banks controlled a significant share of commercial bank deposits: around 30% between 1900 and 1938.[56] The use of such savings to finance international trade has been criticised. However it has to be recognised that the banks also had other uses to which deposits were put, including lending to local governments and, sometimes, involvement in development schemes.

Predictably, the impact of British banks varied between countries and chronologically. The British exchange banks were more single-mindedly devoted to foreign trade finance in India than in China. The Hongkong Bank played an important role in Hong Kong's nascent industrialisation in the 1950s. During this period the Bank accounted for more than half of all bank lending to the colony's manufacturing industries, and provided not only short-term finance for working capital but also medium- to long-term finance for fixed capital.[57] After 1960 it led the branch-banking revolution which accelerated Hong Kong's growth by mobilising private savings for re-investment in business. In 1961 the Hongkong Bank had 16 branches in the colony; by 1971 it had 68, with 250 in 1981.

British business, again most notably before 1914, had a clear impact on economic growth by transferring enterprise and technology into Asia. Its pioneering role in the Thai teak industry (see pp. 133–46), Malayan rubber (pp. 171–3), Iranian oil and banking (pp. 36–8), and Russian oil (pp. 72–4) emerges from these essays. Britain provided the entrepreneurship, management, marketing skills and technology which, for whatever reasons, were absent from those economies at that time, and the development of these new industries was a product of British enterprise. Often British companies pioneered the development of backward regions as they exploited new raw materials or developed new industries. Interestingly, recent research on the growth of Asian NICs suggests that the main

British business in Asia since 1860   27

contribution of foreign investment was in transmitting new methods of production and management.[58]

To argue that British business before 1914 was an important conduit of new products and technologies into Asia is not to accept a 'heroic' view of British enterprise. The Asian economies were not deserts of enterprise or civilisation before the arrival of British business: there were always some powerful indigenous entrepreneurs even in nineteenth-century Iran, the least-developed economy discussed in this volume. Again the essays on Thailand and Malaya stress the great importance of expatriate Chinese enterprise in those countries before the appearance of the British.

Nor was the transfer of new technologies or products to Asian economies necessarily a smooth or beneficial process. Some British companies, like the British oil company in Iran, created industries with enclave characteristics. The British interests active in India lacked the technologies which the Parsee and Marwari industrial groups needed: they approached Germany and the United States to learn the techniques of the glass and chemical industries. The 'transfer' of the managing agency system from the British expatriate firms to the Indian companies is now regarded as unfortunate, given the inefficiencies of that management system. Finally, from the early twentieth century, as we argue in the chapter on Japan, British business could offer a declining number of new products or technologies needed or wanted in Asia.

British business played an important part in integrating Asian economies into the nineteenth-century world economy. The role of British banks and trading companies in this process was obvious, but many British free-standing companies were also involved in export-related industries, often in primary products. It is impossible in this context to discuss the role of exports as an 'engine' or 'handmaiden' of growth: but it is clear that some developing countries achieved substantial gains in per capita output fuelled by primary exports between 1850 and 1914 and again from 1945 to 1973, while others did not. The effect of exports depends on many factors, including whether the challenge of rising export opportunities is met by an adequate production response within the country, the relative size of the export sector, and the disposition of the export proceeds.[59] The impact of oil exports on Iran was fundamental to that country's economic growth in the twentieth century. Conversely, the importance of foreign trade to the large Indian and Chinese economies was always marginal. In 1900 only about 2% of China's national product entered into international trade.

The employment impact of British business was important. In absolute terms the impact of British-generated employment was greater in smaller economies such as Iran than in larger ones such as India and China. Everywhere, however, British companies transferred skills and the English

28   R. P. T. Davenport-Hines and Geoffrey Jones

language to Asians who worked for them, even if discriminatory employment practices meant that few if any Asians were appointed to senior management positions in British ventures until the post-1945 period, or even the 1960s.

During the late nineteenth and early twentieth century industrialising countries both in Asia and elsewhere were predisposed towards 'latecomers' to industrialisation such as Germany, which was seen as the most modern of the European industrialised economies. In Iran, China and elsewhere Germans were recruited to run new national enterprises which challenged British-owned business. The attraction to Germany was partly to balance the British political influence which was perceived to accompany British business in Asia, but also because it was felt that Asian countries had more to learn from another and rapidly developing latercomer than from the world's first industrial nation.[60] Notwithstanding such suspicions and despite the relative decline of British business, it is undeniable that the latter was a major force in promoting modern economic growth in Asia.

1.6 The Asian impact on Britain

During the 1970s and 1980s, as British business in Asia has declined to new levels of insignificance, the impact of Asian business on Britain has risen. As with nineteenth-century British business in Asia, it has taken several forms. Individual Asian entrepreneurs, usually of South Asian extraction but often coming from East Africa, have established strong positions in areas of British manufacturing industry, while small-scale Chinese and Indian businesses have had an impact on the British restaurant and retail sectors. Despite the overall decline in significance of Asian trade for the United Kingdom, Japan and some Asian NICs became important suppliers of industrial goods as British de-industrialisation increased apace. Asian textiles made major inroads into the British market from the 1970s in an interesting reversal of the nineteenth-century trade pattern. In 1986 more than 50% of clothes sold in Britain came from six Far Eastern countries: Hong Kong, South Korea, Taiwan, China, Macao and Thailand.[61] British companies including leading publishers like Macmillan and Longman, have also transferred much of their manufacturing sub-contracting to Hong Kong and other Asian locations, with production exported to Britain.

Another significant development has been the arrival of Asian foreign direct investment in the United Kingdom. Japanese investment in foreign countries expanded in the 1960s, but until the late 1970s largely concentrated on producing low-technology products in tariff-protected markets in Asia or Latin America, or export-platform types of investment using

1.4 *The new Hong Kong head office of the Hongkong Bank, erected in 1985.*

cheap labour in countries such as Taiwan, South Korea and Hong Kong. Since the late 1970s Japanese companies have also undertaken the manufacture of high-technology products in developed countries. Most of this investment has been in the United States, but Britain has been the preferred location in Europe. By the end of 1986 Japanese companies had fifty production sites in Britain, employing around 12,000 people.[62] The British government's liberal policies towards inward direct investment and the fragility of the domestic industrial base were among the influences attracting Japanese companies to Britain. As with nineteenth-century

British companies in Asia, Japanese firms took important roles in transferring enterprise, management methods and technology into Britain. This was vividly illustrated by the Honda group's collaborative arrangement with Rover, the only remaining British-owned volume car manufacturer in the 1980s.

During the 1980s other Asian economies began to make foreign direct investments in Britain. These included Hong Kong – one of whose companies bought the major British toy manufacturer, Matchbox – and South Korea. In 1985 the Sultan of Brunei purchased the prestigious Dorchester Hotel in London's Park Lane. Even the Hongkong Bank, which had never undertaken domestic banking inside the United Kingdom, penetrated British banking in the 1980s. The rebuff of its overtures to the Royal Bank of Scotland in 1982 was followed by expansion of its activities in wholesale and merchant banking, and the acquisition in 1984 of James Capel & Company, one of Britain's leading broking houses. In 1987 the Hongkong Bank purchased a 14.9% stake in the Midland Bank, the smallest of Britain's 'Big Four' clearing banks, under an agreement which included a programme of cooperation suggesting that a full take-over might follow in due course.[63] In the 1980s 'British' businesses in Hong Kong began to receive increasing investment from the People's Republic. In 1987 a Chinese government agency bought a stake of 12.5% in Cathay Pacific Airways, the 'flag-carrier' for Hong Kong which had formerly been largely owned by the Swire group and the Hongkong Bank.

In 1889 Lord Dufferin and Ava, a former Viceroy of India, had reminded the London Chamber of Commerce 'of the enormous benefit' derived by Britain from business in the sub-continent, 'and consequently of the supreme necessity of maintaining to all time dominant and unimpaired England's ascendancy and dominion over her Eastern possessions ... were [it] to be even partially disturbed, there is not a cottage in Great Britain ... in the manufacturing districts which would not ... feel the disastrous consequences of such an intolerable calamity'. After careful analysis, Curzon, in 1894, judged that it was 'only in the East, and especially in the Far East, that we may still hope to keep and create open markets for British manufacturers'.[64] It was a poignant reversal to such attitudes when in 1986 Standard Chartered Bank, one of the last British overseas banks and descendant of the Chartered Bank of India, Australia and China, was saved from a hostile take-over from another British bank by the willingness of rich customers in Hong Kong and Singapore to buy its shares.[65] Such incidents provide an apt epilogue to the rise and decline of British business pre-eminence over the world's most populous continent.

2 British business in Iran, 1860s–1970s

Frances Bostock and Geoffrey Jones*

2.1 The business of imperialism

Iran, or Persia as the country was known in the West until the 1930s, was one of the most under-developed economies in the world in the nineteenth century. A dearth of statistics makes quantification difficult, but there is no doubt that the great majority of the population – which numbered around 10 million in 1900 – experienced extremely low incomes and lived in dire poverty. Most people worked in the agricultural sector, which was largely subsistence in nature, and which suffered periodically from droughts, famines and plagues of locusts. It was a symbol of Iran's lack of development that, despite the country's large size and severe transport difficulties, its first railway was built only in the 1930s. However, the discovery of oil in 1908 made Iran the Middle East's first oil-producing nation. Oil provided the basis for economic growth in the same way as tin and rubber were to do in Malaya. By the 1970s Iran had emerged as one of the most rapidly developing economies in the Third World, and a nation acclaimed in the West as being on the verge of emulating the Japanese 'economic miracle'.[1]

The history of British business in Iran reveals a number of distinctive features. The first is the dominant role played by British business in creating the modern economic sector in Iran before the 1920s. Indigenous entrepreneurship was exceptionally weak compared to that in Japan and India. There was no equivalent to the dynamic Chinese merchants who played major roles in the economic growth of Malaya and Siam. The other significant European investor in Iran – Russia – also made little impact on the economy.

A second noteworthy feature is the close relationship between the British government and British business, a product of Iran's position as a centre of acute diplomatic rivalry. Before 1914 the British and Russian empires competed for influence in the country, which was ruled by the Shahs of the Qajar dynasty. In 1907 the two powers divided the country into 'spheres of influence' which recognised Russia's interest in the north, Britain's interest in the south, and established a neutral zone between the

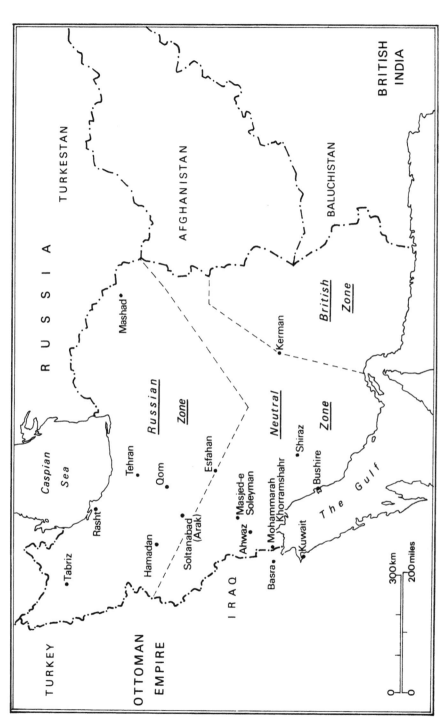

Map 2.1 Iran before 1914

British business in Iran, 1860s–1970s 33

two. The country was a battleground for competing armies in the First World War. The rise to power of Reza Khan, who staged a successful coup in 1921 and established the new Pahlavi dynasty in 1925, was followed by a decline in foreign interference in Iran's affairs, but in 1941 British and Soviet troops invaded the country and deposed the Shah. The last Soviet troops left the country in 1946. Iran subsequently held an important position in the Cold War conflict between West and East. British governments from the late nineteenth century saw British business as an important weapon in the diplomatic struggle against Russia and in the 'regeneration' of Iran.

A third distinctive feature of the experience of British business in Iran is the violence of the reaction against it. British business did not simply wither in Iran, as it did in Japan from the late nineteenth century and in India from the late 1950s. It was greatly distrusted by many Iranians, and from the 1920s Iranian governments cancelled concessions awarded by earlier regimes, introduced restrictions on British-owned ventures, and in 1951 nationalised the biggest British investment in Iran, the Anglo-Iranian Oil Company. British business was ejected from Iran. When it returned, from the second half of the 1950s, its economic importance was minimal.

Recent company histories of British Petroleum, the British Bank of the Middle East and the Inchcape Group, have provided exciting new evidence on the British oil, banking and shipping interests which once dominated Iran's economy.[2] This chapter draws on this new material, together with more patchy data on other British commercial activities. Our survey of British business activity in Iran is divided into three chronological periods. The first period, from the 1860s until the early 1920s, saw the creation of the major British business interests in Iran. The second period, from the 1920s to the 1950s, saw the clash between those interests and nationalist governments in Iran. The third period, after 1954, saw calmer relations between the two parties, but with British business no longer of any great significance. These chronological sections are followed by a brief assessment of the impact of British business on Iran.

2.2 British business under the Qajars, 1860–1925

British business activity in Iran before 1925 was characteristic of British business in most of Asia. There was no sign of the investment by the nascent British manufacturing multinationals which had begun to appear in Japan in the 1900s. Instead, British business consisted of trading and shipping houses, and investments in the extractive and infrastructure sectors, and in banking. Many of the non-trading activities were based on

34   Frances Bostock and Geoffrey Jones

concessions from the Iranian government. These were formerly cast as examples of imperialist exploitation, but are now more realistically seen as a coherent policy by successive Shahs to boost state revenues and attract modern technology and enterprise into the country.[3] However, British enterprises which grew on the basis of monopoly and privileged concessions were highly vulnerable when a government with different development strategies took power in the 1920s.

Before 1918 the British Empire was second in importance only to Russia as a source for Iran's imports and as a market for her exports. In the late nineteenth century British imports were largely cotton goods, and British India supplied tea, sugar and cotton goods, while commodities such as opium and carpets formed the bulk of Iran's exports. At the start of the period much of this trade passed through the hands of agents in Iran who were of non-British origin, but had become British in order to benefit from the protection of the British government. The Greek firm of Ralli and Angelestou and the Swiss firm of Ziegler and Company, based in the northern entrepôt city of Tabriz, and the Dutch company, I. C. P. Hotz and Son, based in Bushire on the Gulf coast, all registered their head offices in London or Manchester in the 1860s for this reason.[4] David Sassoon and Company, Iraqi-Jewish in origin, later followed suit. During the 1890s, however, these 'British' merchants seem to have had less success than 'native' merchants in coping with the difficult trading conditions of that decade, and firms such as Hotz and David Sassoon, who had dominated the export of opium, were all but squeezed out.[5]

A more durable British business presence in Iran was in shipping. In 1861 the British India Steam Navigation Company began a steamer service from London to the Gulf via Bombay, and its London agents, Gray Dawes and Company, established two local partnerships to undertake the necessary agency and handling work – Gray Paul and Company, based in Bushire, and Gray Mackenzie and Company, based in Basra in Iraq. They arranged imports and exports, and also became involved in the forward shipment of goods to the hinterland, arranging mule and camel caravans and charging a forwarding commission on the goods carried.[6] A second shipping company was the Euphrates and Tigris Steam Navigation Company, formed in 1861 by the trading house of Lynch Brothers which had a business in Iraq. This company started a steamer service on the Karun from Mohammarah (later Khorramshahr) to Ahwaz after the Shah opened the river to commercial traffic in 1888.[7] In January 1920 these two shipping and trading groups, which already had close boardroom links, merged their business into one group, the Mesopotamia Persia Company (Mespers).[8]

There was considerable British business activity in the infrastructure and extractive sectors, but with the exception of telegraphs in the former

British business in Iran, 1860s–1970s 35

and oil in the latter, most of this activity was ill-advised, unproductive or fraudulent. In 1862 and 1865 Britain concluded conventions with Iran which allowed the construction of a telegraph line as a link in the overland line to connect England with India. In the next few years, the government of India's Telegraph Department extended its network to Tehran. Siemens, a British company which had close connections with the German Siemens firm, obtained the concession for constructing and working the line from Europe to Tehran, through Russia, to join the British Indian line at Tehran. In April 1868 the Indo-European Telegraph Company was formed to operate this concession – along with similar ones in Russia and Prussia. This company was originally controlled by Siemens, although it also had a director from Reuters News Agency. By 1884, it had established fourteen stations in Iran, manned by British personnel.[9] The spread of the telegraph system, more than anything else, led to the opening up of Iran to the outside world.

From the 1860s to the early 1900s British – and continental European – concession hunters descended on the country in search of bargains. Many of these promoters were interested in the development of Iran's infrastructure, but none of them achieved anything on the scale of Siemens' Indo-European Telegraph Company or the Indian government's Telegraph Department. The most famous project was that of Baron Julius de Reuter. In 1872 de Reuter, a naturalised Englishman and the entrepreneur who had established Reuters News Agency, secured a concession which gave him an almost complete monopoly over the economic development of Iran, including the right to construct railways, exploit the country's natural resources, and to found a national bank. De Reuter seems to have had a serious intention to carry out his obligations, but in the face of Russian government hostility to the concession, British government concern that the proposed railways might present a security threat to British India, and extreme opposition from some Iranian notables, the Shah was induced to cancel de Reuter's concession in 1873.[10] A series of other failed concessions followed, including a lottery concession granted in 1889 and a concession granted in 1890 giving British interests a monopoly over the production and sale of the whole of Iran's tobacco crop. Both these concessions were subsequently cancelled by the Shah, the tobacco concession after widespread protests in Iran.[11]

As elsewhere in Asia, British investors were interested in railway construction in Iran. This seems to have been the main concern of de Reuter in 1872. When, in 1889, he secured compensation from the Iranian government for the cancellation of his original concession in the shape of a new concession to establish a national bank (which was to become the Imperial Bank of Persia), he still seems to have regarded the main purpose of the bank as being to serve as a means of building railways.[12] However, Anglo-Russian diplomatic rivalry blocked all proposals for railway construction. In 1890 Russia forced the Shah to agree that no railway building would take place for ten years, and this 'sterilising agreement' was renewed for a further ten years in 1900.[13] In 1911 various British business interests in Iran combined to form the Persian Railways Syndicate with a tiny capital of £15,000, but owing to the difficulties of securing a concession no serious development work was undertaken before 1914, and, despite another flurry of activity in 1919–20, the venture became moribund after the War. British investment in roads was slightly more productive. The Imperial Bank of Persia secured a road concession soon after its foundation, and built a 97-mile road from Tehran to Qom before further construction ceased in 1894. Later in the 1890s Lynch Brothers constructed a caravan road from Ahwaz to Esfahan. In 1904 the British Foreign Office arranged the merger of the Bank and Lynch's road interests into the Persian Transport Company.[14] This company, however, undertook no new road building.

It was in the extractive sector that British business made its greatest impact. The presence of oil seepages in Iran had aroused interest from the 1860s, and oil rights had been included in the abortive de Reuter concession of 1872. In 1884 Hotz had begun oil drilling near Bushire, but to no effect. In May 1901 W. K. D'Arcy, an English financier who had made his fortune in the Australian gold fields, obtained a sixty-year concession to search for and exploit petroleum throughout Iran, except for the five northern provinces which bordered Russia. D'Arcy found the search for oil to be highly capital-intensive, and in 1905 he had to be rescued by another British oil company, Burmah Oil. In May 1908 oil in commercial quantities was found, and the Anglo-Persian Oil Company was launched in the following year. The first cargo of crude oil was exported in 1912. Two years later, Anglo-Persian, short of development capital and lacking marketing and transport facilities, ensured its independence and subsequent expansion by persuading the British government to acquire 51% of its equity and sign an Admiralty fuel contract with it. In 1912 Anglo-Persian produced 43,000 tons of crude oil. By 1924 annual production was 3.7 million tons.[15]

The Anglo-Persian Oil Company had become the most important British interest in Iran by the mid-1920s. The Imperial Bank of Persia was the second most important. The first Western bank to appear in Iran had been the British-owned New Oriental Bank Corporation, which in 1888 had opened a branch in Tehran and agencies in the major provincial cities of Tabriz, Rasht, Esfahan, Shiraz and Bushire.[16] However, in 1890 the Corporation's assets in Iran were acquired by the newly formed Imperial Bank of Persia, founded on the basis of a concession granted to Julius de

2.1 An oil strike at Masjed-e Soleyman, southwest Iran, in 1909.

38 *Frances Bostock and Geoffrey Jones*

Reuter in the previous year, making it the state bank of Iran with exclusive rights of note issue.[17]

In the period before the First World War the Imperial Bank contrived to develop a banking business, despite early difficulties, not least of which was a rapid depreciation of Iran's silver-based currency in the early 1890s, which forced the Bank to write down its capital by 35% to £650,000 in 1894.[18] The Imperial Bank functioned as a commercial bank, taking deposits, making advances, discounting bills and generally financing trade and commerce. It also functioned as a state bank – issuing bank notes; importing silver for mintage into currency; involving itself in currency control and reform, including the issue of a new nickel currency in the early 1900s; keeping the government's accounts and acting as a recipient of its revenues; and making advances to the government. The Imperial Bank, like British overseas banks elsewhere in Asia, also raised funds for the government on the London market, although the sums involved were tiny compared to those for China, Japan and India in the two decades before 1914. Only two foreign loans were floated on the London Stock Exchange for the Iranian government – for £500,000 in 1892 and £1,250,000 in 1911. The public response to the first loan was so poor that the Bank was left holding most of it until 1900, when the Iranian government used the proceeds of a Russian government loan to repay it.[19]

In contrast to British investment in banking and petroleum, there was little involvement in manufacturing. Indeed, Iran had only a tiny modern manufacturing sector before the 1930s: there was no equivalent to the growth of, for example, the cotton textile industry in India and Japan. However, two British-registered companies, Zieglers and Oriental Carpet Manufacturers, dominated Iran's carpet export industry, which was revived in the late nineteenth century by Western firms introducing quality control and developing export markets. Although little is known about the organisation and capitalisation of these ventures, their importance for the Iranian carpet industry is well documented. Zieglers established itself in Soltanabad (now Arak) in the 1880s, and operated a putting-out system, which was an extension of traditional cottage industry, designed to produce quality-controlled carpets for export. There had been only forty looms in the Soltanabad area in the 1870s. By 1900 Zieglers alone controlled some 2,500 looms in the region. Other British firms emulated Zieglers. In 1906 Oriental Carpet Manufacturers was formed from a merger of six smaller British-owned companies with an interest in exporting to the Ottoman empire. This company established branches at Hamadan, its headquarters, and at other carpet-weaving centres such as Tabriz, Mashad, Seistan and Kerman. Oriental Carpet Manufacturers moved from Zieglers' putting-out system to installing its own looms and employing wage labour to manufacture carpets in factory conditions.

British business in Iran, 1860s–1970s 39

Oriental Carpet Manufacturers and Zieglers dominated the production of carpets for export – especially to European and American markets – until the 1930s.[20]

Although British investment in different economic sectors before 1925 has been treated separately here, an important feature of British business activity in Iran in this period was the strong links between the various companies, both at director level and in terms of equity stakes. The original board of the Imperial Bank included two representatives of the Sassoon family and the head of I. C. P. Hotz. Over the following decades the Bank appointed as directors men associated with the British India Steam Navigation Company, Gray Paul and Gray Mackenzie, and the Anglo-Persian Oil Company. The 1900s saw a series of joint ventures between the British companies in Iran. The Persian Transport Company was jointly owned by the Imperial Bank and Lynch's, while the subscribers to the Persian Railways Syndicate included nearly all the substantial British business interests in Iran – the Imperial Bank, Anglo-Persian Oil Company, the Persian Transport Company, Lynch Brothers, Gray Dawes and British India.

A second noteworthy feature of British business in Iran at the time was its links with British companies active elsewhere in Asia and the developing world as a whole. The late nineteenth century saw the emergence of groups of predatory capitalists attracted to peripheral areas with weak political infrastructures. These groups frequently operated in several countries or even regions. There were particularly strong links between the British parties in Iran and those in China, and to some extent Iran before 1914 can be regarded as 'a poor man's China'. Individuals and enterprises with interests in finance, trade and railways in China seem to have regarded Iran as possessing a similar scope for investment, albeit on a much reduced scale compared to China, and there were also many direct trading links between Iran, India and China, especially in opium and cotton textiles. In the 1870s Hugh Matheson, whose family had widespread trading activities in China, was an enthusiastic supporter of de Reuter's projects in Iran.[21] The Sassoon family interests spanned Iran, the Ottoman empire, India and China. They had been among the promoters of the Hongkong Bank, formed in 1865 and destined to become one of the largest of the British overseas banks.[22] In turn, the Hongkong Bank and the leading China merchants Jardine Matheson were involved in the establishment of the Imperial Bank of Persia. The Imperial Bank's first Chairman, William Keswick, was head of Jardine Matheson and a former Chairman of the Hongkong Bank. Another member of the Imperial Bank's first board was David McLean, a former Manager of the Hongkong Bank's Shanghai branch and a noted Eastern exchange banker and silver specialist. During the 1890s Keswick and McLean were promoters

40   *Frances Bostock and Geoffrey Jones*

of the China Trust, a speculative and unsuccessful venture to 'develop' China's resources. In later years a series of former Hongkong Bank staff joined the Imperial Bank's board, and the close links between the two banks were appropriately consummated in 1960, when the Hongkong Bank took over the Imperial Bank's successor, the British Bank of the Middle East. The British trading and shipping companies in Iran also had many links with India and often operated directly or through associates on the sub-continent. However, the most extensive business link with British India was perhaps the Burmah Oil Company's control of the Anglo-Persian Oil Company between 1905 and 1914.[23]

British business in Iran before 1925 faced a number of problems, of which competition was the least important. This was partly because the Oil Company and the Bank held monopoly concessions. Moreover, although Russia was Iran's largest trading partner before the Bolshevik Revolution, and Russian diplomatic intrigue made difficulties for British business, Russian companies rarely provided strong competition to British interests. This point is clearly demonstrated in the banking sector. A Russian bank was launched soon after the formation of the Imperial Bank of Persia, and from the mid-1890s this was owned by the Russian State Bank. The Russian bank was used as an instrument of Russian diplomacy in Iran, and backed by the resources of the Russian state. It should have been a formidable competitor of the Imperial Bank, but instead its inept management gave few worries to the rival British institution. During the 1900s the Russian bank acted as agent for Russian exporters and stockpiled manufactured goods, especially cotton textiles, and agricultural produce, only to find markets collapsing with the disorder of the Russo-Japanese War in 1904–5, the 1905 Russian Revolution and the Constitutional Revolution in Iran from 1905, and the bank's financial position deteriorated. It was further damaged by making 'political' loans to Iranian notables, practically none of which were repaid. By the eve of the First World War, the Russian bank was bankrupt and moribund. Even periods of Russian political hegemony were not translated into success for the Russian bank. Russia's two large loans to Iran in 1900 and 1902, for example, should have put the Russian bank in a particularly strong competitive position. However, the Imperial Bank's greater technical expertise meant that it, rather than the Russian bank, handled the foreign exchange transactions involved in transferring the two loans to the Iranian government.[24]

The greatest competition to British trading and financial interests usually came from indigenous merchants, frequently Armenian or 'Levantine' in origin. However in most instances the foreign and 'traditional' sectors of the economy were not in direct competition. The Imperial Bank, for example, faced a widespread network of indigenous bankers, or *sarrafs* as they were known, who were mostly concerned with short-term lending and seasonal advances for agriculture, the discounting of bills, and the remittance of funds between towns. High interest rates were the norm. For the most part the modern and traditional banking sectors were not in direct competition, for a large proportion of the population continued to deal with the *sarrafs* for cultural reasons and, particularly, because they were willing to lend without the 'security' demanded by the Imperial Bank. While the Imperial Bank's managers frequently referred to the competitiveness of the *sarrafs*, especially in Tehran, Esfahan, Tabriz and Mashad, and it is clear that the *sarrafs* resented, on their part, the presence of the Bank as a symbol of European penetration, the two continued to co-exist because the indigenous bankers were in a better position to respond to most of the needs of the *bazaar*.[25]

It was fortunate that British business rarely faced strong or direct competition, because in many instances it had inadequate management structures. It was a frequent characteristic of British business overseas in the twentieth century that, although it excelled at opening up new areas of activity, it was less successful in managing the businesses thereby created. This was certainly true in the case of Iran. Before 1922 the Anglo-Persian Oil Company's activities in Iran were run on the widely criticised managing agency system, and even afterwards there were defects in the management structure, for example in the region of technical expertise. The merger of Gray Mackenzie and Lynch Brothers to form Mespers was a failure because of management problems. The Imperial Bank saw constant tension between the London-based board and the Tehran-based Chief Executive.[26]

A more serious problem than competition for British business in Iran before 1925 was the exceptionally underdeveloped state of the infrastructure and the difficult living conditions for European staff sent to the country. Before 1914 a European businessman would often be the only European in a town. Medical care, sanitation, clean water and other such 'Western' facilities were virtually non-existent. The lack of good transport facilities was an enormous problem. The country had no railway and only a limited number of roads – as opposed to rough tracks – before the 1930s, while there was only one navigable river, the Karun in the south-west. Transport of goods, therefore, was usually undertaken by camel or mule caravan, which was both expensive and time-consuming. British goods landed at Bushire or Bandar Abbas on the Gulf could take months to arrive in Tehran or the northern provinces. This was an important reason why British traders concentrated on such crops as opium and silk, or manufactures such as carpets, whose value in relation to bulk was high. Several infant British mining ventures were wrecked by the prohibitive cost of importing plant and machinery, let alone the

42 *Frances Bostock and Geoffrey Jones*

expense of transporting minerals after they were extracted. The need to build an entire infrastructure – a refinery, pipelines, a port, roads, staff accommodation – took the Anglo-Persian Oil Company to the brink of financial ruin before 1914.[27] The absence of an appropriately educated and trained work-force also hindered British businesses. The Imperial Bank, whose managers were British but which relied on locally recruited clerical staff (usually Armenian in the north), had to give a basic training to hundreds of men.

The weakness of the Iranian government provided further problems for British business. During the nineteenth century the Qajars had strengthened the power of the central government, but the Shah's chaotic finances and corrupt bureaucracy limited the effectiveness of the state's power. Central government, for example, was unable to deal with the riots and disorder caused by the activities of the Tobacco Corporation in the early 1890s. Tribal warfare in the south could isolate cities like Shiraz for weeks. During the 1900s Iran approached anarchy. The disorder worsened in the Constitutional Revolution of 1905–9 and Constitutional governments proved no more successful than their immediate predecessors at achieving administrative and financial reform. The result was that British traders and businesses turned to local tribal chieftains for the protection central government was unable to supply. In the south-west the Oil Company, for example, paid the Bakhtiari Khans to protect its business – essentially against the ravages of the Bakhtiari Khans.[28] Central government authority disintegrated during the First World War, leaving British interests to protect their property as best they could. In 1915, Anglo-Persian's pipeline was cut by dissident tribesmen and a German commando, and there was a four-month delay before repairs could be effected; in the same and subsequent years several of the Imperial Bank's branches were occupied and looted.[29]

This sorry tale of chaos and instability did nothing to interest British investors in London in Iran. Occasional bursts of enthusiasm for Iran would end abruptly and be followed by long periods when no British investor would touch any proposal to do with the country. An euphoric boom in Iranian stock around 1890, for example, was ended by the Shah's cancellation of the lottery and tobacco concessions and over the following twenty years it was virtually impossible to raise capital on the London market for investment in Iran. In 1902, when the British government attempted to interest the wealthy City financier, Sir Ernest Cassel, in the development prospects of Seistan (which bordered British India), he observed that nothing would induce him to invest in Iran.[30] When Iran acquired a Constitutional government in 1909, London's money market relaxed its attitude somewhat. During 1910 several banking houses expressed an interest in floating loans for Iran, including Samuel and

2.2 *Imperial Bank of Persia banknote (one toman was equal to ten krans/rials).*

Company and Seligman Brothers. With the help of the Foreign Office, the Imperial Bank beat off this competition, however, and in 1911 floated a loan on the London market for £1.25 million. Unlike for the earlier 1892 loan, there was no difficulty in finding subscribers. However, the honeymoon did not last long, and by the eve of the First World War Iran's name was again unpopular. There was a final surge of British interest in Iran immediately after the War, when the Anglo-Persian Agreement of 1919, a brainchild of Lord Curzon and negotiated with a pro-British government, seemed set to turn Iran into a virtual British protectorate.[31] The Persian Transport Company and the Persian Railways Syndicate were rejuvenated; Mespers was formed in anticipation of new trading opportunities; and a new interest in Iran's prospects was expressed by powerful British industrial groups, including Vickers, Armstrong Whitworth, and Lord Cowdray's Pearson Group.[32] However, the coup d'état of 1921 brought into power a government which finally repudiated the Anglo-Persian Agreement, thus spelling the end once again of the high expectations of British business.

A final complication for British business in Iran was its relationship with the British government. A close relationship with the British govern-

44   Frances Bostock and Geoffrey Jones

ment was almost a prerequisite for survival in Iran, yet it also presented a number of problems. The support of the British Minister in Tehran and of the Foreign Office was essential if concessions were to be obtained and sustained. The lack of such support for de Reuter in the early 1870s, for example, was to a large extent the death knell of his project. Conversely, the negotiations which led to the granting of the D'Arcy oil concession in 1901 were strongly supported by British officials as part of their plan to strengthen British influence in southern Iran, and thereafter the British government or its officials in Iran intervened at crucial moments to sustain the fledgling Oil Company. In 1904 the British Admiralty, who were beginning to appreciate the potential of oil as a fuel supply for the Navy and anxious to have a supply of oil in a region of British political influence, helped to persuade the Burmah Oil Company to rescue D'Arcy. In 1907 a small detachment of Indian troops was despatched to protect the Oil Company's drillings. Finally, in 1914 came the British government's large investment in the company.[33] Other British business interests received support and protection, not always to the extent they desired, but nevertheless a vital assistance to survival in the difficult conditions of Iran.

The upshot was that relations between the British government and British business in Iran were close. The Imperial Bank was not a direct tool of the British state in the way the Russian bank was of the Russian state, but it was expected to serve as an 'agent of Empire'. The Bank channelled British government loans to the Iranian government between the 1900s and the 1920s, and also acted as an agency through which Britain supported strategic commercial and political interests. The government of India subsidised one branch of the Bank near the border with British India at Seistan to the extent of £1,500 a year from its inception in 1903 until 1908.[34]

The need to oblige the Foreign Office left the Imperial Bank and other British business ventures in an awkward position, torn between the conflicting interests of the British government, their shareholders, and the country in which they operated. The Bank, for example, was subject to interference in its lending policies. During the Constitutional Revolution the Foreign Office insisted that no loans were to be made to Iran until a constitutional government was in power. During the First World War the Imperial Bank abandoned any pretensions to being the state bank of Iran and devoted all its resources to supplying funds for the needs of British and Russian troops in Iran. The period after the end of the War saw the blatant use of the Bank by the Foreign Office as an instrument to achieve the ratification of the Anglo-Persian Agreement. The Bank was used to provide compliant Iranian ministers with money – including a notorious bribe of £131,000 paid to Prime Minister Vossuq od-Douleh and two of his ministers to ensure ratification of the Agreement. The Bank felt

British business in Iran, 1860s–1970s 45

particularly unhappy at the policies imposed upon it by the British Foreign Secretary, Lord Curzon, who insisted that no loans should be made to Vossuq od-Douleh's successors until they came up with ratification, even though such loans were merely advances against revenues such as oil royalties which were payable to Iran in any case. Curzon's intransigence continued after the 1921 coup, and even though the Bank's Chief Manager acted against express official instructions on more than one occasion, in providing advances which were desperately needed by the government, the Bank's reputation suffered. Reza Khan unkindly suggested that it might more suitably be retitled 'Lord Curzon's Bank of Persia'.[35]

By 1925 British business in Iran had considerable achievements to its credit. Although the economy remained underdeveloped, the modern oil industry had been created, the carpet industry had been developed, shipping and transport facilities improved, and a nation-wide banking system was in place. British business dominated the modern sector of the economy. Yet, in retrospect, it can be seen that this domination rested on weak foundations. Anglo-Persian and the Imperial Bank operated on the basis of monopoly concessions granted by the Qajar regime, and secured with British diplomatic support. Both the Bank and the Oil Company had close links with the British government. The whole edifice of British business had been built up at a time when Iranian government and business were weak and disorganised, and when foreign competition had been minimal.

2.3 Conflict and contraction, 1925–54

The inter-war years were a difficult period for British business in Iran, even when compared to its troubles in many other Asian countries. Reza Khan's rise to power, culminating in his accession as Shah in 1925, was followed by a drive to reverse foreign political and economic domination of Iran. The first manifestation of this was the cancellation in 1928 of the Capitulations, which had been in force since the Treaty of Turkmanchai a hundred years previously, and which had given foreign trade and commerce a privileged position. Spurred on by the Depression, and to combat the effects on exports of the establishment by Soviet Russia, traditionally Iran's most important market for agricultural produce, of a state monopoly of trade, Iran established in 1930 its own foreign trade monopoly. This was the start of a process of increasing state control of trade and production, which included the introduction of complex exchange control regulations. A state-led industrialisation programme in the 1930s combined the establishment of state factories with protective regulations for privately owned plants. Many of these policies were reversed during

46 *Frances Bostock and Geoffrey Jones*

Iran's occupation by the Allies during the Second World War, but after 1945 there was a renewed surge of nationalistic economic policies, culminating in the Prime Ministership of Mossadeq between April 1951 and August 1953.[36]

British business was buffeted by depressed markets, import restrictions and exchange controls all over Asia, even in the countries of the British empire. However, Iran's historical legacy and the prominent position held in the economy by the Anglo-Persian Oil Company led to serious and acrimonious conflicts between British commerce and the Iranian government. There were major conflicts with the Oil Company in the early 1930s and the early 1950s, and with the Bank from the late 1920s until its withdrawal from Iran in 1952. In inter-war India the long-established expatriate business houses declined, but they were replaced by new forms of British investment, especially direct investment by British-based multinationals. In Iran between 1925 and 1954 the British firms in the extractive and infrastructure industries and banking withdrew or were forced out, but were scarcely replaced. The overall story of British business in Iran in this period is one of conflict and contraction.

By the mid-1920s the Anglo-Persian Oil Company had become the most important British enterprise in Iran. Oil was Iran's largest export. Anglo-Persian's prominence, however, was not accompanied by popularity. As will be discussed below, Anglo-Persian's linkages with the local economy were few, and the company was widely disliked. The fact that the British government was a majority shareholder in Anglo-Persian directly associated the company for most Iranians with British imperialism.

Anglo-Persian's relations with the Iranian government started to sour during the First World War as a result of the Company's claim for compensation for the cutting of its oil pipeline in 1915. Anglo-Persian withheld royalty payments to the government until the compensation had been covered, and the government retaliated with a counter-claim for higher royalties. In addition, Anglo-Persian's definition of the 'net profits' on which royalties were based was challenged. The issue was not finally settled until 1920 when, under the Armitage–Smith Agreement, Anglo-Persian made an immediate lump-sum payment of £1 million to the Iranian government to settle outstanding claims, and the basis of calculation of annual royalties was clarified. However, the Armitage–Smith Agreement was rejected by Iran after 1921, as part and parcel of Curzon's unacceptable Anglo-Persian Agreement, and the basis on which royalties were calculated continued to be an annual source of controversy throughout the next decade. At the end of the 1920s this problem was exacerbated as falling world oil prices led to a decline in royalty payments. The Company and the government engaged in extensive negotiations for

British business in Iran, 1860s–1970s   47

four years after 1928. Anglo-Persian offered shares to the government, and to appoint Iranian directors to its board. However, such offers were of limited importance because the kernel of the crisis was Anglo-Persian's symbolic role as a bastion of British imperialism. The Company's difficulties with the Iranian government culminated in the cancellation of its concession in November 1932.[37] A measure of the strength of feeling regarding the Company is that when its concession was cancelled a two-day national holiday of celebration was declared.

The dispute between the Anglo-Persian Oil Company and the Iranian government became, inevitably, a conflict between the British and Iranian governments, and eventually went to the League of Nations for arbitration. In 1933 a new sixty-year concession agreement was signed with Anglo-Persian, the main effects of which were to reduce the area of the concession to about a quarter of the original, and to introduce a new tonnage basis of assessment for royalty payments. There was also a variety of other guarantees and payments, including a back-payment of £1 million. Overall, however, the Iranian government gained comparatively little out of the dispute. Anglo-Persian, supported by the British government, was still a powerful force.[38]

The Oil Company (which was renamed the Anglo-Iranian Oil Company in 1935) became a renewed target of nationalist discontent after the Second World War. There were further charges that Iran was being denied a rightful share in its most valuable natural resource, and that the British government was responsible for this miscarriage of justice. There was considerable evidence to support such a case. Anglo-Iranian's net profit after taxation rose from £9.6 million in 1946 to a record £18.6 million in 1947, but owing to the British government's wartime policy of dividend limitation, the dividends paid by Anglo-Iranian remained the same. This curtailed the royalty payable to Iran since under the 1933 agreement Iran received annually 20% of the dividend payable to ordinary shareholders as well as the tonnage royalty. Thus the amount received by Iran in 1947 was £7.1 million as compared with nearly £20 million taken by the British government in its 'dual role', as Anglo-Iranian's Chairman put it in 1948, 'of majority shareholder and tax gatherer'.[39] The signing of 50/50 profit-sharing agreements between governments and oil companies elsewhere – in Venezuela in 1948 and Saudi Arabia in 1950 – served to intensify criticism of Anglo-Iranian within Iran.[40]

The idea of nationalisation of the oil industry received its impetus from the attempts of the Soviets to obtain an oil concession in the north in 1944–5. It was first mentioned by the nationalist politician Mossadeq in the Iranian parliament in November 1944, and over the following few years demands for an increased share of the revenues from oil became

48   *Frances Bostock and Geoffrey Jones*

increasingly strident. In 1949 a supplemental Oil Agreement was negotiated which was designed to increase Iran's oil royalties by raising the basic tonnage royalty.[41] This would have had the effect of doubling Iran's royalties in the short term, and increasing them proportionately in the longer term. But the Agreement was never ratified. Nationalist politicians demanded at least a half share in Anglo-Iranian's worldwide profits. However, once again symbolism rather than money was at the heart of the crisis. Anglo-Iranian remained 'the symbol of foreign resistance to the national struggle for progressive socio-political change'.[42]

In the winter of 1950–1, when it was clear that the clamour for nationalisation of the oil industry was gathering force, Anglo-Iranian offered concessions, including a cash advance to the government, and consideration of a 50/50 profit-sharing settlement. By then, however, only nationalisation would satisfy the clamour. In March 1951 the oil industry was nationalised. Between March and October, when the Company's Abadan refinery was closed and Anglo-Iranian's expatriate staff left the country, there were various attempts to negotiate a resolution of the dispute, but to no effect. In October 1951, the oil industry in Iran was effectively shut down.

The following three years provide a classic case-study in the relations between Third World governments and Western business. Diplomatic relations between Iran and Britain were broken off in October 1952 at Iranian insistence. The Western oil companies operated a boycott of Iranian oil which prevented its export, depriving the country of vital foreign exchange earnings. Anglo-Iranian expanded the output from its oil fields in neighbouring Kuwait in order to meet the gap in its requirements created by the loss of Iran. Finally, in 1953, the British government planned a coup – implemented with the help of the American Central Intelligence Agency – which overthrew Mossadeq and restored Reza Shah's son to full powers as Shah.[43]

The political machinations of Britain and the United States allowed the return to Iran of Anglo-Iranian (renamed the British Petroleum Company in 1954), but not on such favourable terms as the Company had secured after the 1932–3 dispute. In August 1954 an agreement led to the return to Iran of Western oil companies, but British Petroleum held only 40% of the shares of the newly formed Oil Consortium, formed to market Iran's oil. The remaining shareholding was initially divided between five American companies, with 8% each; the Anglo-Dutch Shell Group, with 14%; and the French state oil company, with 6%. BP also secured £25 million in compensation from the Iranian government, payable over a ten-year period, as well as further compensation from the other companies in the Consortium. Moreover, although BP lost its monopoly interest in Iran's oil industry, Britain retained through its 40% share and

British business in Iran, 1860s–1970s   49

the Anglo-Dutch Shell Company's 14% share the largest single foreign interest.[44]

Under the 1954 Agreement, the oil industry remained formally nationalised. However, this was little more than a legality since the Consortium had effective control over price and output. Iran did not gain *de facto* control of its oil industry until July 1973 when (as a result of the successful establishment of OPEC by the oil-producing countries as a counterbalance to the power of the Western oil companies) Iran was able to insist on a revision of the 1954 Agreement. Under a new agreement the National Iranian Oil Company took full responsibility for output throughout the area previously controlled by the Consortium, a move which limited BP and Shell, along with the other Consortium members, to the role of mere purchasers of Iranian oil and providers of some technical services under contract.

The Iranian government's clashes with the Oil Company were mirrored by similar conflict with the second most important British business institution in Iran, the Imperial Bank. The Bank does not appear to have been as hated as the Oil Company in Iran. Yet its privileged position as the state bank, freed from all taxation and with the sole right of note issue, its imposing buildings and – for Iran – affluent British managers, served to make it also an obtrusive symbol of British power in the country. As such, it was an inevitable target for Reza Shah.

In 1928 the government created its own bank, Bank Melli Iran, which replaced the Imperial Bank as state bank. Soon afterwards a series of official measures began to handicap the Imperial Bank's commercial business which consisted largely of exchange operations and the finance of foreign trade. In 1930 a law rationed foreign exchange, and the British bank, still the main foreign exchange dealer, found itself compelled to hand over 50% of all its foreign exchange purchases to Bank Melli. The Imperial Bank was eventually released from these restrictions and became, with Bank Melli, an authorised exchange bank, but only after it had agreed to renounce in favour of the Bank Melli its right to issue banknotes. The Imperial Bank continued to have difficulty with exchange controls and foreign exchange restrictions throughout the 1930s. Profit remittance became a problem, and the Bank found itself forced to lend to the government as a *quid pro quo* for permission to remit any profits at all. All this had a crippling effect on the Imperial Bank's business. Between 1928 and 1938 the Bank's deposits declined from £7.8 million to £3.7 million, its advances from £4.6 million to £2.7 million, and total assets from £14.3 million to £7.8 million. The Bank reduced the number of its branches from twenty-five at the end of the 1920s to thirteen by 1939. The Bank's business in Iran made substantial losses for several years in the 1930s, and the Bank only survived on the income from its investments in London.[45]

50   *Frances Bostock and Geoffrey Jones*

The Second World War, however, reversed the melancholy decline in the Bank's fortunes. The Imperial Bank resumed its role as paymaster for the British government, and was freed from the Iranian government's restrictions on profit remittance and exchange dealings. By 1945 the Bank's deposits had soared to £22.1 million, advances to £4.3 million, and total assets to £29.7 million.[46]

The Imperial Bank's respite, however, was a brief one. After 1945 the Bank again found itself under pressure. In particular the British bank faced a determined assault from Bank Melli, whose Governor since 1942 had been Abol Hassan Ebtehaj, an ex-employee of the Imperial Bank who had resigned in 1936 because he was refused any prospect of promotion to managerial rank in the Bank, which was reserved for Europeans.[47] After the War the Imperial Bank, still Iran's foremost exchange bank, found itself the target of Ebtehaj in his determination to make the Bank Melli the effective central bank of Iran.

It was unfortunate for the Imperial Bank that because of the exigencies of providing local currency for Allied troops during the War, and because, also, of a flight of deposits to it as a result of a communist-inspired rebellion in the northern province of Azerbaijan, it was in an extremely liquid position by 1946. In contrast, Bank Melli, faced with the prospect of heavy government borrowing and the financing of large development projects, had a severe liquidity problem. In order to safeguard his bank's position, Ebtehaj wanted the Imperial Bank, as well as the other banks in Iran, to place a proportion of their deposits at Bank Melli's disposal. The Imperial Bank's opposition to any such idea caused Ebtehaj to introduce increasingly restrictive legislation. Although the measures were directed at all banks, it was the foreign banks which suffered most as their position was the most vulnerable. The Ottoman Bank, which had mixed French and British ownership and which had had branches in Iran since 1920, withdrew from the country in 1948. But it was the Imperial Bank – the only authorised exchange bank apart from Bank Melli – which was the main target. Ebtehaj worked hard to get its foreign exchange authorisation removed, or at least subject to the overall control of Bank Melli. He was not successful in the former objective although his efforts caused the British bank considerable difficulties in its foreign exchange operations; but by early 1950 he had succeeded with the latter. When the Bank's concession expired in March 1949, it was forced to change its name, dropping at the government's insistence the title 'Imperial' to become The British Bank of Iran and the Middle East. The Bank was also forced to accept operating restrictions which were much more tight than hitherto – although less tight than Ebtehaj would have liked – including the transfer to Iran of £1 million sterling capital, the redeposit, interest-free, with Bank Melli of 55% of its deposits, and the linkage of the amount of

British business in Iran, 1860s–1970s   51

deposits it could take to the amount of sterling capital it brought into Iran. The British bank's business in Iran soon plunged into unprofitability as these measures took effect.[48]

As it became more and more difficult for the British Bank to operate in Iran, it began to run down its Iranian business and to concentrate on developing its new business on the Arab side of the Gulf, where the Bank had opened a branch in Kuwait in 1942, and in the Levant.[49] The Bank's confidence in its future prospects in Iran was not revived when Ebtehaj was dismissed from his post by the Shah in July 1950. When the Bank's foreign exchange authorisation was withdrawn in September 1951, as a result of the diplomatic wrangle over Mossadeq's nationalisation of the oil industry and the closure of the refinery at Abadan, the Bank's management took the opportunity to close down its business in Iran. The withdrawal of exchange authorisation accelerated a process already well under way: the Bank had begun closing its less profitable provincial branches in 1949, and by early 1951 had decided to move the seat of its Chief Executive from Iran.[50]

Apart from Anglo-Persian Oil and the Imperial Bank, few of the other British ventures which had been established in Qajar Iran survived the Reza Shah era. The Indo-European Telegraph Company went into liquidation in 1933 following the cancellation of its concession. Mespers never achieved its ambitious goals. By the mid-1920s, it had had to write off losses of £210,000, primarily caused by bad debts and overstocking. Although the company did not finally collapse until 1936, dividends were suspended from 1930.[51] During the 1930s the British carpet traders were also squeezed out of business by the state monopoly system.[52] Only the Gulf shipping agencies remained relatively unscathed.

The few attempts to establish new British ventures were unsuccessful. During the 1920s British insurance companies had invested in Iran, and by the mid-1930s there were ten British-owned insurance companies in the country, but legislation in 1936 designed to favour locally owned companies led to their almost total withdrawal.[53] In 1942 a group of British pharmaceutical companies, consisting of Glaxo Laboratories, Boots Pure Drug Company, British Drug Houses, The Wellcome Foundation and Evans Sons Lescher and Webb, incorporated a marketing company called the Anglo-Iranian Pharmaceutical Company Ltd (AIPC). AIPC had a brief and undistinguished career. It was buffeted by the foreign exchange regulations introduced after the Second World War and was put into voluntary liquidation at the end of 1948.[54]

While Reza Shah's Iran was hostile to the older forms of Western business activity, based on exclusive concessions and foreign ownership of important national assets, it did seek – rather in the manner of Meiji Japan – foreign expertise, technical skills and equipment. However, Reza Shah

52   Frances Bostock and Geoffrey Jones

2.3 One of two large span bridges across the Ab-e Cesar River, and one of the seven tunnels through rock, constructed by Costains in its eleven-mile section of the Trans-Iranian railway (the contract value was £1 million in 1936).

British business in Iran, 1860s–1970s 53

was intent on avoiding too great a dependence in any one direction – and particularly in the directions of Iran's erstwhile mentors, Russia and Britain. In the 1930s, therefore, Britain was largely excluded in the search for foreign expertise and the award of supply contracts. Thus when it came to the building of the Trans-Iranian railway, by far Iran's largest and most prestigious industrial project, the early survey and construction work was undertaken by American and German companies. After the Iranian government took over direct control in 1931, a Scandinavian concern was appointed in 1933 as managing agent for the project. Germany provided much of the expertise Iran needed: Germans initially managed the Bank Melli, ran the air services and constructed port facilities. Czechoslovakia provided machinery for sugar mills, Italian engineers helped to establish the glass industry, experts from France and Switzerland improved radio and telegraphic facilities, and Danes provided an entire cement plant near Tehran and built a sardine-packing factory on the Gulf coast. On the whole, British companies were conspicuous by their absence in Iran in the 1930s, although two British engineering contractors – Richard Costain and Nuttall Mowlem – did secure a notable share of the Trans-Iranian railway project in the end.[55]

At the end of the 1930s there was some evidence that British business was prepared to adjust to the new environment in Iran. Certain companies adopted a new means of obtaining large supply contracts – consortium bidding – which was appropriate to negotiating with the large state bureaucracies created by Reza Shah. The use of the consortium idea in Iran was conceived by William Gout, a British subject born in Smyrna who lived in Iran after 1914 and had worked for a British-owned carpet company before becoming an independent merchant in Tabriz. After going bankrupt in 1931, Gout became a commission agent in Tehran for various British manufacturers, and over the following years became convinced that British firms needed to join together to tender for contracts. In 1939 Gout's ideas were vindicated when a consortium of British companies, including United Steel Companies, Dorman Long, GKN and Colvilles, won a contract to supply Iran with 72,000 tons of rails and accessories at a cost of £1 million, although the outbreak of the Second World War meant that barely 10% of the order was delivered. After the War Gout resumed his activity. In 1950 he secured a £3 million contract for the railmakers' consortium in the teeth of German and French competition, and another contract for sixty-four steam diesel locomotives valued at £1.2 million. Gout seems to have stimulated mixed feelings. Sir George Binney, who headed the railmakers' consortium, held a high opinion of him and praised his 'patriotism'.[56] However, a member of the British Embassy in Tehran dismissed him in 1952 as 'an inefficient intriguer with very little political judgement'.[57]

54   *Frances Bostock and Geoffrey Jones*

After the Second World War the most important British supplier of the technical expertise required by the Iranian authorities was Sir Alexander Gibb and Partners, a firm of consulting engineers. In 1944 the Iranian Ministry of Agriculture signed an agreement with Gibb for the survey of a large irrigation and hydro-electric project on the River Lar aimed at damming the Lar and diverting some of its waters onto the Tehran plain.[58] The British Ambassador described the scheme as the 'most promising opening for large scale British enterprise in Persia which has yet appeared'.[59] In fact, the implementation of the Lar project was delayed for a couple of decades, but it did result in Gibb being drawn into other projects, of which a contract to provide a modern water supply system for Tehran, signed in November 1946, was the most significant.[60] This contract lasted until 1956, when Tehran finally got piped water, and Gibb not only served as consulting engineers but also supervised the supply of materials for the project from Britain. Gibb was the only British firm to continue working through the period of crisis when the oil industry was nationalised and diplomatic relations between Britain and Iran were broken off.

Gibb was also able to secure a niche in Iran's planning machinery. In 1949 Iran's first seven-year development plan was approved. A firm of American engineering consultants had acted as initial advisers, and when a new state agency, the Plan Organisation, was set up in 1948 to implement the plan, it too employed American consultants, Overseas Consultants Incorporated (OCI).[61] However, the British government persuaded the State Department that there should be Anglo-American cooperation in this matter, and OCI was persuaded to allot the civil engineering side of its work to Gibb.[62] Gibb's involvement in this way meant that its people became consultants on a number of projects, and they were also able to invite works and supply tenders from British companies. When Gibb served as consultants for the erection of the Esfahan power station, for example, it invited tenders for plant from leading British firms, and Yarrow and Company and Metropolitan Vickers won contracts for the boiler plant and electrical installations respectively with a total value of £550,000.[63] The British government fully appreciated Gibb's role in attracting orders for British industry. 'Despite American competition Gibb's have done a great deal towards enhancing the prestige of the U.K.', a Board of Trade memorandum observed in February 1947, 'and no doubt from many of their plans the U.K. will have a very good opportunity of obtaining the orders for the necessary material.'[64]

Gibb, however, was the main exception in the otherwise general story of the decline and contraction of British business in Iran between 1925 and 1954. By the beginning of 1954, after the crisis over the Oil Company

British business in Iran, 1860s–1970s   55

nationalisation, it was the only British firm left operating within the country. What had gone wrong? Clearly the fundamental problem had been a transformation of the conditions in which British enterprise had flourished. The giants of British enterprise in Iran – the Oil Company and the Bank – had grown on the basis of exclusive concessions negotiated at a time when the Iranian government was weak and British diplomatic influence was strong. The reversal of these conditions during the inter-war years left the British ventures exposed as unwanted relics of British imperial power.

It was sometimes alleged in British business circles that the British government did not support British companies in Iran as actively as other foreign governments supported their own nationals. In the late 1920s the Imperial Bank, which constantly felt it was not given the support it deserved by the British government, blamed the decline of business as a whole in Iran in such terms:

> Of course, the Germans have a most energetic Minister who seeks opportunities, while ours doesn't or cannot, added to which the Germans are much more adaptable than our manufacturers to the needs of their foreign customers – and plus the willingness to take bigger risks to secure trade than we do by longer and larger credit. The real difference in the two country's [sic] method of trading is in the active support they receive from their Government whilst ours leaves us to look after ourselves as best we can.[65]

Twenty years later the Boots' representative in the Anglo-Iranian Pharmaceutical Company discerned a similar lack of Foreign Office commitment to British commerce in Iran, arguing that British diplomats placed the interests of the Anglo-Iranian Oil Company before all else:

> the British Embassy are, in contrast with other embassies here, strongly opposed to irritating the Iranian Government by any kind of threat, because the oil concessions which we hold by the very skin of our teeth are worth millions of pounds monetarily and an incalculable sum strategically.[66]

However, British government support for British companies was far from negligible. The Oil Company on the whole was strongly backed by the Foreign Office, and by British politicians such as Shinwell and Morrison.[67] Moreover, especially after 1945, the British government was very active in encouraging British companies to seek business in Iran. This was primarily because of the large sterling balances accumulated by Iran because of oil revenues and the War. It was regarded as essential that British firms earned as much as they could of Iran's oil income and sterling reserves in order to protect Britain's fragile post-war balance of payments position.[68] The urgency of this matter was increased when a Memorandum of Understanding signed by the two countries in 1947 ensured that

56   Frances Bostock and Geoffrey Jones

Iran's growing sterling balances were convertible into other currencies. During the late 1940s, therefore, British officials were active in pushing often reluctant British companies to undertake work in Iran. A number of British companies had been persuaded to enter 'a market they dislike', a British government official noted in 1950, 'in order to absorb convertible Sterling'.[69] Gibb often expressed frustration at the difficulties of operating in Iran, including delays in securing payment for services, and seems to have persevered largely as a result of British government entreaties. In 1952 Sir George Binney recollected that the 1950 rails contract had been an embarrassment from the outset, 'and we only tackled it because the Treasury and the Board of Trade were anxious at that time that we should endeavour to absorb dollar-convertible Persian Oil royalties'.[70]

The managements of Britain's leading enterprises in Iran were responsible for many of their worst difficulties. Although both the Oil Company and the Bank built up and managed their businesses well, they displayed a lack of sympathy and understanding for post-Qajar Iran. The Imperial Bank was petulant and obstructive when faced by the Iranian government's economic policies in the 1930s, refusing to oblige the government's wishes until it was literally forced to do so. All aspects of the Bank's policies showed a similar insensitivity to the changes which Iran was undergoing. The Bank's refusal to appoint Iranians to management positions, for example, caused much resentment and the fateful loss of Abol Hassan Ebtehaj as well as other senior Iranian staff.[71]

Such policies came under criticism from British government officials, and it is hardly surprising that they did not always give the Bank their whole-hearted support.[72] Similarly, the Eastern Department of the Foreign Office – as opposed to the British Embassy in Tehran which tended to be more pro-Oil Company – often expressed reservations over Anglo-Iranian's policies towards the Iranian government. One British government Minister in October 1951 went so far as to observe that Anglo-Iranian had never made a proper political assessment of the situation it faced.[73] In fact, however, both British civil servants and British businessmen were often unable to free themselves from a vision of Iran as it had been in the nineteenth century. The result was a blindness to legitimate criticisms against British companies, and a view that any difficulties were caused not by an authentic nationalist movement but by a few crazed individuals. Thus during the late 1940s the Imperial Bank blamed all its difficulties on the 'jealousy' and personal animosity of Ebtehaj. Similarly, the British Ambassador in Tehran in the early 1950s painted a most extraordinary word-picture of Mossadeq as an opium-smoking drug addict who spent each day in his pyjamas.[74]

The insensitivity of British business to political changes was unfortunate because from the 1920s, unlike in Qajar Iran, it faced real compe-

British business in Iran, 1860s–1970s   57

tition from other countries. As we have explained above, Reza Shah went out of his way to encourage American and continental European companies to invest in Iran, a trend increased by economic ties developed with Germany in the 1930s. Moreover, companies from these countries also often showed a vigour and interest in the Iranian market displayed by few British enterprises. During the early 1920s German companies began to offer serious competition to British firms in the shipping industry. The German shipping company of Wonckhaus and Company, already known in the Gulf and Karun, established in 1923 a line of small cargo steamers plying between Hamburg and the Caspian via the Russian canals and the Volga. The line won instant popularity with Iranian merchants in the north, enabling them to import bulky items. In addition, Hansa Line steamers began to arrive at Gulf ports, attracting business through the services of an energetic agent based in Tehran.

Throughout the period the British Embassy and British business in Iran were prone to ascribe the success of competitors to a willingness to use bribery, while British firms were portrayed as models of purity and innocence. A British official describing a British success in winning a 1954 rails contract observed that it had been won 'in the face of the most vigorous intrigue and bribery by competitors'.[75] Contracts were indeed often negotiated in suspicious circumstances. In 1950, for example, the Fairmile Construction Company won an adjudication of tenders for the supply of barges for the salt mines at Hormuz called for by the Plan Organisation. Fairmile's had the lowest tender price. But after the adjudication was over, the Plan Organisation informed it that a German firm had undercut it, and asked it to reduce its offer. There had been no German offers in the original adjudication. The Fairmile Company complained bitterly of the 'corruption, intrigue and favouritism' it had faced.[76]

Nevertheless, a series of circulars and pleas from British officials to British firms from the 1920s to the 1950s indicated that British companies in Iran suffered from many of the uncompetitive features which have been diagnosed in other markets. A Board of Trade Circular in 1924 had to remind British merchants that it was helpful to issue suitable trade literature in Persian rather than English; to study more thoroughly the peculiarities of the local market; to issue price catalogues since price was a vital factor in selling; and to establish proper networks of local agents. Such entreaties do not seem to have had a great effect, for in 1946 the British Embassy in Tehran was to be found advising British manufacturers to appoint provincial agents, and to print trade literature in Persian. Again in the mid-1950s, the same points were being made, especially the necessity for British exporters to develop personal

58 *Frances Bostock and Geoffrey Jones*

contacts with the market in Iran, to appoint good local agents, and offer quick deliveries at competitive prices.[77]

2.4 The flawed miracle, 1954–78

The overthrow of Mossedeq and the ending of the oil crisis concluded the period of conflict between British business and the Iranian government. In September 1955, after eighteen months of negotiation, Iran's Council of Ministers granted British (and German) exports 'most favoured nation' status. At the end of 1955, the Iranian Parliament passed a law for the Attraction and Protection of Foreign Investment which provided for the withdrawal of capital in the same currency in which it was imported, for annual profit remittances in that currency, and for equitable compensation in the case of nationalisation. A far more favourable climate was, therefore, created for foreign investment. The Iranian economy, despite cyclical recessions, resumed expansion. Between 1955 and 1975 Iran's Gross National Product (GNP) increased annually by 8.5% at constant prices. By the 1970s there was much talk in Britain of Iran as the 'New Japan': it was only at the end of that decade that the flawed nature of the Shah's Iran became visible to all.

By the mid-1950s Iran's imports from Britain were rapidly recovering from the trough reached during the oil crisis. Indeed, at the end of 1957, the *Financial Times* pointed out that 'Iran is now Britain's best customer in the Middle East.'[78] Within Iran, however, there had been a fundamental change of perspective and the former predominance of British business had been irretrievably lost. British Petroleum was only one of an international group of oil companies, while the British Bank of the Middle East no longer operated in the country. The United States dominated new Western investment in the late 1950s and the 1960s. In April 1958, out of the twenty-eight firms of foreign consultants under contract to the Plan Organisation, only three were British: nine were American and six were French. Between 1963 and 1967 the United States accounted for about 54% of foreign private investment in Iran. Germany and Britain followed with about 8 and 7% respectively.[79] In the 1970s, Japan took over as the leading investor nation.[80] As elsewhere in Asia, British business in Iran from the 1950s played a modest role which hardly reflected its formerly dominant position.

The British government remained eager to encourage British business activity in Iran. The agreement with the Oil Consortium threw into sharper relief than ever the necessity to try and mop up Iran's excess sterling. In mid-1954 the commercial counsellor at the newly re-opened British Embassy in Tehran returned to Britain to talk directly to British business about the Iranian market and its possibilities. 'There is plenty of

British business in Iran, 1860s–1970s   59

business to be done here', he considered, 'and provided British interests accept that the going will be tough, competition severe and the methods used rarely in conformity with the Queensbury [sic] rules, there is no good reason why we should not get our whack.'[81] However, British officials were still more optimistic than British businessmen about the prospects, and generous inducements had to be offered to British companies to sell to or invest in Iran. In 1955 it was arranged that British firms would receive Export Credit Guarantee Department cover on as generous terms as possible so that they were not either deterred from entering the market or forced to increase their prices to the Iranians to take account of increased premium rates or excessive risk.[82] A £10 million line of credit was also offered to Iran, tied to British goods and services. The ostensible object of the credit was to keep Iran economically and politically stable during the period before oil revenues became substantial again. However, British government officials were more concerned with the use of the loan as a means to promote British business in Iran. The credit was, in the words of one official in October 1954, 'a rescue operation for British trade rather than a rescue operation for Persia'.[83]

British foreign direct investment in Iran after 1954 occurred in a number of sectors. Foreigners could own legally only a minority share in Iranian industries, and these new investments all took the form of joint ventures. British banks re-appeared in Iran in this guise. In March 1959 Chartered Bank launched the Irano-British Bank, in which it held initially a 49% stake. In the following May the British Bank of the Middle East, the successor to the old Imperial Bank of Iran, returned to Iran with its own joint venture, the Bank of Iran and the Middle East. Both banks, however, remained marginal in the rapidly expanding and heavily competitive Iranian banking system. In 1962 the two British banks were ranked eleventh and twelfth in terms of asset size of the twenty-seven banks operating in Iran. By the 1970s American banks, notably Chase Manhattan, were the dominant foreign banks in the country.

There was new British investment in Iranian manufacturing. In the 1960s there were a number of joint ventures, especially in the motor industry. The Rootes Group joined with the Iran National Vehicle Manufacturing Company to set up an assembly plant licensed to produce cars modelled on the Hillman Hunter. The first Paykan cars were produced in 1967 from car kits made in Coventry. This operation rapidly became the British automotive industry's biggest export contract, worth some £130 million a year. Leyland established a truck and bus assembly plant in Tehran and a company in Tabriz to build engines for the trucks and buses produced. Dorman Diesel, a joint venture with the British company, was established in Tabriz to assemble stationary engines for deep-well water pumping and electrical power generation in remote

60 Frances Bostock and Geoffrey Jones

areas.[84] British Petroleum resolutely avoided investment in Iranian industry. This was in striking contrast to some of the American oil companies which owned Aramco (especially Mobil), which invested heavily in downstream projects in Saudi Arabia. British Petroleum preferred to search for oil elsewhere in the Middle East, perhaps – as one study has suggested – because of 'disillusionment with its treatment in Iran during the 1940s and early 1950s'.[85]

Many joint ventures seem to have been profitable. They operated in a protected market, and were usually allied with the privileged business elite with close links to the Ruling Family. However, a number of British investments, especially in risky sectors such as agriculture, went awry. In Khuzestan, for example, Shell and Mitchell Cotts established the Iran Shellcott Company, one of a half-dozen agri-businesses set up under pressure from the Shah (who wanted the Company to grow strawberries and asparagus) as a result of the TVA-style regional development of the area in the 1960s. These agri-businesses hoped to grow cotton, sugar beet and cane, and grains on the land irrigated by the Dez and other Karun dams. The British venture, however, was misconceived from the start because little initial research was done before plunging headlong into the operation. Shell had instigated the idea of getting into agri-business in order to do something in Iran unconnected with the oil business. Its research director was advised by the British Embassy that the production of sunflower, or a similar seed oil, would probably be their best tactic, but this advice was disregarded in favour of cotton. The results were disastrous since cotton crops were prone to insect devastation, and in 1976 Shell and Mitchell Cotts withdrew from the venture.[86]

There was evidence of British failure in other sectors. In May 1955 the British contractor, John Mowlem Company, was appointed managing agents for Iran's road reconstruction programme, which involved the building or reconstruction of 6,000 kilometres of road. The contract, which had been won against considerable competition, provided for expenditure over an eight-year period of around £30 million.[87] However, Mowlem seriously underestimated the scale and technical problems of the project, and in 1957 its contract was cancelled. Another failure was in the motor components industry. In 1975 Guest Keen and Nettlefolds agreed with the Iranian government to form a £20 million joint venture plant to manufacture and assemble components, but GKN failed to find a local partner and in 1977 withdrew from the scheme.[88]

In the late 1950s and the 1960s American aid and other links with Iran made it hard for British firms to compete for contracts, or even to attract the best partners for joint ventures. American military and economic aid to Iran totalled $2.3 billion between 1950 and 1970. Loans and credits from the Export-Import Bank, and American official aid, meant contracts

British business in Iran, 1860s–1970s   61

for American firms. American technical assistance programmes, such as Point Four, assisted American companies at the expense of their British counterparts. In 1954 Ewbanks, a British firm of electrical consultants, lost in its bid to act as consultants on a project to build a power station in Tehran to an American firm, whose fees were paid by the Point Four organisation. Ewbanks complained bitterly that British commercial interests

> should be fully aware of something of the intensity of competition in this field that we are encountering from the Americans who through various agency loans, F.A.A. or Point Four are able to cover American Consultants' services without apparent charge to the client. We do our fair share of chasing round the work to get the opportunity of business for Britain, but unlike our competitors, all the costs have to be borne by ourselves and when the Americans are in the field, the dice are very heavily loaded against us.[89]

A Foreign Office official, wondering where the dividing line between the legitimate and illegitimate activities of Point Four lay, idly speculated that if the British Parliament could be persuaded 'to let us spend more money on a Point IV of our own, we could go in for some illegitimate activities ourselves'.[90] Needless to say, no such scheme was established by Britain.

The British companies in Iran in the 1950s and 1960s were often faced by conflicts of business culture. This had always been a problem for British enterprises. Before 1914 the members of the London-based board of the Imperial Bank had been infuriated by the traditional Iranian indifference to the importance of punctuality in repayment of loans, which in Western terms turned a high proportion of the Bank's advances into bad debts. They never adjusted to the fact that, as the Bank's Tehran-based Chief Managers noted, such overdue loans were almost always repaid. However, it was the all-prevalent corruption which most offended British eyes. Iranians were always, a director of the Imperial Bank noted in 1890, 'deceitful and unreliable'.[91] 'Even with the very best of good will', observed one of the Bank's Chief Managers in 1915, 'it is difficult, if not impossible, at times to help so corrupt a people as we have to deal with here.'[92] If the British caricatured Japanese businessmen as 'tricky', they pictured their Iranian equivalents as 'corrupt'.

Corruption, or least what British observers termed corruption, remained a constant feature of Iranian business life after the Second World War. It created particular difficulties for British companies in joint ventures with local partners whom they considered corrupt, and for British firms which had to choose between using bribery to secure contracts or see them pass to competitors. In the second half of the 1950s Iran's Plan Organisation stood aside from the general picture of 'corruption'. In August 1954 Abol Hassan Ebtehaj was appointed head of the

62 Frances Bostock and Geoffrey Jones

Organisation, and his name was a byword in Iran for honesty. Under Ebtehaj, the Plan Organisation adopted a systematic and honest method of allocating contracts. Ebtehaj used two tiers of foreign advisers: a technical group of experts provided through the World Bank who joined the staff of the Plan Organisation, and firms of consulting engineers for individual projects. Contracts awarded after initial survey work went out to international tender.[93] Under this system, British interests got even-handed treatment in the granting of development contracts. However, after Ebtehaj's resignation in 1959 – he was subsequently gaoled for criticising the Shah for corruption – the securing of such contracts again became a matter of the use of 'influence' of various kinds. During the 1960s and 1970s, the nature of Iranian industrialisation, carried out behind high tariff walls, and with the Shah's family heavily involved in business either individually or through the Pahlavi Foundation, created not only acute geographical and sector imbalances in Iran, but ideal conditions for corruption of all kinds.[94] The Shah himself would, often on political grounds, interfere in the awarding of major contracts to foreign firms. In the mid-1970s, an anti-corruption campaign was launched as a result of the problems and excesses which followed the oil boom, and various foreign firms found themselves under attack as a result, including the British sugar firm of Tate and Lyle.[95]

2.5 The impact of British business

A thorough analysis of the impact of British business on Iran would require a paper of its own. Nevertheless, given the domination by Britain of Iran's modern business sector at least until the 1930s, it does seem important to sketch the issues involved in a serious study of this question.

British business enterprise was, as we have seen, largely responsible for opening up Iran to the outside world. For Britain the initial impetus was political and diplomatic necessity, arising out of a concern for its Indian empire, as the case of the Indo-European Telegraph Company and British–Indian Telegraph Department illustrates. The introduction of the telegraph system to Iran in the 1860s and 1870s was a matter of strategic importance for Britain – after the 1857 Indian Mutiny it became vitally necessary to improve communications between Britain and India. The impact on Iran was considerable. The presence of the telegraph facilitated trade and commercial links with Europe and the East, but also exposed Iran to the political and economic interference of the imperial powers and, through the presence of telegraph offices throughout the country manned by British officials, enabled the unprecedented penetration of the country by foreigners. Nor was this exposure to external influence the only result. The telegraph also facilitated communication between Tehran and the

British business in Iran, 1860s–1970s   63

provinces, a process which led to the establishment of closer political and administrative ties and encouraged movement towards a relatively more centralised and autocratic state under the Qajars.[96]

The impact of foreign direct investment on a host economy can be analysed in terms of a flow of resources into that economy. Iran was a 'capital-short' economy in the early twentieth century, and therefore potentially had much to gain from the capital brought in by foreign companies. The initial investments required to start the country's telegraph, modern banking and petroleum sectors were clearly valuable in this respect, but transfers of British capital were not of great significance after 1914. There was little new British investment. One estimate is that total British capital investment in Iran was £19.5 million in 1934.[97] The Anglo-Iranian Oil Company contributed about 5% of Iran's Gross Domestic Capital formation between 1931 and 1951. However, capital transferred by established British companies was probably at least balanced by profit remittances, and the striking feature of Iran's industrialisation drive of the 1930s was its lack of dependence on foreign capital.[98] This remained a feature of the Iranian economy in the 1950s and 1960s. Between 1959 and 1967 foreign capital – of which only a small percentage was British – contributed only 1.4% of GNP in Iran, one of the lowest figures for the developing world.[99] During the mid-1970s the British share of total inward direct investment in Iran never exceeded a derisory 5%, far behind that of both the United States and Japan.

However, British enterprises, especially the Imperial Bank before the 1930s, may have played a significant role in mobilising domestic savings. Although the Bank did transfer funds from Britain to support its business in Iran, it followed British overseas banking orthodoxy by preferring to finance its operations from locally generated resources so far as possible. The Imperial Bank, therefore, can be regarded as mobilising funds which were previously hoarded or used in traditional money lending. The mobilisation of savings in such an economy would conventionally be seen as having a positive economic effect, although more doubts might be expressed about the uses to which such savings were put – the finance of domestic foreign trade, and lending to the Iranian government. The Bank's role in currency matters also contributed to the monetisation of the economy through the issue of banknotes and its efforts to reform the metallic currency of the country.

The Iranian economy experienced a clear benefit from the transfer of enterprise and technology from British enterprises. This was, once again, most important before 1914 when, for a variety of reasons, indigenous Iranian entrepreneurship was negligible and indigenous levels of technology low even by Asian standards. The growth of modern banking, the oil industry and the carpet industry were highly visible demonstrations of

64 *Frances Bostock and Geoffrey Jones*

the impact of British enterprise. After 1914 the impact of British business was less, although Anglo-Iranian before 1952 was a constant source of technological transfer to the Iranian oil industry.[100] Eventually, after 1930, British enterprise was of little importance to Iranian economic development, except in specialist areas. The role of Sir Alexander Gibb and Partners in the 1940s in providing consulting services on a range of projects from irrigation to the erection of power stations was important for British business in keeping the door open for the tenders of British manufacturers to supply machinery, but Iran could have found equivalent advice from elsewhere. Before 1914 Iran needed British enterprise and technology. By the 1950s the British government needed orders in Iran for British industry.

Even in the earlier period the impact on Iran of the Anglo-Iranian Oil Company, the most important British company, was limited because it created an industry with enclave-type characteristics. Because of the geographical isolation of the oilfields, and the decentralisation of government before the mid-1920s, Anglo-Iranian had to provide its own economic and social infrastructure. 'There was little local linkage', BP's historian has noted; 'few local contractors'.[101] The oilfields and Abadan were company towns, and even by the end of the 1930s only about 5% of Anglo-Iranian's total production was consumed in Iran. 'There is no evidence', one writer has observed, 'that the efficient, modern workings of A.I.O.C. had any demonstrative effect on the rest of Iranian industry.'[102] This was probably, however, largely a function of the Iranian economy. Research on Iranian–American joint venture firms operating in the manufacturing sector between 1971 and 1976 has suggested they were not successful in adapting their technology to the economic environment of Iran, because of the lack of skilled labour and the insufficiency of raw materials and parts.[103] The Oil Company faced the same problems. Nevertheless Anglo-Iranian did have important linkages to the Iranian economy. In particular, the royalties paid by Anglo-Iranian to the Iranian government, together with the sales of foreign exchange by the Oil Company to secure the local currency needed for its operations, provided the largest single source of foreign exchange for the economy in the inter-war years.

Suggestions that the Imperial Bank's business was also enclavist, in the sense that it 'discriminated against Persians in giving credit',[104] can be discounted. The Bank undertook lending to local merchants from the start of its operations, and this always formed the mainstay of its commercial operations. Moreover, the Bank's branch network, which covered both the British and Russian 'zones' delineated by the 1907 Agreement, made it the only truly national institution in Iran before the 1920s.

The impact of British enterprise on employment was considerable

British business in Iran, 1860s–1970s   65

before the Second World War. The Anglo-Iranian Oil Company was the largest employer in the modern industrial sector before 1930.[105] The numbers of Iranians employed by the company increased from 1,362 in 1910 to 20,005 in 1930, fell in the early 1930s but rose again to around 20,000 by 1940.[106] No other British venture was such a large employer. The Imperial Bank's locally engaged staff in Iran probably never exceeded 400, and in 1940 it numbered 350.[107]

In addition to providing employment, the British companies also made a significant contribution to improving the quality of the work-force. The Anglo-Iranian Oil Company 'was the only industry that provided training for Iranians in the field of crafts, technology and management'.[108] From the 1920s a growing number of Iranians were given technical training. During this decade a technical institute was built to provide training, and some Iranians were sent to British universities by the Oil Company. Under the terms of the 1933 concession, the Anglo-Iranian Oil Company undertook to train a number of Iranian students annually in Britain. The special training school at Abadan took school-leavers and put them through a full apprenticeship course suited to individual aptitude. Anglo-Iranian's high wages meant that most workers stayed with the company after training, but a minority left and it was observed in the 1940s that many occupations – such as machine attendants and compositors – were filled exclusively by former Oil Company employees.[109] Nevertheless, it has to be noted that the Anglo-Iranian Oil Company's training record compared unfavourably with that of Aramco in Saudi Arabia.[110] The Imperial Bank's staff policies were even less enlightened: it was slower to promote Iranians to management positions and its training was 'on the job'. Nevertheless the basic training it did provide was not available elsewhere in Iran before the 1930s.

Any assessment of the impact of British enterprise needs to take into account its effect on indigenous enterprise. The lack of information about the traditional sector, especially before 1914, makes this hard to gauge, but it does seem that the impact of British companies was not destructive. As we have already explained, the Imperial Bank and traditional *sarrafs* co-existed for decades. In the pre-1914 carpet industry, British firms kept alive a traditional craft and showed how the best advantage could be taken of traditional skills, and local firms followed their example. By the 1920s there were a number of Armenian-owned firms actively involved in the carpet industry in Azerbaijan, and local firms were also well represented in Kerman despite the presence there of Oriental Carpet Manufacturers.[111]

For many Iranians, any positive economic gains for Iran from British enterprise were outweighed by the effect on the country's sovereignty. The ownership of national industries by 'foreign' interests can always be

66 *Frances Bostock and Geoffrey Jones*

regarded as an infringement of a country's sovereignty, but in Iran's case the explicit collaboration between the leading British commercial interests, notably the Oil Company and the Bank, and the British Foreign Office made the problem very visible. There was also widespread resentment at the 'colonial' treatment of Iranians by British enterprises.[112] Iranian government policies towards British companies from the 1920s were directed at least as much against what these companies symbolised as against what they had done or were doing in Iran.

2.6 Conclusion

The experience of British business in Iran between the 1860s and the 1970s provides a particularly dramatic illustration of the changing importance of British enterprise in Asia as a whole. Before 1914 British business established and dominated Iran's modern industrial and financial sector. From the 1920s this domination began to disappear. By the 1960s British enterprise was of little importance in the Iranian economy.

In Japan and India the decline of British business was primarily a function of the rise of strong indigenous business groups. In Iran the government in the inter-war years played a much greater role in both challenging British commercial interests, and stimulating locally owned enterprise. The virulent Iranian economic nationalism, however, cannot be treated solely as an 'endogenous' factor to British business. Iranian policies were a reaction to the close relations between British business in Iran and the British government. In retrospect, it is possible to see the uneasy and ambiguous nature of this relationship. The Bank was never entirely a tool of the Foreign Office, and the Anglo-Iranian Oil Company did not take its orders from Whitehall, despite the 51% government shareholding. But the relationship between British business and government was sufficiently close that it is not surprising that the Iranians missed the niceties of the situation, and that the Oil Company and the Bank became symbols of British imperialism.

How is the performance of British business in Iran to be assessed? A 'heroic' interpretation would point to the creation of a modern economic sector before the 1920s in the face of appalling difficulties such as the almost complete absence of any infrastructure, political chaos and disintegration, and Iran's position as a victim of international diplomatic intrigue. There is no doubt that, as elsewhere in Asia before 1914, British business was a pioneering and entrepreneurial force.

Nevertheless, the overall picture is less complimentary to British business. The major British businesses were founded on the basis of monopoly concessions, secured at a time when British political power was strong and Iranian political power weak. As political circumstances

British business in Iran, 1860s–1970s 67

changed, these ventures ran into difficulties. British business after the 1920s was not entrepreneurial. The Anglo-Iranian Oil Company and the Imperial Bank reacted to adversity by diversifying away from Iran rather than by attempting new approaches within the country. During the 1940s and 1950s the British government had to push British firms to take an interest in the country. British businessmen were too prone to blame their failures on the 'corruption' of Iranians and foreign rivals. Iran, like Japan, acquired a reputation as a 'difficult' market, which was left to others to exploit. The trouble was that Asia, and indeed the world, was full of 'difficult' markets.

3 British business in Russian Asia since the 1860s: an opportunity lost?

Christine White

3.1 Introduction

Any discussion of British business in Asia must necessarily include mention of Russian or modern-day Soviet Asia. Twice as large as the continental United States, Russian Asia encompasses what is known today as Soviet Central Asia, Siberia and the Soviet Far East. Indisputably one of the wealthiest geographical areas in the world, Soviet Asia contains more than nine-tenths of all the Soviet Union's natural resources. While the vast extent of the natural wealth of Siberia and Soviet Central Asia is only now being fully realised, the area has always had a certain lure – the promise of being a virtual eldorado for the bold and determined foreign trader and investor.

It must be noted from the outset that Russia as a whole never accounted for a very large percentage of British foreign investment. Unlike the relatively comfortable investment markets of India and China which had long been recipients of British capital investments, Russian Asia especially represented a large unknown to the British capitalist. The confusing Russian bureaucracy and tangle of prohibitive laws – such as those which forbade foreign ownership of banks and mineral-bearing lands – dissuaded all but the most determined British businessman from entering that market. It was not until the late nineteenth century, concurrent with a large influx of foreign capital to Russia, that the British became acutely aware of the opportunities for investment in that country. British investors concentrated their attentions on the putatively more profitable areas of Russian industry – predominantly the extractive industries, and primarily those of oil and gold. Even so, despite the large British capital participation in Russian oil and gold mining, British investors and merchants on the whole were wary of becoming overcommitted in areas of Russia of which they were ignorant. Further, the refusal to accommodate the Russian preference for buying on credit prevented the British from gaining any appreciable share of the Siberian market, even in cases where the British goods were known to be of superior quality. The British government was concerned over the ground that was being lost in Russia

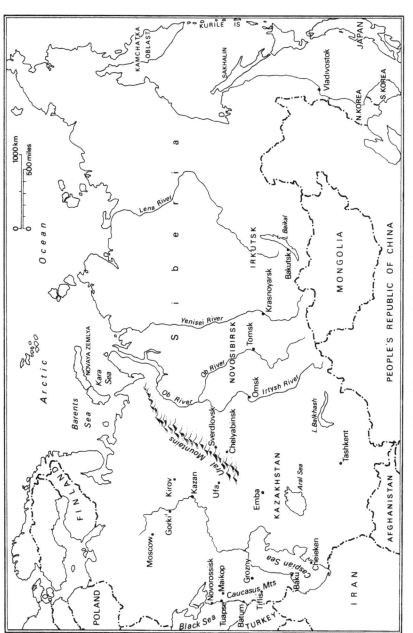

Map 3.1　USSR in Asia, 1984

70   Christine White

to commercial rivals, Germany and the United States in particular. A common thread which runs through some fifty years of Foreign Office correspondence is the complaint over the seeming lack of interest that the British business community had exhibited in the various trade and investment opportunities that were present in the vast area of Russia east of the Ural mountains.

Anglo-Russian commercial relations go back much further than the 1880s, however, and in some respects remained virtually unchanged until the outbreak of the First World War, with some continuity even after the Bolshevik seizure of power. It is surprising to learn that, as one of the foremost industrialised countries of the world, Britain's exports to Russia throughout the period before 1917 consisted predominantly of raw materials and semi-manufactured goods. Like most of Britain's other Asian markets, Russia was consistently viewed as a convenient supplementary market, a market which received intense attention during periods of depressed sales abroad. The later failure of British merchants and entrepreneurs to keep abreast of foreign competition by adapting their business practices and products to suit local conditions resulted in the ultimate loss of considerable opportunities not only in Russian Asia, but in Russia as a whole as well. As the first two of these characteristics span centuries rather than decades, the earliest relations deserve at least a brief mention.

The search for easier, faster and cheaper ways of tapping the riches of Asia prompted the sixteenth-century British mercantile community to explore the possibility of a northern sea route to the East. It was hoped that such a route would open up the riches of the Far East to British merchants directly, eliminating the expense of Turkish, Italian and Portuguese middlemen. Though less immediately obvious, a more important motivation lay in remedying the declining sales of British cloth abroad in the mid-sixteenth century. British textile exports were on average some 25% less after 1550 than during the first half of the century, and as compensation new effort was put into developing foreign trade.[1]

Though it failed to result in a passage to the East, the first of these expeditions – underwritten by a Society which later became known as the Russia Company – did result in the establishment of commercial contacts between Great Britain and Russia.[2] As a result of having financed these voyages itself, combined with the royal grant of exclusive trade privileges, the Russia Company enjoyed the sole right to exploit this new market.[3] Once established, trade with Russia was vigorously pursued by British merchants, though it is interesting to note that, from the outset, Britain suffered almost exclusively from an unfavourable balance of trade with that country until the First World War. Further, the character of Anglo-Russian trade in the late sixteenth century bears a striking resemblance to

British business in Russian Asia since the 1860s   71

that of the nineteenth and early twentieth centuries. Despite the rapid industrialisation of Britain and the persistence of an agrarian economy in Russia, British exports to Russia continued to comprise predominantly raw materials and semi-manufactured goods.[4]

Although it met with considerable success in its commercial relations with Russia, the Company's primary objective in its subsequent expeditions to that country remained 'to learne howe men may passe from Russia, either by land or sea to Cathaia'.[5] While attempts to establish an overland route to China via Russia failed, the search for this route did result in considerable trans-Russian Persian trade, with Astrakhan and Kazan becoming important commercial areas in their own right.[6] Further, Russian territorial expansion during the seventeenth and eighteenth centuries opened up increasing areas of western Asia to British commercial penetration.

British interest in the mineral deposits of eastern and central Siberia arose only during the last quarter of the nineteenth century.[7] World events and changes in Russia after that time significantly altered the British approach to both investment and commerce with that country; periodisation, therefore, is indispensable to understand the course and impact of British business in that area.

Three time periods conveniently present themselves for this study: the thirty years preceding the outbreak of the First World War, the inter-war period, and the period following the conclusion of the Second World War. In each case, a major world event changed the approach and role of British business in Russia. Further, it is necessary to examine investment and trade separately in each period, as they often diverged far from one another. With perhaps the exception of the last period – that is, the more recent trade and 'turnkey' projects of the 1970s and 1980s whose success and impact have yet to be measured – the common denominator of British business in Russian Asia is one of opportunities lost.

3.2 Hostage to Fortune: the British foreign direct investor in pre-war Russia.

While the overall volume and impact of British capital investment in pre-war Russian industry has been much researched,[8] little effort has been made to determine what percentage of that capital was invested in industries east of the Ural mountains. To be sure, foreign direct investment played a much less active role in Russian Asia than in European Russia. Even so, foreign capital as a whole accounted for over 50% of the total capital invested in Russian mining and metallurgical industries at the turn of the century. A cursory examination of British pre-war investments shows that the majority of British direct investment in Russia was

72   Christine White

accounted for by those industries, and a large proportion of these undertakings were located in Russian Asia and the Caucasus. The petroleum industry alone accounted for 171,400,000 roubles – over £18,000,000 – or one-third of all British investments in Russia, the majority of which was invested in oilfields in the Caucasus.[9] Accounting for nearly half of the total foreign capital invested in the Russian petroleum industry, British capital was particularly concentrated in the oilfields of Baku, Emba-Ural, Grozny, and Maikop.

British capital was important in developing the Russian petroleum industry. By 1914, for example, companies wholly or partly British-owned accounted for half of the production of the Grozny oilfields, three-quarters of the oil produced at Cheleken, nearly all of the Maikop production, and the total oil production of the Emba region.[10] A Russian industry that attracted considerable British capital prior to the war, this was one of the few areas of investment that showed any appreciable returns to its British investors – at least during the period up to 1910.[11] In Baku alone – the most important oil-producing field in Russia at the time – there were six purely British concerns operating prior to the war.[12] Three of these companies were devoted exclusively to operations in Baku and accounted for some nearly 20,000,000 roubles of the British capital invested in the Russian oil industry.[13] Only one of these companies – the Bibi-Eibat Oil Co. – operated exclusively through the medium of Russian concerns, though there was extensive British participation in Russian petroleum companies operating in Baku. With Russian law making illegal the foreign ownership of mineral resources in the country, British companies were able to circumvent the restrictions by creating a fictitious Russian concern which then transferred its shares to a British holding company. It was by this means that Shell came to control the Caspian and Black Sea Oil and Trading Company in 1912, one of the many smaller companies that made up its vast petroleum producing, marketing and transport empire in Russia, which supplied oil products to the Asian market.[14]

In addition to foreign direct investment in oil companies, British capital found a ready home in the Russian General Oil Corporation. Incorporated in London in 1912 by a group of Russian banks and several representatives of Russian oil companies, the Corporation was conceived to consolidate the controlling interests of the Baku oil industry. British as well as French capital was invited to participate, and assuming that Russian interests subscribed half of the capital, British participation can be conservatively estimated at nearly 6,000,000 roubles.[15] By 1916, the General Oil Corporation controlled seventeen Russian registered companies.

Another such financial organisation that was particularly interested in

3.1 Bibi-Eibat oilfields, Baku.

the Baku oil industry was the Oil Fields Finance Corporation, comprising the Russian Petroleum Company, the Baku Petroleum Company, 1909, the Russian United Petroleum Company, the European Oil Fields Corporation, the Bibi-Eibat Oil Company, the Amalgamated Russian Petroleum Company, and the Romany Syndicate. Accounting for 17 million poods, or some 2.75 million metric tons, of petroleum output in 1914, the Corporation entrusted a Shell subsidiary, the Petroleum and Trading Company 'Mazut', with sale of its products in Russia. Concerned only with the storage, transport and sale of petroleum products, the Petroleum and Trading Company operated a fleet of tankers and railway tank cars, and controlled a huge storage network.[16]

British interests were by no means confined to the major producing fields of Baku; there was considerable British participation in the Emba-Ural and Grozny oilfields where it was responsible for a significant proportion of the entire oil production. Four of the Emba-Ural companies were wholly British-owned, two British-registered companies and two operating through Russian-registered companies whose entire security issues they held.[17] Further British investment was also made in two local Russian-registered companies: the Ural-Caucasus Corporation and the Emba Petroleum and Trading Company, which had no fields of its own but held securities of other petroleum companies, and which conducted trade in equipment and construction of plants for the petroleum industry. Of the four British companies that operated in the Grozny-Terek district, three were registered as limited liability companies in London, while the

3.2 Plots at Grozny belonging to Spies Petroleum Company.

other was a Russian-registered company with an associated British holding company registered in London.[18] Shell interests were also substantial in the Grozny oilfields.

The highly speculative Maikop oilfields were the most disappointing to British capital. While twenty-five British companies were reported to be in operation at the end of 1914, only eleven of these companies were still operating at the time of the Bolshevik Revolution. Although the majority of those companies founded in the region failed to strike any oil whatsoever, nine British companies produced 99.7% of the entire 1913 petroleum production of the Maikop fields.[19]

British capital was invested in lesser – but by no means insignificant – amounts in other minor oilfields in Russia. Further, there was considerable British interest in the transport, storage and marketing of petroleum products in Russia, and the total amount of British capital invested in the petroleum and allied industries has been estimated at 183,295,400 roubles, or over £129,376,000.[20]

British investments also played a major role in the development of the Russian non-ferrous metals industry; gold, copper and silver–lead mining concerns in Russian Asia and Siberia accounted for the next largest proportion of British capital investment in Russia. Those enterprises in which foreign capital participated were usually formed as joint holding companies and were required under Russian law to employ Russian managers in addition to foreign managers recruited by the company, the Russians being legally in charge while the foreign management retained *de facto* control of the staff and operation of the mines.[21]

Six of the seven British companies involved in the Russian gold industry were wholly British-owned limited liability companies, and together they had a combined capitalisation of over £2 million. British-controlled enterprises were responsible for a significant proportion – some 25% – of

British business in Russian Asia since the 1860s   75

the total amount of gold produced in pre-war Russia. The Lena Gold Mining Corporation, which alone accounted for nearly 40% of the total Russian gold production in 1914, was the largest such concern in the country. Originally established as a Russian limited liability company in 1896, the Lena was unable to provide the necessary capital on its own. In exchange for providing the required financial backing, the Lena Goldfields Company Ltd was allowed to take over the operation of the mines and the sale of their produce. Though it was still registered as legally being a Russian concern, no less than 10,500,000 roubles of the corporation's 16,500,000 roubles total capital was held by the British company.[22]

Another area where British investment played a predominant role was in the development of the pre-war Russian copper industry, where British capital accounted for 56% of the total invested in that industry.[23] Though only five British companies were involved, their combined output accounted for more than half of the total copper production of the country. Three of these companies operated in the Urals, one in the Caucasus, and one in Siberia. As in the case of the British participation in the gold mining industry, all three of the Ural copper concerns were Russian-registered companies owned by British holding companies by the same name. Having thus circumvented the legal restriction on foreign ownership, the Kyshtim Corporation, the Sissert Company, and the Tanalyk Corporation represented a combined British capitalisation of nearly 41 million roubles, or some £4,334,000.[24]

The next largest area of British investment was in the Russian silver–lead industry. The three enterprises involved in this were controlled by British capital: the Ridder Mining Corporation, with a capitalisation of 16,000,000 roubles (or nearly £1,700,000); the Kirghiz Mining Corporation, capitalised at 8,500,000 roubles; and the Russian Mining Corporation, which was capitalised at 350,000 roubles.[25] The Ridder Mining Corporation was founded and financed by the Russo-Asiatic Corporation, a British-registered limited liability company which also controlled the Kyshtim and Tanalyk copper mines mentioned above, as well as the Nerchinsk lead–zinc–silver mines and the Ekibastuz coal properties in Irkutsk.[26] Though these enterprises had not progressed far beyond the organisational and construction stages by the time of the Revolution, there can be no doubt as to the impact that British capital investment had on the development of the Russian silver–lead mining industry. It was noted by P. Aull, of the Soviet Institute of Economic Research, that the British concerns were designed on such a big scale that 'from the moment of the commencement of operations by these ... enterprises the silver–lead industry of Russia would find itself in the hands of British capital, since the productivity of all the other enterprises would be completely lost

76 Christine White

3.3 Share certificate of Russo-Asiatic Consolidated Ltd.

alongside the volume of production of these two concerns'.[27]

British capital was also invested, though to a considerably lesser extent, in other ore mining and metallurgical industries of the Urals and South Russia. As in the case of the lead–silver mines, the participation of British capital frequently had an impact on the modernisation and development of a number of these industries. Further, it seems apparent that British capital found investment in Russian Asia increasingly attractive during the years immediately preceding the war, as reflected in the growing number of British companies in operation there. Until the turn of the century British investments tended to be concentrated almost exclusively in the mining and metallurgical industries.[28] After the Russo-Japanese War (1904–5), however, British capital appeared in a variety of other Siberian enterprises. Mirroring the growing British reliance on Siberian foodstuffs, British capital was invested in the butter export business as well as in certain food processing industries.[29] Further, a list of 'principal interests' belonging to British subjects in the Ekaterinburg district of Siberia in January 1918 listed seven mines and at least five manufacturing and commercial firms whose combined value amounted to over 67.5 million roubles – or some £7 million at the 1913 exchange.[30]

While British investments in Russian Asia seemingly increased during the pre-war period, British trade with Siberia and the Russian Far East was sluggish at best, with 'very few articles of British manufacture ... to be seen in Siberia'.[31] There are, however, difficulties in gathering reliable comprehensive data on the foreign trade of Russian Asia. As Siberia was an integral part of the Russian empire, no separate breakdown of imports or exports are available for it, save perhaps for those that passed through

British business in Russian Asia since the 1860s   77

the port of Vladivostok. The great proportion of Siberian trade was conducted through its western frontiers, mostly by rail, but also by road and water. There are no complete trade statistics, and no breakdown of data at all for trade with individual countries.[32] As late as 1913 Moscow was the chief distributing centre of Russia for Siberia, the Volga District, Central Russia, Central Asia and the Caucasus,[33] although there was renewed interest by British merchants in the establishing of a northern sea route to exploit trade opportunities with Siberia, with Britons pioneering the navigation of the Kara Sea in the 1870s, primarily for commercial purposes.[34] The completion of the Trans-Siberian Railway along with the increased duties imposed on imported manufactured goods in 1891 combined to make the route less than profitable, and the loss of a number of ships and cargoes at the turn of the century as a result of the hazardous navigation conditions and the unpredictability of the arctic climate led to the collapse of British commercial interest in this route, and the brief British monopoly over the route was quickly lost to Danish and German merchants.[35]

It was not until 1912 that British merchants again undertook to navigate the Kara Sea in pursuit of Siberian trade.[36] Despite such displays of interest, British trade with Siberia was always miniscule. Only in the early years of the twentieth century was notice taken of the enthusiastic reports of opportunities for business and trade that had filtered back. Part of the larger and growing political and commercial rivalry with Germany and the United States, the success of these rival traders in Siberia provided cause for concern among British commercial and government circles. Because the region was viewed as an increasingly important source of raw materials as well as a market for British manufactures, there was official concern over the elusive nature of this market to British merchants and moves were made to remedy the situation.

Henry Cooke, a representative of the Board of Trade, made a special mission to Siberia and Vladivostok in 1903 to investigate the existing and future prospects for British trade in Siberia.[37] Like many of the other British consular reports filed from potential new markets at the turn of the century, Cooke's report presents a chronicle of the shortcomings of British merchants and traders in Siberia. Though recommending that those seeking markets should personally examine the country with a view to understanding local opportunities, Cooke went on to point out that the Americans, Danes and Germans had already captured some of the most profitable areas of Siberian enterprise. 'If what remains does not at present offer any vast opening for special branches of British energy, it is, at least, not a market to be passed by.'

But the failure of the British merchant to make any significant impression on the Siberian market remained an irritant to the Board of

78   *Christine White*

Trade. One of the most valuable markets in Siberia was that for agricultural machinery, a business in which the 'Americans are first, the rest, and especially the British, nowhere'. Shops throughout Siberia stocked 'Russian and American' machines rather than 'Russian and foreign'. The promising Siberian market in agricultural machinery was reported to be 'altogether neglected, designedly or otherwise, by the British maker'.[38] While rather more than 10% of the pre-war UK exports of agricultural machines and steam engines were shipped to Russia, only a small proportion was destined for beyond the Ural mountains, the American manufacturers having successfully secured a virtual monopoly there. Kennard states that British-made agricultural equipment accounted for one-quarter of all Russian imports of that classification in 1909. While this may be true, the fact remains that the majority of these goods was sold in European Russia and not in Siberia or the Russian Far East.[39]

Trade in general merchandise was largely in the hands of the Germans, against whose goods British imports 'cut a very pitiable figure in comparison'. Few British firms appeared to have any direct trade with Siberia; instead, British goods were usually forwarded to Siberia via Moscow or other intermediaries.[40] Generally, Siberia (excluding the Russian Far East) received foreign merchandise almost exclusively via Russia proper. Even the vast stocks of American agricultural machinery that annually reached Siberia were imported through European Russia from the Baltic ports, and not from the Far East.[41] Further, the vulnerability of Britain's minimal trade with Siberia is indicated by the fact that 'of the relatively small quantities of British goods imported, fully 90% is ordered in Hamburg by the agents of German firms here. It is obvious that as long as we are dependent upon them for the unimportant share in the trade which we now enjoy, there is little chance of the present condition materially improving.'[42] In short, the British officials despatched to promote their country's business interests in Siberia found that market 'slipping out of [their] hands'.[43]

The reasons for this state of affairs were recognised and lamented.[44] Compared to their competitors, the British seldom adapted themselves or their products to the Russian market. While the Germans and Americans used hordes of travelling salesmen and representatives to promote their goods, the British waited for business to come to them in their city-centred offices. Not only was the effectiveness of advertising overlooked by the British, they also persisted in communicating with their Russian customers largely in English – both in person and through their brochures – frequently giving costs, weights and measures only in English. Their competition not only spoke the language and provided catalogues in Russian, but also gave all specifics in the Russian equivalent. Nor did the British make any attempt to adapt the products themselves – to make

British business in Russian Asia since the 1860s   79

cheaper, more affordable goods. Although often recognised as being of better quality, their higher prices put them at a distinct disadvantage to the wide selection of considerably less expensive German goods available. The Germans and, to a lesser extent, the Americans not only took into account specific Russian needs, adapting their products to suit when necessary, but also accommodated the Russian preference for purchasing on credit – a practice which was anathema to British merchants and bankers.[45] Little was done to redress these shortcomings, despite constant advice from consular representatives that the situation had to be altered before Britain could expect to capture any significant volume of this trade.

It is important to realise that the failure of British trade to capture even a small percentage of the Siberian market, while largely due to the factors outlined above, can also be seen as part of the decline in the British share of the Russian import market as a whole. While British exports did account for 13% of the increase of over 300 million roubles (some £31,712,400) in Russian imports between 1909 and 1913, their proportion in this trade actually declined. During the quarter-century prior to the war, Britain lost its position as Russia's primary trading partner, while Germany came to account for an ever-growing proportion of Russian trade. Further, it is important to realise that raw materials and semi-manufactured goods and *not* wholly manufactured articles represented the largest percentage by value of all British imports into pre-war Russia. These goods also accounted for 48% of the increase in Britain's export trade to Russia between 1909 and 1912.[46] In the five-year period immediately before the War, Britain provided less than 20% of the manufactures of machinery (excluding agricultural machinery) and about 10% of the metal goods and semi-manufactured machinery imported into Russia. Given the nature of the British export trade with Russia, and considering the lack of any industrial base in Siberia, it is not surprising that British trade with that region should be won by the more efficient German merchants.

3.3 A new chance: the Soviet Russian market

Having lost this market largely to the Germans, Britain was given an opportunity by the First World War and 1917 Revolution not only to recapture its former position in Russian trade, but to assert itself over the relatively virgin commercial territory of Russian Asia. Contrary to popular belief, the Bolsheviks were not initially seen as an obstacle to these plans; Bolshevism was perceived as a temporary phenomenon – a belief that widely persisted into the early 1920s. It was maintained that the 'next' Russian government would undoubtedly recognise and honour all debts and obligations. Consequently, there was a move to capture

80   Christine White

whatever opportunities were available while the power vacuum existed. The concern over the fact that their share in this market could easily be lost even before they entered it prompted British merchants to take a new interest in Siberia especially. With American interests in Russia heightened by the increase of trade brought about by the War,[47] considerable Anglo-American competition developed.

Despite the limited nature of British interests in Siberia, its post-war potential attracted attention in both government and commercial circles. The prevailing chaos in Russia presented opportunities for exploitation, and the scarcity of British representation east of the Ural mountains concerned the government in the spring of 1918; 'One wonders', mused Lord Robert Cecil, Under-Secretary of State at the Foreign Office, 'why Siberia has always been neglected by us in the past.'[48] An examination of the possible benefits of an Allied occupation of Siberia was undertaken, the report of which hypothesised that such an occupation would result in the creation of an autonomous state not bound to German peace terms and the destructive trade treaties of Brest-Litovsk. It was believed that this would help to establish British trade in Siberia and, further, would allow for the 'obtaining of concrete securities in concessions (railway, mineral, timber, etc.) against Russia's vast liabilities to the Allies'.[49]

The popular view of Siberia as a land of inexhaustible natural wealth with a vast potential as a market for a multitude of consumer goods held great temptation. In June 1918 it was proposed that, in the event of Allied intervention in Siberia, the British could seek a commercial arrangement with the Siberian Soviets providing for the exchange of surplus stocks in Siberia and Russian Central Asia for goods which were urgently needed in the area.[50] While it was recognised that the organisation of this trade would initially require infusions of capital, admittedly a 'delicate point', it was believed that the risks would be more than offset by the profits to be reaped. Typically, one British consular official remarked that 'so much [natural] wealth abounds everywhere that it is difficult to suggest anything on hard and fast lines – the thing is to be able to exploit and take advantage'.[51]

With regard to Russia generally, there appeared to be a sense of 'business as usual' that pervaded the private sector as well as the government during the early months of the Revolution. The arrival of a commercial mission in June 1918, headed by Sir William Clark (Comptroller-General of the Department of Overseas Trade), shows the prevailing sense of normality. While the mission does not appear to have had its origins in the Foreign Office, the government regarded it benevolently. In response to American pique over the timing and objects of the mission, it was explained that only a small group of commercial experts were 'sent out with [Consul General] Lindley to Russia by His Majesty's Government

3.4 J. Leslie Urquhart (1874–1933) the British mining financier with extensive interests in Asiatic Russia.

to advise them as to the best means of restoring and developing British trade relations and interests in Russia and countering enemy schemes and commercial penetration'.[52] Further, some companies continued their business in Russia unconcerned at the risk of confiscation by the Soviets, despite the Allies' anti-Bolshevik intervention in that country. Vickers, a company that was to have substantial business with the Soviet Union, was

82   *Christine White*

one of the first to conduct negotiations with the Bolsheviks. Change in regime notwithstanding, the company continued to discuss the sale of its Tsaritsyn Ordnance Works to the Soviet government. Despite the increased tension between Britain and the Bolshevik authorities, Vickers concluded what amounted to the first technical trade contract with Soviet Russia in the spring of 1918. While it apparently never came into effect, the contract was to provide the Bolshevik government with continued technical assistance in the operation of that plant over a fifteen-year period.[53]

The Russo-Asiatic Corporation, controlled by the British mining magnate Leslie Urquhart, adopted a different approach to the Revolution. On 15 January 1918 one of the Russo-Asiatic properties – the Kyshtim Mines – was confiscated. This was met with surprising calm both at the mine and at the London offices. Stating that the breakdown in transport had resulted in 'total disorganisation' and that it was a 'practical impossibility' to obtain fuel, food materials and wages, Urquhart's on-site manager observed that the 'stoppage of operations was inevitable and financing through the coming months [would be] most difficult. Today's confiscation may make matters easier when order is restored.'[54] In forwarding this communication to the company in London, the British Consul General in Russia remarked on the wisdom of such a move: 'as regards confiscation of Kyshtim Mines and similar enterprises it must be remembered that it is better to have their property confiscated with the chance of securing damages than be definitely ruined by a few more months working'.[55]

The competitive American presence prevented British commercial interests from gaining a foothold in Siberia. American wartime business investments in Russia tended to concentrate more in Siberia, and though investments there were still comparatively small, there were considerable American trading interests there. The collapse in 1919 of the Siberian Supply Company (the official British organisation set up to handle trade with Siberia) signalled the end of the official preoccupation with capturing the trade of that region. Making clear its priorities, the War Office pointed out that Britain could 'only make an adequate effort in one theatre ... The choice is between Siberia and South Russia and there can be no question on which it falls.'[56] There was, it seems, a clear 'imperial imperative' for the British military intervention in the Russian South and Transcaucasia. While it was stated that any anarchy in the region would pose threats to Britain's entire imperial position in the East, oil played the decisive role in bringing British troops to Transcaucasia. The security of the Russian oilfields as well as the protection of the increasingly important petroleum-bearing areas of Iran were primary concerns of the British. The wartime occupation of the South Caucasus by Turkey and the Bolshevik-inspired

British business in Russian Asia since the 1860s   83

labour uprisings in the Russian oilfields late in 1917 were viewed with alarm in Britain. By the end of 1919 it was openly admitted that parts of the region should be held 'because of the immense value of the oil deposits'.[57] The realisation that crucial supplies could be cut off by the United States – Britain's principal supplier – caused the government to seek other sources and to encourage further entrenchment in those areas where British interests in the industry already existed, such as the oil-bearing regions of Russia.

The absence of authority in Transcaucasia after the Revolution enabled the British to gain control over the petroleum wealth of the area. On 31 October the War Office issued instructions to the British Command in Mesopotamia for the occupation of Baku and its surrounding oilfields. By November 1919 the War Office had extended its liability to include the railway and pipeline that ran between the oilfields at Baku and the Black Sea port of Batum.

The official attempts to ensure a continued British presence – if not dominance – in this industry are striking. In one case, the government went so far as to block the proposed sale of a British petroleum company's interest in the Maikop oilfields, despite the fact that the company had been operating unprofitably there for some time. Throughout the autumn of 1918 the Anglo-Maikop Corporation Ltd had been in correspondence with the Board of Trade's Commercial Relations and Treaties Department concerning the transfer of its properties and interests in the Maikop oilfields to the Moscow Narodny Bank. The Board of Trade was informed that negotiations were conditional on the Corporation retaining one-half of the properties and that joint control and management of the business was to continue for a seven-year period after the sale. The total value of the transaction was placed at £3 million, and the Corporation stated that the shareholders favoured the deal, as no dividends had been paid to them for some time. However, the sale was officially blocked because, the government argued, 'whatever the value the properties may possess today, it must be greater when conditions in Russia improve, so that the refusal can scarcely impose serious hardship to the companies'.[58]

While the government was loath to entertain proposals which involved any diminished British control over such strategic interests as those held by the Anglo-Maikop Corporation, it was quick to support the bulk of applications for the issue of new capital by British concerns, notably by oil companies, with operations in South Russia. There was an overwhelming government sentiment in favour of keeping the oilfields in British hands, even though conditions in the region argued strongly against such action, as being in the better interests of the company. Perversely, it was in this way that the government itself ultimately caused

84   Christine White

the most damage to British business in South Russia, and particularly to those concerned with the Russian oil industry.

Despite the Bolsheviks' expropriation and nationalisation of foreign-owned properties and investments, it was not long before several British businessmen took renewed interest in investment in Soviet Russia. British companies with pre-1914 holdings in Russian industries soon sent representatives to the country to negotiate the 'return' of their properties through concessions. Mining industries again attracted the bulk of the British interest in Soviet Asia, with gold and oil still receiving the most attention.

Pre-war investors in a number of Russian mining industries exhibited a keen interest in reaching agreement for the return of their old properties – even if only in the form of a concession. The protracted and ultimately unfruitful attempts made by Leslie Urquhart to negotiate for the control of the numerous properties formerly under the aegis of his Russo-Asiatic Consolidated Mines is a classic example of pre-war capital interests seeking to recover lost assets through Soviet concessions. When negotiations between the Soviet representative Leonid Krasin and Leslie Urquhart resulted in a concession agreement covering an extraordinarily large area in Siberia,[59] Lenin refused to ratify the agreement. In a purely political move, Lenin used his veto in order to show his displeasure with the British government over other affairs.

Another large British investor in the Siberian mining industry, the Lena Goldfields Company Ltd, achieved better results in its negotiations with the Bolsheviks than had Urquhart. Concluded in April 1925, the Lena Goldfields concession was to run for thirty years, covering not only lands that the company had leased from the imperial Russian government, but properties formerly worked by other companies as well.[60] From the outset, however, the Lena Company had run into difficulties with the Soviets: not only did it fail to receive control of all the stipulated properties, but it was also prevented from disposing of any gold on the open market, though this right was granted to the company in the agreement. Despite this, the Lena Goldfields operated with relatively few problems until 1928, when the Soviet government launched a full-scale attack on the concessionaires. While the official Soviet version of the dispute with the Lena Company attributed the deterioration in relations to the failure of the company to keep its agreement, a more cogent reason was that the modernisation of the properties involved was almost largely complete, and profits had begun to materialise.[61]

British foreign direct investment in the form of the Lena Goldfields concession had a definite impact on the Soviet mining and metallurgical industries in Siberia. In addition to renovating numerous mines and quarries, Lena Goldfields was required to modernise and, in some cases,

British business in Russian Asia since the 1860s   85

construct new plants. By 1929 the company had invested over £500,000 on imported machinery and equipment for these works.[62] Further, the Lena Goldfields accounted for a considerable proportion of the Soviet gold production between 1925 and the termination of the concession in 1930. As a key source of foreign currency, gold was an important export commodity which essentially financed the First Five Year Plan. The efficient working of the Siberian mines by the Lena Goldfields Company Ltd, and the modernisation of the equipment, provided the Soviet government with the invaluable advantage of increased gold production.

While the pre-war operator was welcomed back as a large-scale concessionaire in the case of the Lena Goldfields, the Soviet government was loath to allow foreign capital to regain control of the petroleum industry. Despite repeated attempts by the larger British petroleum companies to conclude concession agreements which would provide for the 'return' of their properties, only one British company – the relatively small Gouria Petroleum Corporation – had managed to conclude an agreement in 1923 for the operation of a producing concession.[63] Foreign participation in the business of transport and the sale of oil abroad were totally different matters, however, and the Shell Group and the British firm of Sale and Company had both concluded agreements of this type by mid-1923.[64]

While the Bolshevik government had ultimately decided against any substantial foreign direct investment in the production side of the Soviet oil industry, advanced foreign technology was none the less actively employed as often as possible. In this respect, British capital and technology played a more important role in the development of Siberian industry through the medium of technical assistance agreements and the direct sale of equipment and machinery to the Soviet Union. Metropolitan-Vickers, for example, received extensive orders for oilfield equipment such as electrically powered pumps, switch gear and other equipment, as part of the oilfield electrification programme. This contract proved to be one of the largest of that company's sale agreements with the Soviet Union.[65] None the less, British domination of the Soviet oilfield equipment market had begun to erode by 1927. General Electric of the USA, whose products furnished the electricity-generating power plant for the oil industry, was increasingly replacing Vickers as the primary supplier of other equipment, and by 1930 American manufacturers had largely taken over the Soviet market for oil equipment. This is hardly surprising as the technology used in the oil industry – including that employed by Metropolitan-Vickers – was largely American.[66]

Even so, Metropolitan-Vickers played a major role in the electrification of the Soviet Union. Between 1921 and 1939 the company handled over £5 million worth of contracts for the sale, construction and installation of

86   *Christine White*

electrical equipment and apparatus in the USSR.[67] With the exception of the Dneipr Dam project, Metropolitan-Vickers had a significant part in virtually all electrical power projects undertaken by the All-Union Electrical Trust.[68] While a large proportion of Metropolitan-Vickers' technical assistance contracts dealt with the development and construction of the European Russian electrical industry, the company also assumed the lion's share of the work in the construction, installation and equipping of power stations in Russian Asia. Among the most important Soviet sales during this period were orders for all the switchgear and transformers for Shatura, Nizhni Novgorod (present-day Gorki), Baku, Chelyabinsk and Ivanovo-Voznessensk; medium-capacity generators for Shterovka; smaller capacity turbo-generators for Irkutsk, Novo-Sibirsk and others; all the switchgear equipment for Volkhov; and equipment for the oil well electrification program for the Baku area.[69] As in the case of the Lena Goldfields concession, however, the Soviets waited until the technology was in place and largely operative before making any moves to rid themselves of foreign concessionaires and advisers. With the arrest and deportation of six of the company's engineers in 1933, the Soviets signalled that they could operate and, to a certain extent, duplicate the technology that they had purchased from the West.

While relations between those companies with pure concessions in Soviet Russia and the Bolshevik government were strained by the end of the 1920s, sales concessions fared considerably better. Like the Shell Group and Sale and Company in the Caucasus, Lord Vestey's Union Cold Storage Company enjoyed good relations with the host government. Having agreed to the transport and sale of Russian animal products abroad in 1924, the Union Cold Storage was handling almost all Russian exports of butter and eggs by the middle of the decade. While the break in diplomatic relations in 1927 disrupted this business, the Union Cold Storage Company concession was the first to be renewed after relations were resumed. A more comprehensive agreement was negotiated in 1928 which provided for an advance credit of £5 million over three years in exchange for the right to handle all exports of Soviet dairy produce for the UK market. The credit was specifically granted to cover purchases of British-made equipment for the Soviet dairy industry.[70]

If the pursuit of concessions was an attempt by pre-war investors to regain control over their properties, and if technical assistance agreements intended to exploit Soviet needs during the First Five Year Plan, the British approach to direct trade with Russia after the First World War still resembled that of the sixteenth century. Russia, and Siberia in particular, was held to be a panacea for the ills of the post-war economic slump, and perceived as a potential 'spill-over' market for British manufactured goods: it was hoped that the vast needs of Russia could be used as a 'safety valve' in the recovery of the depressed post-war market. Siberia – a land viewed as having potentially endless possibilities – especially held forth this promise. Having few indigenous industries, it was popularly believed to be the 'insatiable market'.

The 1921 Anglo-Russian Trade Agreement increased the volume and value of direct trade between the two countries, but this trade did not immediately develop along the lines originally anticipated by either country. Soviet purchases in the United Kingdom remained stable between 1921 and 1923, while the sale of Soviet goods in Britain accounted for an increasing proportion of the total trade turnover. The hope that the normalisation of commercial relations would open up the market and provide a measure of relief for the unemployment and growing unrest in Britain generally failed to materialise.

While British attempts to recapture a portion of the profitable Russian market were initially successful, it was not long before they receded. Though the Soviets courted the West only as long as they required its technology, there none the less appears to have been a preference for the adoption of American technology wherever it was possible. In some instances this meant holding out or taking the lesser of two deals when American technology was involved.[71] In instances where American products and methods had dominated the market since before the war, such as in agricultural machinery, British sales remained residual. While in some cases purchasing habits and familiarity with the product dictated the continued predominance of German goods, in other instances – such as in equipment and machinery for the oil industry – American technology was preferred. When the restrictions on trade with Soviet Russia were removed and direct American assistance became available, the Bolsheviks shifted a significant proportion of this business to the United States. In connection with this, Vickers, who had a considerable business in oilfield equipment with the Soviet Union between 1921 and 1930, had begun to lose out to American manufacturers, particularly to General Electric of the United States, as early as 1927. Further, while Vickers' technical assistance agreement covering the right to produce its patented turbines under licence in the Soviet Union was the first of its kind, this market was soon lost to GE as well.[72] Likewise, by 1930 the Soviets had also decided to utilise American technology in the gold mining industry. Consequently, the Lena, which was 'held predominantly by British interests, could be expropriated without fear that political repercussions would affect further technical acquisitions'.[73]

By the mid-1930s the increasingly isolationist position of the Soviet Union had effectively served to reduce foreign capital participation in Soviet industry. The USSR had become considerably less dependent on foreign technology, and indeed, had again revolted against foreign

88   Christine White

intrusion in this area. No new concessionary agreements had been made since the mid-1920s, and those that were still in operation were being annulled, phased out, or worse.[74] With the conclusion of the Nazi–Soviet Pact in 1939, major Soviet purchases of machinery and industrial equipment were redirected towards Germany, reducing even further the volume and value of British goods to the Soviet Union.

3.4 The eldorado revisited: British technical trade agreements and the development of modern Soviet industry

The period between the end of the Second World War and Stalin's death in 1953 saw a lull in Britain's commercial interest in Soviet Asia.[75] The widening rift between the two countries, combined with the increasing isolation of Stalinist Russia, substantially curtailed post-war British economic interest in the Soviet Union as a whole, and it was not until 1955 that the stagnation of post-war trade had ended. While the percentage of the United Kingdom's world trade accounted for by the trade with USSR as a whole varied little between 1950 and 1985, British interest in participating in Soviet projects increased considerably after 1960 – a fact which was reflected by heightened British competition for Soviet contracts. Further, it is significant that many of the technical assistance and supply contracts undertaken by British companies between the mid-1960s and the mid-1980s were for the construction, equipping and provision of patented production methods for plants, factories and other projects in Soviet Asia.

By the 1960s comprehensive contracts had become the norm, and a number of companies had concluded agreements to supply and set up equipment in Soviet industrial complexes in Siberia.[76] Further, an increasing number of agreements involved the construction and equipment of complete plants. The business to be had was clearly becoming more valuable, and by the end of the decade British companies had secured a number of large contracts for extensive projects in Soviet Asia. One of the first of these, concluded in 1961, was the £2.5 million contract with the British consortium Wycon Services for the construction and equipment of two complete chemical plants near Ufa in Bashkir. In 1964 another consortium of British firms, Polyspinners Ltd, agreed to construct and equip a huge complex at Irkutsk, Siberia, to manufacture Dacron polyester fibre. Although part of a larger agreement, this contract alone was worth some £56 million ($140 million) and represented one of the single largest British contracts with the USSR.[77]

Although the United Kingdom's overall share of Soviet trade declined steadily from the 1960s, with the British share of OECD exports to the USSR falling from 9.2% to 4.9% between 1970 and 1980, British interest

British business in Russian Asia since the 1860s 89

in huge Soviet 'turnkey' contracts had, if anything, sharpened. British companies experienced in doing business with the Soviet government, including John Brown, British Leyland, British Petroleum, Imperial Chemical Industries (ICI), Davy International, Simon Carves, and Courtaulds, faced increasing competition through the 1970s. Coinciding with the energy crisis of the early 1970s, the discovery of vast natural gas and oil reserves in Siberia, combined with renewed Soviet efforts to enlist foreign technical and economic cooperation in the development of Siberian natural resources, ensured that the most advanced technology would be available to the USSR on its terms.

Despite overtures towards closer Soviet–Japanese economic relations, British participation in Soviet projects remained impressive throughout the 1970s and early 1980s. One firm which successfully negotiated several contracts during this period was John Brown Company. A party to the Wycon Services and Polyspinners Ltd contracts of the 1960s, John Brown, either alone or with associates, concluded agreements worth £54 million between 1960 and 1974 and, by the company's own reckoning, had captured new business in the Soviet Union worth £250 million between 1975 and 1985.[78] Nearly half of this amount can be accounted for by contracts supplying technology, expertise and equipment to enterprises in Soviet Asia. More generally speaking, the two single largest Soviet orders placed in Britain under the 1976–1980 Five Year Plan involved work in Soviet Asia.[79]

British capital and technology continued to play an important role in developing key industries in Soviet Asia. By providing construction and engineering expertise as well as the technological know-how and equipment, Britain contributed to the Soviet Union's goal of building what are often touted on both sides as the largest, most modern industrial plants. While the more valuable contracts have inevitably received some attention, technical assistance contracts are generally far less publicised today than they were in the 1930s.[80] There is, therefore, the distinct possibility that such contracts account for a larger proportion of UK exports than is reported in the press.

3.5 Conclusion

There is a remarkable degree of continuity throughout Britain's economic interest in Russian – and later Soviet – Asia. Recent observations made concerning the economic potential of Siberia could easily be mistaken for those made during a much earlier era. In the context of the opening of a 'British Week' in Novosibirsk in 1978, for example, Siberia was again described as 'the Russian El Dorado: a land of boundless natural wealth, a vast unexploited reserve of ... almost every natural

90   Christine White

resource needed for the future development of the Soviet Union'.[81] The possibilities for British trade and technological participation were great; it was only for British business to capture the market from those Japanese and American interests which had long been active in the region. The distinct cooling in Soviet–Japanese and Soviet–American relations during the late 1970s provided a propitious opportunity for 'Britain to strike in the market',[82] notwithstanding that 'whatever opportunities are provided for Western capital in Russia . . . will be laid out strictly on Soviet terms'.[83] It was made clear even during the desperate inter-war period that the Soviet government would forgo much-needed Western trade and technology rather than compromise its principles. The fact that since the 1930s the USSR has been capable of the technology to develop its industries and natural resources – albeit at a greater cost than with foreign participation – enables the Soviets to enforce this conviction. Thus, success in capturing any future business in Soviet Asia depends to a large extent upon the ability of British firms to negotiate mutually acceptable contracts.

Another similarity can be found in the persistent Soviet attempts to press barter agreements and buy-back clauses on Western firms in order to help finance the purchase of their expertise and equipment. Historically a problem in Soviet foreign trade, the Soviet government's chronic shortage of foreign currency has made it necessary to encourage these firms to accept shipments of raw materials as payment against the contracts, or to include as part of the agreement the provision that the company purchase a percentage of the eventual output of the plant it helped to construct.[84] With few exceptions, British companies have been hesitant to enter into such agreements, leaving the way open to West German and Japanese companies in particular, which appear to have had considerably fewer reservations about entering into such contracts – especially when it has involved future supplies of oil and natural gas.

British disinclination to enter into such barter-type agreements was no doubt partially due to the huge trade deficit it has suffered with both Russia and the Soviet Union.[85] Britain continued to rely heavily upon the Soviet Union for supplies of certain raw materials throughout the 1970s and 1980s, a large proportion of which were supplied from Soviet Asia. In 1978, for example, one-fifth of all UK timber, pulp and paper imports, as well as a substantial – and increasing – proportion of Britain's imports of industrial diamonds have come from Siberia.[86]

One difference which does stand out in a comparison of British business in Russian and in Soviet Asia is the nature of British business involvement. Before the First World War, British interests tended to take the form of foreign direct investment in the Russian extractive industries. Notwithstanding the 1917 Revolution, British investors continued to

British business in Russian Asia since the 1860s 91

show some interest in the concessions offered by the Soviets, though this arguably could be representative of the desire of those who lost money and property at the hands of the Bolsheviks to get some of their own back. Post-war British business interests in the Soviet Union have been exclusively commercial, with technical assistance contracts replacing foreign direct investment in the extractive industries. More secure and no doubt ultimately more profitable, this business has been taken over by British engineering and manufacturing firms, and the bold British entrepreneur/ investor in Russia has become a thing of the past.

Despite the recurring image of Siberia as an eldorado, British business had never been unreservedly committed to establishing itself in the region. Unlike its competitors, Britain tended to regard Siberian trade as little more than a means of relieving 'the effects of disturbing cyclical trends of orders from the home market'.[87] Likewise, concern over the trade imbalance tended to wax and wane according to the domestic economic situation. Nowhere is this more evident than in the separation of politics and business during periods of recession in the UK. As in the determination of some British firms to pursue 'business as usual' with the Bolsheviks during the post-war depression, those firms with profitable business relations with the Soviet Union in the early 1980s tended to disregard the political crisis that developed over events in Afghanistan and Poland. Compliance with the Reagan administration's decision to embargo so-called strategic goods that were ultimately destined for the Soviet Union would have meant the loss of British contracts worth approximately £220 million for the Siberian gas pipeline. In the case of John Brown alone this would have meant the cancellation of a contract worth £104 million and the loss of 17,000 jobs at its engineering works in Strathclyde, an area which was already suffering from one of the highest rates of unemployment in the country.[88]

The fact that between 1978 and 1986 – a period marked by official commitments to mutual economic cooperation – no major Soviet contract was concluded with any British company may indicate that British business again lost its way. Even so, it is clear from the 1986–1990 UK/USSR Economic and Industrial Co-operation Programme that both governments remained anxious to expand their economic relations. While the aim of the programme was 'to continue to develop and deepen economic and industrial co-operation on a long-term and mutually beneficial basis', it is obvious that such cooperation would have resulted in Britain benefiting from increased exports of technology and equipment to the Soviet Union – a programme to which the Soviets would have been willing partners, provided that, as always, it was on their terms.[89]

4 British business in India, 1860–1970

B. R. Tomlinson

4.1 Introduction

The Indian sub-continent was host to the largest and longest-lived British business community of any area in Asia in our period, and of any other extra-European location outside the colonies of recent settlement.[1] The diversity of the activities of this community probably exceeded that of any elsewhere, and the rhythm and dynamic of its activities were often faster and sharper than in other Asian or African locations. The history of business activity by British entrepreneurs is an important element in the modern economic history of mainland South Asia, and of the British imperial system as a whole. British firms in India are usually studied as agents of imperial control and exploitation, with their rise, maintenance, and decline being seen as a function of the economic power over production and exchange that foreign capitalists were able to exert in the colonial situation.

To assess such interpretations we must first be clear about whether it is possible to separate out completely the history of private firms from the history of particular industries, of international investment, of colonialism in theory or practice, and so on. The actions of British businessmen in India must be analysed in the context of their own institutions and perceptions, but they cannot be isolated completely from the activities of other public and private agents. The most important of these was undoubtedly the colonial state, which many historians now argue was the crucial influence in creating a distinctive form of capitalism that both stimulated and constrained all other economic operators. To understand the history of British firms in India from the 1860s onwards we must first consider the events of the first century of British rule that shaped a peculiarly 'colonial' economy thereafter.

The break-up of the Mughal empire in the eighteenth century did not lead, as the British liked to believe, to an anarchic collapse into economic parasitism from which only the *pax Britannica* rescued producers and consumers.[2] Instead, effective local political structures which combined administrative control with some elements of socio-economic dynamism

British business in India, 1860–1970   93

and institutional development emerged, rising to prominence independently of the administrative and military systems imported by the British. Recent research stresses the importance of the merchant and service-gentry groups that became the crucial intermediaries between the petty states and the rural productive, revenue-paying base. Such groups attained a strong internal coherence across the urban centres and warrior-states of the Gangetic plain, in the Maratha chiefdoms of western India, in the new mercantilist powers of southern India (notably the Mysore of Hyder Ali and Tipu Sultan), and even in Bengal during the early years of the East India Company's rule there. Indigenous merchants, revenue-farmers, and organisers of new settlement were able to use the supply-lines of courts and armies, and state-organised revenue collection and transfer mechanisms, to organise extensive patterns of inter-regional trade as well as making substantial investments in rural production.

This redeployment of Indian merchant capital suffered a decisive shock with the widespread imposition of British control after 1800. While new definitions of property rights and changing bases of commercial law were an important part of this process, the main destructive force was the new form and activities of the colonial state acting in and for itself. The effect of the coming of Company rule on commodity production, especially in rural areas, is a complex and controversial subject, which we cannot go into here. So far as the intermediaries between the state and producers were concerned, however, the message is much clearer. The East India Company's administrators extensively revised the basis of revenue assessment and collection, and provided new centralised institutions for cash transfer both domestically and internationally. Once the state's own apparatus took over these functions, the scope of private operators, especially of Indian private operators, was considerably reduced. Before the 1850s there was still some room for private enterprise in these activities by Company servants and, once the Company's trading monopoly had been abolished, by formal firms of expatriate entrepreneurs. Such operators required Indian partners, and many of the established native business groups were able to take over this role. But such operations were largely confined to foreign trade and its internal supply by the 1840s, and the international depression of that decade took a heavy toll of many of the old private business empires, British and Indian alike.

In 1858 the administration of British India passed formally into the hands of the Crown, and thenceforth the formal place of private agents in the economic operations of the colonial state was very small. The most significant change was in the financial arrangements for the transfer of government revenues both within India and between Calcutta and London.[3] Spurred on by an awareness of the dangers of commercial instability following the boom and bust of the cotton economy during the

American Civil War, the government of India quickly completed the establishment of its own institutional apparatus for handling official revenues and transfers. In particular, as a result of the collapse of the Bank of Bombay in 1866, the colonial administration set up its own Treasury system, by which revenue within the country was collected, stored and transmitted by its own agents. At the same time, monetary discretion was removed from the local banking system by the withdrawal of the right of even the semi-official Presidency Banks to issue their own currency notes.

While these changes were taking place domestically, the international transfer mechanism for Indian revenues and trade surpluses was being drastically revised in practice by the growth of the Council Bill system. The colonial administration now had heavy expenditures to meet in Britain – the 'Home Charges' that covered defence expenditure, pensions, the maintenance of the India Office etc., and also the debt servicing caused by public borrowing for railway building and other projects. Over the forty years from 1858–9 to 1897–8, service transactions on government account amounted to Rs 542 crores, an annual average of Rs 13.5 crores, with the Home Charges alone running at an annual average of over Rs 10 crores. Over the same period India's total net visible trade surplus was Rs 650 crores, and her total overseas remittances for private dividends, savings and profits no more than Rs 471 crores. To meet these expenditures in Britain the government of India now remitted money to London by auctioning revenue rupees in its Treasuries in India for foreign exchange payable in London. Although alternative methods for transferring trading capital into and out of India still remained, the Council Bill system rapidly became the dominant mode of remittance available to private traders. Over half of India's visible trade surplus of £555 millions between 1872 and 1893, for example, was balanced by the sale of Council Bills through government agencies.[4]

By the last quarter of the nineteenth century the colonial state in British India had largely created its own institutional mechanisms for sustaining itself through revenue collection, expenditure and transfer. The role of private firms in tax farming, and in exchange broking and official remittance that was common in European-controlled areas elsewhere in Asia was virtually non-existent here. Opportunities for accumulation, or the acquisition of market power available to private firms, whether through production, trade or banking operations in the Indian economy were tightly constrained. While the Indian 'great firms' of the eighteenth century were the most obvious casualties of these changes, the Indo-British 'colonial capitalists' of the first half of the nineteenth century also had their wings clipped to a considerable extent.

Recent reinterpretations of South Asian economic history have strongly underlined the point that the colonial state must be recognised as

4.1 The Chartered Mercantile Bank of India, London and China's Bombay office in 1854.

at least a semi-autonomous actor in the larger history of capitalism in the Indian sub-continent. By its attitude to property and tenancy rights in land, its public expenditure priorities, and its monetary policy, the colonial state helped to shape, if not solely to create, a distinctively 'colonial' economy in late nineteenth- and early twentieth-century India in which its own institutions heavily influenced the allocation of land, labour, capital, investment and employment, and also the fields in which these factors were employed. It follows that the socio-economic, and political, context into which any study of British business in India must be set was equally individual and particular. Social structures, economic opportunities, and cultural and ideological systems were all distinctive and each was fed by, and fed off in turn, the peculiarities of a colonial state that was shaped by a longer and more complex history than that of any other European administration in Asia. Thus the criteria by which we should categorise and assess the

96   B. R. Tomlinson

performance and 'achievements' of British business in India may also be particular ones.

Given this sort of background, how should we approach the history of British business in India over the last hundred years or so? If we take the firm as the unit of analysis, and take note of developments in business form and organisation as major indicators of economic change and as signposts to its causality, then our account of British business institutions in South Asia since 1860 can conveniently be split into two halves. The first is the story of the rise, and subsequent decline, of expatriate managing agency houses from the 1860s to the 1940s; the second is the story of the operations of the subsidiaries of British multinational companies, again first waxing then waning, from the 1930s to the present day.

4.2 Expatriate firms and managing agency houses

The managing agency houses run by British expatriate businessmen represent the classic colonial business sector in India. By the late nineteenth century such firms were spread throughout the sub-continent, although the commercial and industrial economy of eastern India, centred on Calcutta, remained the largest single focus of activity. Managing agency houses ran enterprises in banking, trading, plantations, transportation, utilities and manufacturing. It is their activities in this last sector that have been most analysed by historians, and on which we shall focus. British firms, both those based in Britain and in South Asia, were involved in almost all sectors of the 'organised' economy of the Indian sub-continent. In transportation, however, their role was overshadowed by that of the colonial state which was the chief manager of railway activity by the late nineteenth century. In banking, too, the dominance of Europeans was very limited. Their banks financed foreign trade, but the links between the credit used for this and the domestic financial markets were often tenuous, and the public sector again played a major role in making the market for foreign exchange. Certainly, such firms provided a very small percentage of the total liquidity and credit used within the Indian economy as a whole, even before 1914.[5] Focussing on manufacturing enables us to examine the most interesting set of relationships between foreign business and the domestic economy, and also gives us the case most easily comparable with more recent overseas business activity in India.

The available data make it very hard to estimate the size of the expatriate sector with precision. It is conventional to measure capital stock or capital flow figures as proxies for foreign business activity, but these data mask grave uncertainties. (A summary of such estimates, and their deficiencies, will be found in the Appendix to this chapter.) The

British business in India, 1860–1970   97

power of the expatriates is usually thought to have been compounded by the nature of the managing agency system, which (in theory at any rate) achieved a separation of ownership from control in favour of powerful managers protected by legal contract, and able to sacrifice the interests of shareholders in individual companies to the overall corporate plan of their group. This type of dominance was not universal, however, and the effective power of the expatriate sector was sometimes less than it appeared. In trade, as in raw material supply, the expatriates always relied on partnerships and agency agreements with native Indian firms, although foreigners probably had a controlling influence over much of the cash-crop marketing process before 1914. Such firms certainly also dominated the organised industrial sector almost completely at that time.[6] In 1915 almost half of the total employment in industry (excluding public enter-prises and mining) was provided by European-controlled concerns (almost all of them British). So far as large-scale factory industry was concerned, the proportion of employment provided by the expatriate firms was much higher – 100% in jute mills and in dockyards, over 50% in jute presses, leather works, paper mills, and engineering works and foundries, and over 40% in sugar mills and wool mills. The sectors in which they played only a small part were cotton textiles (21% of employment), oil and rice mills, and brick and tile works (minimal). Total employment in the large-scale factory sector was 773,000 persons in 1915.[7]

Information such as this must be interpreted with care, for links between management, ownership and control in Indian private business were often complicated. But, in any case, the influence of the expatriates was clearly in decline by the 1930s. By 1937 employment in their industrial activities was less than 30% of all industrial employment, with clear falls in every sector, especially in iron and steel. Total employment in the large-scale sector was now 1.9 million. In 1944 the largest twenty industrial groups in India provided almost half a million jobs in large-scale industry. Fifteen of these firms, and 70% of the employment, were British-managed, although the employment they created was now only 16% of that in industry as a whole.[8] No convenient comparable estimates exist for the post-Independence years, but by the early 1960s only ten of the top seventy-five industrial groups in India were still run by British expatriate businessmen, and these firms supplied only 11% of the paid-up capital of that sample.[9]

Analysing the history of British expatriate firms raises the issue of the role of political factors in business history in a very direct way. Following the evidence of nationalist businessmen, and some members of the colonial bureaucracy, many historians have stressed that expatriate entrepreneurs in the late nineteenth and early twentieth centuries enjoyed

98   B. R. Tomlinson

a hegemonic control over large swathes of the Indian economy because of their close ties to the colonial regime. If this dominant role of expatriate firms is accepted, then it is also very difficult to explain the spectacular collapse of such firms after Independence except by political explanation. Only by rejecting the notion that the decline of the expatriates was the result of political changes first and foremost is it possible to question the extent of their hegemonic control of the local economy under colonial rule.

There are two ways in which this can be done. One is to argue that the decline of the expatriates, which began well before 1947, came about because of fundamental changes in the structures of the external and internal economies. Michael Kidron's classic study of the subject hints at such an approach by stressing that, in addition to a sympathetic government, the managing agencies depended on being able to call on outside resources of men, money and markets, and hence on a specific form of international economy.[10] Kidron suggests that the rise of new industries in Britain, changes in the British employment and capital markets, and the difficulties that India's traditional exports faced in world markets from the 1930s onwards, all combined with political changes to accelerate the decline of the expatriates. More recent work has thrown further light on some of these ideas. Through a study of one major expatriate firm, Bird-Heilgers, it has been possible to confirm Kidron's suggestions about the problems of capital, liquidity and profitability as major constraints on expatriate firms before Independence. In addition, in the case of jute, the hegemonic power of the established agency houses over production and trade was substantially weakened in the 1930s (if it ever existed at all) by the rise of new industrial and trading groups from within the local economy. These were able, very quickly, to push the expatriates out of much of the export trade as well as out of a good deal of the internal marketing system.[11]

These rival arguments are not mutually exclusive, and it would be unwise to deny too emphatically that the change of administration in 1947, and the disturbed political climate before then, made no difference to expatriate businessmen. But by following up such lines of thinking it is possible to open up the subject more widely than has been done in the past. Once the key to expatriate decline can be glimpsed elsewhere than in the political demise of the colonial government, then fresh assumptions can be made about structure and change in the indigenous economy and its organised business sector. But first we must be absolutely clear about what form of business involvement in India the expatriate firms represented.

Contrary to what is often supposed, the expatriate firms of Calcutta were not simply managers of other people's money. The classic picture of

British business in India, 1860–1970   99

a managing agency as simply an agent, however powerful, running companies with the capital of British investors put up through the London stock exchange is, at best, heavily over-drawn. In jute and coal especially, most of the public companies were floated in India (although that did not mean that Indian investors held a majority of shares in them); even for the sterling tea companies a controlling interest was often held by a group of investors associated with the managing agency itself. The public, either in India or in Britain, were often only admitted to debenture or preference shares, which were sold off through banks in Calcutta or London. There is a real sense in which it can be said that the expatriate business sector from the last quarter of the nineteenth century onwards was a self-supporting, closed world, essentially engaged in recycling the profits that had been made in the great export-led booms of the Indian economy in the 1880s and 1900s.

The activities of most of the modern business sector in the colonial period can perhaps best be explained in terms of theories of business behaviour based on notions of risk, uncertainty and imperfect knowledge. As Professor M. D. Morris has recently argued, the different investment decisions made by various business groups in India were based on different calculations of risk and uncertainty, and differing access to imperfect knowledge.[12] In these circumstances the British firms tended to invest in activities oriented towards foreign markets, while Indians invested in operations to meet domestic demand. In addition, expectations of rates of return were different for the main rival groups of entrepreneurs.

A broader application of this explanation of entrepreneurial decisions makes it possible to explain a number of the distinctive features of business organisation in colonial India. The fact that British firms tended to have good knowledge of overseas markets but poor knowledge of up-country sources of supply and demand, while Indian firms knew more about the internal economy than they did about foreign trade, accounts for the disaggregated nature of so much of the marketing of imported and exportable goods. The integration of production, processing, local and regional marketing, quality control, and so on in the Indian export trades was never anything like as intense as it was elsewhere in Asia (in Japan for example).

The wider problem of atomism in the marketing of all major goods was a function of the same phenomenon. Neither British nor Indian firms in the organised business sector had a good enough knowledge of all aspects of the marketing process to enable them to overcome the problems of risk and uncertainty that impeded the creation of internalised structures to replace the imperfections of existing markets. Thus, in the export trade in primary produce, the forces of indigenous and foreign capitalists were too

100   B. R. Tomlinson

weak to break the hold of local producers and petty traders on up-country marketing for some time. In the industrial sector, too, the textile mills – even those run by large firms of managing agents – were never able to create full networks of vertical and horizontal integration to enable them to overcome the risks and uncertainties of dealing with the 'unorganised' sector of the local economy from which most of their supply and demand ultimately came.

Before 1914 the foreign (largely British) firms were strong enough to prevent native entrepreneurs from creating integrated marketing networks of their own from the bottom up, but they were too weak to impose their own instead. In most of the supra-local economy the result of competition between native and foreign firms was an uneasy compromise characterised by complex patterns of agency agreements between suppliers and producers at many different levels. By the inter-war period, however, a number of changes were taking place which had significant results.

Between 1919 and 1939, especially from 1929 to 1936, considerable advances were made towards the development of 'modern' financial and commercial institutions in India, at a time when the absolute wealth of the economy was probably not increasing. The creation of new business empires by the great Indian entrepreneurs of this period was achieved by a much greater integration of the rural and urban sectors into a single sphere of operations.[13] The switch-back of inflation and deflation between 1917 and 1923, and the prolonged price depression of the years from 1928 to 1933, shook out resources from agriculture and local trading, and led to the retreat of the expatriate managing agency houses from close involvement with up-country markets. The new resources were harnessed, and the markets reorganised, by new Indian business groups that then followed the expatriates into the foreign trade and manufacturing sectors. Thus, as we have already noted, the hold of expatriate firms even over the jute industry of eastern India in the 1930s was being affected by the growth of Indian rivals with much better contacts in the rural producing and trading economy.

Since 1939 Indian firms of this type have gone from strength to strength in their dominance of private enterprise, and may lay claim to being regarded as by far the most successful part of the modern organised business sector. The only challenge to them from private interests has come from the subsidiaries of multinational corporations, many of them British, which have also brought the advantages of internalisation to bear on their Indian operations. This activity first became significant in the 1920s, reached a peak (in terms of involvement) in the early 1950s, and has declined consistently and rapidly from the mid-1960s onwards.

4.3 Multinational enterprise

Poor coverage and definitional confusion make it hard to arrive at precise figures for the extent of manufacturing investment by British multinationals before 1947. The available information suggests that by Independence about half of British private capital holdings in India was direct foreign investment (DFI) in the subsidiaries of British-based companies. Portfolio investment (which can largely be associated with the activities of the managing agency houses) was concentrated mainly in the old staples of tea, jute, coal, shipping etc.; direct investment (which can be associated with the activities of multinational enterprises, or MNEs) was mostly in the 'new' industries of chemicals, processed foods, pharmaceuticals, paints and varnishes, and so on.[14] By 1950 a number of British-based MNEs had become well established in India and, if one looks backwards from the recent past, the historical base of British MNE activity in India is striking. Of 123 British subsidiary companies operating in India in the early 1970s, 24 had been established before 1930, 28 between 1930 and 1945, 34 between 1946 and 1955, 23 between 1956 and 1965, and 9 between 1966 and 1975 (with 5 unknown); of 21 British subsidiaries with assets of more than Rs 100 million in 1975, 13 had been established before 1945, 6 between 1946 and 1955, and 2 between 1956 and 1965.[15] (A list of these firms is provided in Table 4.1.)

Such activities by British MNEs in India have clear parallels elsewhere. The move away from simple exports to DFI fits broadly with the pattern seen in the Dominions, with initial moves in the 1920s reaching a peak in the 1950s, followed by a relative decline from the mid-1960s as British firms turned their attention to European markets.[16] One vexed question is that of the size of the foreign-controlled sector within the modern Indian industrial economy. Estimates of share capital suggest that foreign firms absorbed about 40% of such investment in the 1950s and 1960s, declining to 30% in the late 1970s. But estimates based on total assets or value added are significantly lower.[17] Evidence from the mid-1960s suggests that the total assets of all foreign-controlled non-banking companies amounted to around 20% of the total assets of all such private companies (the British share being about 18%). By the late 1970s it seems that foreign firms controlled about 10% of total industrial output, and owned about 20% of the large-scale corporate sector.[18]

Accounts of the initial investment decisions of such firms usually stress defensive considerations, often resulting from changes in public policy.[19] Some prominent companies certainly began their DFI in the inter-war years to protect an existing market threatened by new local competition as a result of tariff changes (Unilever), and others set up manufacturing plant in India to regain a market lost by new government purchasing policies

102 B. R. Tomlinson

Table 4.1 *British subsidiary companies in India (1975) with assets of over Rs 100 million*

Subsidiary	Parent company	Assets (Rs million)	% ownership by parent	Date of establish-ment
Alkali & Chemical Corp	ICI	248.6	57	1937
Asbestos Cement	Turner Newall	102.8	76	1934
Ashok Leyland	British Leyland	210.1	60	1948
Britannia Biscuits	Associated Biscuits	127.9	53	1918
Brooke Bond (India)	Brooke Bond	419.4	75	1912
Chemicals & Fibres	ICI	201.1	55	1961
Chloride (India)	Chloride	129.7	59	1947
Dunlop (India)	Dunlop	754.9	51	1936
GEC (India)	GEC	392.3	58	1911
Glaxo (India)	Glaxo	296.9	75	1924
Godfrey Philips (India)	Godfrey Philips	116.8	81	1951
Guest, Keen, Williams	GKN	546.3	59	1931
Hindustan Lever	Unilever	791.7	85	1933
Indian Explosives	ICI	656.5	47	1953
Indian Oxygen	BOC	246.0	66	1935
Lucas-TVS	Lucas	143.1	60	1961
Metal Box (India)	Metal Box	364.9	60	1933
Parry & Co.	EID–Parry	113.8	100	1928
Tinplate Co. (India)	Burmah Oil Co.	120.5	67	1920
Tribeni Tissues	Myddleton Investments	119.5	74	1946
Tube Investments (India)	TI	199.1	52	1949

Notes: 'Ownership' is percentage of equity held by the parent company.
Britannia Biscuits, Chloride (India) and Godfrey Philips (India) were no longer listed as subsidiary companies in 1980.
Source: Government of India, *Directory of Joint-Stock Companies in India, 1975*

(GKN). But other firms had different motivations. For companies making products that were hard to ship – such as tin containers (Metal Box), industrial gasses (British Oxygen), and asbestos sheets (Turner Newall) – a move into local manufacture was the only way to exploit new opportunities in South Asia. In addition, a number of paint and electrical equipment firms discovered that setting up a local subsidiary could fit supply to local demand more efficiently than simple imports. Even those firms that did move into India for defensive reasons often used their investment for subsequent expansion into other fields: GKN, for example, did not keep its subsidiary tied to the manufacture of railway equipment but moved rapidly into the production of other items in the parent group's range, such as wood-screws.

The operations of established manufacturing subsidiaries suggest that such companies were exploiting some clear-cut advantages in their Indian operations. Most MNEs vertically integrated their sales and marketing organisations, and provided their own management of production and

4.2 *The Bhandup works in Bombay of GKN's subsidiary Guest, Keen, Williams Ltd which made pressings under Sankey patents.*

distribution. Few used the services of British expatriate companies in the Indian market after the phase of initial penetration was over, even though such agency houses prided themselves on their experience and knowledge of local conditions, and often acted as sales representatives for British exporters in a wide range of goods. Many of them regarded the managing agency houses as inadequate for their requirements; several preferred to use the marketing organisation of another MNE, ICI, for their products until their own sales organisations were ready. This capacity for vertical integration to internalise market imperfections, through the creation of interdependent manufacturing and marketing operations, is a sign of dynamism among British companies setting up in India in the 1930s and 1940s. However imperfect business structures in Britain may have been at this time, the subsidiaries of large British corporations in India were able

104   *B. R. Tomlinson*

to employ the cutting edge of new manufacturing and organisational techniques, and were rewarded with significant growth and success.

The early entry and vigorous performance of British MNEs in India was a feature of Indo-British economic ties in the late colonial and early Independence years. But by the late 1960s such activities seemed to be suffering from a number of severe constraints. British DFI in India was now more concentrated in fewer, larger firms than was the case generally. The Indian sub-continent was the only part of the world in which the fall in the number of large affiliates established before the mid-1960s was not cancelled out by the growth of smaller affiliates of new enterprises. The MNEs that had led the way in India had mostly risen to prominence in the domestic economy in the 1930s and 1940s, and many of them were performing poorly world-wide by the 1960s.[20]

Many of the British subsidiary companies operating in India from the 1920s to the 1970s had a distinctive form, diversifying operations through internalisation but remaining closely identified with a relatively narrow and coherent product range. This has increasingly set them apart from their rivals, both Indian and foreign. The large Indian groups that grew up in the same period have diversified much more widely within the economy, seemingly happy to use their advantages (of management skills, access to capital, relationship with government, and so on) in any field where profits could be made. The recent liberalisation in Indian government economic policies, which has resulted in a loosening of controls, an encouragement of joint ventures and leasing agreements in advanced technology production, has tended to favour new foreign enterprises rather than the established British ones. Few other foreign firms spread themselves as broadly throughout the economy as have the early-entry British MNEs. In 1975 there were 36 Foreign-Controlled Rupee Companies (FCRCs) with over Rs 10 crores in assets; 21 of them were British, 5 American, 3 German, 2 each Swiss and Swedish, and 1 each Canadian, Dutch, and Panamanian.[21] The growth strategy of foreign enterprise in contemporary India concentrates on turn-key projects and royalty and licensing agreements. British firms have been constrained in these fields in part because of the lack of technological edge (and other problems) of the home economy. But in part, also, the earlier presence and heavier involvement of leading British firms in the Indian market may have led to significant problems of adjustment.

The size of the foreign-owned sector of the Indian manufacturing economy was distorted in the late 1960s and early 1970s by new regulations by the Indian government on foreign exchange expenditure and the behaviour of large companies.[22] In practice it was difficult for large FCRCs – those with a foreign holding of 40% or over – to get permission either to repatriate profits or to expand operations. The gross

British business in India, 1860–1970 105

block figures for such companies were thus inflated by retained earnings, but this should not be taken as evidence of business expansion. The Foreign Exchange Regulation Amendment Act of 1973 (FERA) was intended to resolve this problem by allowing FCRCs to expand, provided that they did so by reducing the foreign-owned share holding to less than 40%. However, the large manufacturing subsidiary companies (most of which were British), were slow to conform.

The growth area of new foreign investment in India in the 1970s was in non-direct investment in the service sector, mostly in the form of loan capital going to construction and utilities, often in partnership with public sector firms. In 1977, direct investment amounted to less than 40% of the total foreign private investment in India (having been over 80% of the total in the 1950s and 47% in 1973). Investment in services now made up 46% of foreign private investment, having been 26% in 1973. The lagging of British firms behind their foreign rivals in this field meant that whereas the United Kingdom remained by far the largest single foreign investor in the Indian manufacturing sector in the late 1970s, she had been overtaken by both the United States and West Germany in the much faster growing services sector. Thus by 1976 Britain had been replaced by the United States as the largest national owner of private foreign business investment in the Indian economy.[23]

Reviewing the history of the leading British manufacturing firms in India leaves a strong impression that we are witnessing a distinct, discrete wave of business activity with a clear beginning and also, perhaps, a clear end. The activities of our leading firms seem to have been the result of a specific set of stimuli and responses in the British, Indian and international economic systems in the middle decades of the twentieth century. Many of the subsidiary manufacturing companies established in India by the early years of independence were exploiting a new product or a fresh technique, and were internalising market imperfections to exploit these ownership advantages by the creation of multinational enterprises. But it is also clear that the further expansion of these firms, and the encouragement of large numbers of followers, were discouraged quite quickly thereafter as these bridgeable gaps in market imperfections closed and as fewer new ones opened up. It may well be that by the 1970s Indian corporations had acquired the internalising skills of the first wave of MNEs, and so were able to compete with them effectively, while entry into new fields required an ability to overcome much larger market imperfections that was beyond the reach of anyone in the private sector.[24] In this way the history of British MNEs from the 1920s to the 1970s was similar to that of the expatriate managing agency houses from the 1880s to the 1940s.

4.4 State and enterprise in a colonial context

The relationship between the state, economic development, and private enterprise is the key to unlocking the history of British business in India, but it is one that must be used with care. Stressing the role of the state does not mean taking changes in public policy as the prime mover of all economic change in colonial or post-colonial South Asia. At some points clear links of this kind can be seen, but their significance must be considered in context. The imposition of new administrative forms and institutions in the early nineteenth century did have a decisive effect on some agents of private enterprise, as we have seen. Similarly, public policy in the third quarter of the twentieth century is widely believed to have limited the opportunities of foreign capital and subsidiary manufacturing firms in India. While the Indian government of the 1950s, 1960s and early 1970s convinced itself in public that it was not acting to favour national against foreign businessmen, many of its policies may have had that effect in practice. Its rules on industrial investment, import licensing and corporate expansion served to reduce the advantages gained from management and technical skills that British subsidiaries had hoped to bring to bear on their Indian manufacturing operations. Yet in design, if not in effect, such policies were not usually aimed at foreign firms as such. Rather, they were an attempt to solve the larger and more pervasive problem of generating multipliers and linkages within the national economy, and thereby overcome the structural *stasis* caused by low and skewed demand and static productivity in the economy as a whole. It was these latter problems which must be seen as the crucial bequest of the colonial past, rather than the relatively large share of the private secondary sector dominated by foreign business.

Some aspects of the colonial administration also clearly favoured one part of the business community at the expense of others. Certain private enterprises, almost always British metropolitan or expatriate ones, were able to participate in the economic institutional structure of the colonial government to a limited extent. The most obvious were those that provided private inputs to public services – such as defence stores suppliers and railway contractors in Britain and India, and the shipping lines that secured mail contracts for international and coastal routes. Other private interests were able to force their way into public operations at certain times. The best example here is that of the London-based exchange banks which, from the 1890s to the 1920s, succeeded in effectively sub-contracting the foreign exchange market from the Secretary of State. The most important of these banks were the Chartered Bank of India, Australia and China, the Eastern Bank, the Mercantile Bank of India, the National Bank of India, and the Hongkong and Shanghai

British business in India, 1860–1970   107

Banking Corporation (which was not, of course, based in London).[25] But such dominance was only temporary and, following renewed financial and political pressures traceable to the structural problems of the colonial economy, British manufacturers and bankers were again substantially distanced from the economic infrastructure of the colonial state by the making of new stores purchase rules in the mid-1920s, and the gradual establishment of central bank-type controls by the Imperial Bank of India (founded in 1921) and the Reserve Bank of India (founded in 1935).[26]

For the vast bulk of trading and manufacturing interests even links of this type are far harder to establish. It has been argued that favouritism took place towards British interests in tariff policy, in the allocation of licences for mineral extraction, in the provision of public transportation services, and in the creation of trading networks for export crops between the up-country producing areas and the ports, for example; but the significance of all of these instances can be contested. What is certain is that even if such favouritism did occur, at particular times in particular places, its effect was not strong enough to give British interests enough power to fight off the challenge of both domestic and foreign rivals. One irony here is that links between private business interests and state agencies were probably much stronger in the Indian Native States than in the British-administered areas. But the businessmen that benefited from these links were not British. Even within British India, by the 1920s and 1930s, if not before, Indian businessmen, as well as those from Europe, Japan and the United States, had created market networks of their own within the internal economy that were at least as effective as those of the British entrepreneurs.

The essential point to grasp from all of this is that the operation of the colonial economy in India was often unhelpful to the activities that British businesses might have liked to pursue. In this respect foreign firms, whether expatriate or metropolitan, and indeed the whole organised business sector of whatever race, were largely passive agents within the colonial economy. It was still possible for them to make substantial profits, and undertake considerable expansion, yet they were always acting in the interstices between lines of social, economic and political organisation that were drawn by other forces. One fruitful way to write the history of Indian economic development from the mid-nineteenth century onwards is as the story of forces that opposed and frustrated the development of market capitalism, however imperfect a market we may assume capitalists to require. The 'peasantisation' of the rural economy in the mid-nineteenth century, as alternative nexuses of economic organisation and surplus generation were destroyed, and the subsequent atomism of the agricultural sector, with vertical linkages built mainly on local nodes of social power within the subsistence economy, provided an infertile field for 'modern' business operations. Since it also caused, or accompanied, slow growth in output and stagnant rates of capital utilisation and labour productivity with existing technology, the rural economy subsequently failed to provide any dynamics for operators in other sectors to exploit to any great extent.

The assertion that the structure of the rural economy did not favour the activities of British expatriate and metropolitan firms may cause some surprise. Many historians have argued a contrary case, seeing the monopoly position of certain business houses in trade and manufacture, and links generated by this to capital supply networks, as conferring a capacity for price manipulation and other forms of exploitation that led to considerable extraction, high profits, and business 'success'. This case has been best made for Bengal, especially for the jute economy that linked peasant producers with processors, manufacturers and shippers in Calcutta. Yet even here the dominance of British business houses, as opposed to other foreign or domestic ones, was short-lived and transitory, declining rapidly in the face of new market demand and organisation from the 1920s onwards. Furthermore, it is not clear that the organised business sector as a whole, whatever its racial composition, was the crucial agent of surplus extraction from the bulk of the cultivating population. At times of boom, profits were widely spread within the rural economy; at times of slump, losses affected the secondary sector at least as much as the primary one. The crucial issue is how these profits and losses were distributed within the agricultural sector; here patterns of local social dominance and control separate from the operations of the secondary sector were by far the most important factor. The undeniable fact that an increasingly large number of Bengali agriculturalists experienced a decline in living standards and food intake over the first half of the twentieth century has more to do with the general crisis of the colonial economy than with the extractive operations of the organised business sector that formed so small a part of it.[27]

It was not only the organisation of the internal economy that helped to produce the distinctive form and activities of British firms in India. The changing balance of opportunities and constraints in the metropolitan and international economic systems were often of great significance also. The rise of the India-based expatriate managing agency houses from the 1860s, replacing earlier networks of international or inter-regional trading and banking houses, was heavily influenced by a number of new factors in the structure of the British and international commercial and financial systems.

In the first place, the problems of exchange instability associated with the silver-standard rupee from the 1870s to the 1890s helped to stimulate certain sectors of the Indian economy, but increased risks for some traders

British business in India, 1860–1970 109

and investors. There is a good deal of evidence to suggest that metropolitan interests, and British home-based capital as a whole, became wary of extensive investment in India because of the difficulties in calculating possible exchange losses on the payment of dividends or repatriation of profits. Thus the amounts of capital invested in private or public enterprises were constrained, and South Asia was never the venue for such large-scale metropolitan investment as that which took place elsewhere. Even the British-based trading and banking houses that expanded their Indian operations took a cautious line on this issue, priding themselves on withdrawing balances from India at the end of the trading season, and on minimising exchange risks by limiting asset holdings in India. For the same reasons, those firms whose activities required them to acquire large-scale Indian assets tended to reinvest profits locally, rather than use their local operations as a base for a geographically widespread business network (additional exchange instabilities and remittance difficulties in China and Japan probably contributed to this). The creation of a distinctive rupee currency area from the 1870s to the 1890s helped to establish a certain parochialism in India-based expatriate entrepreneurs.[28]

The structure of expatriate business in India was also affected by the new opportunities for commodity exports from India that arose after the opening of the Suez Canal, assisted by the export price benefits of a depreciating currency. Much of the expatriate sector in the late nineteenth century was based around the procurement, processing and shipping of the main Indian export commodities – raw jute, jute yarn and cloth, wheat, tea, hides and skins, oil-seeds, raw and spun cotton. Local industry and coal mining were largely begun as an adjunct to these enterprises, and to service the transport network (mostly railways) that had helped to create them. With the exception of tea, however, all of these products were the output of the peasant sector of the local economy, not of expatriate enterprise directly. The result was to keep expatriate firms at an arm's-length distance from the local producers, operating in an enclave in the Indian and international economic systems.

India-based expatriate houses tended to lack dynamic connections to the metropolitan economy. It is striking that the great trading groups of the late nineteenth-century imperial economy were based on operations in Africa or South-East Asia rather than in India. Yet these firms still required considerable inputs from Britain. The ability to raise new capital and recruit suitable personnel from the United Kingdom was vital to their operations, but increasingly, and especially after the First World War, changes in the structure of the British capital and employment markets made such inputs hard to sustain. By the 1920s, if not before, the expatriate sector in India was essentially recycling profits made during the great export-led booms of the 1880s and 1900s, and found it increasingly

4.3 The Bombay office of the Mercantile Bank of India in 1950.

British business in India, 1860–1970   111

difficult to respond to the opportunities outside their established fields that were becoming available. It was a short step from here to the constraining club-like atmosphere of the expatriate business community of Calcutta in the first half of the twentieth century. Beyond this lay the nemesis of the 1940s when many expatriate firms found themselves subjected to asset-stripping take-overs by their erstwhile Indian rivals.

The subsidiary companies of British multinational firms, which became the dynamic sector of foreign business enterprise from the 1930s onwards, also entered South Asia through a particular window of opportunity. New patterns of income and demand distribution provided a market for a range of consumer goods for Indian domestic consumption, many of which could be manufactured locally. At the same time, the emergence of a distinct imperial economic nexus for British manufacturers (based, perhaps, more on the collapse of the rest of the international economic system than on any positive factors), made India a logical place for such operations. But manufacturing for local demand, and subject to local restrictions, required particular skills that were not necessarily of much use anywhere else. Most importantly, perhaps, raw material supply problems and labour productivity difficulties meant that the Indian manufacturing base was often of little use as a platform for exports to other markets. The synergic systems associated with modern multi-national enterprises have usually by-passed the road-blocks of the South Asian economies.

For all these reasons the activities of British firms in India were considerably marginalised within the international business world as a whole, while their influence in mainland South Asia itself was more wide-ranging than pervasive. In addition, as we have seen, British businessmen were often distanced from the operations of the colonial state and of its post-colonial successors. Furthermore, the British metro-politan administration of the imperial period perhaps did little to encour-age the activities of British firms in the long run, however much it may have attempted at times on behalf of particular home producers of export goods. Some contemporaries certainly suggested that official agencies in other countries were helping their nationals to undercut the position of British businessmen in India. Japanese trading firms in the 1900s and 1920s, for example, benefited considerably from officially sponsored links with shipping and banking interests (some of which, like the Yokohama Specie Bank and the NYK shipping line, were themselves semi-official bodies). Similarly, German firms were allegedly able to operate a success-ful ring in the purchase of hides before 1914 because of support from within a domestic economy in which official influence on business structure was extensive.[29] Set against this, the securing of private business interests in India was always a marginal part of the government of India's

112   B. R. Tomlinson

'imperial commitment', and one that was heavily limited by the more important requirements of official finance. Thus, in the inter-war period, the need for balanced budgets and deflationary policies to defend the rupee and facilitate the official remittance mechanism to London meant that the sort of expansionary programmes of public works that colonial governments in Africa were persuaded to undertake (with consequent new business for British industrial and banking firms) were not implemented in India. Nor was the home government ever so willing to offer financial support for the development of the Indian economy in the 1930s as it was to underwrite reconstruction in China, for example. The use of the British government's influence to push through currency reform, organise loans and subsidise exports (through the Export Credit Guarantee Scheme) in China had no equivalent in India.[30]

Since 1947 the main link between official action in developed countries and the Indian economy has been via aid programmes. A clear correlation can be established between the volumes of certain types of aid and the activities of businessmen from donor countries. Here too, it can be argued, British businessmen were at a disadvantage as British aid disbursements in India have been significantly lower, and significantly less import-directing (being single-tied not double-tied for most of our period), than those of others.[31] The major expenditure programme on capital from Britain in South Asia since 1947 was that of the Indian and Pakistani sterling balances from the late 1940s to the mid-1950s. The existence of these balances, and the promise they seemed to hold for extensive exports of British equipment and expertise, was a powerful inducement to British firms to set up subsidiaries in India in the years just before and just after Independence. But the spending of these balances in practice was never directed whole-heartedly towards the sustaining of British private interests in South Asian official development programmes. The rigorous exclusion of India and Pakistan from the imperially based reconstruction plans of the post-war British government was striking. The British government's main concern in practice over the sterling balances was how to prevent them being spent on the heavy industrial capital goods on which any domestic reconstruction effort would be based. One result was to limit the ability of British firms in India to participate in the national development schemes that required just the same type of inputs.[32]

4.5 Conclusion

In conclusion, we return to the question of what lessons an account of the history of British business in India will teach. Are we to assume that such a history will tell us something about the British national economy

British business in India, 1860–1970   113

and its recent structural problems? Or are we to assume that it will tell us something about the history of India, because of the link between British firms and British imperialism? The above account suggests that neither should be expected. British firms in India were operating in a particular and specific environment; in any case it is not at all clear that 'British' is a meaningful collective adjective to apply to individual firms, or groups of companies, that happened to be owned or run by citizens of the United Kingdom. The links between 'British' firms and the 'British' colonial state (if that is a useful description either) were not simple or unambiguous. So far as political alignments were concerned, for example, colonial business-men were often critical of the colonial administration, and frequently aligned themselves with locals to defend 'Indian' interests against 'imperial' ones. Indeed, the government of India itself sometimes opposed London's plan from a desire to restrain imperial demands on India's scarce resources, or excessive favouritism to British metropolitan inter-ests.[33] What the history of such firms in India can do is to help us to illuminate certain aspects of the larger socio-economic historical canvas on which their activities were painted. By analysing the sort of interpreta-tive issues that this chapter has tried to raise, we may better appreciate some of the salient features and dynamics of recent Indian, and British, economic history. Business history is a useful instrument for looking at parts of that larger subject in more detail and, with luck, for clarifying its structure somewhat. We should not ask for anything more or less than that.

The distinctive problem that has faced British firms in India over the last hundred years has been that of control over their environment, with success attending those able to adapt to changes in it, or to adopt new techniques to minimise resulting uncertainties. The expatriate managing agency houses that rose to prominence in the late nineteenth century were successful largely because they provided the organisational skills needed to coordinate India's new export-oriented primary produce sector. The heavy investment in management, organisation and plant that distin-guished British subsidiary companies in their expansionary phase was the basis of their success at a time when older types of firm (represented by the expatriates) were failing. But such investment was only viable if no external mechanisms for drawing together the necessary inputs for manufacturing and trading operations were available. Since the 1960s, broadly speaking, new sources of supply of technology, expertise, capital, and market skills have appeared in the Indian and international business sectors. The result is that firms with lower overheads have been able to operate more successfully, while the early entrants have found it hard to adapt. Set up to operate in the colonial economy at points in time when the externalities were unfavourable, British expatriate and multinational

114 B. R. Tomlinson

companies in India adopted particular forms that were necessary for immediate success, but which also limited their options for future evolution. They were the product of a particular time, as well as of a particular place.

Appendix. Statistical estimates of British business activity in India

British firms in India were a large and obvious presence in the hundred years after the abolition of the East India Company. But calculating the size and range of their activity is a difficult task. A number of sets of statistical estimates do exist, both from Indian and British data, that attempt to measure the volume of British private investment. But few of these capital stock estimates are as careful or as analytically rigorous as might be expected. Furthermore, they are flawed by the use of book, not market, values, and of historic prices. The figures given in Table 4.2 are the best of such estimates available. They are based largely on the work of Dr Banerji, which represents the only careful attempt to get to grips with the problems of capital in non-listed firms and partnerships, and of foreign capital in rupee companies. They are also the only estimates that are comparable over time, at least for the colonial period.[34] It is worth noting that throughout the late nineteenth and early twentieth centuries foreign public investment (in government stock and guaranteed railway investments) probably exceeded foreign private investment. Foreign public investment in India was 61% of the total in 1898, 60% in 1914, 52% in 1921, and 50% in 1938.[35] For the post-1947 period, the estimates of the Reserve Bank of India are the standard source. These are given in various issues of the Reserve Bank's *Bulletin*, and in two special studies: *Census of India's Foreign Liabilities and Assests as on 30th June 1948* (Bombay, 1950), and *Foreign Collaboration in Indian Industry – Survey Report* (Bombay, 1968). These estimates are conveniently summarised in M. Lipton and J. Firn, *The Erosion of a Relationship: India and Britain since 1960* (London, 1975), chapter 6.

Estimates of capital stock are usually concerned with one of three issues: the sources of British investment income; the degree of foreign control over the domestic economy; or the possibility of disturbance to the Indian balance of payments. Those concerned with different questions often had different assumptions and came to different conclusions, and also had different political contexts. Dr Banerji's estimates have been produced as part of an investigation of India's balance of payments accounts. They are therefore concerned with likely inflows of capital and outflows of current invisibles. For these purposes estimates of paid-up share capital are appropriate, as well as being the most easily available (in

British business in India, 1860–1970 115

a rough-and-ready form, at least). But it is less clear that capital stock figures are appropriate for measuring economic power, or fluctuations in foreign business activity. For economic power, asset values of foreign-controlled groups would be of more use (if one wished to accept the theoretical assumptions of such an analysis). Some estimates for the 1930s and 1960s can be found in C. Markovits, *Indian Business and Nationalist Politics, 1931–1939* (Cambridge, 1985), Appendix I; Government of India, *Report of the Monopolies Inquiry Commission, 1965* (New Delhi, 1965), vol. II, Appendix D; and Government of India, *Report of the Industrial Licensing Policy Inquiry Committee* (New Delhi, 1969), Appendix III. However, these are not complete and cover only a relatively short period. For business activity we lack the precise estimates of annual expenditure on fixed assets that are available for Indonesia, and are set out in P. Creutzberg, *Changing Economy in Indonesia*, vol. 3: *Expenditure on Fixed Assets* (The Hague, 1977). One available indicator of annual flows of real investment to India in the inter-war period is the index of the value of imported machinery calculated by Professor Bagchi in *Private Investment in India, 1900–1939*, Table 3.2. This shows that such investment boomed in the early and late 1920s, slumped in 1930–1, and exceeded its 1930 level consistently from 1933 onwards, reaching a peak again in 1938. Much of this new investment was in activities directed towards the domestic economy, many of which were pioneered by Indian, rather than expatriate, businessmen.[36] An alternative data source for calculating fluctuations in foreign business activity derived from import figures for machinery etc. is A. Maizels, *Industrial Growth and World Trade* (Cambridge, 1963), and also R. Batchelor *et al.*, *Industrialisation and the Basis for Trade* (Cambridge, 1980). In these volumes India and Pakistan are one of the geographical units of analysis.

The structural shift in foreign business activity in the 1930s away from the export market and towards import-substituting industrial enterprises to meet domestic demand is an important feature of the history of British firms in India. Unfortunately, hard data with which to map it is again difficult to find. The best information available is that concerned with the activities of companies in groups run by British managing agents, as compared to those in groups run by their Indian rivals. Such evidence suggests that, by the 1930s and 1940s, British expatriate businessmen were trying to diversify into the 'new' industries of the Indian domestic economy, but were less successful at this than were Indian entrepreneurs or the early-entry MNEs. As Dr Banerji's figures show, British holdings of shares in rupee and foreign industrial companies (including mines and plantations) declined from approximately 72% in 1921 to 53% in 1938.[37] Sectorally, these data show declines in British share holdings in jute mills, cotton mills and coal mines, with rises in electricity and telephones, engineering, tea plantations, sugar mills, railways, and miscellaneous enterprises.

116 B. R. Tomlinson

Table 4.2 *Total British long-term private business investment in India, excluding banking and insurance, 1921–60 (in Rs crores)*

	1921	%	1938	%	1948	%	1960	%
Plantations	26.16	13	40.07	17	40.00	24	77.60[a]	18
Oil	13.29	6	27.04	11	17.90	11	116.90	26
Utilities and transport	55.30	27	53.42	23	25.30	15	32.80	7
Mining	25.70	13	21.00	9	9.20	6	10.40	2
Manufacturing	25.21[b]	12	25.06[b]	11	56.90	35	143.70	35
Miscellaneous	57.87	28	68.14	29	14.20	9	19.70	4
Trading	–		–		34.70	21	23.60	5
Financial	–		–		5.50	4	17.50	4
TOTAL	203.53		235.08		203.70		441.70	

[a] Revalued in the 1950s

[b] Jute, cotton, sugar and engineering only

Figures for 1921 and 1938 are for whole sub-continent (excluding Burma); figures for 1948 and 1960 are for Indian Union only.

The Reserve Bank of India, *Census of India's Foreign Liabilities and Assets 30.6.48* gives a total figure of British private business investment of Rs 230.14 crores; this includes banking, insurance and short-term investment.

Total foreign private business investment was Rs 243.49 crores in 1921, Rs 303.18 crores in 1938, Rs 255.80 crores in 1948 and Rs 566.40 crores in 1960.

Sources: A. K. Banerji, *India's Balance of Payments 1921–2 to 1938–9* (London, 1963), pp. 171, 175; Reserve Bank of India, *Bulletin* (October 1962), p. 1542.

5 Early British business in Thailand

Malcolm Falkus*

5.1 Political, economic and social context of Siam

British business enterprise and capital investment in Thailand (known as Siam before 1939)[1] prior to the Second World War have received no systematic study from British historians. From a British perspective, and viewed solely in quantitative terms, such neglect is hardly surprising. Southeast Asia was of relatively small significance for British business outside of the great trading entrepôt of Singapore, and capital investment in the region was dwarfed by comparison with holdings in the United States, India, and the white Dominions. Even within Southeast Asia Siam did not loom large: British long-term investment in Siam in 1914 probably totalled less than £2 million compared with investments of around £16 million in Burma and £25 million in Malaya at the same date. Outside of empire countries British interests in the Dutch East Indies were more substantial than those in Siam, and were probably some three times greater in aggregate in the late 1930s.[2]

British enterprise in Siam is of interest partly because it is a case-study of investment in a region which was able to retain political independence, the only Southeast Asian territory not to fall under the sway of a colonial power before 1914; and partly also, from the perspective of Siam, because foreign enterprise, and especially British enterprise, was of considerable significance. The significance of foreign enterprise to Siam lay in both political and economic factors. Politically, foreign enterprise raised delicate and complex issues for the Siamese government. On the one hand the granting of foreign concessions was one way to assuage the appetites of hungry colonial powers, a token of good intentions on the part of the Siamese to modernise their country and allow foreigners access to markets and resources. On the other hand the extension of foreign enterprise brought dangers and problems: the possibility of foreign intervention to protect national interests, and the extension of extraterritorial and other privileges which the Siamese had been obliged to grant to Western powers in the mid-nineteenth century.

For Siam's economy the importance of foreign enterprise grew out of

118 *Malcolm Falkus*

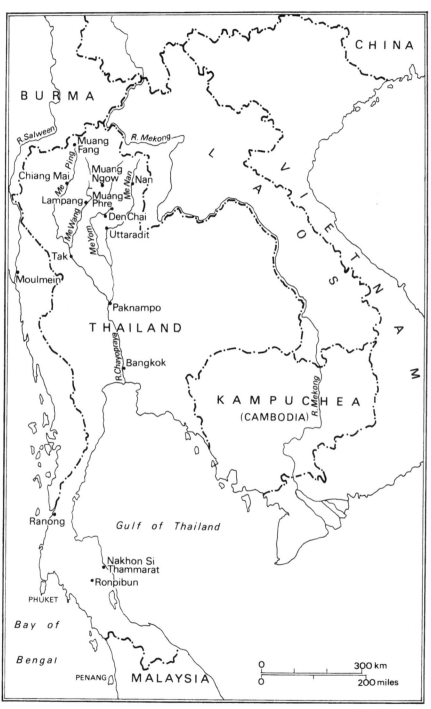

Map 5.1 Modern Thailand

Early British business in Thailand 119

the country's continuing economic backwardness and the very limited supplies of native capital and labour to move outside the traditional rice economy. Prior to 1914, and to a large extent even down to 1940, economic change and modernisation were synonymous with the extension of the foreign sector.

Foreign economic involvement came principally from two sources, Chinese and European. Of these the former was by far the more long-standing, pervasive, and significant. The role of the Chinese has been analysed in many studies and will not be discussed here.[3] Suffice it to say that the Chinese dominated, in many cases exclusively, virtually all the non-traditional occupations in nineteenth-century Siam. While the vast majority of the Siamese, more than 80%, lived in the rice villages and undertook such traditional pursuits as village-based handicrafts, fishing, boat-building, and boating, the Chinese were the middlemen, shop-keepers, traders, and businessmen. The Chinese provided the link between village and town, and in turn dominated the urban economies. Bangkok was very much a Chinese city, some commentators suggesting that one-half of the population may have been Chinese in the second half of the nineteenth century.[4] Nor were the Chinese confined to Bangkok; they were to be found throughout the country, being especially prominent in the southern provinces where they dominated tin mining until after 1900. Many Chinese reached high levels within Siamese society, even the ranks of the nobility. In the south, some of the powerful provincial governors were Chinese. Mostly, though, the Chinese provided an unskilled labour force in urban centres and in mining, and from the second half of the nineteenth century large numbers arrived each year from China directly or from the Straits Settlements. In the 1880s and 1890s as many as 15,000 a year entered the country, while in the prosperous years between 1913 and 1929 some 95,000 came each year.[5]

Unfortunately there is no way of estimating the 'role' of Chinese investment in Siam's economy. Even the numbers of Chinese, due to inadequate registration, a high degree of cultural assimilation, and the inclusion of those born in the country as Thai nationals in national censuses after 1913, can be estimated only imperfectly, and estimates vary widely.[6] The only estimate of foreign capital in Thailand before 1940, made by Helmut Callis in 1941, had to exclude the Chinese.[7]

The role of the Chinese in Siam was not without significance for Western enterprise. In many ways the Chinese provided complementary services for Western firms, linking import–export houses in Bangkok with markets and sources of supply in the interior. All major Western firms established in Bangkok employed Siamese-speaking Chinese *compradores* who were vital to Western firms in developing links with the native economy and with Chinese enterprises.[8]

120 Malcolm Falkus

The Chinese in Siam were significant for Western business in two other respects. Through their numbers, influence, capital resources and enterprise the Chinese were powerful competitors for the West in a number of fields. Two opposing tendencies can be found, illustrated by tin mining and rice milling. In the former case, Western enterprise could long make little headway in the face of Chinese competition. Cheap labour-intensive technology favoured Chinese methods of production, and only when rising costs and the availability of new capital-intensive technology occurred after around 1905 did Western firms make significant inroads. In rice milling there was a reverse trend. The first steam rice mills were set up in the 1850s and 1860s by Western firms, but after the 1880s the relatively simple technology and low capital costs involved proved well within the compass of Chinese entrepreneurs. Thus the Western mills passed steadily into the hands of Chinese, while new mills after about 1880, with one or two notable exceptions, were mostly erected by Chinese.

The Chinese were influential in another way. Some, including a number of the leading merchants, came from the Straits Settlements. In the south, for example, there was an influx of capital and labour from Penang and Singapore into the tin areas around Phuket in the 1860s and 1870s.[9] Chinese from the Straits, like the Burmese foresters and the Shan sapphire miners in northern Siam, were British subjects. This, in view of the extraterritorial privileges granted under Siam's treaties with the West, was a serious issue for the Siamese government, for it meant that the extension of Chinese or Burmese enterprise from British possessions inevitably involved dealings with the British government. The potential danger of British intervention to safeguard 'British' interests was a real one, as events in Malaya in 1874 made only too plain, and was an additional factor in the delicate balance which the Siamese government was obliged to keep between permitting sufficient Western penetration to satisfy the great powers, but at the same time safeguarding Siam's independence and social cohesion.

Western enterprise developed in Siam from the 1850s and was prominent mainly in the import–export business of merchant houses, in shipping, in banking, in the opening up of Siam's teak resources, and in tin mining (the latter not until the opening years of the twentieth century). In all these fields British, and especially Scottish, entrepreneurs played a pioneering and dominant part. In a few other areas, too, Western enterprise played a considerable role. Danish initiative and capital, for example, was largely responsible for Siam's first railway, opened in 1893, a small narrow-gauge line twelve miles in length between Bangkok and Paknam, and for a tramway company, started as a horse-tramway in 1888 but electrified and extended in 1893.[10] In 1898 Danish capital also took over an ailing American electricity supply company which later amalga-

Early British business in Thailand   121

mated with the tramway company (and which continued in operation until taken over by the Thai government in 1950).[11] There are various other examples of Western enterprise in Siam before 1914, in a few manufacturing concerns (for example a British brick and tile firm in Bangkok in the 1880s), in the Bangkok Dock Company (formed in 1865 partly with British capital), in the occasional grant of mining concessions for gold and precious metals, in sugar plantations (for example a British company capitalised at £100,000 received a 25,000 acre concession in 1869), in hotels, in river steamers, and in a variety of other fields.[12] But the significant point is the relatively small-scale nature of Western enterprise outside the operations of the trading companies and the teak and tin firms.

British pre-eminence in Siam may be illustrated in a variety of ways. Britain remained Siam's principal source of imports from 1856 until the 1930s, while British empire countries were the largest markets of Siam's exports. Britishers always made up the greater part of the foreign community in the country; for example in 1889 around 40% of all foreign residents from Europe and America were British.[13] More British than any other nationality were employed by the Siamese government as foreign experts and technicians, while British subjects always held the important position of Financial Adviser (instituted in the 1890s and continued until 1950). Britain long remained the country most favoured by Siam's elite to provide foreign education for their sons. In 1930 there were 200 students in England, compared with only 50 in the United States and 40 in France.[14]

Britain also dominated Siam's banking. The first bank to be established in the country was the Hongkong and Shanghai Banking Corporation, opened in Bangkok in 1888. The dominance of Western banking had been firmly established before 1914. Following the Hongkong Bank in 1888 came the British Chartered Bank in 1894 and the French Banque de l'Indochine in 1897. The first Siamese bank, the Siam Commercial Bank, was not founded until 1906; even then the bank had German and Danish interests and remained under European management until 1941 (German until 1917, English thereafter). In 1909 came the opening of the first Chinese bank, the Sze Hai Tong Bank. Banks, though, played only a small role in the Siamese economy prior to the Second World War. Their business was largely confined to financing the foreign trade sector. European banks only lent large sums to the well-established European business concerns, and the negotiations for such loans normally took place in Europe rather than in Bangkok. A measure of the small role of banks in the economy is that the total of loans and advances given by the commercial banks came to only 25.6 million baht in 1939 (the value of rice exports alone was four times that figure).[15]

Table 5.1 illustrates the continued importance of tin and teak among Siam's exports, though their value was always dwarfed by that of rice.

122 *Malcolm Falkus*

Table 5.1 *Composition of Siam's exports (% of value), 1890–1938*

Year	Rice	Tin	Teak	Rubber	Other
1890	69.7	11.1	5.5	–	13.7
1906	69.1	11.0	11.2	–	8.7
1926–7	69.1	9.5	3.4	2.2	15.8
1937–8	44.5	13.1	5.4	19.9	17.1

Sources: J. Ingram, *Economic Change in Thailand, 1850–1970* (Stanford, California, 1971), p. 94; *Statistical Yearbook for Siam for 1937–8 and 1938–9* (Bangkok, 1939)

Table 5.2 *Tin output in Siam and British share, 1907–37*

Year	Output (tons)	% British and Australian firms
1907–8	4,381	–
1916–17	8,906	37
1926–7	7,397	35
1936–7	13,386	68

Sources: *Commercial Directory for Siam, 1929* (Ministry of Commerce and Communications, Bangkok, 1929); Ingram, *Economic Change in Thailand*, p. 100; Wilson, *Thailand, a Handbook of Historical Statistics*, p. 153.

Since Britain had come to dominate teak by 1890 and tin by the 1920s Table 5.1 gives some indication of Britain's overall role. Table 5.2 further shows the share of tin output taken by British and Australian companies.

Unlike tin, only a part of teak output was exported. Most teak exports went through the port of Bangkok (which are the figures shown in Table 5.1), but some teak was exported through Burma and Indochina while perhaps one-third to one-half of total output found its way to local markets.[16] By 1914 nearly all this timber was handled by Western firms, very largely British. It should be noted that since teak and tin were highly localised their regional impact was greater than national totals suggest. By the late 1930s rubber had also become a significant export but production here was almost entirely in the hands of smallholders, and, unlike in Malaya, involved virtually no Western enterprise.

How large was British capital investment? Table 5.3 presents estimates of Britain's share in long-term capital investment in Siam between 1880 and the 1930s.

The figures are only very rough guides to trends and orders of magnitude. Over and above the well-known definitional and statistical problem of compiling such estimates, the lack of data for Siam makes such an exercise possible only within very wide margins of accuracy. Moreover a considerable proportion of British investment in Siam was undertaken by large

Early British business in Thailand 123

Table 5.3 *Foreign long-term capital investment in Siam, 1880–1938 (£000)*

	British	%Teak	%Tin	All Countries	%British
1880	50	–	–	56	91
1900	826	84	–	1,033	81
1914	1,640	73	10	2,050	79
1927	6,250	32	58	8,330	76
1938	11,100	22	67	14,800	74

Note: This British long-term investment was virtually all 'direct', resulting from investment by 'free-standing' companies registered in London or in various empire countries.
Sources: Inchcape Archives: Annual Reports of Borneo Co. Ltd, and Anglo-Thai Co. Ltd. Callis, *Foreign Capital,* pp. 59–70. F. Birch, *Tropical Milestones: Australian Gold and Tin Mining Investments in Malaya and Thailand 1880–1930* (unpublished MA thesis, University of Melbourne, 1976)

trading companies, like the Borneo Company Ltd and the Bombay Burmah Trading Corporation. Such firms had operations in many different countries and even from company balance sheets it is often impossible to allocate investment among the different territories, nor is it possible to distinguish between fixed and working capital (the latter much more significant).[17] Again much of the 'British' investment came from companies registered in India, the Federated Malay States, the Straits Settlements and Australia. The assumption that all the investment can be counted as British is open to question.[18] On the other hand some Chinese, Siamese, Danish and other non-British registered companies certainly attracted British capital, although to what extent cannot be determined.

It is worth drawing attention to three points in connection with Table 5.3. First, the dominance of teak and tin in British holdings is very clear, most of the growth in teak investment taking place before 1914. Secondly, the figures given for British and total foreign investment are considerably smaller than those given elsewhere, especially before the 1920s. Ingram, for example, puts total teak investment at £900,000 in 1895, and British investment alone in teak at £2 million in 1899 and £3 million in 1924.[19] These figures are all based on contemporary estimates by British consular officials whose concept of 'capital' appears to have been the actual value of teak logs cut in the forests and in transit to Bangkok at any one time.[20] My estimates are those for investment in sawmills, buildings, expenditure on machinery and communications in the forests, advances to foresters and purchases of elephants, as far as these can be estimated from company balance sheets and other sources.

Thirdly, Table 5.3 is interesting for what it does not show: that is, extensive investment outside of teak and tin. For example, unlike in other

124 Malcolm Falkus

countries, British investment in railway construction, urban infrastructure, plantations, and so on, was extremely limited and this lack of diversification deserves comment. Lack of profitable outlets for investment, given the economic backwardness of the country and poor internal communications, was certainly part of the answer. But there was also a great reluctance on the part of the Siamese government to permit large-scale capital investment, and especially to allow any one country to become too powerful.[21] The history of railway construction is interesting in this respect.[22] Western firms and Western governments were certainly anxious to participate in railway construction in Siam from the 1880s but not until 1890 was a Railway Department set up by the government. The government was naturally fearful of undue British influence in the northern areas bordering Burma or in the south adjacent to Malaya (where Siam claimed suzerainty over the states of Kelantan, Trengganu, Kedah and Perlis, all ceded to Britain in the Anglo-Siamese agreement of 1909). At the same time the French were threatening in the east (Laos was taken in 1893 and in the same year two French gunboats forced their way up the Chaophraya River to Bangkok), and the Germans too were anxious to increase their influence in Siam. All this determined the Siamese government to control its own railways and to provide the capital as far as possible out of internal revenue and to avoid foreign loans. The first government railway was projected from Bangkok to Korat in order to strengthen Bangkok's position in the eastern areas at a time of French expansion. The initial contract went to the Scottish firm of George Murray Campbell, financed by Jardine, Matheson and Company, and work started in 1892. Ayuthaya was reached in 1897 and Korat in 1900, the line eventually being extended from Ayuthaya to the north. However, the arrangement with Campbell proved disastrous: the British firm engaged in constant wranglings with the Siamese government and German engineers.[23] Eventually in 1896 the contract was cancelled and from then on the entire railway system (with the exception of some small private lines) was constructed by the Siamese government, though with the continued assistance of foreign technicians. The reluctance of Siam to become embroiled with foreign firms was evidently widely known: in 1896 the British firm of Livesey, Son and Henderson wrote to the Foreign Office asking for Lord Salisbury's help in securing the contract for the Bangkok–Chiengmai rail link, but the Foreign Office replied that it was unlikely that the Siamese would react favourably to any such proposal.[24]

One result of these decisions was that Siam floated very few foreign loans, and had one of the lowest rates of public indebtedness in Southeast Asia.[25] Railway loans were raised in 1905 (for £1 million), 1907 (for £3 million), and in 1909 (for £4.75 million). The first loan was floated in London and Paris, the second in these centres and partly also in Berlin,

Early British business in Thailand 125

while the third was a loan from the Federated Malay States explicitly for the completion of the southern railway linking Bangkok with the Malayan border. Only two more loans were issued, in 1922 and 1924 for £2 million and £3 million respectively, both raised entirely in London.

The Siamese government was reluctant to permit foreign control of its railways; it was also determined to keep foreign enterprise in Siam within limits, prohibiting tin mining to foreigners outside the south and controlling the extension of foreign enterprise in the provinces. Thus the rather limited scope of Western enterprise in Siam may be explained partly by Siam's backwardness and partly by wariness on the part of the Siamese government, each reinforcing the other.

The extent and character of Western enterprise in Siam was conditioned as we have discussed, by the political independence of Siam and by the prevailing economic and social environment. Siam in 1914, and even in 1940, was a poor, sparsely populated, and overwhelmingly agrarian country.[26] Lying wholly within the tropics, Siam's economy was based on peasant-cultivated rice. The bulk of Siam's population lived and worked in the rice villages. Even when traditional restrictions on mobility and occupation were loosened during the reign of King Chulalongkorn (1868–1910) and the tentacles of the market spread gradually into the largely subsistence rural economy, the Siamese themselves showed little inclination to forsake their villages and customary occupations as rice farmers. Rice production expanded, and the proportion of the crop exported rose from 5% in 1855 to 50% in 1900, but virtually all the intermediary stages between the village and final export from Bangkok were in the hands of non-Siamese, as already mentioned.[27]

Numerous examples of social and economic backwardness might be given. For example, the last vestiges of slavery did not disappear until 1905; until 1932 Siam remained an absolute monarchy, and the ancient system of ranks, the *sakdina*, continued to be the basis of a rigid social stratification until that date. Not surprisingly, therefore, many of the new urban and middleman jobs created by growing commercial change came to be performed by alien groups not subject to traditional restrictions. Internally, too, there was little capital for development. Government revenues were restricted by the poverty of the country, by the restrictions on revenue-raising imposed by the Western treaties, and by the semi-autonomy of the northern teak areas and the southern tin regions, where much of the revenue went to local rulers, the *chaos* in the north, the *rajas* in the south, before effective measures of centralisation took place around the 1890s.

Modern communications long remained underdeveloped. Even in 1913 less than 1,600 miles of track was open to rail traffic in a country the

126 Malcolm Falkus

size of France, and no line reached the tin or teak districts. The second largest city, Chieng Mai in the north, was only linked by rail with Bangkok in 1921, and there was no direct road link until 1940. Indeed, a national highway system was not created until after 1950 and as late as 1935 Bangkok was not linked by road with any other major town. The comment made in 1912 that 'outside the town of Bangkok there are very few made roads anywhere in Siam and none at all in the central part' remained largely true until the 1930s.[28] In the 1930s, despite the existence of a railway network then amounting to some 4,000 miles, more than 80% of rice exported from Bangkok was carried by water from the interior to the rice mills.[29]

Siam's natural resources were not especially rich, although since so much of the country long remained unexplored there were always rumours of abundant mineral wealth, gold and precious stones, petroleum, and coal. In fact tin was easily the most important mineral resource, and the other great national resource was timber, especially the teak forests in the north.

Even from this cursory outline of Siam's backwardness it will come as no surprise that the pattern and extent of British enterprise should differ markedly from that found in many other parts of the world. Clearly the opportunities for capital investment were limited. The main export staple was produced by village peasants working with traditional technology, and the movement of rice from the villages did not involve large expenditures on infrastructure. Industrial development beyond simple agricultural and industrial processing was virtually non-existent, while only in Bangkok was there a significant demand for such urban enterprises as tramways, hotels, dock facilities, and the like. The absence of a large colonial administration or Western settler community meant also that the call for goods and services catering for Western tastes was limited.

5.2 The phases of British enterprise in Siam

British enterprise in Siam may usefully be divided into three phases. In the first, between the 1850s and the 1880s, British business was largely confined to the trading activities and agency business of a small number of import–export houses. British enterprise was then concentrated almost entirely in Bangkok, through which the great bulk of Siam's foreign trade passed.[30] There was little long-term capital investment beyond the erection of warehouses and other commercial buildings and the building of rice mills and sawmills connected with the export trade. By the 1870s British shipping had become dominant in Siam's trade, carrying a large proportion of both exports and imports.

From the 1880s to 1914 came a second, much more active phase in

Early British business in Thailand 127

British business as Siam's economy became integrated more fully into the international economy. This period was notable for the rapid growth of Siam's foreign trade, for the continued expansion of Western banking, for the development of Bangkok (including the Western-financed urban infrastructure, already mentioned), and for the construction of railways. As far as British business was concerned, though, the principal development was the extension of enterprise into the outlying parts of the country, involving considerable capital investment and a greatly extended Western stake in Siam (with important political implications for the Siamese government). There were two main areas of enterprise, both involving a great deal of pioneer exploration in little-known areas. In the 1880s British firms began to take a direct part in the exploitation of the teak forests in the north of the country, while after 1905 British and Australian (especially Australian) concerns became involved in tin prospecting and mining in the southern provinces.

The rapid development of Western enterprise in the north and south of the country was one reason for the impetus towards much greater control over the still largely autonomous outlying provinces pursued by the Siamese government in the 1890s. The need for government revenue, the desire to prevent the indiscriminate exploitation of natural resources, and the political dangers of increased Western interests in parts of Siamese territory bordering colonial or disputed areas all impelled the Siamese government towards centralisation. In 1891 a Royal Department of Mines was set up in Bangkok, followed by a Forest Department in 1896. The working of these departments, both under the direction of British officials in the service of the Siamese government, considerably altered the conditions under which Siam's natural resources were exploited. By 1909, when a new system of forest leases came into operation, both mining (where new leases had been organised in 1901) and forestry were able to move into a more regulated phase.

From around the death of King Chulalongkorn in 1910 until the outbreak of a Second World War British business developed along the lines already laid down in the previous three decades. British pre-eminence among the import–export houses in Bangkok remained, though challenged increasingly in the 1930s by German and Japanese firms and also by growing American business.[31] British firms remained dominant in the teak business, while in tin they increased their stake at the expense of Chinese firms. There was, though, strikingly little diversification into manufacturing enterprise, plantation agriculture, or into other areas of the country beyond those already penetrated by teak and tin enterprises.

The most active field for British investment after 1910 was in tin mining, where there were peaks of investment during the prosperous First World War years and again in 1926–7, and by the latter year investment

128 *Malcolm Falkus*

in tin had outstripped that in teak. The Great Depression in the early 1930s saw considerable rationalisation in the tin industry, with Siam joining international restriction schemes and becoming subject to quotas after 1931. Most of the independent Western companies (many of them Australian-based) came under the control of large London-registered holding companies. As far as teak was concerned, investment and the scale of production grew little after 1909, the areas of forest leases at the rate of output being subject to the agreements of that year. By the late 1930s Britain's overall share of Siam's trade and shipping was declining in the face of competition from German, Japanese, American and other rivals. A growing national consciousness, too, and attempts by the government to encourage Siamese-based enterprise in trading and manu-facturing and the raising of tariff barriers after 1926 made the economic climate for foreign firms increasingly difficult.

The remainder of this chapter will be largely concerned with the developments in British business before 1914, that is during the pio-neering phases when Britain obtained a clear dominance among Western countries, a dominance which was to remain until the Second World War.

5.3 British business from 1855 to the 1880s

In the 1850s Siam was opened 'rather abruptly' to the West as a result of the commercial treaty signed in 1855 between the British and Siamese governments.[32] The treaty was negotiated on behalf of the British government by Sir John Bowring and came into force in April 1856. Its major provisions were (1) the removal by Siam of a large range of trade restrictions, prohibitions and monopolies; (2) the limitation of import duties to 3% *ad valorem* and export duties to 5%, for revenue purposes; (3) the right of British subjects to trade at all Siamese seaports and to reside in Bangkok; (4) British subjects to be under the jurisdiction of a resident British Consul rather than under Siamese courts. Thus the treaty involved considerable inroads into Siam's sovereignty and traditional forms of government revenue: free trade, extraterritorial privileges, and lack of customs autonomy were the concessions wrested from Siam by the British. Following the Bowring Treaty, similar treaties were signed with the United States and France in 1856, Denmark and the Hanseatic Cities (1858), Portugal (1859), the Netherlands (1860), and most other Euro-pean trading nations in the succeeding years.

Bowring's successful mission was the culmination of various efforts by Western powers, Britain above all, to open up trade with Siam. In the early nineteenth century Siam had been largely isolated from contact with the West. Such foreign trade as then existed was conducted as a royal monopoly, operated either directly by the king or, from the 1820s,

Early British business in Thailand 129

through tax farmers.[33] Trade was mainly conducted with China, and shipped in Chinese vessels, although after 1826 direct trade between Bangkok and Singapore grew. But political and economic circumstances in Southeast Asia were changing rapidly as Britain established herself as a major power in the region. In 1786 Britain had acquired Penang; in 1819 Raffles founded Singapore and in 1824 possession of Malacca was confirmed by treaty with the Dutch; in the First Burmese war, 1824–6, Britain acquired Assam and Tenasserim, and in the Second, in 1852, seized lower Burma. As a result of the Opium Wars (1839–42) Britain forced China to open its doors to trade, and to concede both territory and extraterritoriality. In 1841 Hong Kong became a British colony. America too was extending her commercial interests in Asia, and in 1854 Commodore Perry's gunboats forced Japan to end over two hundred years of isolation. British merchant houses established themselves throughout the East, particularly in India and Singapore, considerable impetus stemming from the abolition of the East India Company's China monopoly in 1833. For Siam the development of Singapore was especially significant, and became, in Francis Hyde's memorable phrase, 'the pivot of the chain between the age of steam and steel and the ox-cart and rickshaw; between capital-intensive economies and peasant cultivation.'[34] Before 1833 Singapore had been used by independent agency houses as a means of overcoming the East India Company's China monopoly, and some of the early Western contracts with Siam sprang from the activities of such firms.

Against this background there were various attempts by Britain to gain a commercial footing in Siam.[35] Two British missions in the 1820s, an American mission in 1831, and British and American missions in 1850 failed to achieve their objectives. By 1850 the Western powers were getting increasingly exasperated, and there was talk by both the British and American envoys of that year of the use of force.[36] Fortunately for Siam the accession to power in 1851 of a forward-looking monarch, Rama IV (King Mongkut) brought to the throne a king who was well aware of Western strength, had studied the English language, and was convinced that Siam, too, could benefit by commercial contact with the industrialising economies.

In view of the commercial pressures which had been building up before the 1850s it is not surprising that the Bowring Treaty should have been followed by an influx of import–export houses into Bangkok, or that British firms should have predominated. The first post-treaty firm, though, was the American J. S. Parker and Company, a branch of Heard and Company in Hong Kong, which opened in April 1856. A month later the Borneo Company Ltd opened its branch, followed by D. K. Mason, both of them Singapore-based British companies. By 1858 several more British companies had set up, including S. P. Goodale and Company, and

130 *Malcolm Falkus*

Table 5.4 *Number of foreign vessels entering Bangkok, 1848–73*

1848	9	1860	265	1865	159	1870	278
1856	141	1861	309	1866	166	1871	310
1857	204	1862	318	1867	451	1872	344
1858	229	1863	326	1868	219	1873	286
1859	457	1864	457	1869	311		

Sources: Bangkok Calendar; GB and US Consular Reports, various dates; C. M. Wilson, *State and Society in the Reign of King Mongkut, 1851–1868: Thailand on the Eve of Modernization* (unpublished PhD thesis, Cornell University, 1970), Appx P, vol. II, pp. 983–4

Hamilton Grey, while the large American firm of Russell and Company also opened an office. A French concern, Remi Schmidt, opened in 1857, and the 1858 treaty with the Hanse Cities was followed by the opening of two important German houses, A. Markwald and Pickenpack Thies.[37] Nearly all these early firms were branches of companies already established in Asia, the British being based mainly in Singapore, the others in China.

Siam's trade grew substantially after 1856, yet the optimistic expectations held by many Europeans and Americans of a rich internal market for Western goods and large-scale exports of sugar and other goods to Europe were not fulfilled. The majority of the trading companies, especially the smaller concerns, failed, and others amalgamated. By 1880 not a single American firm remained.[38] The difficulties encountered by Western business firms were many: inadequate knowledge of the Siamese language and ways of doing business in Siam; hostility from the established Chinese merchant community and dependence upon the Chinese for contacts with the Siamese; and, above all, the fact that Siam possessed a poor underdeveloped economy whose size and wealth had been greatly exaggerated. The total population of the country in 1855 may have been as low as 2–3 million, and was certainly no more than 5 million; even in 1911 it was only 8.3 million, and in 1937, 14.5 million.[39] As pointed out already, the economy was largely subsistence in nature, with only a limited circulation of money outside the capital. Not until the 1860s did metallic money replace cowrie shells for small transactions,[40] while until after 1900 the predominant form of money in the north was Indian rupees and in the south Mexican and Straits dollars.[41]

Another problem for Western firms was the substantial variation in business from year to year. Rice quickly established itself as the staple export but the quantity exported depended on the yield of the harvest; this in turn determined the demand for imports. Table 5.4 shows both the expansion of business in the port of Bangkok after 1856 and the uneven development of trade thereafter. The year 1865, when only 36,718 piculs

Early British business in Thailand 131

Table 5.5 *Nationality of ships arriving in Bangkok, 1861–86*

	1861–2 Tonnage	%	1863–4 Tonnage	%	1882 Tonnage	%	1886 Tonnage	%
British	30,233	22.2	57,508	34.5	117,762	58.3	140,213	70.5
American	26,246	19.3	4,972	3.0	664	0.3	1,737	0.9
Siamese	47,078	34.6	46,859	28.7	33,849	17.1	10,142	5.1
Other	32,392	23.8	56,359	33.8	46,162	23.3	46,715	23.5
Total	135,949		166,698		198,437		198,807	

Source: GB and US Consular Reports, various dates

of rice were exported compared with 2,409,748 piculs the year before was a particularly difficult year for the Bangkok trading houses (one picul = 60kg.).

From the outset British shipping, strongly supported by the trading companies as agents for the main shipping lines (such as the Borneo Company for Holt's Blue Funnel steamers) carried more trade than that of any other Western nation, dominating the direct trade with Europe. Prior to the American Civil War, American sailing vessels were also prominent in the carrying trade while small Siamese ships took a large share of the local Asian trade. But with the advent of steam shipping British dominance increased, and remained overwhelming until the 1890s, when German shipping came to the fore. The shares of British, Siamese, and American ships are given in Table 5.5.

In 1898 British ships still accounted for 76% of the total tonnage arriving in Bangkok compared with only 7% owned by German lines. Thereafter there was an abrupt change. In 1899 the shares were 67% and 19% respectively, while in 1900 British lines accounted for only 38% of the tonnage, and German shipping for no less than 51%. The principal cause of this British decline was the sale in 1899 by Holt of the East India Ocean Steam Ship Company to North German Lloyd. The only regular line between Bangkok and Singapore therefore passed to the German flag, while in 1900 the Scottish Oriental, which dominated the Bangkok–Hong Kong route, was also absorbed by the German company.[42] Since roughly three-quarters of both Siam's imports and exports were centred on these two ports the impact on British shipping was dramatic.[43]

From the 1850s the main activities of British and other Western firms in Siam were importing, exporting, and general agency business, the latter initially mainly for insurance and banking companies connected with the finance of trade. Thus in 1862 the Borneo Company Ltd represented three insurance companies, the Netherlands Indies Sea, the Bengal, and the North China, and later added others. The same company were agents for

5.1 Siam Forest Company's teak logs on the River Me Wang, c. 1905.

the Chartered Mercantile Bank of India, the Oriental Bank Corporation and the Northern Bank of Scotland.[44] The German firm of Pickenpack Thies were agents for the Hongkong and Shanghai Bank and the Bank of Rotterdam.[45] This latter example emphasises a point which could be multiplied in many instances, that the nationality of the trading house was not necessarily a guide to the nationality of the agencies it handled. British firms were represented in Bangkok by American, German, Danish, Dutch and other houses; in turn the British firms often represented Western companies of various nationalities.

There was some diversification into the processing industries for export, a necessary step in the building up of wholly new lines of business. Until the 1880s Western firms dominated steam rice milling. The first British steam rice mill was erected in 1863 by A. M. Odman and Company, who also owned a sawmill, and in 1865 the Borneo Company became joint partners in this venture, renamed the Bangkok Rice Mill.[46] The earliest Western mill had been erected by an American company in 1858, but it was taken over by Pickenpack Thies after a few years. In 1865 another German firm, Markwald, also established a large rice mill. There were also several Western sawmills. During the 1860s the Borneo Company's exports of teak grew, and this developing business was followed by the building of a large new sawmill in Bangkok in 1870.[47]

Western dominance of rice milling was not destined to last. By the

Early British business in Thailand 133

1870s there were growing complaints of excess milling capacity and low profits, and the Western firms proved unable to compete with the Chinese. As a result most of the Western mills, including the Bangkok Rice Mill and the American Steam Mill, were sold to Chinese entrepreneurs. Of the 27 steam rice mills in Bangkok in 1889, 17 were owned by Chinese, while by 1919 Chinese owned 56 out of 66.[48]

5.4 Teak and British enterprise

Prior to the 1880s Western firms had remained largely on the periphery, as it were, of the Siamese economy, located exclusively in Bangkok, and having dealings with the interior only through the agencies of Chinese middlemen. Between 1880 and the outbreak of the First World War the nature of Western enterprise and its degree of involvement in Siam's economy changed markedly. The numbers of trading firms expanded as the Siamese economy itself developed and rice exports grew rapidly. This meant more and increasingly diversified imports and an extension of agency business. Shipping grew considerably, while from the 1880s foreign banking houses were first established in Siam. Most significant was the development of Western enterprise in teak and tin, and in this section we shall examine the growth of British involvement in the opening up of Siam's forest resources before the First World War.

Teak was a valuable hardwood, used extensively in shipping and for railway sleepers (especially in India), for which no adequate substitute existed. The properties of durability and resistance to fire and to the ravages of insects had made teak the principal material for Chinese junks for centuries, and it was also widely used in the construction of temples, palaces and other important buildings in Southeast Asia. With the destruction of European oak forests teak became used for European wooden sailing vessels and, later, for the decks of iron steamships.

The supply of teak was limited, confined almost entirely to the monsoon forests of southern Asia. By around 1850 the once abundant resources of south India had been virtually exhausted by indiscriminate and unregulated felling. Following British territorial gains in Burma in 1826 (especially the province of Tenasserim) Moulmein developed as an important teak exporting port, drawing supplies both from Tenasserim and, increasingly, from Siam. This Siamese teak was certainly being worked by Burmese foresters in forests belonging to the Chief of Chieng Mai in the 1830s, and during the 1860s and 1870s it is probable that Siamese teak came to form the bulk of Moulmein's exports, the teak being floated into British Burma along the Salween River.[49]

In 1852 Britain acquired the provinces of Lower Burma, and Rangoon began to develop as a teak exporting port, drawing supplies from the Pegu

134 *Malcolm Falkus*

forests which were worked under rather primitive conditions. Following the Indian Mutiny in 1857 the demands for Burmese teak for the Indian railways increased considerably, and out of this growing demand developed the firm of Wallace and Company, formed in 1862 to exploit a timber concession acquired from the still independent Kingdom of Burma. In 1864 the Bombay Trading Corporation was floated in Bombay to take over the assets of Wallace and Company, which included the forest concessions in Upper Burma, sawmills in Rangoon and Moulmein, and ninety elephants (17 employed in the mills, 73 in forest work).[50]

At this stage it is necessary to say something about the teak business itself in Siam.[51] Teak was found almost exclusively in the northern provinces (often called the Laos provinces by Europeans) whose forests were owned by the local *chaos* such as the Chiefs of Chieng Mai or Lakon (Lampang). Prior to the 1880s these Chiefs leased forest concessions to mainly Burmese contractors who normally employed Burmese or other local non-Siamese labour. Such workings were normally small-scale, in the vicinity of rivers. The felled logs would be dragged to the rivers by elephants and floated to mills, finding their way to markets in the interior, or to Moulmein or Bangkok. European firms wishing to purchase teak would usually buy the timber on arrival in Moulmein or Bangkok.

Teak extraction was arduous, time-consuming, and involved an initial outlay of considerable sums of money. This arose from the nature of the teak forests and of the timber. Teak grows in the forests alongside a wide variety of other trees, so that each individual teak tree to be felled needed to be selected, marked, cut, and then dragged by elephants through the thick forests to the river systems. Moreover fresh-cut teak cannot float and only dead trees two years old or more could be put into the rivers. The European system was to 'girdle' the trees about two or three years before felling, cutting round the bark so that the trees died, and dried out where they stood. The felling was done during the rains between July and October. If the rains failed it was impossible to transport the logs and a whole year had to elapse before movement could recommence.

Elephants were essential for forest work, for dragging felled trees to the rivers, for pushing the logs into the water, and for freeing floating logs from obstructions on their journey to rafting stations or mills. In 1912 a report in *The Times* suggested that 'probably no business in the world is more absolutely dependent on the services of an animal than is the teak industry on those of the elephant'.[52] The northern chiefs, as forest owners, normally advanced money and elephants to the forest contractors, and would receive substantial royalties on the felled timber.

It is evident that forest working on any considerable scale required large capital investments in elephants and advances to the forest workers. From the time of selecting and marking a teak tree to its eventual arrival in

5.2 *Elephants of the Siam Forest Company at work in Muang Ngow district.*

Bangkok the process took on average five or six years. The logs were floated individually down the various tributaries of the Chaophraya River (if going to Bangkok) where they would be assembled into rafts of some 120 to 150 logs at some convenient rafting station, such as Raheng (Tak). An elephant could cost several hundred pounds (a good 'tusker' perhaps £500 or £600) and as many as fifty or sixty could be required in a single forest, as well as for transport and for work in the rivers. The need for large sums of money in order to work forests on a large scale clearly favoured the British companies, who were also in a position to import the Indian rupees necessary to pay the Burmese foresters until the early years of the twentieth century.

Before 1880 British firms had made a number of attempts to gain direct central control over Siam's forest resources, either by leasing forests themselves and employing contractors, or by making arrangements with the Burmese lessees. The problem faced by the British firms was that the northern provinces were largely autonomous, and neither the extraterritorial privileges to British subjects nor the rights of residence and commercial activity granted under the Bowring Treaty extended to these northern districts. Moreover communications with the north were difficult; the normal journey time down-river from Chieng Mai to Bangkok (a distance of about 500 miles) would take about three weeks, while the

136 Malcolm Falkus

journey in the other direction could take three or four months. When an American Presbyterian missionary, Daniel McGilvary, arrived to start a mission in Chieng Mai in 1867 he was only the third Westerner to make the journey from Bangkok.[53]

During the 1860s British interests in Siamese teak increased. A certain Captain R. C. Burn from Moulmein in Burma leased a forest from Chief Kawilorot of Chieng Mai, but in the absence of maps and adequate legal controls a series of disputes arose. Burn claimed that the Chief had leased the same forest to more than one lessee and complained to the British Consul in Bangkok, T. G. Knox, that his Burmese foresters (British subjects) had been killed by the Chief when they entered the forests to which they were entitled. In 1866 the Consul delivered an ultimatum to the Bangkok government; either they must discipline the Chief and ensure adequate protection for British subjects or he would regard Chieng Mai as an independent territory and 'act accordingly'.[54] He pressed for the appointment of a British Vice-Consul in Chieng Mai. At about this time, too, the Borneo Company attempted without success to obtain teak leases in the north.[55]

The Bangkok government, faced with the dilemma of resisting growing British pressure or interfering with the customary authority of the northern *chaos*, was able to parry British demands for a time. In 1874 a treaty was signed between the governments of India and Siam with the aim of regulating the granting of teak leases in the Salween area and increasing Bangkok's jurisdiction in the north, but the practical effect of these measures was very limited.

By the early 1880s both external and internal circumstances were impelling changes. In British Burma, strict conservation by the State Forestry Department (established in 1858) limited the forests available for exploitation, while in the still-independent Kingdom of Burma the Bombay Burmah Trading Corporation was having increasing difficulties with its forest leases. As a result neither the quality nor quantity of teak reaching Rangoon was satisfactory. Meanwhile a boom in British ship-building between 1881 and 1884 and the rapid development of Indian railways (where mileage nearly doubled in the 1880s) caused a surge of demand and rapidly rising prices. The Bombay Burmah Trading Corporation, which controlled most of the supplies reaching Rangoon, declared a dividend of 25% in 1883.[56] In 1882 a Dane, Captain H. N. Andersen, loaded the royal sailing barque, the *Thoon Kramom*, with teak and sailed for Europe round the Cape. The voyage produced a huge profit and further attracted attention to Siam's teak resources.[57] Andersen himself remained interested in teak, forming the trading company Andersen and Company in 1884 and acquiring a major forest concession in Phrae in 1894. In 1897 he founded the famous East

5.3 *European forest managers with their foresters in Chieng Mai, 1893.*

Asiatic Company in Denmark, which took over Andersen's enterprises in Siam.

The internal situation in Siam was also ripe for greater Bangkok control over the northern provinces. The death of the conservative ex-Regent in January 1883 cleared the way for a new treaty with the British. The Treaty of Chieng Mai signed the same year replaced the 1874 treaty and made a number of detailed provisions concerning teak leases, but its real significance lay in three factors: first, it extended (and modified at the same time) the extraterritorial privileges of the Bowring Treaty to the north, providing a resident British Vice-Consul in Chieng Mai; second, it established the right of the Bangkok government to a measure of control over the terms of forest leases and to a share of the revenue produced; and third, the treaty opened the way for Western firms to cut logs themselves, instead of buying them from native foresters.[58] Nevertheless, the practical effects of the treaty were extremely limited. The northern *chaos* were able to retain almost complete control over the granting of leases and the gathering of royalty payments for more than a decade.

The growing significance of Siamese teak can be seen from the figures for exports from Bangkok. In 1872 these had amounted to a value of

138 *Malcolm Falkus*

Straits $104,369 and in 1880 were still only $193,330. In the following three years their value rose quickly to $279,989 in 1881, $378,294 in 1882, and $735,366 in 1883. Burma remained the leading teak exporter down to 1940 but by 1896 Siam was supplying at least one-quarter of world markets. Altogether Siam's teak exports grew from under 20,000 tons annually in 1882–7, valued at £130,000, to around 90,000 tons in 1903–4 to 1908–9, valued at nearly £1 million.[59]

The Borneo Company, dissatisfied with having to purchase teak in the open market in Bangkok, where it had little control over quality or quantity, decided to appoint agents in the north who would contract on behalf of the company with the independent foresters. Accordingly, in 1884 the company appointed Dr Cheek as its agent in Chieng Mai and Louis Leonowens as agent in Raheng (Tak). Both were remarkable individuals. Marian Alonso Cheek was an American missionary who had joined Dr McGilvary's mission in Chieng Mai in 1875. By 1882 he had acquired both a harem and an interest in teak, supplying the Borneo Company in that year (with teak).[60] Louis Leonowens was the son of Anna, the famed governess to the children of King Mongkut between 1862 and 1867. Anna had been recommended to the king by the Borneo Company, and Louis had been brought up in the royal palace alongside the future King Chulalongkorn, who succeeded to the throne of Siam in 1868 as a boy of fifteen. Louis, who had left Siam in 1867, returned in 1881, and was made a Captain in the king's army.

It is worth noting that the Borneo Company established close relations with Siam's royal family from the beginning of its operations in Bangkok. Not only was there the Leonowens connection, but there were several references in the company minutes to the cordial interest shown by King Mongkut in the affairs of the company. More remarkable was the correspondence between King Mongkut and the company's Managing Director in London, John Harvey, shortly before the king's death in 1868. The king approached 'my worthy private friend' with a request for some confidential help with investments in London should any disaster happen to the throne and 'miserable mischief' befall his children.[61]

The Borneo Company, with the help of its agents, rapidly became the largest teak firm in the country. Both Cheek and Leonowens leased forests in 1885, the former with the help of an advance from the royal palace, and that same year the Borneo Company also took a six-year lease on a forest near Chieng Mai. A company minute of 11 March 1885 confirmed 'the engagement of Captain Leonowens for up-river work in the teak forest under Dr Cheek and the remittance for Dr Cheek of such sums as were required to complete payment for wood secured under his agreement with the company'.[62] Cheek worked for the Borneo Company until 1889,

5.4 *Siam Forest Company office at Bangkok, c. 1910.*

Leonowens until 1895, and they were both responsible for providing the company with many valuable teak leases.

During the 1880s two more British concerns, the Siam Forest Company and the Bombay Burmah Trading Corporation, also became interested in the northern forests, though neither became significantly involved until the following decade. The Siam Forest Company grew out of the Bombay firm of Ewart, Latham and Company. This firm in 1883 acquired the agency of the Bombay Saw Mills Company Ltd, whose traditional source of teak was Rangoon, where the Bombay Burmah Trading Corporation was the chief supplier.[63] The Bombay Burmah at that time obtained most of its teak from its forest concessions in independent Upper Burma. By the early 1880s there was growing dissatisfaction with Rangoon timber on account of both its high price and poor quality, and in 1883 Bombay Saw Mills sent a representative to Rangoon to try to negotiate a new source of supply. The representative, Mr C. H. Dennis, found that not only did the Bombay Burmah Trading Corporation have a virtual monopoly of Rangoon teak, but even this company was having difficulties getting supplies from Upper Burma due to friction with the Court of Ava which, eventually, was one of the causes of the Third Burmese War in 1885. At the same time the more easily worked Burmese forests were becoming exhausted, which was resulting in rising costs and lower-quality timber.

In Rangoon Dennis learned of the growing interest in Siamese timber

140 *Malcolm Falkus*

and in 1884 he was sent to Siam and negotiated a major forest concession with the ruler of Lakon (Lampang). This was for the valuable Me Ngow forests. Accordingly, Ewart, Latham registered the Siam Forest Company in Bombay in 1884 with a paid-up capital of Rs 100,000 to exploit these forests. In fact the terms of the lease were not settled at once, and the lease eventually came into effect on 1 January 1886, lasting for a period of ten years.

In return for a payment to the Chief of Lakon of some Rs 8000, and royalty payments on teak logs varying from Rs 4 to Rs 1 (depending on the size of the logs), the company obtained rights of working extensive forests covering around 2,000 square miles.[64] The company's method was to contract actual forest work to Burmese and other foresters, and to advance money to these men on the security of their elephants.

The expectations of the promoters in 1884 proved wildly optimistic. Dennis had estimated that timber could be floated from the forests to Bangkok in about three months, that some 35,000 trees stood already girdled, waiting to be felled and floated, and that an annual supply of 20,000 logs would reach Bangkok. In fact no timber reached Bangkok until 1890, and by the end of 1891 only 4,315 logs had arrived, with a further 20,670 put into the rivers.[65]

Various circumstances contributed to the company's misfortunes. Its European employees in the forest headquarters, Dennis and Phare, proved incompetent, one report claiming that 'the funds of the company were being squandered in riotous living and gambling with the Chief of Lakon'.[66] Both Dennis and Phare were dismissed in 1889 by the company's Chairman, John Ryrie, who travelled himself to Lakon to see the affairs on the spot. There were also the immense problems of pioneering in a remote region, dealing with people unfamiliar with Western ways, and organising a business in an often hostile environment. The fifty-mile journey between Lakon town and the forest camp at Muang Ngow took four days each way under favourable conditions, while the journey between Bangkok and Lakon could take several months. Another problem was that the time taken between cutting the logs and their eventual arrival in Bangkok was much greater than anticipated, which meant that far more capital than expected had to be tied up in advances to contractors. Instead of the three months forecast by Dennis in 1884, by 1892 the company had realised that 'the average time required to float timber in Bangkok is about 24 months from the main forests'.[67] And, of course, the additional period required for marking, felling and dragging in the forests added years to the time a particular tree would take to reach Bangkok as a log.

The years 1888–92 happened to see a succession of extremely poor floating seasons with inadequate rains so that logs piled up on the river

Early British business in Thailand 141

banks and little arrived in Bangkok to be sold. Not only the Siam Forest Company, but the Borneo Company, Dr Cheek (who in 1889 started his own forest concern with heavy borrowing from the Siamese government), and Louis Leonowens all got into difficulties in this period. The Siam Forest Company tried unsuccessfully in 1892 to refloat the company in London with an increased capital, but not until 1897, when conditions in the teak market were much more favourable, was this possible. The new company was then floated in London with an authorised capital of £50,000 (£30,000 paid-up) to take over the assets of the Bombay concern. At this stage the total investment in the Bangkok sawmill and other property was put at nearly £12,000 while the estimated value of logs actually felled or in transit was nearly £37,000.[68] This proved to be a turning point in the affairs of the company. Renewed interest was taken in the working of the Me Ngow concession and the company bought timber from Leonowens and other lessees. Business expanded rapidly with the arrival in Lakon in 1902 of an able manager, W. A. Elder, and by this time the company was diversifying into new fields. In 1897 the newly floated Siam Forest Company absorbed the sawmill and timber business of F. S. Clarke and Co., a Bangkok agency firm, and by 1908 had completely taken over all the agency and other interests of Clarke's. Clarke's business in 1899 was bringing a revenue of around £4,000 annually and 'increasing all the time'.[69] Among its agencies were the Siam Forest Company itself, a French mining company, a sugar refining company, the National Bank of China, and the Commercial Union Insurance Company. Clarke's bought consignments of goods from Europe, chartered steamers for Chinese rice millers, bought Japanese coal from Mitsui and Company, and purchased opium on behalf of the Siamese government. They sold Siamese rice, pepper, hides and other commodities in Europe. Clarke himself had entered the service of the Borneo Company in London in 1867 and had spent ten years in Siam with the company between 1872 and 1882 before leaving to found his own firm; he had been involved with the formation of the Siam Forest Company, and had acted as agent for the company from the outset.

Thus by 1908 the Siam Forest Company had become a trading and agency business, and from this date the general and agency business (especially the rice trade, the company acting as agents for D. M. Horne and Company) began to rival that of timber. Eventually in 1917 this pattern was recognised when the company was re-designated the Anglo-Siam Corporation Ltd.

Once the capital resources of the Siam Forest Company had improved, with better teak deliveries and newly raised capital in London in 1897, the diversification of interests was a logical step. Dependence on a single product, teak, was dangerous in view of the sudden fluctuations in world

142 *Malcolm Falkus*

demand on the one hand and the inelastic nature of supply on the other. At the same time the limited markets in Siam, the importance of personal contacts in business dealings, the shortage of managerial skills, language problems, and so on, all made a diverse portfolio of agency work a sensible means of operating.

The Bombay Burmah Trading Corporation was the third great British company to become involved in the teak business in Siam. Although its entry was later than the Borneo or the Siam Forest Companies, it had, in fact, become the leading teak firm by the mid-1890s and retained that position until the Second World War.

Representatives of the Corporation had visited Chieng Mai in 1884, although nothing came of this at the time. However, the outbreak of the Third Burmese War in 1885, which ended the independent Kingdom of Burma, brought a major upheaval in teak supplies which considerably enhanced interest in Siam. Even when conditions in Upper Burma had returned to normal, the imposition by the British authorities of strict conservation measures, the increase of royalty payments, and a feeling in Rangoon that the power of the Bombay Burmah Trading Corporation was too strong, all combined to turn the Corporation's attention eastwards. In 1889 the Corporation built a sawmill in Bangkok and in 1891 sent a representative to Chieng Mai. In the latter year it obtained its first forest concession in Siam, the Me Song forest near Lakon.[70] It was at this time that poor floating seasons were causing great difficulties for independent operators like Cheek and Leonowens (who had parted from the Borneo Company in 1895 after accusations that he worked timber concessions on his own account), and for small Siamese, Burmese, and Chinese lessees. As a result, both the Borneo Company and the Bombay Burmah were able to purchase a number of valuable leases by paying off the contractors' debts. For example, the original Burmese lessee of the Me Song forest, Moung Kalah, owed Rs 30,000 to a Siamese lady in Raheng. The Bombay Burmah paid off this debt, in return acquiring Moung Kalah's 5,000 logs in the river, his future output of logs, and mortgages on his eighteen elephants.[71] More significantly the Corporation was able to reach agreement with the Siamese government in 1892 to take over the debts of the bankrupt Dr Cheek, paying 400,000 baht for the promised delivery of 20,000 logs in 1892 and 1893.[72] Later, in 1897, it also acquired the output of some 8–10,000 logs annually from the forests leased by Leonowens, who then entered the service of the Corporation, remaining until 1901.[73]

In 1893 the Bombay Burmah Trading Corporation took the important decision to acquire forests on an extensive scale. Since it was difficult to get original leases in the Corporation's own name (partly because of suspicions that it had been responsible for the Burmese War) the Corpor-

Table 5.6 *Annual teak output sent to Bangkok, c. 1902*

Producers	No. of logs per annum
Bombay Burmah Trading Corporation	35,000
Borneo Company	10–12,000
Siam Forest Company	6–7,000
L. T. Leonowens	8,000
East Asiatic Company (Danish)	3–4,000
Chinese producers	10–12,000
'native' producers	20–25,000

Sources: R. H. Macaulay, *History of the Bombay Burmah Trading Corporation Ltd 1864–1910* (London, 1934), pp. 71–3, 111–12; Inchcape Archives, Annual Reports of Borneo Company Ltd and Siam Forest Company Ltd.

ation decided to proceed as it had with the Me Song: take over the debts of foresters and, if possible, renew the leases in the Corporation's name when they fell due. As a result, the Bombay Burmah acquired forest rights in Lamphun and in Phrae and Nan (though operations in these latter provinces were a costly failure), but their main holdings were in the Salween basin and in the Chieng Mai and Lakon forests.

The entrance of the aggressive and experienced Bombay Burmah Trading Corporation brought a new era to the teak business in Siam. The Corporation introduced the methods used in Burma, directly working the forests themselves under European supervision instead of contracting with small foresters or with agents like Cheek and Leonowens. The Corporation purchased elephants and began the systematic girdling of trees rather than felling them green and allowing them to dry where they lay (an inefficient method, since the logs might well not be dry when eventually dragged to the river, and hence would not float). Stimulated by this competition the Borneo Company also began the direct exploitation of its forests, as did the Siam Forest Company and other European firms.

The relative position of the different producers at the opening of the twentieth century is shown in Table 5.6.

Thus of a total annual output in the region of 100,000 logs some two-thirds were produced by European firms, nearly all of whom were British. Indeed, the two great trading companies, the Borneo and the Bombay Burmah, alone accounted for over two-thirds of European output. British dominance was in fact far greater than these figures suggest. The Bombay Burmah controlled most of the Salween forests, producing some 40,000 logs a year for Moulmein. Also, most of the first-class quality teakwood, and hence the more valuable part of total output, was produced by the Europeans. Finally, most of the Chinese and

144 Malcolm Falkus

'native' output was bought by the large companies and often their forests were leased under agreements with the Europeans.

The growing dominance of the large British concerns presented the Siamese government with a dilemma. By 1895 the three major British companies had control of large areas of the northern forests, and the government watched with concern as the financial difficulties of the small foresters and the greed of the provincial rulers combined to accelerate the process. Attempts by the government to favour Siamese lessees or to stay the advance of the British proved ineffective. At the same time the Siamese government, under the growing influence of the able Prince Damrong, was engaged in a process of bringing the outlying provinces under central control.[74] As part of this process, it was decided to set up a Forest Department which would serve several purposes: it would help to control the northern forests and bring an increasing share of the revenue to Bangkok; it would reduce the independence of the northern states, and give Bangkok more influence in areas where there was potential friction with the Western powers; it would provide a powerful counterpoise to the Western companies; and it would allow some measure of conservation of forests which was increasingly necessary in view of the anarchic state of leases and terms under which the forests were being worked.

Accordingly, the Siamese government requested the loan of a forest officer from India, and Herbert Slade arrived in March 1896 to establish a Forest Department.[75] This was the start of a rather hectic period during which new forms of leases with the Forest Department replaced those with the chiefs, large forest areas were closed to exploitation, and royalty rates increased. Slade's Report to the Bangkok government in 1896 drew attention to the need to bring the granting of leases under central control, and, as Macaulay has put it, 'it may truly be said that it was through the Forest Department that the Siamese Government inaugurated the system which ended in its securing absolute control of the Laos States'.[76] By 1900 Bangkok had asserted full control over the affairs of Chieng Mai and Lakon, the most important states as far as the Western teak leases were concerned. After difficult negotiations, Slade reached agreement with the principal teak firms that half the forest areas would be closed and new leases substituted for the old ones. These came into effect in 1901, and their main features were the cessation of fresh girdling, an increase in royalty payments, and terms for the leases which would run from six years from the expiry of the old ones (which were generally for three years). These leases were made directly with the Forestry Department rather than with the chiefs. In 1909 there was yet a further reorganisation of the leases which this time gave the companies a more permanent stake in Siam's forest industry. New leases were signed for thirty years, dividing the leased forest areas into a closed and open portion, each to be worked

Early British business in Thailand 145

for a period of fifteen years. Girdling of large trees was once more permitted, and royalty rates were increased again. At the same time the forest leases were rationalised into large blocks, to permit better supervision and working, and the total number of teak leases was, in consequence, reduced from 105 to 40 (and by 1929 had been further reduced by amalgamation to 28).[77] These various changes all strengthened the position of large companies with extensive capital resources, and so consolidated the control by British firms.

Thus by 1914 the conditions under which British enterprise operated in the Siamese teak districts were very different from those in the early 1880s. No European had leased a forest until 1884 and none directly worked a forest until 1888.[78] The forests then were worked mostly on short leases by small contractors leased directly from the provincial *chaos*. By 1914 British enterprise was dominant, with three British trading and agency companies, the Bombay Burmah, the Borneo, and the Siam Forest, controlling the bulk of supplies. Another London firm had also been established in 1905, when Leonowens registered a company under his own name in London with a paid-up capital of £105,000 to take over his forest and other business. This move marked the entry of another major British trading house, Guthrie and Company, into Siam with Sir John Anderson, for Guthries, on the board of the new company. Also in 1905 Guthries registered in London another company, the Siamese Trading Corporation, with a capital of £10,150, to take a £10,150 stake in L. T. Leonowens Ltd. By 1914 the pioneering phase of exploration and often indiscriminate exploitation of the forests was over. Regulation, control and extensive leases of known forest resources now characterised the teak business, and this pattern continued throughout the inter-war years.

In this examination of the dominance of the British companies several points have emerged. One is the movement of the teak 'frontier', from southern India, to Lower Burma, to Upper Burma, and so to Siam, as supplies were either exhausted or came under more stringent control. Another factor was the importance of the Indian market as a source of demand and also of the supply of capital through the activities of trading houses. In many ways the growth of British business in teak, as in Siam's economy generally, can be seen as part of a developing Asian economy, with trading firms already established in Asia being drawn towards the exploitation of Siam's resources as world conditions of supply and demand changed.

Why was the teak business dominated by trading firms rather than specialist companies (as was the case, for example, as we shall see in tin)? The reason is partly that teak had long been a staple export from the port of Bangkok, and some of the Western trading firms had invested in sawmills. Involvement in sawmilling led naturally to a search for cheaper

146 *Malcolm Falkus*

and more assured sources of supply. Also, being dependent on the success of the rains for floating timber, teak supply could fluctuate considerably from year to year, locking up large sums of capital for several years. The risks involved help explain why trading companies, with a more diversified spread of activities, came to dominate teak. It is notable that neither Cheek nor Leonowens could maintain independent teak operations, and L. T. Leonowens Ltd was established in 1905 as a general trading and agency company, with interests in tin as well as in forests. The Siam Forest Company, too, had become a general merchant and agency house by 1908.[79]

5.5 Tin and British enterprise

British enterprise in Siam's tin resources was markedly different from that in teak. The major differences may be summarised in the following points. (1) Whereas Western investment in teak coincided with the large-scale entry of Siam's teak into world markets in the 1880s, investment in tin came many decades after Siam's tin had begun to be exported on a significant scale. Even in 1914 London-registered companies had made only a modest start, whereas Australian-registered companies were much more significant. (2) Teak investment was mainly undertaken by major trading companies, tin normally by specialised tin dredging companies. (3) Western enterprise in tin involved the introduction of new capital-intensive technology, especially dredging, while teak, particularly in the early stages, continued to be extracted by traditional methods. (4) The main British teak firms developed from established businesses in Asia. In the case of tin, capital and enterprise were initially launched from the metropolitan countries (Australia and Great Britain), although after the First World War British enterprises registered in Malaya and the Straits Settlements became significant. (5) Whereas the northern *chaos* in Chieng Mai and Lakon had been very willing to grant teak leases to British firms, British tin enterprise had to face considerable opposition both from Chinese competitors and from the local provincial governors, themselves often Chinese and leading tin entrepreneurs. (6) Once started, British tin enterprise tended to expand and to control an increasing share of Siam's total output down to the Second World War. This was due to the inherent superiority of dredging, which remained beyond the capital resources of all but a handful of Chinese concerns before 1940; Western control was furthered by the Great Depression of the 1930s and the adherence of Siam to various international restriction schemes after 1931, which saw the collapse of many independent firms and the dominance of major London-based holding companies. In order to explain the pattern of Britain's investments in Siam's tin resources – its late start and the early promi-

Early British business in Thailand 147

nence of Australian companies – it is necessary first to make a few points briefly about Siam's industry and its place in world markets.

Tin, prior to the Second World War, was mined almost exclusively in the southern peninsular provinces, mainly on the Western side, and very largely in the 'tin island' of Phuket. From the 1850s the tin mining of Phuket and some of the mainland mining areas underwent a period of rapid growth built almost exclusively on Chinese enterprise, capital and labour.[80] Much of this Chinese enterprise came from the Straits Settlements, and the great bulk of the tin output was exported to world markets via Penang.

From a period of considerable expansion between the 1850s and the 1870s Siam's tin industry went through one of stagnation and difficulty in the last quarter of the nineteenth century. Partly this was due simply to the rise of Malaya as the world's largest source of tin. So productive were Malaya's mines that despite soaring Western demand for tin, tin prices tended to fall. At the same time the great demand for Chinese labour and capital for these Malayan mines also affected Siam unfavourably.

By around 1900 the situation was changing. World demand continued to expand but costs of production in the Malayan mines began to rise as the easiest deposits were worked out. Supply no longer kept up with demand, so that tin prices began to rise. There naturally occurred a search for new supply sources and for the adaptation of more capital-intensive Western technology to existing areas of mining which could be mined economically by Chinese methods only as long as the rich, easily won tin deposits held out. This was the background against which Western interest in Siam's tin deposits, and the willingness of the authorities to allow such enterprise, developed after 1900.

During the second half of the nineteenth century the southern tin districts, like the northern teak provinces, enjoyed a large measure of regional autonomy. The local southern provincial governors (called *rajas*) were often Chinese, and took an active part in tin mining and smelting. They drew up and granted tin leases and sometimes worked mines directly, advancing money and equipment to the miners.[81] Not unnaturally the local governors tended to favour Chinese entrepreneurs, especially since the business interests of the governors might include lucrative sidelines such as opium supply, transport activities, gambling monopolies, and the like.

A considerable part of Siam's tin output was controlled by a handful of powerful Chinese families connected through business dealings or family ties with the provincial governors. Most remarkable of these business empires was that of the Khaw family, whose wide-ranging activities stretched far beyond tin and far beyond Siam's borders.[82] By the 1890s the Khaws owned the Penang-based Koh Guan shipping and trading company

148 *Malcolm Falkus*

as well as having extensive tin and other interests. The leading figure was Khaw Sim Bee, who was governor of Trang province between 1890 and 1900. When he was created High Commissioner for the Monthon of Phuket in 1901, the Khaw interests were paramount in Siam's richest tin regions.

Chinese mining enterprise was favoured not only by the local business elites but also by technical factors. Methods of production were labour-intensive and the Chinese used simple techniques which were well suited to the rich alluvial deposits of Phuket, while Chinese immigrants from the Straits Settlements and the southern provinces of China made up the bulk of the labour force. Chinese tin enterprises, with their close-knit organisation and control over labour supply, were in a much better position than Western firms to operate the simple open-cast mining which prevailed until the end of the nineteenth century. This competitive strength of the Chinese was a feature not only in Siam but elsewhere in Southeast Asia, in Malaya, Burma, and in the Dutch East Indies.

There was an additional reason for the poor showing of Western enterprise. The Bangkok government was hostile to the spread of British business in the southern provinces for political reasons, while the British government, also for political reasons, was hostile to the spread of Western enterprise from anywhere else.[83] Bangkok had witnessed with alarm the control of Perak, Selangor and other Malay states after 1874 and feared that Britain was anxious to use commercial penetration as an excuse for political control. The tin districts of the south were especially vulnerable since they bordered the northern Malay states over which Siam claimed sovereignty and which were ultimately ceded to Britain in 1909. Prior to 1891 only thirteen mining concessions had been granted to Westerners since the Bowring Treaty, mostly speculative and ephemeral ventures seeking gold and precious stones. One or two tin concessions were granted, but these, too, were short-lived.[84]

As in the case of the northern provinces, Bangkok made efforts for fiscal and political reasons to assert its control over the southern provinces from the 1870s. During the 1890s the tin districts were brought within Prince Damrong's new administrative structure,[85] which involved the installation of a Bangkok-appointed High Commissioner. A Department of Mines was set up in 1891, under British officials. In 1896 the Department was placed under the Ministry of the Interior and in 1898 sent its first Mines Commissioner to Phuket. But the established policy of resisting Western enterprise and favouring the Chinese continued, and even strengthened. This anti-Western policy was not confined to tin mining, but extended to other forms of mining, plantations, forest concessions, and railway development. For example, when in 1889 Tan Kim Chiang gained mining and forest concessions in various parts of the country, including Yala in the South, Tak (Reheng) in the north, and

Early British business in Thailand 149

Chantaburi, he was restricted to operating on his own account, and not in conjunction with any British company.[86]

Siam's reluctance to permit Western business concessions in the south continued up to the First World War and was frequently commented upon by British consuls and British businessmen at the time. Such reluctance was one reason for the very small Western interest in Siam's rubber plantations, in contrast to the situation in Malaya.[87] As mentioned already, Prince Damrong (who remained Minister of the Interior from 1892 until 1915) and other members of the government were deeply suspicious of the British. Under the Anglo-Siamese Secret Convention of 1897 the Siamese had been obliged to give Britain the dominant voice in the southern regions. The American General Adviser to the Siamese government said of this Convention that 'it not only makes Britain a partner in the commercial development of the region, but the dominant partner'.[88] After 1897 the Siamese were under constant British pressure to open up the southern provinces to Western enterprise, to improve communications, and in other ways to encourage the economic development of the region.[89] Ironically the British strongly supported the appointment of Khaw Sim Bee as High Commissioner of Phuket, doubtless feeling that such an able administrator, with strong Penang business connections and a British subject, would favour British interests. Thus in 1900 the British Consul in Penang put pressure on Bangkok to make Khaw Sim Bee High Commissioner of Monthon Phuket. In the event, though, the new Commissioner was anything but favourable to British interests. Sir John Anderson, the Consul General, wrote in 1906 that 'so far as Puket is concerned no enterprise will ever get a fair chance so long as it is run by the present High Commissioner who has his finger in every pie, and by himself or his family levies toll on everything'.[90] Khaw Sim Bee, with full support from Prince Damrong, continued to obstruct British enterprise in Phuket throughout his period of power (ended by assassination in 1913).

The major exception to this anti-Western policy was Khaw Sim Bee's remarkable connection with Australian tin mining enterprise, which developed in the early years of the twentieth century and resulted in Siam being the first country in the world where the technique of bucket-dredging was used for tin mining. The story of this enterprise has been ably discussed by Dr Cushman and Francis Birch, and will be only briefly outlined here.[91]

In 1902 the Koh Guan Company purchased in Penang four New Zealand steamships through the agency of Captain Edward Miles, an Australian. Miles was at that time also an agent for Henry Jones and Company, an Australian firm with interests in tin canning. As a result of the shipping transaction Miles met members of the Khaw group in Penang.

150 Malcolm Falkus

This transaction had a dual significance for Western enterprise. On the one hand the Koh Guan Company's fleet was considerably strengthened, and began to challenge the powerful British Straits Steamship Company. This latter enterprise had been set up in 1890, and monopolised the shipping of tin ore from Malaya to Singapore, where the British Straits Trading Company had established a modern smelter in 1887. In 1902 and 1903 both the Straits Trading Company and an American smelting firm endeavoured to move into Phuket, the Straits Trading Company buying ore there in 1904.[92] This presented a challenge to the Khaw interests who responded by strengthening their fleet and, in 1907, forming both the Eastern Shipping Company and the Eastern Smelting Company in Penang to compete with the British. Both the Penang companies, though, were later taken over by British interests.[93]

The second significance of the Miles–Khaw transaction led directly to Australian involvement in Siamese tin production. Towards the end of the nineteenth century both the Siamese government and Khaw Sim Bee were increasingly anxious to expand the development of Siam's tin resources, which had languished from the 1880s. One way of sustaining such expansion was to encourage Western enterprise and new technology, but, as I have stressed already, British involvement was viewed with distaste.

Out of Miles' business in Penang came a suggestion from Khaw Sim Bee that Miles might introduce 'modern European methods' to a tin mining site in Phuket which the Commissioner was anxious to develop.[94] Miles visited Phuket in 1905 and offered to mine, not the site which Khaw Sim Bee had suggested, but the harbour area where there were already several hundred Chinese working by building primitive dams and using their traditional methods. The technology Miles proposed to introduce was imaginative and hitherto untried in tin mining: that of the bucket dredge. Miles had seen bucket dredges operating in New Zealand. The idea was that continually moving buckets would scoop up the ore-bearing gravel, which would then be washed in the dredge with water pumped up from the ground (or in this case the harbour), and the debris ejected. The dredge would then move to another place and continue the process. A dredge was an expensive piece of equipment. The average cost of a dredge in Siam in 1914 was £18,000. But dredging had very low operating costs and a single dredge might have a working life of several decades; therefore dredging could be profitable in areas of poor-quality or deeper ore where the labour-intensive Chinese methods used would be inadequate.[95]

In return for a twenty-five-year lease Miles offered to pay a royalty on the tin mined and to deepen the harbour, which had silted up, and build a new dock. This proposal was quickly considered and approved by Prince Damrong and by a special commission in Bangkok, and an agreement was signed in September 1906. In the following month, the Tongkah Harbour

5.5 The first tin mining dredge in Siam at Phuket, c. 1907.

Tin Dredging Company was registered in Tasmania with an authorised capital of £150,000 with Miles himself, Henry Jones, A. W. Palfreyman (an Australian business associate of Jones), and the Khaw family as major shareholders. The original paid-up capital, though, was just £17,500 of which some half came from the Penang Chinese. The company ordered its first dredge in 1906 from William Simons and Company in Renfrew, Scotland (designed largely by Miles himself). The dredge was shipped in dismantled form to Prai Dock, on the mainland opposite Penang, and there re-assembled and towed to Phuket. It began work late in 1907, the first ore being dredged in January 1908. So successful was the venture that by the end of that year two more dredges had been ordered, and by 1911 the company had five dredges in operation.

The Tongkah Harbour Company was a spectacular success, and stimulated by this a second Australian company was formed in 1909 to take over the Phuket 'government compound' – the area originally offered to, and rejected by, Miles. The Tongkah Compound Company, financed in Melbourne, was formed by A. W. Palfreyman, and included Khaw interests also. This company, too, was spectacularly successful. It had a dredge working in 1912 and was able in 1913 to distribute dividends of £67,000, which was more than its paid-up capital of £50,000.

Following these successes the Miles–Khaw group turned its attention to the Renong region, an area on the mainland of the western side of the

152 Malcolm Falkus

peninsula, about 120 miles north of Phuket. In 1913 three further Melbourne-registered dredging companies were set up by Miles in the region, the Deebook Dredging, Katoo Deebook Dredging, and Bangnon Valley Dredging. In 1916 Miles also formed companies to prospect and mine on the eastern side of the peninsula, this time without Khaw involvement; these were the Ronpibon and the Ronpibon Extended Companies.

The first two Australian tin concerns were located in the rich Phuket area, where Khaw Sim Bee had been careful to deny London-based companies access. Outside Phuket, however, two London companies were in operation in Renong before the First World War. These were the Renong Tin Dredging Company and the Siamese Tin Syndicate. Both were floated by Guthries and formed by a group headed by Herbert George Scott, the Director of the Department of the Mines in Bangkok; Sir John Anderson, for Guthries; and Louis Leonowens, in whose company Guthries also had an interest.

These companies grew out of the Temoh Gold Hills Company Ltd, which had been formed in the 1890s by Thomas Scott, a senior partner in Guthries and relative of Herbert George Scott, and by the financier Chachick Paul Chater. The subscribed capital was £135,000 but not much is known of the activities of this company. In 1904, when the gold mine was running out, the company began prospecting in the Renong district and discovered tin. On the advice of the brilliant mining engineer, E. T. McCarthy, it was decided to exploit the tin by the use of bucket dredges. Further prospecting was necessary and the Renong Mines Company was formed to prospect for tin in the Renong region. As a result of favourable prospects the Renong Dredging Company was incorporated in London in July 1908, with a paid-up capital of £29,000. Their first dredge – the first land-dredge to be used in Southeast Asia – began work in March 1910. The company was soon in a position to order two more dredges, and in 1913 a new company, the Renong Tin Dredging Company, was formed to enlarge operations and take over the assets of the former concern.[96]

The Siamese Tin Syndicate was formed with an authorised capital of £120,000, Scott obtaining a concession from the Siamese government 'to discover unowned and valueless land which would pay to work'.[97] The search, with six or seven boring gangs, covered huge areas of Pangnga, Takuapa, Bangnon and Renong. For long the search was unavailing. His assistant later recalled that 'for more than two years we suffered these recurring disappointments and it was really marvellous the way H. G. Scott stood it. In London the shareholders were restive and the Chairman resigned, stating he had no faith in Siam as a mining proposition.'[98] Eventually, though, in December 1909, suitable deposits were found at

Early British business in Thailand 153

Table 5.7 *Share of British and Australian companies in Siam's tin production, 1910–18 (000 tons)*

Year	Australian companies	British companies	% of total output
1910	1,250	–	25
1911	1,140	120	26
1912	1,990	150	36
1913	2,110	210	34
1914	1,600	830	37
1915	1,870	1,020	32
1916	1,970	1,470	40
1917	2,430	1,710	45
1918	2,230	1,880	47

Source: F. D. Birch, *Tropical Milestones*, p. 170

Ngow in Renong. Two dredges were ordered, and the first commenced work in 1912; by 1913 a third was in operation, and the company paid its first dividend of 10%.

It is difficult to avoid the conclusion that the Siamese were prepared to allow Western interests to develop in the southern tin mining regions only where close personal connections in official circles were involved.[99] Thus prior to 1918 only one Australian-based company outside the Miles–Khaw–Palfreyman nexus had obtained a mining concession, while at that time the two Scott-backed concerns were the only London companies. At this stage the Australian firms were clearly dominant, in terms of numbers, capital and production, although, as Table 5.7 shows, this dominance was lessening.

Several interesting questions suggest themselves about this early Western involvement in Siam's tin. Why was Australian investment favoured in Phuket, but not investment from Great Britain? Did the Siamese distinguish between Great Britain herself and another empire country? Why, outside Phuket, were two London-based companies nevertheless permitted to prospect and produce? Why, after such a slow start, did British firms come to dominate Siam's tin production during the inter-war years?

Dr Cushman suggests that Khaw Sim Bee was willing to work with Miles because he was independent and 'stood outside the larger British business and political community'.[100] This would obviously minimise the political implications of Western involvement. There was evidently, too, an element of shrewd opportunism in Khaw Sim Bee's original approach to Miles in Penang. In addition it is possible that both the Commissioner and Prince Damrong may have been convinced of the need for some Western involvement and visible signs of commercial progress in order to

154 *Malcolm Falkus*

stave off what might become irresistible British pressure to modernise the southern provinces. What is clear is that an association with Miles offered Khaw Sim Bee opportunity both for acquiring Western technology and for maintaining an interest in an important tin-producing concern which would ship its ore with the Eastern Trading Company. It must be emphasised again that the Khaw interests were represented in both the Miles company and the Tongkah Compound Company, and in many subsequent Australian ventures. In 1913 Penang investors (including the Khaw family) had perhaps one-fifth of the capital of the two Tongkah companies in 1913.[101]

Between 1918 and 1940 the structure of Western enterprise in Siam's tin mining changed. Before 1930 a great many new enterprises, Chinese and Western, were registered, and among the Western firms those emanating from Great Britain or Malaya and the Straits became increasingly prominent. In 1928, in the wake of a considerable mining boom in 1926–7, the paid-up capital of the London–Malayan concerns amounted to about two-thirds of the total of Western capital invested in Siamese tin.[102] Nevertheless, Australian companies remained significant and even increased their share of total output in the late 1920s.[103] Meanwhile the near-monopoly position of the Khaw–Miles interests among Australian concerns which had existed in 1918 declined as new Australian groups (financed mainly in Sydney) became prominent. The decline of Khaw influence set in after the assassination of Khaw Sim Bee in 1913, while in 1915 Prince Damrong, who had been a powerful supporter of Khaw Sim Bee, left the Ministry of the Interior. The climate for Western enterprise became more favourable as the superiority of dredging became clearly evident (only a handful of Chinese concerns had dredges before 1940) while the 1909 Anglo-Siamese Treaty had finally settled the vexed question of Siam's southern borders and so lessened political tension in the region. The southern railway, too, brought new opportunities for mining investment.

The Great Depression of the 1930s brought further changes. With falling prices after 1929 (at a time when many of the boom companies floated in 1926–7 were coming into operation) and with the adherence of Siam to international tin restriction schemes in 1931, there were many bankruptcies among both Western and Chinese firms. This resulted in a concentration of holdings, and in particular the growing control of large London-registered holding companies with world-wide interests, such as the Anglo-Oriental. Many Australian concerns were absorbed by the holding companies in these years, including the Tongkah Harbour Dredging Company, which was taken over by the Anglo-Oriental in 1934.[104]

Early British business in Thailand 155

5.6 British business in Siam before 1940

This chapter has attempted to outline some of the main features of British business in Siam before 1940, concentrating on the initial phases of what turned out to be a long-lasting pre-eminence. Attention has been focussed on investment rather than on trade and shipping, although here, too, Britain always played a significant role in Siam. Prior to the 1930s Depression Britain always provided the bulk of Siam's imports (mostly textiles) either directly or via Singapore. Thus in 1928–9 Britain still accounted for 17.6% of total imports (excluding those from Singapore and other ports of transhipment), far more than any other country.[105] However, during the Great Depression the situation changed, with the Japanese and the Dutch East Indies supplying growing proportions of reduced totals. By 1933–4 both Japan and the Dutch East Indies exported more to Siam than Britain, Britain's share being 13.3%, that of the Dutch East Indies 15.7%, and Japan's 19.2%. By 1936–7 Japan's share had risen to 28.3%, while Britain's stood at only 11.6%.

Siam's shipping continued to be dominated by European countries in the inter-war years, as it had been before 1914, though Germany, the principal carrier in 1913, never regained more than a small proportion of total tonnage. In the 1920s and 1930s Norway, Britain, Denmark and the Netherlands carried the bulk of Siam's foreign trade, Britain's share of inward tonnage being 22.5% in 1913–14, 33.9% in 1928–9, and 22.5% in 1938–9. For a time Japan's share of shipping increased dramatically, from just over 39,000 tons in 1928–9 to nearly 215,000 tons in 1936–7, at which stage Japan accounted for 16.0% of Siam's inward tonnage. Thereafter, though, Japan's military involvement in China led to a sharp reduction in her merchant activity.

Where capital investment was concerned, Britain retained its dominant place until the Second World War, as we have seen. Perhaps more impressive than the actual overall totals of capital investment by British firms was the great diversity of business represented by the British trading companies, their regional impact in opening up hitherto unexploited areas, and their pioneering of new developments in Siam, hence acting as agents of modernisation. British enterprise in Siam was characterised by direct investment by 'free-standing' companies; portfolio investment, so characteristic of British involvement elsewhere, was in Siam largely confined to the very limited government foreign loans raised between 1905 and 1924.

Let us look very briefly at these features of British trade, since examples have already been given. The agency business of the Western trading companies brought a vast range of modern business to Siam, much of it connected with the development of international commerce, as we have

156 Malcolm Falkus

seen: insurance, banking, commodity imports and exports, mining, forestry, and steam rice and saw-milling. We find the Borneo Company exploring for lead ore in the 1870s, owning pepper plantations in Chantaboon in the 1880s, and investing in the Bangkok Dock Company in the 1890s.[106] The Siamese Tin Syndicate had several interests outside mining, including a 3,000-acre coconut plantation on its land in Renong in 1911. Louis Leonowens, in addition to his teak and tin concessions, had interests in railway projects, and bought the famed Oriental Hotel in 1891 from its founder, the Dane H. N. Andersen, while still an employee of the Borneo Company. Andersen in turn promoted an electricity company in Bangkok, electric tramways (the first running in 1893), and, together with an Englishman, Captain A. Loftus, projected Siam's first private railway.[107]

British enterprise was important in its regional impact, too. The exploitation of teak forests brought prosperity and trade to the hitherto remote northern areas and was crucial in Bangkok's growing control over these regions. The Borneo Company dominated the import trade of Chieng Mai and Lampang in the late nineteenth century, bringing textiles, watches, kerosene, and other Western products to these areas. In the south, too, although the impact of Western firms was limited, such regions as Renong were opened up by British and Australian tin concerns. Perhaps as noteworthy as the pioneering activity of British firms before 1914 was the continuance of British pre-eminence thereafter. To some extent this is to be explained by the sound basis laid by the Borneo Company and the other trading and tin enterprises. To some extent it was due to the First World War, which reduced German enterprise and influence in Siam at a time when it was growing strongly, and ushered in a period of prosperity in tin mining of which Australian capital, especially, was able to take advantage. But partly also it must be explained by the striking lack of structural change in Siam's economy, which left little room either for other Western or for Siamese enterprise in new-developing sectors. Such changes had to await the changed political and economic environment which followed the Second World War.

6 British business in Malaysia and Singapore since the 1870s

Jean-Jacques van Helten and Geoffrey Jones*

6.1 A British success story

The experience of British business in Malaysia and Singapore since the 1870s can be characterised as a success story within successful economies. During the nineteenth century Singapore grew as a prosperous entrepôt and the premier British port in Southeast Asia. From the 1960s independent Singapore underwent rapid industrial development, ranking with Hong Kong, Taiwan and South Korea as one of Asia's Newly Industrialising Countries, and achieving, by the 1980s, one of the highest per capita GNPs in the developing world. Peninsular Malaya, also under British control, experienced accelerating economic growth from the late nineteenth century through the production and export of tin and, later, rubber. An estimate – admittedly highly fragile – of per capita incomes in 1929 placed Malaya well above Japan, and far in excess of India and China.[1] Over the last thirty years the country has developed as 'one of the great post-colonial success stories',[2] its rich natural resources being supplemented by a burgeoning industrial base and a new petroleum sector.

British business was a dynamic element within these economies, although it was only one factor among several which contributed towards their growth. In the first half of the nineteenth century many British agency houses were established in Singapore. These houses diversified their activities, in many cases becoming involved – alongside other types of British enterprise – in plantations in Malaya, and also spreading to other Southeast Asian economies. British banks pioneered modern banking in the region. After the Second World War the relative importance of British business declined, yet there was no wholesale collapse. In 1962 Malaysia was the sixth largest recipient of British direct investment (excluding oil, banking and insurance), with India just ahead in fifth place. British companies became involved in new forms of economic activity, especially manufacturing. During the 1970s the traditional British agency houses which had dominated Malaya's extractive sector fell under local control in a spectacular series of boardroom battles and corporate take-

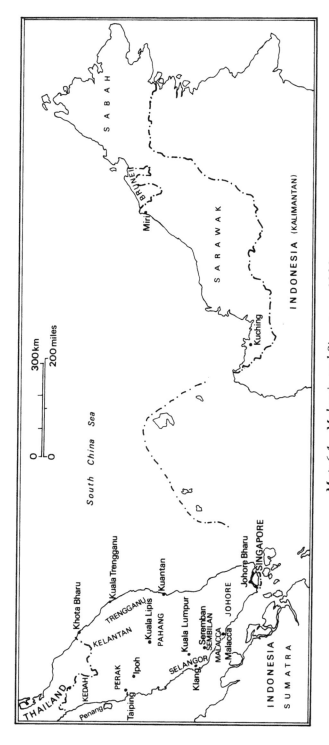

Map 6.1 Malaysia and Singapore, 1988

British business in Malaysia & Singapore since the 1870s 159

overs. However, the level of British private investment remained high. Overall, and at the risk of gross over-simplification, the long-term performance of British business in Malaysia and Singapore appears more dynamic and 'successful' than that of its counterparts in Iran, Japan or even India. This chapter will offer some explanations for this.

Before proceeding, however, it is necessary to clarify the unusually complex political history of the region we shall be discussing. Britain's presence dated from the period of rivalry with the Dutch which led, in 1786, to the acquisition of the island of Penang, near the strategic sea route through the Straits of Malacca. In 1819 Sir Stamford Raffles founded Singapore on land leased by him for a reluctant East India Company from the Sultan of Johore, and the place soon turned from a mangrove swamp into a flourishing port. In 1824 the British also finally acquired the former Dutch port of Malacca. Penang (with Province Wellesley on the mainland), Singapore and Malacca became the Straits Settlements, administered until 1858 by the East India Company, then by the India Office, and from 1867 until 1942 as a British Crown Colony. Between the 1870s and 1909 British protection was extended over the mainland of Malaya, which was divided into several states. In 1874 the Sultan of Perak accepted a British Resident. In 1895 four states in such treaty relationships with Britain – Perak, Selangor, Negri Sembilan and Pahang – formed the Federated Malay States. Meanwhile, in the south of Malaya, Johore state signed a treaty of protection with Britain in 1885. In 1909 Thailand ceded to Britain suzerainty over the four remaining Malay states in the north – Kelantan, Trengganu, Kedah and Perlis – and these together with Johore became known as the Unfederated Malay States.

This curious political patchwork remained in place until after the Second World War, when attempts to form a unitary state led to the creation of the Federation of Malaya in 1948. This united the Federated and Unfederated Malay States with Malacca and Penang, but made Singapore into a separate colony. The Federation became independent from Britain in 1957. In 1963 the Federation of Malaysia was formed by a merger of Malaya, Singapore and two former British colonies located 400 miles across the South China Sea, Sabah (formerly British North Borneo) and Sarawak. Sabah had been administered by the British North Borneo Company under a Royal Charter between 1881 and 1946, when it became a colony. Sarawak was ruled between 1841 and 1946 by three generations of the English Brooke family who governed as Rajahs: it was a British protected state from 1888 and become a colony in 1946. In 1965 Singapore left the Federation to become an independent republic.

6.2 The growth of Singapore

Singapore holds a pivotal position in the story of the expansion of British enterprise in Southeast Asia and China in the nineteenth century. In the fifty years after its foundation by Raffles, the trade of Singapore expanded. Singapore's excellent harbour and sheltered anchorage, its nodal position at the tip of the Malay Peninsula, and the policy originated by Raffles that it should be a free port were key factors in this expansion. After the 1870s Singapore's growth accelerated as the economic development of surrounding areas, and especially of its natural hinterland of Malaya, enhanced the port's position. Meanwhile the opening of the Suez Canal in 1869 made Singapore the focal point of steamship lines along the route between Suez and Shanghai. Singapore's foreign trade (measured by value) expanded over nine times between 1870 and 1913.[3]

The same factors which encouraged Singapore's growth as a trading centre also made it an attractive base for British agency houses, of which about twenty had been established at the port by 1846.[4] Two of the earliest were Boustead and Company and the predecessor to Guthrie and Company, both founded in the 1820s. These firms, usually sole traders or partnerships, started with little capital, relying on credit from British suppliers of imports to undertake business turnovers well above their own resources. From the middle of the nineteenth century these houses began to diversify from purely trading activities along the lines previously taken by British merchants in India and China. Guthries, for example, became agents for British banks and shipping lines. There were some minor investments in agriculture and more substantial moneylending activities – mostly on-lending the funds of resident Europeans to Asians. The Borneo Company formed a close relationship with the Brooke dynasty which enabled it to monopolize the exploitation of gold and other minerals in Sarawak, and it also became a leading force in the teak industry in Thailand.[5] Most dramatically, in the decade after the great rubber boom of 1905, the agency houses diversified into primary commodity production in Malaya. Singapore acted, therefore, as the base from which British enterprise spread out into neighbouring regions.

Singapore was also the initial location of the British overseas banks. The Oriental Bank Corporation established the first bank branch at the port in 1846. It was joined by branches of the Chartered Mercantile Bank of India, London and China in 1859 and, rather belatedly, the Hongkong Bank in 1877. These banks were concerned, as elsewhere, with the finance of foreign trade, but they also issued banknotes for the Straits Settlements until 1899, when the Straits Settlement government assumed sole responsibility for the issue of currency notes. In a similar pattern to that of the agency houses, the British banks expanded outwards from their Singapore

British business in Malaysia & Singapore since the 1870s 161

bases. Chartered Mercantile opened a branch in Penang in 1859; the Chartered Bank of India, Australia and China followed in 1875; and the Hongkong Bank in 1884. These branches provided the basis for expansion into the Malay States from the late 1880s.[6]

British traders and banks were important forces in Singapore's nineteenth-century growth – but they formed only part of a dynamic business community. In particular Chinese merchants played a critical role in Singapore's growth as a regional trading centre, in which direct trade with the United Kingdom formed only around a third of total trade by the time of the First World War. Chinese merchants at Singapore, for example, supplied Siamese rice to the markets of Malaya and the Dutch East Indies. Singapore acted as a centre for the spread of Chinese labour and capital to elsewhere in Southeast Asia. Chinese merchants acted as middlemen between the Western and Asian traders, importing Asian produce into Singapore and selling it to European merchants. While import and export business with Western countries was handled mainly by Western businessmen, intra-Asian trade remained largely in Chinese hands. The activities of the Western and Chinese traders were frequently complementary to one another, and there were considerable connections between the two sectors. British agency houses and banks, for example, provided credit to Chinese firms, importing the *compradore* system from China to facilitate their dealings with the Chinese merchants. Singapore's growth was a product not of British business but of 'Sino-Western enterprise'.[7]

British business in nineteenth-century Singapore flourished, therefore, in a congenial environment. A favourable geographical situation, a stable British colonial government following laissez-faire economic policies, and a dynamic local – especially Chinese – business community were all positive factors. Similar considerations help to explain the growth of British business activity in Malaya itself from the 1870s.

6.3 British business and Malayan tin

The extension of British political control over Malaya after 1874 provided the conditions for the economy's growth through specialisation in the production of rubber and tin for the world market. Malaya offered ideal conditions for foreign investment in these commodities, for its rich natural resources were combined with a low population density. The population of Peninsular Malaya was only 2.3 million in 1911, rising to 4.9 million by 1947. As in the Straits Settlements, the British administration provided an effective framework for increased economic activity. Initially officials were motivated by a limited desire to increase tax revenues by encouraging the growth of the tin industry, but this evolved into an enthusiastic campaign by men like Sir Frank Swettenham to

6.1 *Sir Frank Swettenham (1850–1946), who became a British official in the Straits Settlements in 1871 and whose career in the region culminated in his appointment as High Commissioner for the Malay States and Governor of the Straits Settlements (1901–4). He was thereafter director of several rubber companies.*

British business in Malaysia & Singapore since the 1870s 163

Table 6.1 *Tin and rubber production in British Malaya and world market share, 1890–1960*

Year	Tin production (000 tons)	% world tin production	Rubber production (000 tons)	% world rubber production
1890	27	41	–	–
1900	43	51	–	–
1910	46	40	6	7
1920	37	30	174	51
1930	67	37	452	54
1940	83	35	547	39
1950	58	35	694	37
1960	52	32	708	35

Sources: Lim Chong Yah, *Economic Development of Modern Malaya* (Kuala Lumpur, 1967), p. 94, Appendices 2.1 and 4.3. World rubber production has been estimated at 13,000 tons in 1890 and 32,000 tons in 1900 (J. H. Drabble, *Rubber in Malaya, 1876–1922* (Kuala Lumpur, 1973), p. 19). Malayan rubber production was insignificant at these dates: it reached 1,000 tons in 1907.

promote the economic development of their territory. They combined a welcoming attitude to foreign capital with public infrastructure investment to 'open up' the country. Government building of the railway and roads had the greatest developmental impact, but there were other activities ranging from irrigation works and agricultural loans to the promotion of labour migration to Malaya.[8]

Changes in the world market led to an accelerating demand for Malaya's raw materials. Demand for tin rose as the tinplate industry in Britain and, more importantly, the United States expanded following the widespread usage of canning. Tin prices increased by one-half between the 1850s and the 1890s.[9] Other sources of supply declined with the contraction of the old Cornish tin industry and a gradual fall in Australian production, particularly after 1882. From the second half of the nineteenth century there was an equivalent growth of world demand for rubber products following a chain of discoveries and inventions from the vulcanisation process, which enabled the manufacture of pliable and durable rubber products, to the invention of the pneumatic tyre in 1888.[10] As Table 6.1 illustrates, British Malaya emerged as one of the world's major tin and rubber producers.

British investment in Malaya from the 1870s until the 1960s was overwhelmingly concentrated in tin and rubber (together with palm oil which became important from the inter-war years). According to one contemporary source, some 93% of the estimated total British investment in Malaya in 1930 of £108 million was in plantations and mines.[11] Britain was the dominant foreign investor in both industries. In 1920 some 96% of foreign (non-Chinese) capital in the Malayan tin industry was British,

164 Jean-Jacques van Helten and Geoffrey Jones

while British interests were almost as dominant among the foreign investors in rubber. However the roles of the British in the development of the two industries were quite different, as were the forms of British corporate involvement, and it is necessary to discuss the two industries separately.

In many Asian economies before 1914, British enterprises introduced new products and industries. However, they performed no such role in the case of the Malayan tin industry, which owed its vigorous growth in the nineteenth century almost entirely to Chinese entrepreneurs. During the eighteenth century Chinese had been active in the smelting rather than in the mining of Malayan tin (which was in Malay hands), but the discovery of rich ore resources in 1848 in the Larut district of Perak was followed by a wave of Chinese immigration. Conflict between Chinese miners which the Malay chiefs were unable to control was a major factor behind the British political intervention in Perak in 1874.[12] However the Chinese took advantage of the new British-imposed political stability, and tin production soared. Following British intervention output of tin from Perak expanded from 650 tons in 1874 to 10,000 in 1884, and in the thirty years before the First World War the industry expanded rapidly. Malayan tin production reached 51,000 tons in 1913, of which 75% was produced by Chinese. It was not until 1929 that tin production by Western-owned firms in Malaya exceeded that of Chinese enterprises.

The extension of British control over the Peninsula was followed by the first Western investments in the industry, but these initial ventures were very unsuccessful. The first European mining company, the Société des Mines d'Etain de Perak, was established by French entrepreneurs in Paris in 1883. This was followed by the Gopeng Company (later Gopeng Consolidated) in 1892, established by Cornish interests seeking to diversify from their own collapsing tin mining industry.[13] There was a strong Cornish influence in many of the subsequent British tin companies in Malaya. Gopeng, with its administrative base at Redruth in Cornwall, developed as one of the large groups which dominated the Malayan tin industry from the 1920s. The late nineteenth century saw a wave of company promotions – between 1882 and 1900, forty-seven British-registered companies were floated to work Malayan tin with a total authorised capital of £4.8 million – but most of these failed. The actual amount of capital issued was probably around £1.9 million.[14]

There were several reasons for the failure of British entrepreneurs to establish a firm foothold in the tin mining industry before 1900. Although British mining expertise was well developed and the British were applying technical and managerial skills successfully elsewhere – from the Witwatersrand to the copper mines of South Australia and the diamond deposits of Central Brazil – few of these skills, at first, were in demand on

British business in Malaysia & Singapore since the 1870s 165

the alluvial fields of the Malayan interior.[15] As in Siam, the large surface deposits could be easily mined by the Chinese using labour-intensive working methods. There were no lode mines in Malaya except in Pahang, where British capital and enterprise were active. For the most part, British mining companies quickly discovered that they did not possess a technological advantage over their Chinese counterparts.[16]

Chinese mines possessed other comparative advantages over British firms. They employed Chinese labourers, many of whom were indentured, before 1914 when the system was abolished. Other Chinese workers were employed under profit-sharing schemes. On British-owned mines the supervision of workers had to be done through a supervisor or Chinese overseers, which was both costly and time-consuming.[17] The result was that British mines had to pay their workers more than was paid to Chinese workers on Chinese-owned mines. Significantly, as relative newcomers to the field, British companies sometimes had difficulty in acquiring mineral-bearing properties as all the best ground was held by the Chinese or Malay smallholders.[18]

By the early 1900s, however, once the more easily accessible and rich ore deposits were exhausted, British mining companies found themselves in a more competitive position. The crucial innovation was the introduction of bucket-dredging, first developed in New Zealand in the 1880s. This allowed British firms to enter tin mining without trying to compete directly with the Chinese for either labour or land.[19] Dredges could operate in swampy areas where drainage would have been impossible, work low-grade deposits profitably through economies of scale, and operate on ground that had previously been worked by the Chinese using open-cast methods. Imported technology gave the British companies for the first time a strong comparative advantage within the industry, which was strengthened by the fact that the high initial capital outlay involved in dredging was no obstacle to British entrepreneurs with access to the London capital market. British investment in Malayan tin mines surged ahead, buoyed by both high tin prices and the reduction in real working costs following the introduction of Western technology.

Few Chinese capitalists took up the challenge of dredging. As a result a major segment of the Malayan tin industry fell into the hands of British firms. One possible reason why the Chinese did not adopt dredging was lack of capital. From the outset Chinese merchants and traders had invested heavily in the industry across the Peninsula, largely in the form of advances to tin miners and by supplying very modest fixed capital for mining operations in the form of tools, pumping machinery and so on. Other Chinese merchants had tied their capital up in tin-ore dealing and the operation of opium and gambling dens for the workers. But the long-term financing of extensive dredging operations was either beyond

166 *Jean-Jacques van Helten and Geoffrey Jones*

the resources of the Chinese community or they did not wish to become involved in it. Such financial commitment over an unspecified time-horizon was also in direct conflict with the primary aim of many (but not all) Chinese in Malaya to remit a large part of their savings to China.[20] However, fears that the colonial administration would favour Western companies, and the availability of more attractive investment opportunities were probably factors at least as important as capital shortages *per se* in explaining the failure of the Chinese to adopt the bucket dredge.

Before the 1920s British investment in Malayan tin mining consisted of a large number of 'free-standing' companies of the kind discussed in chapter 1. In this respect there was a contrast with rival tin producing countries such as Bolivia and the Dutch East Indies, where there was more concentration in the ownership structure of the industry. The Malayan tin companies focussed their attention on Malaya and, significantly, played no part in the development of Siam's tin industry before the First World War. As elsewhere in Asia, the British 'free-standing' companies were divided into 'sterling' companies, registered in the United Kingdom, and locally registered firms, with their capitals denominated in Straits dollars. This difference in domicile did not reflect fundamental differences in capital ownership, for the large majority of the capital in the dollar companies seems to have been 'British', although often coming from locally resident Europeans, such as members of the Malay Civil Service, as well as from other expatriate business interests. As in Siam, there were also substantial Australian 'British' capitalists active in Malayan tin before the late 1920s. Yip estimated that in 1920 the capital of British-registered tin mining companies amounted to £3.6 million, with the sterling equivalent of the 'dollar' mining companies at around £1.5 million.[21] The average size of all the companies was small. The thirty-seven British-registered firms in 1920 had an average capital of around £100,000. The largest was the Pahang Consolidated Company formed in 1906 and active in capital-intensive lode mining, which had a capital of £475,000.[22]

Average declared dividends of tin mining companies floated in London varied from 4.0% in 1911 to 17.4% in 1920, when the tin price was £296 per ton compared to £192 per ton nine years previously. In the absence of reliable data to measure the internal rate of return, dividend payments are the only, if fallible, measure of financial success of British firms in the industry. The high 'mortality rate' of mining companies in Malaya and elsewhere, the use and abuse of vendors' shares and insider trading, and the generally speculative nature of mining investments whereby greater profits were made by investors in share dealing than in actual mining, mean that dividends are crude indicators of the profitability of an enterprise.[23] Nevertheless, the expansion of the industry in the early part

British business in Malaysia & Singapore since the 1870s 167

of the century suggests that, at least for those investors who came in on the ground floor of a flotation and whose mine was well capitalised, the financial rewards of investing in Malaya were not inconsiderable.

Colonial government legislation also eroded Chinese dominance over the tin mining industry, even though these measures were not necessarily taken to further British business interests. From the 1890s onwards, for example, the ability of the Chinese secret societies to control tin mining workers was broken by legislation. This and other measures helped to open up the labour market and led to a flow of miners to British-owned mines. The higher wages that resulted from these developments further undermined the Chinese mines' position as low-cost producers. Colonial fiscal policies also eroded their hold, as between 1895 and 1912 the government, in the interest of fiscal stability, abolished opium and gambling farms, thereby curbing the supply of ancillary profits to the Chinese mine-owners. It was also a matter of official policy to encourage British business, as was made clear by the Perak government's Mining Code of 1895, the model for all subsequent legislation that encouraged the development of more technically advanced methods of mining, as well as by other forms of legislation, notably land alienation.[24]

British business achieved a dominant position in Southeast Asian tin smelting earlier than in tin mining. The pioneer British venture was the Straits Trading Company, which was established in 1887. The firm erected a smelter on the island of Pulau Brani, off Singapore, in 1890, and a more modern smelter in Penang in 1902. By that date the firm processed 50% of the tin exports of the Straits Settlements. There were also a large number of Chinese tin smelters, but their product had a high impurity content, and they could not match the economies of scale achieved by the Straits Trading Company.[25] In the 1900s the British position was challenged by Khaw Sim Bee, a Chinese who combined service as a Siamese bureaucrat with control of a large commercial empire based at Penang. In 1907 the Khaw group purchased a modern smelter which another Chinese had established in Penang in 1898. The locally registered Eastern Smelting Company was formed, and by 1910 it accounted for 29% of total tin shipments from the Straits. In the following year, however, the firm was sold to British interests and re-registered in London, apparently because of an inability to raise sufficient finance.[26]

There were two related trends in the inter-war Malayan tin industry: the concentration of ownership in the Western sector, and participation in international cartels. A post-war slump in tin prices led to the first steps in cartelisation. The British colonial government adopted a rescue policy based on a domestic price-supporting programme and close cooperation with the neighbouring colonial government in the Dutch East Indies. The colonial government's policies stemmed less from lobbying by British tin

168 Jean-Jacques van Helten and Geoffrey Jones

interests than from concern about tax revenues. In the early 1920s taxes on opium, which was smoked by Chinese workers in the tin industry, were the government's largest source of revenue, and officials were determined that the industry could not be allowed to falter.

Cooperation with the Dutch administration, sealed by formation of the Bandoeng Pool in 1921, demonstrated that by withdrawing around one-sixth of total world output from the market and holding it as buffer stock, international tin control could work.[27] It was only after 1923, as tin prices were once more rising (reaching £200 a ton), that stocks were gradually released onto the market. Indeed, by 1925, after the Bandoeng Pool stock had been released, it became clear that, with a booming automobile industry in the United States, world capacity to consume was running ahead of world output and a tin shortage was developing. By 1926–7, once tin had reached £290 a ton and a scramble for tin mining company shares was on, a plethora of mines was floated on the London Stock Exchange and the total issued capital of British-registered mining companies in Malaya shot up from £3.6 million in 1920 to £18.7 million in 1927, with the sterling equivalent of the 'dollar' mining companies reaching £2.2 million. Overall, foreign investment in Malayan tin doubled between 1920 and 1927, with 85% of the increase coming from Britain. Malayan tin output nearly doubled over the 1920s (see Table 6.1), with two-thirds of this increase occurring between 1926 and 1929.[28]

The upsurge of British investment in Malayan tin mining was accompanied by concentration in the industry. The ownership of tin, like that of many other commodities in the 1920s, also acquired an international dimension, with Malaya's production coming under the control of enterprises with world-wide interests. The two main developments were the formation in the 1920s of the London Tin Corporation (LTC) and the establishment of Consolidated Tin Smelters. Within a decade LTC and its subsidiary, Anglo-Oriental (Malaya), secured control of twenty tin companies accounting for about a third of Malaya's production. During the 1930s this group, as chapter 5 relates, also absorbed many of the Australian tin companies operating in Thailand. LTC rarely had majority ownership of these enterprises, but exercised control through a combination of management and interlocking directorships. It was controlled by its Chairman, John Howeson – originally called von Ernsthausen – who emerged as the leading figure in the British tin industry in the 1920s.[29] The remaining British tin producing companies in Malaya also became linked in this period, sometimes under the management of agency houses such as Guthries. By the end of the 1930s there were still around eighty separate tin mining companies in Malaya, but ownership was highly concentrated.

The Howeson group was impressive. It secured control of British tin companies in Thailand and Burma, and by the 1930s also accounted for

British business in Malaysia & Singapore since the 1870s 169

around half of Nigeria's tin output. In Malaya the group introduced much-needed managerial rationalisation among the companies it controlled. However Howeson also pursued more controversial business tactics. He specialised in the creation of secret tin stocks to maintain prices. In the mid-1930s he extended his operations to other commodities, devising a scheme to corner the world market in shellac and white pepper. He was eventually gaoled in 1936 for issuing a fraudulent prospectus.[30] The great 'pepper scandal' left LTC debilitated for a time, and the Bank of England became involved in the reconstruction of the group and the appointment of successors to the disgraced Howeson.[31]

The Malayan tin smelting industry underwent similar concentration in the 1920s, and a substantial sector fell under the influence of the Bolivian millionaire Simon Patiño. Patiño controlled a large share of Bolivian tin production – roughly half by the 1930s – and in 1916 acquired control of Europe's largest tin smelter, the firm of Williams, Harvey of Liverpool. In 1929 Patiño formed a new British-registered holding company, Consolidated Tin Smelters, which purchased the Eastern Smelting Company, which left only one large independent smelter in Malaya, the Straits Trading Company. Patiño also took an equity stake, probably in the region of £700,000, in the London Tin Corporation: an alliance favoured by the British government which was anxious to counter the strong American influence in the world's metals industry.[32]

The concentration of ownership in Malaya's tin industry and its integration with interests operating in other tin producing countries provided the conditions for the formation of the International Tin Council following the signing of the first International Tin Agreement in 1931. This Agreement was signed by the governments of the Federated Malay States, the Dutch East Indies, Bolivia and Nigeria, and it became the basis of what was to become the world's largest running commodity agreement, which endured until 1985. Contemporary critics alleged, with justification, that the scheme's origins were related to the speculative activities of LTC, whose heavily 'over-capitalised' producing companies and large stocks of tin were threatened by sharp falls in the price of the commodity at the end of the 1920s.[33] LTC was certainly behind the voluntary restrictions scheme launched under the aegis of the Tin Producers Association, representing around 90% of British tin mining interests in Malaya, Burma and Nigeria, and when this proved ineffective was active in encouraging the Colonial Office to secure a wider international agreement which enabled them to dispose of their stocks.[34] Howeson became a leading figure in the International Tin Council, and clearly had designs to bring the whole world tin industry under his control.

British Colonial Office officials found 'some truth' in the criticisms of LTC's influence, but also accurately observed that they were 'very far

170 Jean-Jacques van Helten and Geoffrey Jones

from the whole truth'.[35] Whatever the activities of British speculators, a 50% collapse in the price of tin between 1927 and 1930 prompted all producers to move in the direction of restrictive schemes. The 1931 Agreement restricted output on the basis of an allotted standard tonnage and percentage quota based on 1929 output figures. Enforcement and output from non-member countries were constant problems: nevertheless two further Tin Agreements were signed, in 1934 and 1937.

The Tin Agreements were successful in sustaining prices and almost certainly saved the world industry from ruin in the 1930s. However the scheme was criticised in Malaya, and it is probable that the ownership structure in the Western sector of the industry – whose production by the 1930s was far in excess of the Chinese sector – worked against Malaya's interests. The Malayan industry was low-cost in world terms, and it might have been expected to do well in the difficult circumstances of the Depression. In fact, Malaya's quota was underassessed compared to those of other countries such as Thailand. The result was that Malaya's share of world tin output declined in the 1930s, from 37% in 1930 to 28% in 1939, though a surge of production in the first year of the Second World War raised Malaya's share to 35%. LTC's investments in high-cost tin mines elsewhere influenced the quota allocated to Malaya. In the late 1930s LTC made substantial investments in the Nigerian industry, culminating in 1939 in the creation of Amalgamated Tin Mines of Nigeria, then the world's largest single tin producing company.[36] The consolidation of the Malayan industry had made production in that country dependent on the global price and production strategies pursued by Western corporate oligopolists.

Beyond the Malay Peninsula in Sarawak, British enterprises were also active in mineral production, although there was no tin industry. The Brooke government established coal mines in the late nineteenth century. In the second half of the 1890s gold replaced coal as Sarawak's most valuable mineral product. The Chinese had been mining gold since at least the 1820s, but the industry was revolutioned when the Borneo Company introduced modern methods of extraction. Gold exports dramatically increased from 984 ounces in 1898 to 24,192 in the following year. When rising costs led to the withdrawal of the Borneo Company from gold mining in 1921, the industry reverted into Chinese hands.

From the early 1920s until the late 1950s – when bauxite production became important – Sarawak's leading mineral product was petroleum. In 1909 the Shell Group (40% British- and 60% Dutch-owned), which owned large oilfields in the Dutch East Indies, was awarded the exclusive exploration and production rights for Sarawak for 75 years. Shell had failed to find oil in neighbouring British North Borneo, but in 1910 oil was struck at Miri. By 1913, when the first crude oil was exported, production

British business in Malaysia & Singapore since the 1870s 171

had reached 26,000 tons. Sarawak oil, however, was not the equivalent of Malayan tin. The 1913 production level was much less than 1% of world oil production. During the 1920s there was expansion, as Sarawak Oilfields (a locally incorporated subsidiary of Shell formed in 1921) introduced new technology such as rotary drilling. Inter-war production peaked at 750,000 tons in 1929, but declined over the following decade. The industry never developed on the scale of that of the Sultanate of Brunei, where another Shell subsidiary had discovered oil at Seria in 1929. In 1951, after a period of recovery following the destruction of the oilfields at the onset of the Japanese invasion in December 1941, Sarawak's production was 52,000 tons (compared to Brunei's 5 million tons). Throughout the 1950s, however, Shell's oil refinery at Lutong in Sarawak (established in 1919) refined most of Brunei's oil, and was Sarawak's most important industrial installation.[37]

6.4 Rubber and the agency houses

Rubber was the second major industry on the Malay Peninsula which concerned British business before the 1960s. In contrast to their role in the tin industry, British interests performed a pioneering role in this industry; it was, as Allen and Donnithorne would have it, 'one of the greatest achievements of Western colonial enterprise'.[38] The story of the introduction of rubber seeds into Malaya in the 1870s from Brazil, via Kew Gardens and Ceylon, has been often told. British planters in Malaya became interested in the product after prices of their main product, coffee, began to fall in the mid-1890s, and by the turn of the century there were areas of rubber in many places along the west coast of Malaya. After 1900 accelerating demand in the West created a boom. Malayan rubber exports reached 33,000 tons in 1913 and 200,000 in 1919, by which time it had replaced tin as the country's largest export.[39] The colonial government pursued an overall policy of trying to develop Malaya's agriculture through a combination of planters – especially Europeans – specialising in producing crops for exports, while indigenous Malays were encouraged to concentrate on food production. Within this context the British administrators encouraged European cultivation of rubber: in the Federated Malay States after 1905, for example, the policy was to alienate land with road frontage to estate ventures rather than to smallholders. Smallholder entry into the industry was not hindered but overall government support for British rubber interests was far more important than for British tin ventures.

The plantation sector of the rubber industry was initially in the hands of individual estates owned and managed by British planters. However, this system was unable to generate the funds required by the industry, whose expansion required the opening up of new areas of jungle. This was both capital-intensive and involved a waiting period of five or six years before an estate was ready for tapping. Limited companies were formed to assist in raising capital. As in the tin industry, some companies were British-registered 'sterling' ventures while others were locally registered. There were also some rupee companies registered in Ceylon, an indication of the interest taken in Malaya by British planters in that colony. The first 'sterling' company specifically concerned with rubber cultivation was the Selangor Rubber Company, registered in Glasgow in 1899; several other Scottish-registered companies followed in the early 1900s, reflecting the Scots origins of many of the planters. The dollar rubber companies, like their tin equivalents, seem to have found most of their funds from locally resident Europeans, but there were also Asian investors in, and even Chinese control of, some of the companies formed in the 1900s.[40]

As the boom in rubber demand in the early 1900s led to the spread of plantations over large areas of south and west Malaya the agency houses which had developed in nineteenth-century Singapore became involved in the industry. Plantation companies enlisted their help to float new companies in London, in which the agency houses often took some shares. The agency houses in turn were frequently appointed managing agents and secretaries of the new companies. By the 1920s the Guthrie group of companies had become the largest of the Malaysian rubber groups: Bousteads and Harrison and Crosfield also became extensively involved in rubber. Occasionally planting interests also diversified into other activities. The most famous example was Sime Darby, formed in 1902 from a group of Malacca rubber estates, which by the inter-war years had emerged as a full-scale agency house active in several sectors apart from rubber.

These events had a marked impact on the character of the British agency houses. They assumed limited-liability status: Guthries took corporate status in 1903, Harrison and Crosfield in 1908. There were several amalgamations between firms. The management of plantation companies necessitated a new range of skills: agriculturists and other specialists were recruited to assist in the administration of the estates. The agency houses also made further diversifications into, for example, motor-car distribution. In 1925 the Borneo Company formed a new subsidiary, Borneo Motors Ltd, which developed a large import and retail business.[41]

The other major British investment in the Malayan rubber industry was a precursor of the more familiar form of direct investment by foreign-based multinationals which was to come to the fore in the post-Second World War period. In 1910 Dunlop, the leading British rubber goods and tyre manufacturer, embarked on a strategy of backward vertical integra-

British business in Malaysia & Singapore since the 1870s 173

tion by acquiring rubber estates in Malaya. By 1915 when a wholly owned subsidiary, Dunlop Plantations Ltd, was formed, the company held one of the largest tracts (well over 6,000 acres) in the country.

The example of the British estates soon encouraged Malays and Chinese to enter the industry and a smallholding sector developed. In 1921 smallholdings accounted for 41.5% of the total planted acreage of rubber in Malaya. By 1930 the percentage had reached an inter-war peak of 48%, but it fell sharply after 1933 to reach a low of 32% in 1939, before recovering to 39% in 1940. This was partly because of government policies, especially the restrictions on exports discussed below, but also partly because of constraints within the general economic and social structure of the industry.[42]

There was an interesting variation from the Malayan ownership structure in the rubber industry in Sarawak. Commercial rubber planting began there in 1905, but the Brooke family discouraged large-scale capitalist development which they felt would dislocate the lives of the indigenous population. Thus, although the Borneo Company established a plantation in 1902, rubber production in Sarawak developed as an overwhelmingly smallholder operation, with substantial Chinese participation. In 1940 only 7% of the 239,557 acres of Sarawak under rubber were in the hands of estates (compared to 61% at that date in Peninsular Malaya). By the inter-war years rubber was Sarawak's leading export. The second most valuable export, pepper, was largely in the hands of small Chinese farmers.[43]

During the inter-war years Malayan rubber, like tin, was the subject of a number of restrictive international commodity agreements, which had some costs for the industry in general and the smallholder sector in particular. In 1920 there was a dramatic fall in rubber prices, which led to a sharp fall in government tax receipts, forcing many British-owned estates (many of whom had followed improvident dividend policies) to the edge of bankruptcy and led the British government to fear the American take-over of the Malayan plantation industry. It was against this background of rumours and impending default that the Rubber Growers' Association (RGA), established in London in 1907 and representing 'sterling' companies with estates in Ceylon, the Dutch East Indies and Malaya, first mooted the idea of restraints on the output of rubber. After the failure of voluntary restrictions by producers, the British government was persuaded to intervene, and in 1921 Sir James Stevenson was appointed to chair a committee, dominated by RGA members, to advise on remedies for the rubber industry. Stevenson strongly advocated restrictions on output. The planters in the Dutch East Indies refused to participate, and so the Stevenson Scheme, with restriction of output based on a stipulated percentage of the 'standard output' of each plantation,

174 Jean-Jacques van Helten and Geoffrey Jones

became mandatory only in the British empire on 1 November 1922. In a pattern which was later to be repeated, the average assessment per mature acre of Malayan smallholding was only about one-half of that of estates, revealing a distinct bias towards the British-controlled sector. However recent research has convincingly demonstrated that the British Cabinet decision to accept the Stevenson Scheme stemmed from broad 'imperial' considerations to prevent the Americans taking over the ownership of the British rubber plantations rather than 'sectional pressure from producers'.[44]

The Stevenson Scheme collapsed in 1928. It had short-term success in assisting a recovery of rubber prices and a reduction of stocks before 1925, but the overall result was hardly favourable to Malaya. As American demand for rubber expanded in the mid-1920s, the Stevenson Scheme in Malaya stimulated the spread of rubber planting to other parts of Southeast Asia, especially the Dutch East Indies. In the 1930s more wide-ranging commodity agreements had the same effect. In 1934 the governments of Britain, the Netherlands, India, France and Thailand signed an International Rubber Regulation Agreement.[45] Quotas were allocated to each country, based on average exports for the years 1929–1932, and new areas of planting were forbidden. As with tin, Malaya's share of world production of rubber fell under these agreements, from 54% in 1930 to 39% in 1940 (see Table 6.1). The spread of technical change within the Malayan industry also slowed down in this period, especially in the smallholder sector.

The restrictive agreements of the 1930s again favoured the British-owned plantations as against the smallholders, who were greatly under assessed. The reasons for this lay more in the colonial government's concern for its revenues than in the lobbying of the RGA, which actually suggested more liberal quotas for the smallholders.[46] Under the restriction schemes of the 1930s the earnings for the British rubber companies increased, but the Malayan industry as a whole, 'especially in its smallholding sector ... was prevented from deriving full benefit from its low cost advantages'.[47] The high-cost British estates would, indeed, have hardly survived smallholder competition without official protection.

It would be misleading to characterise the British plantations in the inter-war years as stagnant. One noteworthy development was the introduction of large-scale palm oil production into Malaya. In 1875 seeds of the West African palm from Ceylon had been planted experimentally in Singapore. However it was not until 1917 that the first commercial planting in Malaya was undertaken by a Frenchman: this estate and other oil palm plantations were subsequently acquired by the Franco–Belgian group Socfin which possessed large palm oil estates in Sumatra, and which became a substantial producer in Malaya. During the 1920s the depressed

6.2 *Ten-dollar note issued by Chartered Mercantile Bank of India, London and China at Penang, 1886.*

state of the rubber market and the relatively high price of palm oil encouraged British estates to experiment with the crop, with Guthrie companies playing a prominent role. Malayan palm oil production reached 3,300 tons in 1930, around 1% of world production. The 1930s saw further substantial growth as unused land was taken into cultivation in Johore, Perak and Selangor. The fact that palm oil was not subject to an international commodity agreement, and that its production was directly encouraged by the governments of the Federated Malay States and Johore as a means of diversifying the economy, encouraged this expansion. By 1940 Malayan production stood at 58,000 tons, or 12% of world production. The industry was almost entirely in the hands of British and other Western-owned estates as a consequence of the size of investment necessary in processing facilities, and it was not until after 1957 that substantial smallholder participation was encouraged.[48]

6.5 British banks in Malaya

The establishment of a modern banking system in Malaya was – as with the rubber industry – the product of British enterprise. In the late nineteenth century the British overseas banks established in the Straits Settlements extended their activities. The lead was taken by the Chartered Bank, which opened branches (or agencies as they were then known) at Taiping and Kuala Lumpur in 1888. Further branches followed at Klang

(1909), Seremban (1910), Malacca (1911) and Ipoh (1912).[49] The Hongkong Bank was rather slower to expand beyond Singapore and Penang, but the five years before the First World War saw a sudden spate of openings of new branches at Malacca (1909), Kuala Lumpur (1909), Ipoh (1910) and Johore Bharu (1910).[50] Finally the Mercantile Bank of India (which had emerged in 1892 from a reconstruction of the old Chartered Mercantile Bank of India, London and China) took the lead in opening branches on the east coast of Malaya, at Kota Bharu (1911), Kuantan (1926) and Kuala Trengganu (1936).[51] A single branch of the Chartered Bank of India, Australia and China opened in Kuching, the capital of Sarawak, in 1924 was the only modern bank in Sabah and Sarawak until after the Second World War.

As everywhere in the East, the British overseas banks were primarily concerned with the finance of trade, both internal and external, and exchange operations. Their customers included the British agency houses, though sometimes these firms had sufficient resources to finance their own business. The various banks tended to have long-standing arrangements with particular houses, which were sometimes cemented by interlocking directorships. In 1941, for example, the Mercantile Bank elected Sir John Hay, Chairman of Guthries, to its board in the hope of receiving more of that firm's business. The immediate result, however, was the loss of the business of Guthries' rivals, Sime Darby, to Mercantile's rivals, the Chartered Bank.[52]

The British banks also acted as government bankers to various authorities in Malaya. The Chartered Bank was banker to the government of the Federated Malay States. The Hongkong Bank was appointed banker to the Johore State Government in 1910, a position it retained until 1966. The Mercantile Bank was government banker in the three east-coast states where it had branches, Kelantan, Trengganu and Pahang. The government deposits at these branches were indispensable to the Mercantile Bank's business for there was comparatively little exchange or trade finance business to be had in the inter-war years.[53] Surplus government and other balances were lent to Mercantile's Singapore office enabling it to finance commercial operations.[54]

In Malaya, as elsewhere in Asia, the British banks also conducted an extensive Chinese business assisted by *compradores* employed by the banks, who guaranteed loans in return for commission on business introduced or guaranteed.[55] Chinese business was important for all the banks, but especially for a smaller one such as the Mercantile Bank which held few of the accounts of the British agency houses which usually went to the Chartered and Hongkong Banks. A Chinese rubber firm was described as the 'lifeblood' of Mercantile's Singapore branch in 1946.[56] The Mercantile Bank also had substantial 'bazaar' business in the

6.3 *The Penang office of the Hongkong and Shanghai Bank in the late nineteenth century.*

inter-war years, lending funds in Kuala Lumpur and other branches to Chettiars, originally a South Indian caste of money-lenders, who on-lent them at higher rates of interest.

The British banks faced little competition from local rivals before the 1930s. The first Singaporean Chinese bank was founded in 1903, but it was not until the following decade that three effective Chinese institutions emerged, which came together as the Overseas Chinese Banking Corporation in 1932.[57] This was a well-managed, conservative bank which soon made inroads into the businesses of the British banks even before the Second World War.

Between the 1920s and the 1950s a fixed pattern of business evolved in Malayan banking which gave it some semblance to the oligopolistic structures in the Western-owned sectors of the rubber and tin industries. The Chartered and Hongkong Banks stood at the apex of the banking system in Malaya and Singapore. 'The Chartered and Hongkong Banks have grown immensely powerful', Mercantile's Singapore manager bemoaned in 1949. 'They control practically all the cash and dictate to the exchange market in collusion with one another.'[58] The two banks divided up the business of Malaya's two leading industries: Chartered had the lion's share of the tin business while Hongkong Bank had much of the rubber trade. The banks were also established in different geographical areas: Mercantile's branches were concentrated on the east coast, Hong-

6.4 The Kuala Trengganu agency of the Mercantile Bank of India, 1940.

kong Bank's on the west coast, and Chartered's in central and northern Malaya. As in the tin industry, business strategies were influenced by considerations outside Malaya. Mercantile's Singapore Manager, for example, was warned in 1952 by his superiors not to encroach on the business of the Hongkong Bank for fear of 'unpleasant repercussions elsewhere': the Hongkong Bank had the power to destroy Mercantile's small but lucrative business in Hong Kong and its ire must not be aroused.[59] Yet there was competition within this oligopolistic structure. There was rivalry between Chartered and the Hongkong Bank and between them and other banks. The timing of Mercantile's expansion on the east coast in the inter-war years was conditioned by fears that the Chartered Bank would pre-empt them. In 1927 Mercantile's Singapore Manager was ordered by his London office to ask the governments of Kelantan, Trengganu and Pahang where they wanted future branches to be opened: 'it is of paramount importance that we should not be forestalled in opening an agency by another Bank'.[60]

6.6 British business since 1945: diversification and *Bumiputra*

The most striking aspect of the history of British business in Malaya and Singapore since the Second World War was the extent to which the large British groups which had been formed in the early decades of the century retained their leading positions in the local economies until the mid-1970s, despite the granting of independence from Britain in 1957. Commodity production, in turn, remained the backbone of the Malayan economy. In 1960 Malaya produced 32% of the world's tin and 35% of the world's rubber, and its position as a leading world commodity producer was strengthened over the following two decades. In 1980 Malaysia produced 40% of the world's tin, 50% of its rubber, 60% of its palm oil and most of its pepper.

The tin industry remained largely in British hands: the London Tin Corporation, for example, controlled 15–17% of Malaysian production in 1975. Malaysia's largest rubber plantation estates were in the hands of the British agency houses, led by Guthries, Sime Darby and Harrison and Crosfield. Sime Darby in 1975 was the largest foreign-owned company on the Malay Peninsula. In addition after the War there was a new entrant to the plantation sector in the form of the Anglo-Dutch multinational Unilever. In 1947 Unilever acquired a war-damaged plantation in Johore. By 1960 the company owned 11,400 planted acres in Malaya, mostly for palm oil cultivation, and although this formed only a small proportion of Unilever's world-wide plantation interests, it proved – in the words of one of the firm's historians – an 'excellent investment'. Unilever also established a palm oil plantation from virgin jungle in North Borneo in 1960.[61]

British control over the tin companies and agency houses was maintained in the post-war period despite a shift in equity ownership from Britain to Malaya and Singapore. For example, while in 1954 nearly 78% of shares in 'dollar' tin dredging companies were held abroad, mainly in Britain, by 1964 this had fallen to 36%.[62] Even the ownership of some of the agency houses shifted away from Britain. In 1976 Sime Darby estimated that only 10% of its shareholders were domiciled in Britain, compared to 48% in Singapore, 36% in Malaysia and 6% in Hong Kong.[63] Political uncertainties – the Emergency from 1948–1960, independence, uncertainties over Singapore's position, 'confrontation' with Indonesia between 1963 and 1966, British withdrawal from East of Suez – all acted to deter British investors from buying Malaysian stocks, facilitating the transfer of shares away from Britain.[64] Yet through interlocking directorships and strategic minority shareholdings the agency houses retained control of many tin and rubber companies, while houses such as Sime Darby retained British boardrooms and senior

180 *Jean-Jacques van Helten and Geoffrey Jones*

managements by keeping the confidence of their increasingly predominant but fragmented Asian shareholders.

The transformation in the business of the agency houses was equally notable.[65] They moved from plantation management and trading to manufacturing. In 1970 at least 70% of British investment in Malaysia was still in agriculture and mining. Yet the 1960s in particular saw the growth of manufacturing investment and by the end of that decade the estimated book value of British holdings in local manufacturing was £19.2 million or 10.5% of total British investment in Malaysia. To the surprise of some observers who anticipated that the agency houses would not favour local manufacturing because of their vested interests in the primary sector and importing, the firms played a leading role in promoting and channelling British investment into manufacturing. The agency houses had traditionally acted as agents for distributing and selling British goods in Malaya. When independence and the erection of some protective tariff barriers in the 1960s, along with increased international competition, threatened these markets, both the British manufacturers and the agency houses faced a loss of business which made a strategy of local manufacture desirable. The agency houses smoothed the entry of British firms into local manufacturing and made available their marketing, financial and managerial expertise in the local market to the newly established companies in the manufacturing sector. Some of the agency houses acquired manufacturing operations on their own account. By the 1970s British manufacturing concerns in Malaysia covered a wide variety of industries with well over half of manufacturing establishments in the groups covering food, drink and tobacco manufacturing; chemical, rubber and metal products manufacturing; and the processing of agricultural products.

The British agency houses did not restrict their diversification to Malaysian manufacturing. During the 1950s many of them began to pursue strategies of vertical and horizontal integration which took them both into neighbouring countries, such as Thailand, and industrialised countries, especially Britain, Australia and the United States. In the early 1950s, for example, Harrison and Crosfield acquired a fine chemicals manufacturer in the United States. In the 1960s Guthries invested in rubber goods and carpet manufacturing in Britain. These new investments necessitated changes to corporate structures, with the agency houses constructing 'pyramid-shaped' organisations which comprised a British-registered company controlling a range of often locally registered companies in Malaysia and elsewhere.

The operations of British business continued to be assisted by a 'favourable' political context, despite the military and political instability in the region for much of the two decades after the end of the Second

British business in Malaysia & Singapore since the 1870s   181

World War. British administration lasted a decade longer than in India, and economic policies remained sympathetic to British commercial interests if by no means the result of pressure from them. Rubber policy until the mid-1950s, for instance, continued to favour the estates. Only in 1955, as independence approached, were policy changes made which began to restore the competitive advantages of the smallholders.[66]

British policy-makers would have been reluctant to adopt policies which might have disrupted the activities of the British commodity producers because of Malaya's significance in the Sterling Area in the post-war period, when sterling's role as an international currency came under increasing threat.[67] During 1948 and 1949, when Britain ran huge deficits with the Dollar Area, Malaya emerged as one of the very few Sterling Area countries whose current accounts with the Dollar Area were in surplus, particularly because of rubber exports to the United States. Its dollar earnings were boosted by the 1950–1 commodities boom during the Korean War: the value of Malaya's rubber exports, for example, accelerated from 558 million Malayan dollars in 1949 to 2,279 million in 1951.[68] Malaya in this period was 'the principal dollar earner of the Sterling Area', and on one calculation over the three years 1948–50 it contributed net about $US 650 million to the Sterling Area's reserves.[69] In the mid-1950s Malaya remained, in the words of a Foreign Office report in 1956, 'the largest earner of non-Sterling currency' of all the Sterling Area countries in Asia: its dollar surpluses on current account of $US 37 million in 1954 and $US 68 million in 1955 were unrivalled.[70] By the first half of the 1950s, too, Malaya had emerged as the United Kingdom's second most important trading partner in Asia, after India, and the second most important area for British investment, again after India.

After independence the Malaysian government continued to welcome foreign capital, and steered clear of a direct interventionist role in the industrial sector on the lines pursued by Indian governments. A number of British civil servants remained in post for some years after independence, and even subsequently an 'old boy network' between British executives and Malaysian civil servants persisted.[71]

Singapore after its withdrawal from Malaysia in 1965 was an even more hospitable location for British business. With the loss of open access to its natural hinterland, the government decided to pursue a policy of export-led growth. Foreign manufacturing companies were attracted to Singapore by a variety of incentives schemes, by political stability, by restrictive labour legislation and by government infrastructure investment which made the island an attractive site. Singapore also retained the traditional free-trade policy, avoiding export restrictions, and taxes and foreign exchange controls.[72] As a result of these factors foreign companies played a preponderant role in Singapore's growth as a major manufactur-

182 Jean-Jacques van Helten and Geoffrey Jones

ing centre. In 1982, foreign companies accounted for 55% of the industrial labour force and over 70% of manufacturing exports; whole industries – such as petroleum, electrical machinery and electronic products, and chemicals and pharmaceuticals – were in foreign hands.

British business interests were active in Singapore's post-1965 growth, but perhaps the main noteworthy aspect has been their 'surprisingly small contribution to manufacturing development in Singapore in view of [Britain's] long colonial tradition there'.[73] In 1965, Britain was the largest single source of Singapore's foreign direct investment (29% of the total). By 1982 it was in third place with 16.3% – behind Japan and the United States.[74] British investments were heavily concentrated in food and, especially, petroleum and chemicals. The British share of foreign direct investment in manufacturing was kept high by its part ownership of the Shell Group, which had erected the first petroleum refinery in Singapore in the early 1960s. Shell's operations were the largest single foreign investment in Singapore even in the mid-1980s. However there was evidence during this decade of a renewed interest by British companies in Singapore as a base for manufacturing. This seems to have been mainly in response to Singapore government incentives for foreign investors, though uncertainties about the political future of Hong Kong also enhanced Singapore's attractiveness as a host economy.

British banks remained powerful influences in independent Singapore: although again there was a loss of relative importance which was perhaps surprising in view of their one-dominant hold on the island's banking sector. In 1984 the Hongkong Bank and Standard Chartered Bank (the successor to the old Chartered Bank) were ranked tenth and eleventh amongst Singapore's banks in terms of asset size, behind not only locally registered institutions, but American and Japanese banks and even Crédit Lyonnais of France.[75]

In Malaysia, the general thrust of government policies towards foreign capital was the same direction as Singapore's, at least until 1970, but a more nationalistic tone was audible during the 1960s. The banks were the first British business interests to be affected. During the 1950s the British banks had faced growing competition from the Chinese banks, but competition was intensified in 1960 when two locally registered banks were established – Malayan Banking Berhad and the United Malayan Banking Corporation. These banks competed vigorously for deposits, and for government business which had been the mainstay of several of the branches of the British banks. Within two years the two Malayan banks had thirty and twenty-one branches respectively in the Federation, and their initial progress was facilitated by the transfer to them of considerable government accounts.

The growth of local banks created considerable problems for the

British business in Malaysia & Singapore since the 1870s 183

British banks which had traditionally focussed their business strategies on exchange banking. There was little emphasis on attracting local deposits, which were often provided in sufficient amounts by government funds. *Compradores* were allowed commission on the foreign exchange business they introduced, rather than on any deposit accounts they might attract. Branches were usually located in the centre of business areas of Malayan towns – the best location for attracting foreign exchange business. During the early 1960s, however, the indigenous banks began to compete for exchange business with the British banks. They found themselves having to grant overdrafts or packing credits in order to keep foreign exchange business. This, in turn, obliged the British banks to raise more local resources to fund such lending. However, attracting local deposits was by then more difficult because of the competition of the local banks.[76] The result was extremely uncomfortable: as early as December 1961 Mercantile Bank was bemoaning the 'veritable onslaught on our business resulting from the establishment of so many new banks'.[77]

The British banks responded, in part, with resignation to a situation which was becoming ever more common in many developing countries. 'Nothing we or the other foreign banks can do will prevent the growth of indigenous banking Companies', the Chief Executive of the Mercantile Bank wrote to his Manager in Kuala Lumpur in 1960. 'What we can do is to fight a stubborn rear-guard action whenever this is necessary.'[78] In Mercantile's case, the 'rear-guard action' included a new determination that all its British staff had to speak Malay and to recruit Malays to work in the bank.[79]

These measures were arguably a case of 'too little, too late', for by the mid-1960s the growth of indigenous banks was reinforced by official restrictions on the activities of foreign banks. In 1962 Mercantile's Kuala Lumpur Manager attended a conference with the Governor-designate of the new Central Bank where the latter expressed his opinion that it would only be necessary for foreign banks to open in ports. This opinion provoked an outbreak of hackneyed metaphors in the Bank's London office: 'This is the thin edge of the wedge and the writing is on the wall for foreign banks.'[80] There was, in fact, writing on the wall, for in 1965 foreign banks were prohibited from opening further branches. In the same year a decree excluded all foreign assets in the composition of liquid assets for the purpose of calculating official liquidity ratios: a device to force the banks to undertake more local lending. In the 1970s the lending policies of the banks were subject to even more direct influence, as they were obliged to make a certain proportion of the loans to 'priority' sectors, notably manufacturing and also small-scale firms: one result of these policies was a fall in the Hongkong Bank's loans to agriculture

184 Jean-Jacques van Helten and Geoffrey Jones

from 34% to 15% of its total lending between 1972 and 1981, and a corresponding rise in its loans to manufacturing from 20% to 27%.[81]

Despite these restrictions, British and other foreign banks continued to play a much larger role in the Malaysian economy than in many other Asian economies, such as those of India or Japan, where they were allowed to operate. As at 31 December 1985, the Hongkong Bank was Malaysia's third largest bank in terms of assets, and the fourth largest in terms of deposits. Standard Chartered was in fourth and sixth positions respectively. The two British banks remained the largest foreign banks in the country.

It was not until the 1970s that British preponderance in Malaysia's tin and rubber industries was challenged and overturned. The background was the launching of the New Economic Policy in 1970 as a response to ethnic riots in the previous year. The NEP aimed to restructure the ownership of Malaysian industry, and in particular to increase the ownership shares of the ethnic Malays or *Bumiputras* ('sons of the soil') who formed the majority of the population. The plan formulated under NEP launched a twenty-year strategy to reduce the foreign ownership of Malaysian business enterprises to 30% (from an estimated 62% in 1970); to increase the ownership of non-Malay Malaysians (Chinese and Indians, in practice) from 34% to 40%; and to expand *Bumiputra* ownership from an estimated 4% to 30%. This shift in ownership was not, however, to be achieved by forced sequestration, but by gradual reallocation in the context of a growing economy. In the tin and rubber industries *Bumiputra* policies were implemented by state-owned companies – financed by buoyant government revenues stemming from Malaysia's strong economic growth – in an adroit series of Stock Exchange manoeuvres which defeated British capitalists at their own games on their own home ground.

It was probably the British financier Jim Slater who explained the possibilities of using the London Stock Exchange to further the aims of the NEP to the Malaysian government, and in particular to Tunku Razaleigh, the Chairman of the state-owned oil company Pernas in the early 1970s and later Finance Minister. Slater's property company, Slater Walker, acquired the Singapore firm of Haw Paw in 1971, which was then used as a vehicle to buy a large majority stake in the London Tin Corporation. Slater subsequently approached Tunku Razaleigh who purchased the shares in LTC in 1975. An attempt by Pernas to take full control of LTC was prevented, however, by a major scandal in Singapore concerning Slater and Haw Paw: a scandal which provoked Singapore's Prime Minister to remark that 'there were no English gentlemen left'. However, in 1976 Pernas did launch a successful bid for LTC's shares on the London Stock Exchange in alliance with Charter Consolidated, the British sub-

British business in Malaysia & Singapore since the 1870s   185

6.5 Sime Darby meets Bumiputra, as seen by the Far Eastern Economic Review in 1976.

sidiary of the South African-owned Anglo-American Corporation which had purchased the British-owned Tronoh group of Malayan tin companies in 1965. The Pernas bid made skilful use – probably thanks to Slater's tutoring – of the 'dollar premium' to increase the value of its offer: under British exchange controls operative before 1979, British residents had to pay a premium when they brought back foreign currencies, and this automatically raised the cost and value of foreign stocks to British investors. LTC's and Charter's tin interests were subsequently merged into the Malaysian Mining Corporation, 70% controlled by the government.[82]

During the second half of the 1970s the great British agency houses, which had become visible and unwanted symbols of the colonial past, were brought under Malaysian control in a spectacular series of boardroom coups and share manoeuvres. The agency houses had attempted in some respects to 'localise' themselves: especially after 1957 they had begun to appoint nationals to management posts, and during the 1960s and early 1970s publicly quoted local companies had been registered, which allowed a local shareholding to develop. However in the mid-1970s the government resolved to accelerate this process. Sime Darby, Malaysia's biggest industrial and plantation group which already had (as explained above) only a small British shareholding, was the first bastion to crumble. During 1975 and 1976 Pernas built up a 9% stake in the company, but instead of pursuing an expensive strategy of buying further blocks of shares launched a boardroom coup in November 1976 with a proposal that four of the six British directors due for re-election should be voted out of office and replaced by four Malaysians. The past record of the British management was not ideal – the former Chairman had just served an eighteen-month prison sentence in Singapore for criminal breach of trust – and the coup was successful. The British Chairman resigned, and three Malaysians were elected to the board. There followed a process of slow Malaysianisation. In 1978 the head office moved to Kuala Lumpur; in 1980 legal domicile was shifted from Britain to Malaysia; and British senior managers were slowly replaced by Malaysian nationals.[83]

The other bastions of British business followed one by one. Guthries, unlike Sime Darby, had a large British shareholding and a small Asian one: around 20% in 1979. In 1979 and 1980 it fought off take-over bids from Pernas. However in September 1981 it fell victim to a spectacular 'dawn raid' when a Malaysian government agency (PNB) purchased 8 million of its temporarily depressed shares in a few hours: a 'masterful deal' in the words of one British broker, which, according to another observer, left Guthries' British executives 'with their trousers down around their ankles'.[84] A similar fate befell Harrison and Crosfield, the last remaining large British agency house, in the following year.[85] By 1982 control of most of Malaysia's plantations and tin mines had been brought home.

The early 1980s saw the nadir of British–Malaysian business relations. The British Conservative government's decision in 1980 to raise university fees for foreign students – a move which caused considerable hardship for Malaysia's 16,000 students in Britain – provoked the government into a 'Buy British Last' campaign. Substantial British direct investment, however, remained in the country: Shell, for example, produced with Exxon most of Malaysia's oil and gas. An extremely severe recession in 1984–6 following a collapse of commodity prices promoted a reversal of hostile policies towards British and other foreign investors. Foreign companies were no longer restricted to a 30% maximum holding in their Malaysian associates, provided these associates exported at least 20% of their production, and in certain circumstances foreigners were to be allowed to acquire majority stakes of up to 80%. The fact that the foreign share of Malaysian equity was already far below the 30% target set for 1990 clearly made these measures more politically acceptable. In July 1987 a visit by the Malaysian Prime Minister to London which was specifically designed to attract British investment into Malaysia marked a formal ending of the period of political tension with Britain. Even before this step, in 1986, Britain was the third largest foreign investor in Malaysia, after Singapore and Japan.[86]

6.7 Conclusion

The history of Singapore and Malaya before the First World War provides a prime example of the vigour of British business enterprise in Asia in that period. Singapore was transformed into the dominant entrepôt of Southeast Asia, albeit by the joint efforts of British, Chinese and other Asian traders. Modern banking facilities were provided first in Singapore and then over Peninsular Malaya as British protection was extended. The tin industry was built by the Chinese, but in the 1900s British companies introduced new technologies which transformed the industry. British interests virtually created Malaya's rubber and palm oil industries. Sarawak's modern gold and petroleum industries were the product of British enterprise.

During the inter-war years the era of pioneering was replaced by one of consolidation and participation in international cartels. While it would be plausible to cast British business in this period as restrictive and in some cases corrupt, the mergers in tin and the control of the plantation companies by the agency houses seem — although the evidence is still sparse — to have brought managerial and technical benefits to those industries. In the comparative perspective of the other countries considered in this volume, the most striking feature of British business in the region since 1945 has been its survival and, indeed, growth. The willingness of the traditional agency houses to diversify into manufacturing in the 1960s was an unexpected sign of entrepreneurial vitality. If in the 1970s and 1980s some of the old bastions of British business were left with their 'trousers down around their ankles', for the most part British enterprise continued to prosper, even though it became relatively less important for the local economies.

It is not necessary to espouse a romantic view of British business to argue that it made a positive contribution to the Malayan and Singaporean economies. It was by no means solely responsible for their growth, but the introduction of new products, technologies and services formed an indispensable part of that growth. The major period for which such an optimistic interpretation looks tarnished is the inter-war years, when Malaya (and non-British rubber and tin producers in Malaya) was probably treated unfairly in the international commodity agreements. However the responsibility for any misallocation of quotas rests far more with the British and colonial governments (pursuing their own strategies and interests) than with private British business. And the price stabilisation schemes at least guaranteed an income for Malaya's two leading industries without which the whole economy would have been in serious trouble.

Why has British business been 'successful' in Malaysia and Singapore over the last hundred – or more – years? Clearly the geographical location and natural resources of the countries provided an excellent base. The low population density gave British planters the opportunity to introduce rubber and, later, palm oil production. A dynamic local business community, the Chinese in particular, provided partners and a means to engage in inter-Asian commerce. The Chinese also provided competition which may have encouraged a vigorous British response.

However, the fundamental difference between Malaysia and Singapore and many other countries was political. The British colonial governments were not the 'tools' of British business: they had their own concerns and ideologies. Yet the policies they pursued – free trade in Singapore, then the 'opening up' of Peninsular Malaya under British political influence from the 1870s supported by substantial infrastructure investment – provided the ideal conditions for British business to flourish. The British rubber companies were given particular assistance by the colonial administration, which for a number of reasons discriminated against smallholders over a long period. The British estates would, arguably, not have survived smallholder competition in the inter-war years without such official protection. In the early 1920s the British government also acted to protect the British estates from American predators. The British tin interests, however, received less direct government help.

The colonial heritage gave British business a powerful position when independence came in 1957: the willingness of the new sovereign governments to continue the general economic policies inherited from the past enabled British enterprise to continue to exist and expand. Malaysia came nearest to disturbing the favourable political context with its *Bumiputra* policies in the 1970s: yet even then the challenge to British business came not from expropriation or penal taxes or controls but by boardroom coups and 'dawn raids' on the London Stock Exchange. By the mid-1980s, moreover, a more hospitable climate for British investment had been restored. Malaysia and Singapore, therefore, provided the conditions for British business to succeed in those sectors in which its greatest strengths have been over the last century: extractive industries, commerce and banking.

7 British business in China, 1860s–1950s

Jürgen Osterhammel

7.1 Introduction

The historical role of foreign business in any comparatively less developed country can be analysed from at least four different points of view. From a *global* perspective that takes 'international society' or the 'modern world-system' as its principal unit of reference, foreign business is one among several mechanisms which contribute to the integration of 'peripheral' societies into universal political, economic and cultural structures as they have been shaped by Europe from the early modern period onwards. In this view, foreign business is a vehicle of general processes of system-building; its overall effects can alternatively be interpreted as inculcating modernity and occidental rationality into non-Western civilisations or as incorporating the agrarian societies of the East and South into the world-system in positions of inferiority and dependency. An *imperial* perspective adopts a more narrow focus. It looks out into the world from one of the dynamic capitalist centres and examines business operations in terms of the projection of metropolitan resources (people, technology, commodities, capital, etc.) into areas of the globe that have been linked up with a particular imperial system either through direct rule ('formal empire') or through indirect control ('informal empire'). In business history, this corresponds to a view from headquarters and to an analysis in terms of entrepreneurial strategies. By contrast, an *expatriate* perspective shifts the angle of observation to foreign enterprise 'on the spot'; it tells the story of Western firms and businessmen operating in non-capitalist or semi-capitalist economic environments and non-Western cultures. Finally, the *indigenous* (or host country) perspective poses the most difficult question of all, that of the 'impact' of the West on 'Third World' economies and societies. In particular it examines the ways in which various indigenous groups and classes respond to intrusion from abroad.

Of course, these four approaches are by no means mutually exclusive. On the contrary, it is a challenge to historical interpretation to try to connect the different levels and perspectives in a manner that combines

190 *Jürgen Osterhammel*

empirical richness and theoretical subtlety.[1] This chapter pursues a much more modest aim. It takes up the expatriate perspective, with occasional glances at the imperial and the indigenous side, and attempts a bird's-eye view of the activities of British business in China over roughly a century from the opening of China's interior in 1860 to the final winding-up of British business there in the mid-1950s.

7.2 The nineteenth century: the age of trade

In the nineteenth century, the Asian empires east of India were one by one opened up by the force of Western arms. Their military might was broken; their rulers were humbled; they had to accede to the diplomatic conventions of the European powers such as the stationing of permanent representatives abroad, the establishment of Ministries of Foreign Affairs and finally the acceptance of the standards of international law as they had emerged in early modern Europe;[2] treaties were imposed upon them that granted privileges to Western traders and travellers, soldiers and missionaries; native political and administrative institutions, especially those connected with the collection of revenue, were subjected to varying degrees of foreign control; eventually, spheres of influence were carved out, protectorates declared and territories brought under colonial rule. By 1910, Burma, the principalities and kingdoms of Malaya and Indochina, the Philippines, Korea, large areas in Central Asia, one Chinese province in its entirety (Taiwan), and parts of the province of Shandong had been absorbed into the colonial empires of Britain, France, the United States, Japan, Russia and Germany. They joined the old Dutch empire in the East Indies. China, of course, escaped partition and wholesale occupation. In this, however, it was not unique, Japan and Siam sharing the same good fortune. China's uniqueness lies in the fact that it had been connected with the international economy long before it was incorporated, from 1842 onwards, into the international political system. In a sense, this was also true for Japan: until about 1680, European merchants regarded Japan as a more promising trading partner than China.[3] But Japan strictly enforced its own seclusion,[4] whereas China allowed maritime trade along its south-eastern littoral, increasingly concentrated on the port of Canton (Guangzhou), to grow into one of the most important sub-systems of the international economy in the eighteenth century.

By 1715 the commercial mechanisms of the Canton trade had been established in their basic form.[5] On the Chinese side foreign trade was conducted as 'administered' trade – in the words of a modern historian, 'perhaps the most efficient mechanism for exchange between societies that differed in economic assumptions but were not prepared to press their case against each other too vigorously'.[6] On the Western side, chartered

British business in China, 1860s–1950s 191

companies predominated, chief among them the British East India Company (EIC). The EIC stood at the centre of a vast intercontinental trading network; it was a huge and complex organisation by the standards of the time and operated in the manner of a 'pre-modern multinational organization'.[7] The EIC lost its India monopoly in 1813, but retained its monopoly of the China trade for another twenty years.[8] Yet, from the late 1780s onwards, the predominance of the EIC was increasingly eroded by two new factors in Far Eastern business. One factor was the American private traders who had firmly entrenched themselves in the Canton trade by the 1820s.[9] The second factor was British agency houses extending their activities from Bengal to the China coast. They soon became indispensable to the Company as, among other things, the main suppliers to the Chinese market of opium and cotton goods, thus financing the EIC's export of tea from Canton.[10]

A number of agency houses fell victim to a series of crises that affected the fragile credit basis of the 'private' China trade.'[11] But when Britain sealed its victory in the first Opium War with the Treaty of Nanjing (1842), several British firms were ready to exploit the new opportunities offered by a system of limited free trade that included the opening of five 'treaty ports' (among them Shanghai), the cession of Hong Kong, the abolition of the Chinese monopoly, the establishment of consular representation, and the fixation of a uniform and 'moderate' tariff. However, the more extravagant hopes were soon dashed. While the illegal opium trade continued to grow, Western legal trade, especially that in British cotton goods, came up against Chinese resistance in various forms: a simple lack of demand for Western commodities, the resilience of indigenous trading networks, high taxation of imported goods outside the treaty ports, and a general defensive reaction which the British were quick to denounce as Chinese 'xenophobia'. A second treaty settlement was imposed on China in 1858 and 1860: another twelve treaty ports were opened (at least on paper) to commerce; extraterritoriality was extended; the entire interior of China was made accessible to foreign travellers; above all, foreign shipping was now allowed to enter the river Yangzi – China's main artery for traffic between the coast and the interior.

The years from 1860 to 1895 saw the rise of Sino–Western commercial capitalism in and around the major treaty ports.[12] There was little change in the composition of foreign trade, opium from India continuing to be the leading import item until 1890, with tea and silk contributing the bulk of China's exports. The import of cotton piece goods increased considerably, but the allegedly limitless potential of the Chinese market for the sale of European manufactured goods was still not realised. By 1896 China absorbed (in value terms) little more than about 8% of the exports of the British cotton industry compared to 27% for India.[13] Still, the entire

192 *Jürgen Osterhammel*

foreign trade of China was handled by foreign firms, and the most important of them were British. Throughout the 1860s opium was the mainstay of their business.[14] In the 1870s, the largest firms reduced their dependence on opium and began their transformation into managing agencies increasingly concerned with auxiliary services – shipping, insurance, banking and treaty port utilities.[15] The buying and selling of commodities was downgraded to one of several lines of business; it was increasingly done on commission rather than on the firm's own account. When large companies, such as the old opium traders Jardine Matheson & Co. and Dent & Co., decided to diversify, this was partly in response to growing competition in the old lines of trade. The improvement of overseas communication, especially after the introduction of the telegraph in the 1870s,[16] and the easier availability of credit due, among other factors, to the founding of 'local' banks, above all the Hongkong and Shanghai Banking Corporation (1866),[17] attracted a multitude of adventurous businessmen. In the 1890s there were about 400 British firms in the treaty ports.[18] Only a handful of them, however, extended their activities beyond Shanghai and Hong Kong and engaged in mass distribution of goods; the majority catered to the needs of Europeans and wealthy Chinese in the treaty ports.

Even those British firms which, in the nineteenth century, established agencies outside Shanghai and Hong Kong seldom managed to assume direct control of 'up-country' trade for any length of time. The distribution of cotton imports remained firmly in Chinese hands,[19] and the foreign exporters of tea and silk received the finished product through long chains of indigenous middlemen.[20] The China market not only proved remarkably resistant to penetration by foreign business organisations, but the Chinese also quickly learned to seize the new opportunities. From the very beginning of treaty port trade, Western merchants had to rely on the expertise and the business connections of their Chinese *compradores*. These *compradores* and their associates soon began to invest in foreign firms, thus benefiting, among other things, from extraterritorial protection. A considerable number of small British companies virtually subsisted on Chinese credit and most of the large multi-functional China houses took Chinese capital into partnership.[21]

Several of the early industrial ventures initiated by foreigners were also supported by Chinese investors. For example, Jardine Matheson's 'Ewo Silk Filature', opened in Shanghai in 1882, was financed 40% by foreign and 60% by Chinese capital.[22] In general, there was little foreign industrial investment before 1895, and the shipyards, silk filatures and brick tea factories (the latter in Russian ownership) that had been established in Shanghai, Hankou and elsewhere[23] were justly regarded as illegal by the Chinese. The most spectacular industrial enterprises of the

British business in China, 1860s–1950s 193

period were those sponsored by high Chinese officials as part of their programme of 'self-strengthening';[24] they relied heavily on imported machinery and raw materials and on the highly paid services of Western experts – some of them of dubious qualifications.[25] Western firms did not regard these official ventures as serious competition. They rather sought to cooperate with those factions within the Chinese bureaucracy that were inclined towards development and modernisation, sometimes, as in the case of Jardine Matheson, eager to attain the position of a 'special agent to the Chinese government'.[26]

By the mid-1890s the structural foundations had been laid for the further expansion of British business in China: the legal framework of the unequal treaties had been worked out; the instruments of foreign influence and coercion, ranging from consular networks to gunboat fleets, had been deployed; a few old-established British firms had managed to transform themselves from opium-trading agency houses to widely diversified managing agents and were ready to take the next step towards being fully developed investment groups;[27] several other large companies had entered China after 1860, most prominent among them Butterfield & Swire (1867); banking and insurance requirements could be met by facilities specifically tailored to local needs. Cooperation at various levels with Chinese merchants had been practised and routinised to the extent of the emergence of a kind of symbiotic Sino-foreign commercial capitalism; the Imperial Maritime Customs had been thoroughly reorganised from 1861 onwards by the energetic Ulsterman, Sir Robert Hart;[28] the main shipping routes in ocean traffic as well as in Chinese coastal and inland waters had been explored and were now regularly used by steamships under the British flag;[29] finally, Shanghai had outstripped all the other treaty ports and had evolved into a second centre, next to Hong Kong, of the British mercantile system in China. However the disproportionate growth of the expatriate communities of Shanghai, and the increasing concentration of foreign business there at the expense of treaty ports like Hankou or Fuzhou, was a symptom of the difficulties in penetrating or replacing the commercial institutions of a tightly organised pre-modern society.

7.3 Completing the system, 1895–1914

Imperialism in China was never the unchallenged domain of any one great power. From its very beginning in 1842, the treaty system, with the most-favoured-nation clause as an essential component, was a multinational instrument. Even so, there can be no doubt that Britain predominated among the foreign powers in China – in political-military as well as in economic terms – until the last decade of the nineteenth century.

7.1 *The Shanghai manager of the Hongkong and Shanghai Bank (A. G. Stephen, who became Chief Manager of the Bank in 1920) poses seated, around 1910, with his* compradore *standing behind him.*

Thereafter, new powers appeared on the scene and others increased their aggressive policies. Against these late-comers, Britain found itself in a basically defensive position; this became apparent, at the latest, with the conclusion of the Anglo–Japanese Alliance in 1902. It is, however, easy to exaggerate the importance of the numerous 'scrambles' and diplomatic rows over China between the European and American powers around the

British business in China, 1860s–1950s 195

turn of the century. Below the level of high diplomacy, cooperation between the representatives of civilisation (including the Japanese who had been promoted to the status of 'honorary whites', especially after their victory over Russia in 1905)[30] in a 'semi-barbarian' environment characterised the daily routine of foreign preponderance. Moreover, the dramatic struggles between the powers during the period 1895–1905 soon gave way to a new unanimity and fairly clear demarcation of interests. On the eve of the First World War the governments of the major powers and the heads of East Asian big business were looking back at two decades of largely successful joint subjugation and *mise en valeur* of China.

During that period the emphasis shifted from trade to investment. Investment in sectors of the economy not immediately connected with foreign trade became the most promising form of expansion for British business in China. Investment in turn stimulated various new lines of trade. An increasing proportion of imports comprised equipment for the railways, factories and mines that now appeared in China. British investments in China in 1914 have been estimated at around US$600 million (equivalent of around £120 million), two-thirds of which were direct investments and one-third obligations of the Chinese government.[31] The total was the equivalent of about one-third of British investments in India and Ceylon. Among non-colonial recipients of British investments in Asia, Africa and Latin America, China (including the Crown Colony of Hong Kong) ranked third after Argentina (US$1,550 million) and Brazil (US$700 million), and before Japan and Mexico (US$500 million each).[32] In other words, China received more British capital than any other Asian country except India.

According to C. F. Remer's estimates, about US$100 million, that is, one-fourth of total British business investments in China, went into manufacturing.[33] The establishment of manufacturing industry in the treaty ports was legalised by the Treaty of Shimonoseki in 1895. A great variety of small industrial enterprises sprang up, but only very few large-scale British plants were constructed. Significantly, the early attempts to gain a foothold in the silk reeling industry had to be abandoned and were never again revived. From around the turn of the century, the silk industry was almost exclusively developed by Chinese capital, although the export of silk remained entirely in foreign hands.[34] By far the most important industrial newcomer to China was the British American Tobacco Corporation (BAT). Soon after the foundation of BAT in 1902 as a result of an alliance between the American Tobacco Company and the Imperial Tobacco Company of England, the new firm applied its innovative recipe – the integration of mass cigarette production with mass cigarette consumption[35] – to China, taking over two existing

196 *Jürgen Osterhammel*

7.2 *A sampling crew and advertising placard bearers for British American Tobacco's Swallow brand at Kirin, central Manchuria.*

Western-owned cigarette factories in 1902 and building new plants in Shanghai, Hankou, Mukden (Shenyang) and Harbin. By 1915, these factories employed 13,000 workers – more than any other Chinese or Western industrial enterprise in China. In the same year BAT valued its China branch at US$16.6 million.[36] The majority of BAT's capital was in American hands until at least 1915 and an American, James B. Duke, was Chairman of BAT's board until 1923.[37] Its history as a British-based multinational should therefore properly be told in the next section of this chapter.

The other major industrial enterprises were initiated by the two leading general-purpose investment groups – Jardine Matheson & Co. ('Ewo') and John Swire & Sons who were represented in China by the partnership of Butterfield & Swire ('Taikoo').[38] Swires never went into large-scale manufacturing in the treaty ports, preferring investment in Hong Kong, where the Taikoo Sugar Refinery was opened in 1884. Originally it was intended to supply sugar to Japan, Australia and the United States, but from 1898 China was its principal market.[39] A smaller sugar factory had already been established by Jardine Matheson in 1876. Both companies also possessed huge dockyards in Hong Kong: Jardine Matheson owned the Hongkong and Whampoa Dock Company Ltd (established in 1865) and Swires the Taikoo Dockyard (founded in 1908). In 1895 Jardine

Matheson opened a cotton mill in Shanghai; a second mill was added in 1914. In contrast to the mass manufacture of cigarettes, industrial cotton spinning and weaving was not entirely new to China. The foreigners entered a field that had already been pioneered by Chinese officials and entrepreneurs.[40] By 1913, Western-owned factories, among which the Ewo mills were the largest, accounted for some 27% of spindles installed in the whole of China.[41]

A second field of investment that was effectively closed to foreigners during the nineteenth century was mining. Although the Treaty of Shimonoseki did not explicitly permit foreign investment in mining, the example of manufacturing industry proved to be contagious. Moreover, mining interests also profited from China's reduced ability to withstand the invasion of foreign capital. Foreigners who wished to open a mine in China were still required to obtain a licence from the Chinese government, but such licences were now often granted, sometimes in response to direct pressure exercised by foreign diplomats, sometimes because the Chinese government – desperate to raise funds in order to be able to pay the indemnity to Japan – was hoping for revenue from increased mineral taxes.[42]

In 1898–9, the golden years for concession hunters, British subjects obtained five concessions and licences for exploiting coal deposits.[43] However, several of the concessionaires lacked the financial resources actually to open and work coal mines; moreover, from 1903 the Chinese leaders in the capital and in the provinces implemented a defiant policy of withholding new permits and recovering alienated mining rights. On the eve of the Revolution of 1911 which toppled the monarchy, four out of five concessions had been redeemed or had proved to be unenforceable in the face of local opposition.[44] The only concession that was actually worked was that granted to the Pekin Syndicate, an Anglo–Italian combination, for the exploitation of coalfields in Henan province. The Syndicate produced its first coal in 1907. In 1914 its annual output amounted to 482,000 tons.[45] Opposition from a rival Chinese mining company was overcome when, in 1915, a joint sales organisation was established.[46] The main effect of this arrangement was political: the Pekin Syndicate became largely immune to pressure from the Henan provincial government.

British control of China's most important modern coal mine, Kaiping in Hebei province (North China), did not derive from any concession. The Kaiping mines had been established in 1878 as a semi-official company; in the early 1880s they were a 'going concern'.[47] Production expanded during the 1890s; simultaneously the mine fell increasingly under foreign financial control.[48] An outright foreign take-over was made possible in 1900 when during the rebellion of the Yihetuan (the 'Boxers') Kaiping's

198 *Jürgen Osterhammel*

Chinese management sought protection under the British flag. Clever manoeuvering on the part of two 'advisers' to the Chinese government, the German Gustav Detring and the American Herbert Hoover, ensured that within months ownership of Kaiping had passed into the hands of the newly formed Chinese Engineering and Mining Co. Ltd, an Anglo–Belgian syndicate based in London.[49] To counter the further expansion of the British Kaiping mines, Yuan Shikai, the Governor-General of Zhili (Hebei) established the Luanzhou Mining Co. Ltd in an adjacent area. In 1912, a joint organisation was formed under the name of Kailuan Mining Administration (KMA) to be responsible for mining operations and the selling of coal. In other respects, the two partners remained independent, but *de facto* control rested with the foreign side and in particular with the almost omnipotent British General Manager.[50] Throughout the first half of the twentieth century, the KMA continued to be the largest and most modern coal mine in China outside Manchuria. Among many British contemporaries it enjoyed the reputation of being 'an outstanding example of successful co-operation between Chinese and foreign interests',[51] while Chinese authors complained about the continuous usurpation of Chinese rights by the British partners.[52]

Remer estimated British investment in Chinese coal mining at US$15 million in 1914.[53] This is much less than investment in each of the categories of manufacturing, import–export, banking and finance, and real estate holdings at Shanghai (no less than US$87 million!) and elsewhere. The KMA was a powerful company with an enormous impact on the history of mining in China, but on the whole coal mining was only of subordinate importance within the system of British economic interests in China. Most importantly, the KMA and, to a much lesser extent, the smaller Pekin Syndicate were integrated into this system as suppliers of fuel to steamers and railways, power stations and steam-powered factories. Both exported only a fraction of their output, and although foreign-produced coal was not exclusively consumed by expatriate customers, coal mining certainly fulfilled an important function in relation to other British business interests.[54]

In several ways, mining and railways were closely connected. Railways were indispensable for the transportation of coal; in turn, they were one of its major consumers. Also, the development of railways as well as that of mines required concessionary permission from the host government since both fields were considered closely related to the question of national sovereignty. There were a number of 'colonial railways' in early twentieth-century China: the Russian Chinese Eastern Railway, the Japanese South-Manchurian Railway and the French Yunnan Railway. These lines were fully owned and politically controlled by foreigners. The British possessed only a small section of this kind: that part of the Canton–

British business in China, 1860s–1950s 199

Kowloon Railway, opened to traffic in 1910–11, that crossed the territory leased in 1898 and ended at the southern tip of Kowloon peninsula. British interests in Chinese railways were financial and ought to be classified as portfolio investments. In other words, British capital was invested alongside and in various combinations with funds from other capital-exporting countries in the construction of railways which remained under the at least nominal ownership and under the operational control of the Chinese authorities. In contrast, for example, to Argentina there were no major British-run railways in China. Of course, profitable opportunities existed for British bondholders and British financial middlemen, the most important of whom was the British and Chinese Corporation, established in 1898 as a joint venture of the Hongkong and Shanghai Banking Corporation and Jardine Matheson & Co. The Corporation was a major factor in the financing of China's railways: 'Between the Sino–Japanese War [1895] and World War I, the Chinese signed contracts for foreign railway loans that totalled about £75,000,000. Of this sum, at least £16,000,000 consisted of loans arranged exclusively by the British and Chinese Corporation, while another £22,000,000 consisted of loans in which the corporation shared in the syndication.'[55] Providing funds for the construction of railways, however, did not automatically lead to a comparable volume of sales of railway materials. On the contrary, competitive bidding for construction was the rule. As a result Britain, which was by far the leading source of railway loans to the Chinese government during the period 1898–1912, only came fourth behind Belgium, the United States and Germany as a supplier of rails and rolling stock.[56]

Financial railway concessions differed in the terms of control obtained by the foreign leaders. The differences were mainly in control of construction, control of expenditure and control of receipts. The outcome of bargaining depended in each individual case on a number of factors: availability of capital from alternative sources, cooperation or competition between different foreign interests, policy and scope of action of the Chinese side (which comprised the central government as well as provincial elite groups), diplomatic support by representatives of the foreign powers, etc.[57] Much more than any other field of British economic interests in China, the financing of Chinese railways was a matter of international diplomacy, top-level negotiations with the Chinese authorities, and cooperation between the British government and private companies, above all the Hongkong and Shanghai Banking Corporation.[58] Railway questions were debated at the highest echelons where the more mundane interests of merchants and manufacturers were seldom attended to. Yet ultimately the era of fully fledged railway imperialism (apart from the special case of Manchuria) was little more than a spectacular interlude

200 Jürgen Osterhammel

that did not survive beyond the First World War. By 1911, 2,488 miles of line built under foreign financial concessions had been opened to traffic; between 1912 and 1927 only 1,083 miles of this type of railway were added.[59] When China declined into the turmoils of military factionalism and internal war from the late 1910s onwards, the railways suffered enormously. Those railway loans that were mainly secured on current earnings went into default, and by 1930 hardly any railway loan was serviced at all.[60] An adjustment of China's railway debts was negotiated between 1933 and 1937. This was the condition for China's renewed ability to raise loans in international capital markets.[61] After 1911, China's railway development proceeded comparatively slowly. By 1928, its railway mileage (including Manchuria, not including Taiwan) was less than one-sixth that of British India and roughly equivalent to the mileage of Bavaria and Saxony put together.[62] After about 1914 foreign financiers of China's railways were primarily occupied with limiting and recovering their losses rather than with plans for new expansion.

7.4 Holding the line, 1914 to 1937

Writing two years after the Japanese attack on Pearl Harbor, E. Manico Gull, the experienced Secretary to the London-based China Association, characterised the years from 1842 to 1914 as 'our cock-of-the-walk period in China'.[63] During the inter-war period the British position in China declined when seen in relation to the rapid expansion of Japanese investment in China and to the rise of the United States and, in the early 1930s, Germany as the most dynamic trading nations in China. The international economic situation was more unstable than before 1914, a harsher commercial climate prevailed in the Far East, and the political consensus among the foreign powers that had been the hallmark of the imperialist *belle époque* was seriously impaired during the First World War and ultimately collapsed in the Manchurian Crisis of 1931–2. Still, it is easy to paint too gloomy a picture and to assume from the decline of British business elsewhere in Asia that a similar trend occurred in China. In fact, it may be argued that British business coped fairly well in circumstances that were dominated by the growth of indigenous and third-country competition, by the decline of British military power and political influence in the East, by civil war and the rise of nationalism in China and, in the early 1930s, by the Great Depression. When the war between Japan and China began in the summer of 1937, important sectors of British business in China had good reasons for looking forward to a prosperous future.

Compared to the preceding decades the period 1914–37 (to paraphrase E. M. Gull again) gains in interest what it loses in simplicity.[64] It is indeed difficult to chart the course of British business during these eventful years and to arrive at meaningful generalisations. A suitable starting point is perhaps the question: what had changed by 1936–7, compared to the situation in 1914?

In absolute terms, British investments in China were about double the amount of those in 1914, while the British had managed to retain their share of about 35% of total foreign investment.[65] This was achieved in spite of the fact that British interests except BAT and the Hongkong and Shanghai Banking Corporation were virtually excluded from Manchuria after 1932. Direct investments accounted for an even larger share than before of British capital invested in China, the proportion of obligations of the Chinese government (foreign borrowing by private Chinese individuals and firms was negligible)[66] having declined from 34 to 13%.[67] Even if we take a sceptical view of the high estimates for British investments in 1936, the fact remains that there was no economic retreat from China parallel to the contraction of British military power and diplomatic influence in the region. The continuing existence or even the expansion of business investments, of course, has to be separated from the question of returns on these investments. Data are scarce and difficult to interpret, but it is safe to conclude that most of the leading British firms quite successfully weathered a sequence of political and economic crises which caused some major Chinese enterprises to fail. Some companies, like Dodwell & Company (the shipping agents and import–export merchants) and the Hong Kong-based Green Island Cement Company suffered substantial losses in the early 1930s; the Kailuan Mining Administration experienced difficulties between 1929 and 1936; the Pekin Syndicate got into political trouble in 1925 and kept its mines closed between 1927 and 1933; and the China General Omnibus Company did not earn profits for several years in the early 1930s. On the other hand, BAT, the Ewo Cotton Mills and some of the public utility companies in Shanghai were highly successful throughout the period. Others, like the Hongkong and Shanghai Banking Corporation and the Chartered Bank of India, Australia and China, suffered a reduction of profits during the first half of the 1930s, but recovered towards the end of the period.[68]

If we compare the distribution of British investments in 1914 and in 1936, it is obvious that development occurred within the basic structures inherited from pre-war imperialism. The system of 'unequal treaties' had been partly eroded on paper and more radically undermined in practice, but survived until the advent of the Imperial Japanese Army. More importantly, the British 'business system'[69] of 1936 was a direct continuation of that of 1914. No entirely new fields of investment were opened up in the meantime, and no new type of enterprise had appeared on the scene. Geographically the patterns of penetration had undergone no qualitative change, but only a shift of emphasis. Hong Kong remained slightly more important than Shanghai as a port for overseas shipping, while Shanghai was the centre of coastal and river shipping, the largest emporium in the country, and by far the most important industrial and financial centre. Hankou (from 1926 part of the municipality of Wuhan) on the middle Yangzi and Tianjin (Tientsin) in North China were centres of secondary importance; the other treaty ports, including such big cities as Canton and Qingdao (Tsingtao) were only significant to foreign firms with a regional specialisation. Only the few giants of British China business maintained representatives outside the largest centres. At the small ports, 'the kernel of the community consists of agents of Jardines and Butterfield & Swire, the APC [Asiatic Petroleum Company] and BAT, the Commissioner of Customs, and, if the place is sufficiently important, the consular representatives of the leading foreign powers'.[70] With the rise of civil disorder in the interior provinces during the 1920s, business representation in the hinterland declined even further. Shanghai became more than ever the pivot of British business in China.

Part of the growth of British direct investments during the inter-war period can be explained by this very growth of Shanghai. Between 1914 and 1936 Shanghai's population trebled to around 3.8 million, leaving Hong Kong, with 1 million, far behind. There were only about 10,000 residents of British nationality, but their real-estate holdings in the International Settlement and the French Concession were considerable, especially those of several land investment companies. The value of their properties skyrocketed in the 1920s[71] and thus boosted the estimated total of British investment, even though this was caused by market appreciation rather than by fresh investments.[72] Little import and export of capital was involved. As Remer has pointed out, 'a large fraction of the real estate ... has been purchased from income received within China and brings into existence income which is expended in China'.[73] However, it is important to note that a large proportion (at least some 36% in 1926)[74] of land registered in the names of British subjects was actually owned by non-British, i.e. mostly Chinese. A second aspect of the rise of Shanghai was the growing demand for the services of public utility companies most of which were in British ownership: waterworks, power stations, gasworks, telephone and public transport companies. These companies usually held monopolies in the International Settlement. They profited from the dramatic growth of the Chinese population and expanded their activities in order to meet the increasing demand. To a considerable extent the influx of Chinese into Shanghai was caused by mounting violence and poverty in the interior provinces. The prosperity of much of British business in Shanghai was therefore not unrelated to the unsettled conditions in China.

The other main beneficiaries of unrest in China were the foreign shipping companies. Whereas Chinese ships were in constant danger of being molested or commandeered, ships under the flag of one of the treaty powers were fairly safe from interference. The biggest British shipping company was Swire's China Navigation Company, followed by Jardine Matheson's Indo-China Steam Navigation Company. In the early 1930s, the two British lines carried roughly two-thirds of freight in Chinese coastal shipping; on the Yangzi river route their combined share was considerably lower. On the whole, more than half of steamer traffic in Chinese waters was of British hands.[75] Remer estimated that around 1930 shipping accounted for some 13% of British direct investment in China.[76]

Import–export, including the processing of raw materials (tung oil, eggs, raw cotton, etc.) continued to be the most important single category of investment. Jardine Matheson and Butterfield & Swire occupied leading positions in this field, but the bulk of investments derived from trading companies of medium size and a higher degree of specialisation such as Arnhold & Company; Gibb, Livingstone & Company; or Dodwell & Company. A feature of the post-1914 period was the shift away from the old staples. On the import side, the sale of British cotton piece goods declined dramatically during the 1920s and collapsed in the early 1930s. This was caused by the proliferation of cotton mills in China, by the total obsoleteness of British marketing techniques and by the Chinese import tariff of 1933.[77] The spectacular loss of the cotton piece goods market contributed to the impression that the days for British business in China were numbered. To some extent, this loss was offset by rising sales of industrial machinery. By 1937 three-quarters of the textile machines installed in China had been imported from Britain; even some of the giant Japanese cotton mills in Shanghai, Qingdao and Tianjin preferred British machinery.[78] The shift towards industrial equipment required new adjustments. Cotton goods were traded on commission, and their distribution to the Chinese customers remained, as in the nineteenth century, entirely in Chinese hands. Now engineering departments had to be established, technicians had to be hired and service had to be provided to industrial customers.[79] On the export side new investments were necessary for the processing of raw materials. Hardly any British capital had been employed in the preparation of tea and silk for export. With the commodities that rose to prominence during the inter-war period this was different: tung oil (by the mid-1930s China's leading export item) had to be refined, eggs had to be frozen or converted into powder, etc.[80]

Manufacturing for the Chinese market did not develop as rapidly as some enthusiasts for import substitution were hoping. The alleged 'unlimited possibilities'[81] for cotton spinning in the treaty ports were tested by Japanese and Chinese rather than by European and American business. In

204 Jürgen Osterhammel

fact, the number of spindles in Jardine Matheson's Ewo Cotton Mills slightly declined between 1925 and 1934. The only new venture was a small cotton mill established in 1934 by the British-owned China Printing and Finishing Company, which now added spinning and weaving to its established business in printing and dyeing of cotton cloth. In 1936, the British mills accounted for 4.1% of spindles, 6.9% of looms and 6.9% of the work-force in China's cotton industry.[82] Lancashire never moved into import substitution. The only genuine import-substituting enterprise in textiles was a medium-sized (1,120 workers) factory for woollens opened in Shanghai in 1934 by Patons & Baldwins; the main motive behind this venture seems to have been to surmount the Chinese tariff barrier.[83]

Perhaps surprisingly, given that China was widely regarded as a promising market, that wages were extremely low, and that legislation favoured foreign investment, China did not significantly share in the considerable new investment by Western multinational enterprises in the developing world.[84] There were three main reasons for this. Firstly, China did not have protective tariffs before 1933. Secondly, China was a *potential* market, not yet able (as Henry Ford, for example, understood)[85] to absorb significant quantities of manufactured consumer goods other than textiles and drugs (including tobacco). Thirdly, the political situation was highly unsettled and discouraged investors. Chiang Kai-shek's National Government achieved a reasonable degree of effectiveness only in 1935, at a time when the Japanese left little doubt as to their long-term aspirations on the mainland.

Among British-based multinationals only Lever Brothers took up production in China. In 1911 Lever Brothers (China) Ltd was incorporated as a sales subsidiary. It was later transformed into the China Soap Company which started production at Shanghai in 1929. Five years later it employed some 1,000 Chinese workers and provided about one-half of the output of soap in China. A smaller factory for the production of margarine was opened in 1932.[86] The China Soap Company obtained a large proportion of its raw materials from Imperial Chemical Industries (ICI).[87] ICI itself never started production in China, but evolved into one of the most important British exporters to China, yet without challenging the German chemical concerns as principal suppliers of indigo and dyes to industrial and handicraft spinners and weavers throughout China.[88] ICI instead concentrated on artificial fertilizer and soda ash. Following the German precedent, ICI's predecessor, Brunner Mond, at an early stage moved from treaty port trade to the organisation of its own country-wide distribution network. In the early 1930s ICI employed 130 Europeans and 500 Chinese who in turn supervised more than 1,000 Chinese agents; these sold fertilizer directly to the Chinese peasants and were paid on a commission basis.[89]

British business in China, 1860s–1950s 205

7.3 British American Tobacco's railway carriage with sleeping and living accommodation and storage and display area, for its peregrinatory sales force.

Even more extensive than ICI's distribution network was that organised by APC for the sale of kerosene – the famous 'oil for the lamps of China'. The early imports of kerosene, especially during the 1880s when kerosene began to replace the vegetable oils traditionally used for lighting, had been conducted through agency houses. In 1885 Standard Oil opened its first office in Shanghai; in 1914 it began setting up a nation-wide sales system.[90] APC came into being in 1902 as a joint selling organisation of the British Shell Transport and Trading Company and the Royal Dutch Company. After the merger of the two partners in 1907 it became their subsidiary responsible for sales in Asia, Australia, New Zealand and East Africa. Following the pioneering Standard Oil, APC established its own distribution network. In the 1920s, it encompassed the whole of China with the exception of the thinly populated provinces of Inner Asia. On the eve of the war, APC had a share of 44% of the Chinese petroleum market; 37% of the trade was conducted by Standard Oil, 11% by Texaco and 8% by others (mainly agents for the Russian Neftsindikat).[91]

APC came second on the list of British-based multinationals in China, being overshadowed by BAT, whose up-country selling organisation was the most extensive in the country. BAT was the principal spearhead of the

206 Jürgen Osterhammel

commercial penetration of the China market by British business, and was pre-eminent in *industrial* penetration. By 1935 it employed around 21,000 workers in its factories in Shanghai, Hankou, Tianjin and Qingdao and accounted for about 60% of industrially manufactured cigarettes in China.[92] BAT was a classic case of a market-oriented subsidiary. It was a fully integrated business organisation that controlled its own supplies (tobacco grown by Chinese peasants dependent on sales to the company), the entire process of manufacturing including such auxiliary services as printing, packing, advertising and marketing down to the level of Chinese retailing. BAT's phenomenal growth from its foundation in 1902 until 1936 was perhaps the most spectacular success story in British, or even Western, business in twentieth-century China.[93]

It is extremely difficult to arrive at summary conclusions about British business in China during the period from 1914 to 1937. The British business system was composed of hundreds of enterprises of different sizes representing a broad range of types of expatriate business: old-style commission houses; widely diversified investment groups; banks and insurance companies; public utility companies; sales subsidiaries of multinational corporations; partners in Sino-foreign mining enterprises; real-estate companies, shops, department stores and hotels in the largest treaty ports; dockyards; the unique case of BAT; and finally a variety of specialised firms catering to the luxury market in Western-style goods, such as Mr Jack Case, gentleman tailor at 41B Kiangse Road, Shanghai, Adolph Frankau & Company, manufacturers of briar pipes, smokers' sundries and fancy leather goods, or S. Moutrie & Company, makers of pianos and organs who produced especially for the use of missionaries 'excellent portable harmoniums, which can be folded up into a small space'.[94] Did they share a common experience?

Firstly, they were not the only foreigners in China. Mr Moutrie may have dominated the market in portable harmoniums and BAT certainly was the only major foreign cigarette manufacturer in China. Most others, however, had to face third-country competition. In general commission business, German firms managed to revitalise the excellent connections they had built up before the First World War. As early as 1925, it could be said of Siemssen & Company that 'probably no firm in Shanghai represents a larger number of European houses',[95] and that meant not only German clients. Around the same time, Siemens and other German firms successfully re-entered the market for electrical equipment.[96] The Japanese formed by far the largest foreign communities in China. They maintained the most widely spread banking network and came second among foreign nations in shipping (the leading line was the Nisshin Kisen Kaisha) and coal mining; they exercised financial control over a large part of Chinese iron ore mining and iron industry; above all, they owned the

British business in China, 1860s–1950s 207

7.4 *Advertising hoardings on the building site of Shanghai's most luxurious department store, Whiteaway Laidlaw, show some of the variety of British business in the former treaty port.*

largest and most successful cotton mills in China. The Americans were ubiquitous in trade of every description.

In many cases market-sharing agreements were openly or tacitly concluded. APC was on friendly and oligopolistic terms with the American oil companies and ICI with the German dye manufacturers, whereas there was stiff competition with Japanese importers of chemicals.[97] In shipping, rate wars occurred intermittently from the 1870s onwards; pools were formed and dissolved in an almost cyclical pattern. Anarchy prevailed on the Yangzi between 1925 and 1935, when a new pooling agreement was concluded between the British, Chinese and Japanese Lines.[98] Another highly competitive market was that for railway equipment. Here, the British fared reasonably well only because the remitted British share of the Boxer Indemnity had to be used by the Chinese government for purchasing equipment in Britain – at prices that were fixed about 25 to 40% above the market level.[99]

Secondly, Chinese participation and cooperation were essential to the conduct of all kinds of business. Of course the Chinese were consumers of

208 *Jürgen Osterhammel*

imports and of the output of foreign-owned factories in the treaty ports; they were the producers of export commodities; and they were the labourers in foreign-owned plants and mines, the seamen manning foreign ships and the domestic servants attending the 'better sort' of expatriates – as opposed to the 'poor whites' who flocked to Shanghai after the Russian Revolution, during the Great Depression and as refugees from fascism in Central Europe. But there were also those who performed functions of a *compradore* type, that is, linking the British business system to the indigenous economic environment. Smaller firms confined to Shanghai invariably had their 'house *compradore*', even if he came increasingly to be styled a 'Chinese manager'. The Hongkong and Shanghai Bank had unsuccessfully tried to circumvent the 'compradoric system' as early as 1866. It appointed its last *compradore* in 1953, and the post was only abolished in 1965 upon his retirement.[100] Even BAT, APC and ICI with their modern forms of organisation, where commissioned agents were replaced as far as possible by salaried employees, still had to rely on middlemen of various kinds for rooting their distribution systems in local Chinese trading networks. As a rule, Western marketing was adapted to, rather than imposed upon, indigenous commercial structures and practices.

Thirdly, competition from Chinese entrepreneurs was not entirely absent either. In general, Western technological superiority was obvious everywhere. Modern technology was Western technology. But, on the one hand, pre-modern and non-industrial forms sometimes proved highly efficient or even superior to their modern rivals – examples were transport by junk, handicraft weaving, and coal production in man-powered 'native pits'. On the other hand, some Chinese rapidly adopted modern techniques of production and management. In the late nineteenth century the official or semi-official enterprises of the Self-strengthening Movement relied on Western technicians, while young Chinese were sent abroad in ever-increasing numbers for vocational training.[101] Towards the end of the century, China was 'developing a coterie of highly trained merchant-managers able to initiate and manage foreign-style industrial enterprises'.[102] In the early twentieth century, these groups became part of a small class of urban entrepreneurs.[103] Some members of this class effectively challenged foreign hegemony over the modern sector of the Chinese economy, especially between 1915 and 1928. Modern banks developed rapidly and in partial competition with foreign banks. The same was true for insurance companies. Services for which Chinese customers had hitherto depended on foreigners became available from indigenous firms. In the 1930s ICI encountered strong competition from the Chinese-owned Yongli Company, whose very existence was chivalrously praised by one of ICI's directors as 'a tribute to Chinese technical

British business in China, 1860s–1950s 209

skill and commercial enterprise'.[104] ICI estimated that, between 1934 and 1936, it had lost an annual average 20,000 tons of business in soda ash to Yongli. ICI repeatedly offered market-sharing agreements which Yongli proudly refused.[105] In the 1910s and 1920s BAT fought fierce battles with Nanyang Brothers, the leading Chinese cigarette manufacturers.[106] In the mid-1930s, the two British shipping lines faced aggressive competition from the Sichuan-based Minsheng Co. which had been established in 1925.[107] In engineering, Chinese business advanced considerably after the turn of the century and was increasingly able to replace imported equipment with Chinese-manufactured machinery.[108] In Shanghai and elsewhere modern Chinese department stores forced several British rivals out of business.[109] In many cases the secret of success was not wholesale adoption of Western management methods but a skilful blending of elements borrowed from abroad with traditional Chinese forms of organisation, especially family and regional connections.[110] Taken as a whole, the counter-attack of Chinese private capitalism before 1937 never posed a mortal threat to foreign business. But a menacing trend was obvious.

Fourthly, British business in China became the target of repeated strikes and boycotts, many of which were of a political nature and were motivated by resentment against the foreign presence in general. Anti-imperialist activities reached their peak in the mid-1920s; they much declined in number and intensity in the early 1930s, when Japan became the chief enemy and Chiang Kai-shek's military dictatorship restrained popular protest. British firms were not seriously harmed by Chinese mass action, but growing resistance was widely perceived as being a *long-term* threat. A related aspect was the increasing involvement of the Chinese state in the modern sector of the economy. The growth of 'bureaucratic capitalism' in the 1930s[111] had ambivalent consequences: on the one hand, plans for state-sponsored industrialisation seemed to create new opportunities for British suppliers of capital goods; government business promised to gain a new importance. On the other hand, the Chinese government was increasingly able to bargain for better terms with its British partners. In the long run, this would not have meant the expulsion of British business from China. Quite to the contrary, the developmental programmes of the 1930s were based on large-scale participation of foreign capital. But the Chinese insisted on terms of equality or reciprocity and were no longer prepared to tolerate the legal privileges derived by foreigners from the unequal treaties. British business responded in different ways. The large companies with their country-wide interests were willing to compromise and to cooperate with Chiang Kai-shek's government, to support the abrogation of the surviving unequal treaties, and to recognise China's full sovereignty. Those firms, however, that depended

210   *Jürgen Osterhammel*

on their privileged position in Shanghai, were ardent defenders of the semi-colonial *status quo*, above all of the continuing existence of extraterritoriality.[112]

Fifthly, and finally, what role was played by the British government? Until the mid-1920s the British stood fast against the demands of Chinese nationalism. The most important task of the British diplomatic and military apparatus in China was that of guaranteeing the system of privileges. Within this framework, British firms were largely left to fend for themselves; again banking was a major exception.[113] When the British attitude to China 'softened' in the closing years of the 1920s,[114] this was not so much evidence of far-sighted statesmanship as the result of Britain's declining ability to defend its interests with the traditional tools of coercion. It was also the consequence of the Guomindang regime's willingness to look after British interests. From the diplomats' point of view, while the chief problem of the 1920s was anti-imperialist revolution, the chief problem of the 1930s was Japanese expansion on the Asian mainland. Officials at the Treasury and the Board of Trade took a less defensive and more sanguine and combative view. Their most effective spokesman was Sir Louis Beale, the Commercial Counsellor at Shanghai. Beale regarded China as a country on the threshold of an unprecedented process of industrialisation, repeating the story of Japan on a far grander scale. He noted that Britain's most important customers were developed rather than backward countries, and advocated British participation in the development of China, even advising British firms to lower their profit expectations and to grant more favourable terms to China in order to assist the growth of the Chinese economy. According to Beale's reasoning, a high standard of living for the Chinese people would benefit British business. In order to compete with Japan, Germany and the United States, British firms should modernise their marketing and managing techniques in China, abandon the old habits of treaty port trade and cut out superfluous middlemen.[115] Beale's 'modern' concept paralleled ideas discussed in the boardrooms of the big China companies. Predictably, it was violently resented by the 'Old China Hands' in the treaty ports. Yet, the steadfast defenders of the old semi-colonial system had few friends left in British official circles. By 1937 a powerful alliance was being forged between the Guomindang regime and its state capitalism, British big business, and modernisation-oriented officials like Beale and the Chief Economic Adviser to the Cabinet, Sir Frederick Leith-Ross.

7.5 A small rise and a deep fall, 1937 to 1957

With hindsight, the decline of British business in China began with the outbreak of war between Japan and China in July 1937. During the

British business in China, 1860s–1950s 211

subsequent period, the Chinese economy was largely shaped by non-economic forces. The same is true for British business in China. Business history as a separate field of investigation is therefore much more difficult to isolate from its political context than in earlier periods.

The fate of British business in East Asia during the sub-period that ended with the attack on Pearl Harbor in December 1941 is closely connected to the geography of Japan's military advance in China. In addition, from September 1939 the war in Europe had radical effects on the Far Eastern scene. Shipping may illustrate the complex ways in which the military situation determined business operations:

> After the outbreak of the Sino–Japanese War in July 1937 there was a great increase in passenger and other earnings owing to the flight of Chinese refugees both southward and westward. Chinese tonnage began to hide itself and Japanese tonnage to be requisitioned. In 1938 Chinese tonnage disappeared almost entirely; there was little Japanese tonnage available, yet the transfer of population, plant and materials of all kinds towards the west created a great demand for river tonnage up to the middle of the year. Thereafter the Yangtze was closed to all but Japanese tonnage ... But for the effect of the war in Europe on freight markets earnings would have fallen to very little in 1940. They were kept up, however, by world scarcity of tonnage, the China coast fleets enjoying a stronger charter market.[116]

Ironically, the era of the treaty ports culminated in an artificial boom. Until the end of 1941, Hong Kong and the International Settlement at Shanghai, due to their non-combatant status, were the only economic centres on the China coast untouched by the conflict; when Japanese naval artillery bombarded the Chinese quarters of Shanghai, they carefully aimed their shells across the International Settlement and the French Concession.[117] After the outbreak of war in Europe new markets were available for the industries of Shanghai in the Pacific area and in Africa.[118] The cotton industry of Shanghai, which had been cut off from its Chinese hinterland since the end of 1937, especially benefited from the opening up of these new 'forelands' overseas.[119] The major British firms reported excellent results. As late as 1940, it was 'business as usual'[120] for the Hong-kong and Shanghai Banking Corporation. In 1939 Unilever achieved record sales and ICI saw all its expectations surpassed,[121] while BAT and the Ewo Cotton Mills earned profits that exceeded anything previously experienced.[122] The KMA, situated as it was in territory that had already been under *de facto* Japanese control well before July 1937, had a record of friendly relations with the Japanese who had been relied upon since 1935 to quell unrest among the Chinese miners.[123] The mines survived the first phase of the war unscathed and were able to report record sales and exports for 1939 and 1940.[124]

Pearl Harbor, the subsequent occupation of Hong Kong and of the

212 *Jürgen Osterhammel*

foreign enclaves at Shanghai, the internment of British nationals in Japanese camps and the expropriation of British property[125] concluded, almost exactly a century after the Treaty of Nanjing, the age of treaty port imperialism. After the Japanese surrender, many British firms hurried to reclaim their properties and to rebuild their China business. Above all, Britain accomplished the remarkable feat of recapturing Hong Kong against the opposition of the Chinese government and with the reluctant connivance of the United States.[126] Material destruction of British properties in China had been surprisingly slight. The Foreign Office estimated the war losses amounted to little more than 11% of the total value of British business investments (shipping excluded) in China in 1941. The most important causes of loss were the deterioration of stocks (especially BAT's tobacco stocks at Shanghai) and the decay of mining equipment. Few buildings were seriously damaged, and only a small amount of machinery had been removed by the Japanese.[127] On the contrary, some British firms discovered that their factories were better equipped than before. However, the Chinese government regarded as enemy property those machines that had been installed by the Japanese.[128] Only after difficult negotiations was most of this material released to the British firms.

There were additional reasons for British businessmen to be unhappy with the situation in China. The Guomindang government continued to operate some of the state monopolies that had been established shortly before and during the war; foreign shipping was (quite legally and in accordance with the treaty of 1943 that had terminated extraterritoriality) excluded from the Yangzi route;[129] businessmen were as appalled as many Western diplomats by the corruption and inefficiency of the regime; a special complaint on the part of foreign employers was that the government was no longer able to control labour and keep down demands for higher wages.

British trade *with* China stood up well against overwhelming American competition. Since, however, China was not a hard currency market, the Board of Trade, for the first time in the history of Anglo-Chinese commercial relations, *dis*couraged exports to China.[130] British officials 'on the spot' could do little in support of British trade *in* China. The Chinese civil war was experienced like a natural disaster, beyond the reach of any of the foreign powers. By 1948, it had become obvious to most that the Guomindang regime was doomed and that a policy had to be worked out as to future relations with the Communists.[131] A more realistic appraisal of the political situation in China, however, went hand in hand with a good deal of wishful thinking. As late as November 1948, the Consul-General at Shanghai, Sir Robert Urquhart, still believed that Britain was in a position to teach the Communists a 'lesson of how to deal

British business in China, 1860s–1950s 213

with foreign installations'.[132] He even recommended that British businessmen 'should make plain to the communists that if any of the standard tricks are adopted, of establishing communist controls, etcetera, they will stop business'.[133]

In the event, things turned out quite differently. The new authorities were in no mood to be bullied by foreign capitalists or even to negotiate compromises with them. The People's Government moved rapidly to establish total state control of foreign trade and to withdraw all privileges from foreign enterprises. Alien companies were 'protected' by the government as long as they complied with Chinese laws which meant, among other things, functioning in a very inferior position within the network of a planned economy and paying high taxes.[134] British firms were slowly squeezed out of China rather than expelled in one dramatic gesture. Their large amount of immovable assets now became a tremendous liability because these assets were difficult to liquidate. The schedule was in each case fixed by the Chinese. Many firms were refused permission to close down since this would have made workers redundant. Some of them had to maintain a full payroll of idle workers for several years. A number of companies were forced to remit funds from Hong Kong in order to cover current expenses and meet the tax demands of the Chinese authorities.[135] The outbreak of the Korean War prolonged this phase of 'hostage capitalism'. Only after the Korean armistice was the Chinese government willing to complete negotiations about the closure of British firms.[136] BAT left China in 1952, Jardine Matheson & Co. and Butterfield & Swire in 1954; it was not until 1957 that the last British firm, Patons & Baldwins, was allowed to withdraw.[137]

One of the most irritating experiences of British businessmen was the realisation that they no longer mattered. They had seriously underrated the incorruptible intransigence of the new men and women in power. For the first time in living memory, indigenous rulers were unimpressed by the foreigners' alleged superiority. The belief that British business was 'indispensable' to China was shattered. There was no clearer illustration of this than a British manager's sigh of exasperation:

> It is simply not possible to 'go to the Authorities and ask . . .' London principals can be assured that we exist in a vacuum; we have no direct access to anyone and little indirect access, and nobody appears to be interested in us except our Labour and the Tax Gatherer.[138]

The Chinese economy did, after all, survive without the benefit of British participation and advice – a lesson which the most powerful of all British companies, BAT, found especially hard to learn. For decades, BAT had eschewed American or British diplomatic support and had relied on its own strong bargaining position *vis-à-vis* the Chinese authorities. BAT

214 Jürgen Osterhammel

executives were confident that a weak and poor China would continue to require British capital and expertise and that the firm's well-tried strategy of making 'its own way with the Chinese in Chinese style' would work equally well with the new regime.[139] This was a serious error of judgment. BAT, the epitome of British manufacturing and trade within China, was removed as unceremoniously as any other British company.

7.6 Conclusion

A few general points about British business in China can be made in terms of the four basic perspectives outlined at the beginning of this chapter. From a *global* perspective, British business played its most important part during the early stages of the incorporation of the Chinese empire into the emerging world economy. The economic invasion of China, starting from the undermining of the East India Company's conservative monopoly by private traders during the first three decades of the nineteenth century, was spearheaded by the British. They organised the opium trade which remained the prop of the China trade through most of the century. They led the first military expeditions against China, worked out and implemented the institutions of informal control which became the underpinning of the 'imperialism of free trade'[140] and assumed leadership among the foreign business communities in the major treaty ports. And it was the British who built the first foreign factories in China, developed the first large-scale (semi-) foreign coal mines, and contributed the largest individual share of foreign loans to China before 1914. From the 1890s, however, it is no longer possible to speak of British supremacy in East Asian business and diplomacy. The most significant new forms of China's integration into the international economy were henceforth pioneered by other trading nations: direct up-country distribution by the Americans (Standard Oil, BAT) and the Germans (IG Farben), market-oriented mass-manufacturing using Chinese labour and raw materials by the Americans (BAT) and the Japanese (cotton spinning), large-scale exports of agricultural commodities by the Japanese (soybean trade in South Manchuria), and export-oriented industry also by the Japanese (light industry, mainly sugar, in Taiwan; heavy industry in Manchuria). The British were no longer the foremost commercial innovators among foreigners in China. Endless lamentations about the inadequacy of British 'trading methods'[141] were a symptom of a shift in economic leadership that involved much more than mere differences in marketing technique.

From an *imperial* perspective, China never lived up to the hopes of those who enthused about its unlimited potential as an outlet for the products of Britain's manufacturing industries. When British exports of

British business in China, 1860s–1950s 215

cotton goods began to decline, in East Asia they declined even more rapidly than elsewhere. Exports of cotton piece goods to China, Hong Kong and Japan fell from 773 million square yards in 1913 to 18 million in 1935, of which 7.7 million went to China.[142] The loss of the Chinese cotton market was only partly offset by an increase in other export lines. In the long run, Britain's share in China's imports (not including the import of British-made goods via Hong Kong) declined from 33% in 1868, to 17% in 1913, 12% in 1936 and 8% in 1948. Britain's share in the total value of China's foreign trade plummeted even more drastically: from 45% in 1868 to 6% in 1948.[143] Export of capital from Britain to China was a much more limited affair than trade. It was largely confined to the three decades preceding the First World War, and, of course, not all the capital funnelled through London was of British origin. After 1914, portfolio investments largely ceased to be made and little fresh capital was exported from Britain for direct investment in China. The growth of business investments during this period was mainly due to 'local' factors, especially the reinvestment of profits earned in the Far East.[144] Finally, emigration has to be considered as an aspect of an 'imperial' connection to the metropolis. According to Remer, there were about 20,000 British subjects living in all parts of China by 1930.[145] Other estimates are somewhat higher and arrive at a total of about 28,000 for the mid-1930s.[146] The great majority of these persons was in one way or another connected with business and its protection.

From an *expatriate* perspective, two things are obvious. Firstly, British trade (in the widest possible sense) *in* China was vastly more important than British trade *with* China. The British commercial establishment on the China coast fulfilled many more functions than just acting as an intermediary between the British metropolitan economy and the economy of China. British trading houses held agencies of firms of many nationalities; conversely, there were manufacturers in the United Kingdom who sold their products through German or American merchants. At least until the First World War, the Hongkong Bank was a truly international bank which enjoyed strong support, especially from German firms, and which had a number of Germans and other foreigners on its Board of directors.[147] Some important British firms in China had only a very tenuous connection to the metropolis. BAT used Chinese resources to manufacture for the Chinese market; the semi-British coal mines did not export to the United Kingdom; the Taikoo and Ewo steamer fleets in Chinese waters catered mostly for indigenous demand, etc.[148] The most significant link to the home economy was the repatriation of profits – if and to the extent that it occurred. Secondly, British business in China was part of the East and Southeast Asian regional economy. Continuing the tradition of the 'country traders', British firms played a crucial role in the commercial exchanges between India, China, Hong Kong, Singapore and the various parts of Malaya, the Philippines, French Indo-China and the Dutch East Indies. British shipping lines occupied a particularly strong position in intra-regional traffic, especially since China failed to develop an ocean-going merchant navy.[149] They also competed with American, Canadian and Japanese lines for trans-Pacific business.[150] Hong Kong, Shanghai and Singapore were the entrepôts around which this Southeast Asian sub-system of the international economy was arranged. In all three centres, British business cooperated with Chinese merchants and entrepreneurs in many different ways.

From an *indigenous* point of view, it is increasingly more difficult, the more we approach the recent past, to identify a particular *British* impact as distinct from that of transnational entities such as 'industrial capitalism', 'multinational enterprise' or 'modern technology'. Perhaps the only safe conclusion is that there is no other Western country (Russia may, for the present purpose, count as a partly Asiatic power) which has had as many points of economic contact with China over such a long period of time as has Great Britain, even if the British impact lost much of its intensity and distinctiveness in the twentieth century.

8 British business in Japan since 1868

R. P. T. Davenport-Hines and Geoffrey Jones*

8.1 Diseases and miracles

The stark contrast between the business histories of Britain and Japan over the last hundred years is a commonplace. A century of relative industrial decline has transformed the world's first industrial nation into the poor relation of the developed European economies. Over the same period Japan, only emerging from feudal isolation in the 1850s, has become the world's second largest industrial economy. The temptation to resort to clichés to explain these contrasting economic performances is almost overwhelming. We hope, however, to provide more specific insights into the Japanese 'miracle' and the British 'disease' by examining an area where British and Japanese business interacted directly: British economic activity in Japan.

Since 1868 British business in Japan has followed a course of early success and pioneering followed by decline and insignificance. This is well illustrated by the Japanese import statistics given in Table 8.1. Until the mid-1880s Britain was the leading exporter to Japan, reflecting its mid-nineteenth-century industrial hegemony, but thereafter its importance receded, with some correlation to its decline as an industrial power. This chapter will show this was the normal pattern for all forms of British business in Japan, and that while no foreign capital or expertise made an outstanding impression on Japanese business, there were particular features which put Britain at a disadvantage.

The reasons for Britain's poor business performance in Japan provide important matters for debate. There is a strong and pervasive tradition in British business circles that the Japanese market, Japanese companies, business–government relations, and Japanese culture had special characteristics which worked against foreign business interests. There is validity in this approach, as we will show, but we also argue that it is in the 'diseased' British economy rather than in Japan that the more fundamental causes of poor British performance are to be found. Our approach is to take a long-term view of mercantile contacts, technology transfer, foreign direct investment, financial services, and trading relations over the

218　*R. P. T. Davenport-Hines and Geoffrey Jones*

Table 8.1 *British imports as a percentage of total Japanese imports, 1875–1965*

Date	Total Japanese imports	Total British imports to Japan	%British imports
		(million yen)	%
1875	29,976	14,690	49
1880	36,627	19,626	54
1885	29,357	12,457	42
1890	81,729	26,619	33
1895	129,261	45,172	35
1900	287,262	71,638	25
1905	488,538	115,380	24
1910	464,234	94,701	20
1915	532,450	58,084	11
1920	2,336,175	235,353	10
1925	2,572,658	227,292	9
1930	1,546,070	92,561	6
1935	2,472,236	82,160	3
1940	3,453	11	0.3
1945	957	–	–
1950	348,196	2,414	0.7
1955	889,715	13,650	1.5
1960	16,168	357	2.2
1965	29,408	585	2.0

Source: Nihon Ginko Tokei-Kyoku (1966)

period since 1868, believing that the gains from such a speculative survey will outweigh the losses caused by dealing superficially with some subjects.

8.2　British business and Meiji Japan

The role of foreigners and foreign capital in Japan's economic growth after the Meiji Restoration in 1868 has been under-rated by some Western historians. It is certainly true that Japan had very high rates of domestic savings and investment (unlike the rest of Asia), and did not depend upon foreign capital for its business development. Much of the literature presents a picture of a strong nationalistic government promoting industrialisation by subsidies to local entrepreneurs and state factories. The Meiji government is cast as seeking to minimise foreign influence in Japan, although the contemporary struggle of the Western powers to partition China, and exploit its wealth, makes the Japanese response seem reasonable and even laudable. The contrast with other pre-1914 developing economies, such as Russia – where the heavy industrial sector was largely owned and managed by Western Europeans – and India – whose

British business in Japan since 1868 219

modern industry was substantially all British-controlled – seems stark. In reality, however, foreign business has been important in Japan's economic history, even if its contribution took different forms from those in Tsarist Russia or British India. As Allen and Donnithorne observed in 1954, 'although foreign enterprise never had a dominant role in the creation of a modern Japanese economy, its contribution was indispensable in the Meiji era and was far from negligible down to very recent times'.[1] In the second half of the nineteenth century, after the Chinese merchants, British business was the most influential section of foreign business activity in the Japanese economy, although it soon declined to nugatory significance.

It is certainly true that there were formidable political obstacles to foreign business in Meiji Japan. For a period before the revision of the Commercial Law in 1899 and the end of extraterritoriality, foreign direct investment was only permitted in the various treaty settlements in Japan. Subsequently foreigners were freed from practically all legal impediments to engaging in direct investment nation-wide. They were, however, prevented from investment in a number of 'strategic' sectors, such as national banks and transport companies. Moreover, whatever the legal situation, in practice government officials did not want foreign *control* over any Japanese business and sought by a number of means to direct foreigners into portfolio rather than direct investments.

Within the overall context, the specific diplomatic relations between Britain and Japan were not particularly conducive to British business activity in that country. For several decades after 1868 there was 'much distrust of Britain in Japan' because of British naval power, and the 'hauteur and condescension' of the long-serving British Minister at Tokyo 'left the impression that Britain had scant sympathy for Japan'. As late as 1893 one diplomat at Tokyo was unsure if Japanese power would turn 'out to be bubble or nugget', adding 'in England we regard it as a practical joke ... but I shouldn't wonder if it turned out wrong'. As signified by the Anglo-Japanese alliance of 1902, there was a moderation of this attitude which affected business opportunities, but mutual suspicion had undermined the alliance by 1911, and after its abrogation in 1923, Anglo-Japanese relations gradually deteriorated, providing an indifferent context for business understanding and some incentive to disinvestment.[2]

Western enterprise in Japan after the Meiji Restoration took a variety of forms. Foreign teachers, managers and technical experts were extensively recruited by the Meiji government. The government hired some 3,000 foreigners between 1868 and 1912. About half of these were British, and the British comprised two-thirds of the foreign nationals who were employed by the Public Works Ministry, which sponsored major technological projects and model industries. Scots were particularly prominent.[3] These individuals seldom performed entrepreneurial func-

8.1 Colonel the Master of Sempill, head of mission to reorganise Japanese Imperial Air Service during the 1920s.

tions, but in other ways their contribution to the growth of modern business in Japan was important, and their role persisted after the Meiji era. Just as collaboration with the Royal Navy was crucial to the development of the modern Japanese navy in 1873–94, so, similarly, when it was decided to create an aircraft industry in Japan in the early 1920s British experts, together with a designer and technical staff from Sopwith Aviation, went out to Japan.[4]

The work of British technical experts in Japan is marginal to our main theme and has been covered by other writers. However, one feature of their experience is worth noting. From the beginning of the Meiji era the Japanese government deliberately excluded foreign experts from a permanent role in Japan. They trained the Japanese, and then left. While in 1853–68 foreign experts had been known as *okakae* (tutor), after 1868 they were normally referred to as *oyatoi* (hired menial). 'The Japanese only look upon foreigners as schoolmasters', one British journalist who had worked in Japan observed in 1881. 'As long as they cannot help themselves, they make use of them; and then they send them about their business.'[5] The idea that the Japanese were only interested in foreigners to learn, borrow or steal from them, and would then ungratefully eject them from Japan and use the newly acquired skills against their teachers,

British business in Japan since 1868 221

remains axiomatic to many British businessmen even today. It helps, in part, to explain the deep suspicion of Japanese business practices held in the West: a point which will be developed later in this chapter.

Cultural misunderstandings have nevertheless distorted perceptions of the complex process of technological transfer. For many years some Japanese engineers were so keen to adopt or imitate the wonders of Western technology that they declined to modify it to suit local needs, despite the advice of *oyatoi* engineers, whose dissatisfaction at being ignored (expressed to businessmen and consular officials) contributed to Britain's pessimistic view of Japanese economic prospects. Many early Japanese technologists responsible for contact with Westerners were so bewildered by the expertise which they learnt that they exaggerated Japan's technological retardation; but when imported technology was properly adapted to the needs of local industry, it was more effective than either *oyatoi* or their pupils often credited.

British business, as opposed to British technical experts, made its greatest contribution to Meiji economic development in the external sector of the economy. In the early Meiji period, up to the mid-1880s, Japan imported substantially from Britain, while before 1914 Britain supplied, for example, all the spinning equipment for the Japanese cotton and silk spinning industries. Platt Brothers of Oldham in 1882–3 designed and provided all the machinery for the Osaka Spinning Company, even importing Lancashire red bricks, and supplied technical advice to the company for three decades. Platts took Osaka through a rapid transition from mule to ring spinning in the 1890s, at a time when British cotton-spinners obstinately adhered to the increasingly archaic mule, and, given the rapid diffusion of new industrial techniques that prevailed in Meiji Japan, this facilitated Japan's assault on British export markets after 1919.[6] It has been estimated that in 1887 nearly 90% of Japanese foreign trade was handled by foreign merchants, falling to 60% by 1900.[7] Comparative statistics are lacking, but the share of British merchant houses in Japanese foreign trade was much lower than that of Chinese merchants, who were responsible for the overwhelming majority of Japanese exports to Asia (which increasingly outranked the importance of exports to the West).[8] Indeed Japan's trading links were strongest with Asia rather than with Europe, and the participation of British mercantile houses in this was necessarily limited.

Japan was part of a world-wide phenomenon in which British merchant houses by the 1890s had lost their pre-eminence while German and American merchants grew in importance. Simultaneously Japanese enterprises began to enter the foreign trade sector. In 1876 the famous Mitsui Bussan Kaisha was established, and this pioneer of Japanese general trading companies soon secured a share of Japan's raw silk exports. By the

222 R. P. T. Davenport-Hines and Geoffrey Jones

1900s Japanese firms had largely wrested control of the foreign trade sector from expatriate merchants. The question of the reasons for the rapid loss of influence of the British and other foreign merchants has provoked much discussion, especially in Japan. It is true that for three decades after 1868 merchants at treaty ports had severe restrictions on travel or building factories imposed on them, but Allen and Donnithorne's argument about the highly integrated character of Japanese business development seems helpful in this context. The Mitsui *zaibatsu* (business group), for example, controlled a range of industrial, shipping and financial activities, and this facilitated the Mitsui Bussan Kaisha's expansion of foreign trade (particularly through its coal exports to Southeast Asia, which had reached a considerable volume by the 1890s).[9]

This decline of the British merchant houses typified the British business experience in Meiji Japan. It was accelerated in the 1880s by closer commercial links with Germany, provoked by Japanese admiration for Bismarckian political institutions. In several sectors British enterprises underwent a process of 'marginalisation' after initial dominance. By the inter-war years foreign merchants played only a small role in Japan's foreign trade. They accounted, for example, for about 16% of raw silk exports in the mid-1920s, falling to about 4% in the mid-1930s. Only in a few spheres, where Japanese enterprise was for some reason weak, was a substantial foreign role preserved. The most prominent of these sectors was petroleum, where the Rising Sun Petroleum Company – a subsidiary of the Anglo-Dutch Shell Group – and American oil interests dominated the import into and refining of oil in Japan.

A similar process can be observed in the shipping industry. The first British shipping firm to establish a regular line of steamers to Japan was the Peninsular and Oriental Steam Navigation Company, which began to ply between Shanghai and Japan in 1859. In the 1870s the Blue Funnel Line began operating to Japan, and by the following decade had secured 70% of the total carrying trade between Britain and Japan.[10] The Meiji government made it a major priority to reduce the country's dependence on foreign shipping companies. As early as 1875 Mitsubishi began to operate ships between Shanghai and Japan, and in 1885 the government sponsored an alliance of shipping concerns under Mitsubishi's control to create Nippon Yusen Kaisha (Japanese Shipping Company), which was subsequently heavily subsidised. Nevertheless even by 1913 foreign ships, many of them British-owned, still carried over 50% of Japan's trade.[11] By 1930, however, the proportion had fallen to 30%.

A third area of British business activity to undergo the process of marginalisation was banking. Table 8.2 lists the foreign banks operating in Japan before 1914. Five British overseas banks opened branches in Japan before the Meiji Restoration. Two of these were rapidly overcome

British business in Japan since 1868 223

Table 8.2 *Foreign banks in Japan, 1860–1914*

	Date of first branch	Date bank closed in Japan
British (and British Indian) banks		
Chartered Mercantile Bank of India, London and China (later Mercantile Bank of India)	1863	1886
Central Bank of Western India	1865	1866
Oriental Bank Corporation (later New Oriental)	1865	1892
Commercial Bank Corporation of India and the East	1865	1866
Hongkong and Shanghai Banking Corporation	1866	
Chartered Bank of India, Australia and China	1880	
Other Foreign Banks		
Russo-Chinese Bank (Russian)	1898	
International Banking Corporation (US)	1902	
Deutsch-Asiatische Bank (German)	1905	
Banque Franco-Japonaise (French/Japanese)	1912	

by the Overend and Gurney banking crisis in Britain in 1866. Of the remaining banks, the Hongkong Bank was the strongest. It opened branches in Yokohama (1866), Kobe (1872), Osaka (1872), Nagasaki (1896), Shimonoseki (1906) and Hakodate (1919).[12] The arrival of the Chartered Bank of India, Australia and China in 1880 brought another leading British overseas bank to Japan, and over the following two decades these two banks were the dominant foreign banks. Later, in 1906, an Anglo-Japanese Bank was formed in London with nominal capital of £2 million and a board of directors from other British domestic and overseas banks, such as the London Bank of Mexico and South America, the Union Bank of Australia and the Imperial Bank of Persia. A local board in Japan was envisaged with the powerful Kihachiro Okura as a member. It was intended not only to finance Anglo-Japanese trade, but also to open branches in Japan, but little seems to have eventuated: the venture's name was changed to the Commercial Bank of London in 1913 and it was liquidated in 1914.[13] It was only in the 1900s that non-British foreign banks became significant.

The lending activities of the British banks were largely confined to financing foreign trade, but here their role initially was significant. 'For two decades after the opening of the country', Allen and Donnithorne observed, 'they were indispensable to the conduct of Japan's foreign trade.'[14] However, British banks by the turn of the century also began to be 'marginalised'. The abolition of extraterritoriality in 1898 and the decline of foreign merchants contributed to the recession of the British banks' importance, but the critical element once again was the development of competing Japanese institutions. In 1880 the government spon-

224 R. P. T. Davenport-Hines and Geoffrey Jones

sored the creation of the Yokohama Specie Bank, supplying funds to the new institution at low interest rates, and giving it a monopoly over Japanese exports. The British banks were left to engage in an unbalanced import business. By the 1900s the Mitsui, Mitsubishi and Sumitomo banks had begun foreign exchange transactions, albeit on a limited scale. They all shared a determination that their banks and their country should not be dominated by the foreign banks. The Japanese attitude is reflected in the instructions sent by a director of the Mitsui Bank in 1898 to his overseas managers:

> You should not bow down before the Hongkong and Shanghai Banking Corporation but raise your head high and associate with them on equal terms ... In this way the HSBC will recognise the strength of the Mitsui family and will be willing to make finance available to us.[15]

Although 'marginalised' in the provision of foreign trade finance by the 1900s, British banks kept an active role in Japan for a time through their access to the London capital market. The Oriental Bank floated in London the new Meiji government's first two foreign loans, in 1870 and 1873. The Japanese government did not enter overseas capital markets again until 1897, when the country's adoption of the gold standard led to a sharp improvement in her credit rating and the possibility of raising capital abroad on favourable terms. There followed a period of substantial central and municipal government borrowing abroad. Between 1899 and 1914 foreign investors lent about £200 million to the Japanese government, which recent writers have argued played an important role in meeting Japan's trade deficit. The Hongkong Bank, as the 'senior' foreign bank in Japan, was prominent in arranging these loans, and between 1897 and 1930 that bank was involved in issuing government (including municipal) loans with a total value of £250 million. However, the Hongkong Bank never had exclusive relations with the Japanese government, and saw its function as being more concerned with developing regional trade, for example between Japan and Australia. The loans were almost invariably issued by syndicates comprising, in addition to the Hongkong Bank, other British overseas banks (especially Chartered Bank), British domestic banks (especially Parr's Bank, which became part of the Westminster Bank after 1918), British merchant banks (especially Barings and N. M. Rothschild) and the ubiquitous Yokohama Specie Bank.[16] Parr's was particularly prominent, apparently because one of their staff had been seconded to Japan as an *oyatoi* training bankers in the Meiji period.

British business, therefore, played a substantial role in the initial development of the external sector of the Meiji economy, through the activities of British merchants, shipping companies and banks, but by

British business in Japan since 1868 225

1914 only the role of British banks in raising foreign capital for Japan remained really significant. In contrast, British direct investment in Japanese industry was never large. The Japanese government resolutely retained in national hands the control and ownership of the railways – a sector which attracted much foreign investment in other developing economies. In Argentina, for example, British-owned companies controlled 70% of the rail mileage and virtually all the major lines in 1914.[17] Occasionally British merchants became involved in domestic Japanese manufacturing or extractive industry: the case of Thomas B. Glover and the Takashima coal mine has received considerable attention.[18] But Glover's involvement in coal production, which contributed to the bankruptcy of his firm, was exceptional.

The late nineteenth century saw the emergence of the modern manufacturing multinational enterprise, with the United States, Germany and Britain as the leading home economies.[19] In Japan there was an inflow of foreign direct investment after revision of the Commercial Law in 1899, although the collapse of the silver price in Japan in 1897 deterred some foreign capital. In the electrical goods sector, the Nihon Electric Company and Shibaura Electric Company formed joint ventures with American companies, Western Electric and General Electric respectively.[20] However, there was much less British than American multinational investment in Japan. Japanese sources suggest that the USA accounted for the greatest proportion of foreign direct investment in Japan (which is estimated to have risen from US$50 million in 1913 to US$120 million in 1929), although American foreign direct investment in China was twenty times as large as that in Japan by 1931. Of 84 joint ventures identified in 1932, 36 were American, 21 were British and 17 were German. Only a few instances of British multinational investment in Japan are identifiable before 1914.

One of the more significant ventures was the building of a factory at Kobe in 1909 by the Dunlop Rubber Company, which pioneered the Japanese rubber industry, retaining (together with other foreign firms) a dominant position in the sector until the Second World War.[21] In 1905 Nobel's Explosives, Armstrong Whitworth and the British subsidiary of a German explosives group established a cordite factory in Japan.[22] In 1907 Vickers and Armstrong Whitworth established, in a joint venture with Japanese industrialists, a steel and armaments factory, Nihon Seikosho, at Muroran.[23] The size and long-term impact of this company, also known as the Japanese Steelworks, exceeded that of Dunlop's subsidiary, although in Seikosho's case British participation steadily declined. In 1910 Babcock & Wilcox, which had a Japanese sales branch associated with Mitsui since 1906, established a factory. By 1914 this venture (Toyo-Babcock) employed 300 men.[24] In 1907 J. and P. Coats launched a joint venture, Teikoku Cotton, with Japanese partners. In addition, some British firms licensed technology to Japanese firms. In the shipbuilding industry, for example, Parsons made a licensing agreement with Mitsubishi in 1904 under which the Japanese company obtained the use of the patent for the Parson turbine, together with substantial technical assistance.[25] Overall British foreign direct investment in Japan was in response either to tariffs, as in the cases of Babcock & Wilcox and Dunlop, or to government pressure for local manufacture, as in the case of the armaments companies and Nobel's.

The main explanation for the limited amount of British investment is clear. British multinationals before 1914 established factories in the heavily populated markets of North America and continental Europe, and Japan's developing economy held little attraction. In addition, the fact that the Japanese government often directly promoted new industries – such as the steel industry in the 1900s – reduced the scope for foreign companies, as the prospect of competing with state-owned or subsidised concerns was hardly an inviting proposition. Allen and Donnithorne suggest that foreign business opinion lacked confidence in Meiji Japan's economic prospects,[26] although the Anglo-Japanese treaty of 1902 provoked a short spate of investment, while Japan's victory over Tsarist Russia in 1904–5 was for several years 'cited as a vindication of organisation, dedicated patriotism and scientific method in the supreme test of war' in some business circles. Thus the chairman of Britain's largest rolling stock manufacturers devoted much of his speech at the company's annual general meeting of 1904 to praising the Japanese as 'a great progressive people' of 'phenomenal' efficiency and 'prowess'. Another English financier, Lyttelton Gell, wrote in 1904:

> I shall turn to the Japanese, for they at least can think, and act and be reticent! ... I fail to see any Western people in a position to set the Japs an example in ... their organization, their strategy, their virile qualities, their devotion and self-control. Above all, their national capacity for self-reliant self-sacrifice and their silence.[27]

In 1905 Lord Revelstoke of Barings expected 'good business coming on from Japan', while another merchant banker, Vicary Gibbs, found that 'at present' British investors 'are greedy takers of Jap things'.[28] This commercial enthusiasm receded in the decade after 1905: overall, while groups of British businessmen before 1914 were at times ecstatic over the economic prospects of countries such as China or Iran, pessimism about Japan was orthodox as late as the 1950s.

It is unclear whether the few British companies which did establish foreign factories in Japan before 1914 experienced greater problems than in other countries. Early British multinationals were handicapped by

British business in Japan since 1868 227

deficient management structures which made the management of foreign subsidiaries difficult.[29] As Japan was on the other side of the world from Britain these problems may have been acute. Certainly Armstrong Whitworth suffered in this respect. 'The creation of a new industry at so great a distance from England is a difficult task', one representative wrote from Japan in 1909, 'and it would be idle to blind ourselves to the fact that in the laying out of the shops, there has been great waste of money.'[30]

Some British businessmen disliked life in Japan. A future director of Fairfields Shipbuilding, for example, observed in 1911:

> This is a pretty stodgy country ... to live in: it may be alright for a 6 weeks tour with a nice bit of fluff! But to live and work in ... well all I can say is ... give me China.[31]

Expatriate British businessmen before 1914 often disparaged foreign countries, and it is unclear whether Japan was seen as particularly unpleasant. Much business and consular comment of this period on Asiatic peoples was disfigured by racial and other prejudice. Before the abolition of extraterritoriality, the typical visitor to Japan (as indeed to China) looked entirely 'through treaty-port spectacles' and reported the Japanese as 'devoid of integrity and morality ... grasping, unreliable, rude and even dangerous' because he had read this embittered diatribe 'every day in his treaty port journal'.[32] It is certainly the case that English-language newspapers in Asiatic ports, written by disappointed exiles, poisoned perceptions of the Chinese and Japanese by their rancour and racial contempt, while the English community in one treaty port was well described in 1898 as 'cocktailing, kicking coolies, riding ponies (and American ladies) deploring exile from a mother country – which does not really miss them – and generally living on the fat of the land, with a new crisis or bogey every morning'.[33] Yet however egregious were the expatriate communities, studies conducted in the 1980s indicate that expatriate business people living in Japan still experience severe culture shock and stress. Research at Waseda and Tokyo universities has isolated several factors which cause such stress, including the extreme difficulties of assimilation into Japanese society, and certain features of Japanese cultural behaviour, including 'smiling with no particular meaning, excessive attention to cleanliness, slurping soup, and staring at foreigners'.[34]

There were constant comments from British businessmen before 1914 about what one Armstrongs man termed 'Japanese trickery. They will get everything and give nothing.'[35] Stories of the ruthless pursuit of Western technology by Japanese became commonplace. In 1925, for example, an Armstrong Whitworth director told one British Admiralty official how

> whenever the Japanese place an order with an armament firm, it is their custom to send sufficient Inspectors, of various classes, to deal with an order some

228 R. P. T. Davenport-Hines and Geoffrey Jones

twenty times the size ... these Inspectors roam the works, with notebook in hand. They look at any drawings laid out and are indignant if requested to move on by the Foreman ... a Japanese [in 1913] was caught in the act of extracting dimensions etc., from an Admiralty gun drawing, and was much aggrieved when his notebook was taken away and torn up by one of the firm's representatives.[36]

The Japanese reputation for being inveterate and unscrupulous copiers by the late 1930s had spread even to Davenport's joke shop, in London, which exported jokes, tricks and stage comedians' and magicians' equipment to Japan. 'The Japanese don't invent much in the way of jokes', the shop's proprietor observed. 'They chiefly copy other people's inventions.'[37]

Nevertheless accusations of 'imitation' need careful interpretation. Japanese industrialists also keenly imitated each other as part of the general process of 'diffusion of presumptive best practice [which] seems to have been extremely rapid in Meiji period manufacturing'. According to a foreign observer in 1896, there was uniform practice and no secrecy between Japanese cotton mills, although foreigners were regarded with suspicion.[38] Some so-called imitations included novel devices or refinements whose possibilities had not occurred to unenterprising Western merchants in Asia, or to foreign manufacturers whose knowledge of local markets was minimal. This ignorance of local demand made it hard for Western observers – even professed Japanese specialists – to appreciate the ingenuity of adaptations to meet consumer wishes, and led to bitter comments when the Japanese 'imitations' proved more competitive. This tendency was strongly pronounced in textiles and pottery: it was in fact a manifestation of Japanese superiority over British business in collecting and analysing commercial intelligence on local markets, a superiority which was pronounced even before 1914.

In a further sense complaints about 'trickery' and 'imitation' were based on cultural divergences. The Japanese professed that in commercial matters, the infrastructure of information (including economic geography, publicly quoted prices etc.) should be disseminated as widely and openly as possible, even if it was of commercial value. As a case-study of the textiles sector concludes, 'the spirit of technological cooperation that seemed to exist among competitive firms' meant that 'the cost of acquiring technological information for any given Japanese spinning firm was extremely low by international standards', indeed 'unique'.[39] In contrast with Britain, for example, Japanese consular reports were distributed free of charge, through chambers of commerce, commercial museums, and provincial departments of commerce, while technical drawings, patents and names of potential customers were often officially reprinted for local circulation. British officialdom, however, under pressure from business interests, and reflecting the profound and inhibiting traditions of secrecy in English society, had none of the openness of the Japanese. Information was jealously guarded, particularly where costs or pricing were concerned, to the detriment of British business; companies were not only worse informed about local markets in consequence, but adhered to traditional forms of competition rather than cooperation, or consortium bidding, meanly hugging individual short-term advantages, and ultimately losing their market position.[40]

Notions of Japanese 'trickery' became widespread. A British writer on 'Commercial Morality in Japan' observed in 1896:

> the standing complaint among foreign merchants in Japan [is] that the native trader will not honourably fulfil his engagement if by so doing he is likely to suffer loss. On the one hand, orders given and contracts signed are regarded by the Japanese as so much waste paper when the market declines; while, on the other, the foreign merchant is held strictly to his agreement should the prospective loss be his.[41]

Japanese 'trickery' did not encourage British businessmen to participate in Japan's development, although it is arguable that Japan evolved these 'unequal tactics' as a counterbalance to the 'unequal treaties' whose practical effects persisted for at least a decade after the abolition of extraterritoriality in 1898.

The British sometimes had problems in adjusting to other Japanese negotiating techniques. 'When the Japanese want a thing they always begin to run the article down', wrote the Tokyo representative of Sir Robert Hadfield, the Sheffield shell and special alloy manufacturer. 'The more they do, you may be sure they intend to buy. If they crack a thing up you may as well pack up and get a move on to another customer.'[42]

8.3 The inter-war years: British influence in decline

British business influence in Japan, already in decline from the late nineteenth century, receded even further after the First World War. The other chapters in this volume have demonstrated a similar trend elsewhere in Asia, but the 'marginalisation' of British business in Japan exceeded that in either, say, Iran or India. There was not only an acceleration of Japanese industrialisation during the European war, but also there were rapid changes in factory organisation and a more aggressive commercial policy in foreign markets such as China. Traditional British business activities in Japan were limited after 1918. Only a few British technical experts were employed in Japan. British merchant houses were significant in only a few specialist sectors: Brunner Mond, for example, maintained a large chemical-importing business in the early 1920s.[43]

230 R. P. T. Davenport-Hines and Geoffrey Jones

In the banking sector, although there was some branch expansion after 1918 – the Hongkong Bank opened a branch in Tokyo in 1924 – the overall significance of British banks in the Japanese financial system declined. However the Hongkong Bank, for example, retained some business in the foreign trade sector – financing, in the 1920s, silk exports to New York and providing finance for trade to places where the Yokohama Specie Bank had not yet penetrated. British banks also continued to operate in foreign capital markets, although there was a relative decline as the New York market increased in importance. The Hongkong Bank, usually in alliance with the Westminster Bank and the Yokohama Specie Bank, arranged the issue of a series of Japanese loans in London. The most notable of these were the South Manchurian Railway Company 5% Sterling Loan for £4 million in 1923, the Japanese Government 6% Sterling Loan of 1924 for £25 million, the City of Tokyo 5.5% Loan for £6 million in 1926, and the Japanese Government 5.5% Conversion Loan for £12.5 million of 1930. The 1924 and 1926 loans were used, in part, to provide the funds needed for the rebuilding of Tokyo after the 1923 earthquake. The British insurance market also undertook some business with Japan. In 1941 British companies had £275,000 worth of contracts of insurance and re-insurance with Japan,[44] although this is a tiny figure which may have stood higher before the deterioration of the Far Eastern political situation in the late 1930s.

The 1920s was a period of considerable world-wide expansion by British and American multinational companies. In the case of American companies, important investments were made in Japan in this period, often in joint ventures with Japanese companies.[45] American rubber and sheet glass manufacturers established factories in Japan. ITT established a substantial manufacturing operation. IBM built a wholly owned subsidiary in Japan in 1937. Perhaps most importantly, American car companies pioneered the Japanese motor-car industry. Ford built a factory at Yokohama in 1925 and General Motors followed a year later with a works at Osaka. Toyota developed links with the American Motor Corporation as part of its search for mass-produced middle-market goods. These factories essentially assembled knocked-down kits imported from the United States.[46] By October 1929 the United States direct investment in manufacturing in Japan had a book value of $US 40.3 million.

British multinational investment was much less extensive. In 1927 Columbia Graphophone, a British gramophone and record manufacturer, acquired the Nippophone Company of Japan, but this was an isolated incident. The British armament companies hoped as early as 1920 to withdraw from their joint ventures, although it proved impossible wholly to liquidate their investments before 1941.[47] By 1940 British companies

British business in Japan since 1868 231

8.2 Sir David Low depicts the British view of Japanese competition, c. 1934.

had investments in only seven manufacturing enterprises in Japan, three 100% owned and four with some Japanese capital.[48] Only three of these ventures were of significance – the factories of Dunlop, Babcock & Wilcox, and J. and P. Coats. A Federation of British Industries Report in 1934 noted the neglect of Japan by British multinational companies in comparison with their American counterparts:

> If tariffs or cost of production prevent certain goods from being imported, British manufacturers should consider having their products manufactured in co-operation with Japanese concerns. For some reason British manufacturers have lagged behind their American competitors in this respect.[49]

Indeed, by the inter-war years the main interest in Japan of British companies was not as a market for investment, but as a dangerous competitor in third-country markets. Japan's industrial base had been considerably strengthened during the First World War. During the 1920s Japanese exporters began to compete with British firms exporting a range of commodities, and the 40% depreciation of the yen in the early 1930s accelerated the Japanese export drive. Numerous British companies felt the impact of Japanese competition. For example, Kenricks, the hardware manufacturers, found its Eastern markets damaged by competition from low-priced Japanese rice bowls, tumblers and chamber pots. From the late

232 R. P. T. Davenport-Hines and Geoffrey Jones

1920s Courtaulds began losing its markets in the East and Australia to Japanese rayon producers.[50]

Japanese competition was widely regarded in interwar Britain as 'unfair'. A British government memorandum written in 1948 recalled Japanese competition in the textile industry in the inter-war years in the following terms:

> The power of Japanese competition was based on excessively low wage rates. In addition, Japanese merchants were unscrupulous in imitating designs, trade marks, packaging and other features in commercial goodwill. It was considered that Japan had cotton exports in mind in fixing an exceptionally low exchange rate when the yen was devalued in 1931 ... Japanese competition was a unique phenomena [sic] in modern commercial experience in that it combined Western efficiency with oriental living standards ... Normal competition is a proper factor to be reckoned with in international trade, but Japanese competition is entirely abnormal in character.[51]

Yet this view was exaggerated in the 1950s as a substitute for more conscientious analysis. The Economic Adviser to the British Mission at Tokyo noted in 1951 that although 'The terms "Japanese competition" and "unfair competition" [were] practically synonymous' before 1941, it was 'dangerous ... to assume that Japanese competition is unfair simply because it can produce and sell more cheaply than its U.K. counterpart'. In cotton textiles, for example, 85% of Japan's output was exported, compared with 30% of Britain's, not because Japan had 'a rice bowl economy', but because 'technically, the Japanese industry was fully as efficient as Lancashire's' with mills 'amongst the most efficient and modern in the world'.[52] These were facts which the British were slow to face.

If in the Meiji period British businessmen in Japan were irked by Japanese 'trickery' in the plagiarism of their products, in the inter-war years the Japanese were cast as combining 'trickery' with the ruthless exploitation of their own people to ruin British export markets. In the sporting images beloved by Britain's ruling classes, the Japanese did not 'play the game'. Certainly, unlike British manufacturers, they played the game to win rather than to lose.

Why was there not more British foreign direct investment in inter-war Japan? The liquidity problem of much of British industry in the 1920s, culminating in the Depression after 1929, was one factor. Another was the hostile environment created by Japanese governments, especially in the 1930s when nationalistic and autarchic policies made the operation of multinational companies in Japan almost unviable. In 1934 a Petroleum Control Act imposed price controls and compulsory stockpiling requirements on the foreign oil companies in Japan, although they seem to have successfully evaded these regulations.[53] In 1936 it was decreed that only

British business in Japan since 1868 233

companies with over 50% Japanese-owned equity would be permitted to assemble or manufacture motor cars in Japan. As a result Ford and General Motors withdrew, leaving the Japanese market to Nissan and Toyota.[54] More specifically, the deterioration in Anglo-Japanese political relations after the invasion of Manchuria in 1931 proved a further obstacle to British business: as one diplomatic expert on the Far East wrote, 'The Japanese have ever since regarded us as the ringleader of the anti-Japanese crusade and Japanese public opinion has been extremely bitter against us.'[55]

By 1931 Dunlop was so alarmed by the growth of nationalistic feeling in Japan that the company began to search for local partners. However, Japanese exchange-control laws made it impossible to repatriate to Britain the proceeds of any sale of equity in the Japanese subsidiary. By 1939 the British company would have sold the whole of Dunlop Japan if it could have remitted its capital, but as this proved impossible no sale had been made before the attack on Pearl Harbor.[56] Babcock & Wilcox had a similar experience. In 1927 it sold a share of its Japanese subsidiary to Mitsui Bussan Kaisha, the Mitsui *zaibatsu* being the dominant buyer of Babcock & Wilcox boilers in the 1920s. Throughout the 1930s Mitsui pressed for majority control of the subsidiary, and by 1939 Babcock & Wilcox had become convinced that its business could not prosper under British control. However, no agreement could be reached on a sale of a further proportion of the equity, primarily because of the problems of exchange control. In the circumstances, the preference of British multinationals for, say, Australia rather than Japan in the inter-war years was entirely rational.

The nature of the Japanese labour market, and Japanese labour laws, also discouraged some British companies from investment in Japan. In 1924 Rowntree, the British chocolate manufacturers, considered taking an equity stake in a Japanese chocolate venture. This would have been the British company's first foreign direct investment. For a time the scheme stimulated considerable enthusiasm at Rowntree, whose Quaker directors contemplated with missionary zeal the prospect of helping a Japanese company 'whose chocolates [were] almost nasty'. However, the discussions were abandoned when Rowntree insisted that its Japanese partner would have to adopt the benevolent and paternalistic employment conditions it maintained in its British factories.[57] Meanwhile, Dunlop's attempts to sell off part of its Japanese subsidiary were complicated by Japanese legislation which apparently obliged the British company to pay its Japanese workers a 'discharge allowance', even though only a change in ownership was contemplated and not the closing of the factory.[58]

There is perhaps a more fundamental explanation behind the paucity of British foreign direct investment in both inter-war and post-1945

234 *R. P. T. Davenport-Hines and Geoffrey Jones*

Japan. Japanese businessmen, and the Japanese government, explicitly sought foreign enterprise only if it brought new technologies and skills to Japan. In 1920s, as Mira Wilkins has shown, American partners were sought by Japanese companies 'eager to obtain US technology'.[59] By the inter-war years Britain had little that was new or innovative to offer Japan, in contrast to the early Meiji period when British banks and shipping expertise did bring needed skills. The British economy offered a combination of decaying staple industries and a range of 'new' industries many of which developed either through foreign direct investment in Britain or by using licensed foreign technology. A considerable number of the British multinationals of the period, outside the consumer goods sector whose products were unlikely to find favour in the low per capita income Japanese market, grew on the basis of imported – often American – technology. ICI and Metal Box were two examples. British industry had little that the Japanese wanted.

8.4 British business and the economic miracle

During the Second World War all British assets in Japan were sequestrated, and during the period 1946–52 the British occupation zone (unlike that of the USA) did not include any industrial areas or major commercial ports. After the war, however, British companies with pre-war Japanese links seemed eager to return to the country. In 1947 a Hongkong Bank representative arrived in Japan, and in the following year the Bank's branches at Yokohama and Kobe were re-opened. Over the following years a moderate business was attained, the Bank financing trade between Japan and the Sterling Area and China, and serving the needs of foreign customers in Japan. In the autumn of 1947 representatives from Babcock & Wilcox, J. and P. Coats, and Dunlop, the three British companies with substantial investments in pre-war Japan, pressed General MacArthur for permission to re-acquire their properties and resume business; disingenuously, but significantly in view of Anglo-American trade rivalry, he disavowed any power to help in the matter.[60] A contrary case was the armaments company Vickers, which in 1952 declined to have restored on favourable terms its 70,490 shares in Seikosho which had been seized by Mitsui in 1941–2. Vickers, for political reasons, would not contemplate any direct participation in Japanese industry, although for an additional subscription of 23.26 million yen (about £23,000) it could have recovered the shares, then paying dividends of 20%.[61] Other British interests regained long-lost market positions in the peculiar circumstances following Japan's defeat and occupation. In 1946–7, for example, British ships carried about two-thirds of the commercial cargo imported into Japan.[62]

There seemed, in the late 1940s and early 1950s, a number of

British business in Japan since 1868 235

Table 8.3 *Geographical sources of technology supplies to Japan,
1950–64*

	Licensing agreements lasting over 12 months %	Licensing agreements lasting under 12 months %
United States	60.0	53.0
West Germany	11.6	22.8
Switzerland	7.0	4.5
United Kingdom	5.3	3.1
France	3.5	5.7

Source: Y. Tsurumi, *Technology Transfer and Foreign Trade. The Case of Japan, 1950–1966* (New York, 1980), p. 246.

opportunities for a renaissance of British business influence in Japan. In 1948 the Japanese Prime Minister suggested that the British-owned British American Tobacco Company (BAT) should take over the Japanese government's tobacco monopoly. The Prime Minister put forward this idea, according to a hopeful British government representative, partly to 'set a precedent for substantial foreign investment in Japan, which is one of the policies of the Democratic–Liberal Party'.[63] The British Foreign Office was enthusiastic about the scheme, but BAT did not wish to become involved. In 1953 a prominent Japanese industrialist, Baron Okura, visited Britain and expressed considerable interest in British aircraft manufacturing, suggesting he might license British technology in this field, 'if and when Japanese rearmament became practicable'.[64]

However, despite these hints of a British business renaissance in Japan, British companies made remarkably little impact in the forty years after 1945. British business was irrelevant to the 'miraculous' growth of the Japanese economy in the 1950s and 1960s. Britain supplied 1.5% of Japan's imports in 1954, and 2% in 1965. A major factor in the 'miracle' was the rapid absorption of foreign technologies by Japanese industries through skilful use of international licensing agreements. Between 1950 and 1964 3,200 licensing agreements were concluded between Japanese licensees and foreign licensors, two-thirds of which had a contractual life exceeding twelve months and the remainder with a contractual life under twelve months. Britain's overall insignificance as a supplier of technology to Japan in this period is illustrated in Table 8.3.

One of the few instances where British technology was used by the Japanese was in the motor-car industry. Following encouragement by the Ministry of International Trade and Industry (MITI) to remedy the absence of medium-sized cars in its product range, Nissan in 1952 signed a technical agreement with Austin Motors (which was then merging with

236 R. P. T. Davenport-Hines and Geoffrey Jones

Table 8.4 *British foreign direct investment in Japan, April 1982*

Date of Foundation	Manufacturing companies			Other companies[a]		
	Wholly owned	Joint venture	Total[b] capital (*million yen*)	Wholly owned	Joint venture	Total[b] capital (*million yen*)
Pre-1970	4	25	62,876	12	6	3,474
1971–6	4	26	9,610	16	14	1,757
1977–82	5	17	12,677	5	13	982

Notes (a) This category includes commerce, banking, insurance, real estate, transport and services.
   (b) This is the total capital of companies containing British foreign direct investment.
Source: List of European Community Companies' Investments in Japan, April 1982, Department of Trade, London

Nuffield to form the British Motor Corporation) whereby the Japanese company assembled and later built Austin cars. Royalties payable to the British in the years 1954–9 totalled 600 million yen or about £600,000. Austin engines and bodies were of great use in developing both trucks and Datsun motor cars, but its chassis and other components were the source of many problems to Nissan, whose product development and production techniques were outpaced in this period by Toyota, which designed new cars of its own without foreign help. The tie-up with Austin stimulated Nissan's product and production technology, although after the arrangements ended 'Nissan engineers realised that they had not acquired any technology from Austin that was unavailable through "indirect" methods – copying from foreign firms, or studying literature that was publicly available.' This was not a straightforward transfer of technology, as Nissan redesigned or improved the British models.[65]

There was little British foreign direct investment in Japan after 1945. Table 8.4 analyses total British foreign direct investment in Japan in April 1982, which amounted to 54,729 million yen (£125.8 million) invested in companies with a total capital of 91,376 million yen (£210 million).

Many of the British ventures were tiny. Four Shell companies accounted for two-thirds of the total capital of the manufacturing companies established before 1970. Foreign oil companies' subsidiaries suffered through MITI's policies, but Shell fared better than others, while Shell's local management and strategy were highly regarded by the Japanese. The importance of joint ventures in the manufacturing sector is also clear, though wholly owned subsidiaries were more popular in services and sales companies. Only a few British or part-British companies were of any significance to either the Japanese economy or their parent groups. One exception was the pharmaceuticals industry, which will be discussed

British business in Japan since 1868 237

below (p. 242). Another was that of industrial gases. In 1982 BOC, the industrial gases company, secured control of Osaka Oxygen, a rare example of a take-over of a Japanese company by a foreign company. Osaka Oxygen was ranked a weak third in Japan's industrial gases industry, but the company was notoriously unprogressive and was part of one of Japan's most technologically backward industries. In 1987 Osaka Oxygen remained in third place with about 10% of the market.

Dunlop's experience provides a poignant if extreme illustration of the general post-1945 performance of British multinationals in Japan. Dunlop, having re-acquired its Kobe factory in the late 1940s, turned its Japanese company into a 40%-owned joint venture, Sumitomo Rubber Industries (SRI), in 1963. SRI remained heavily dependent on British Dunlop's technology until the end of the 1970s. During the early 1980s, however, Dunlop virtually collapsed, and in 1985 it was dismembered and partly absorbed by the British conglomerate BTR. In 1984 SRI purchased the 40% stake Dunlop held in it. Subsequently, SRI purchased for £45 million Dunlop's tyre factories in Britain, France and Germany. 'We have changed the master/student relationship', SRI's Chairman later commented on the remarkable shift of power between Dunlop and its erstwhile Japanese subsidiary.[66]

Indeed, taking a wider perspective, the 'master/student relationship' between British and Japanese business had by the mid-1980s been completely transformed from the situation after the Meiji restoration. Licensing agreements with Japanese firms were hailed as a key strategy in saving Britain's only independent car maker; British government agencies scrambled to attract small Japanese electronics assembly plants; and Japanese management techniques were praised as a model for British labour management policies. The teachers had become the taught. Even in the financial sector – practically the only part of the British economy which was internationally competitive by the mid-1980s – Japanese institutions made remarkable inroads on the British market. During 1986 Japanese banks accounted for 25% of all loans booked in the United Kingdom, although their penetration of the purely domestic banking market remained small.

The undistinguished performance of British business in post-war Japan needs to be put in the context of the considerable obstacles faced by all foreign companies in that country. Even more than in the inter-war years, Japanese government policy between the 1950s and the 1970s discouraged foreign direct investment and even many categories of imports. The preamble to the Foreign Investment Law of 1950, which gave the government powers to screen all international licensing agreements involving Japanese industries and foreign direct investments in Japan,

238 R. P. T. Davenport-Hines and Geoffrey Jones

stipulated that foreign business in Japan was to be strictly regulated to conform to national policy goals:

> The purpose of this law is to create a sound basis for foreign investment in Japan: by limiting the introduction of foreign investment to that which will contribute to the self-support and sound development of the Japanese economy and to the improvement of the international balance of payments by providing for remittances arising from foreign investment, and by providing for adequate protection for such investment.[67]

In accordance with the 1950 law, MITI pursued a consistent policy of locating the best foreign technology to import to Japan, while obstructing foreign direct investment in the country. Many American companies wanted to invest in 'fast-growing Japan', Mira Wilkins observes, but 'they were often thwarted'.[68] Powerful American multinationals found themselves curbed by MITI. In the 1950s, for example, IBM established a wholly owned subsidiary against the wishes of MITI, which wanted a joint venture. MITI launched a campaign against IBM, and wrecked its business by banning imports of computers, and especially the importation of production machinery to manufacture computers. In 1960 IBM was forced to concede to MITI's wishes, agreeing to let Japanese computer manufacturers purchase, for a 5% royalty on sales, all basic computer patents held by IBM. IBM also agreed to concentrate on exporting computers made in its Japanese factory, and to restrict both the models and units of IBM machines sold in the domestic market.[69]

The brunt of MITI's interventions came in industries which were seen as significant to 'self-support', such as cars, computers, steel, petroleum or aeronautics, and of these only the first two sectors were integral to the economic 'miracle'. MITI's interference with market mechanisms produced longer-term structural inefficiencies which are only now becoming apparent, and in some cases at least MITI served as a bogey or as an alibi for Western failure. The impact of Mercedes-Benz and BMW on the Japanese car market suggests that MITI did not create obstacles for British Leyland which were wholly insurmountable.

After Japan joined the Organisation for Economic Cooperation and Development (OECD) in 1964, there were growing international demands that the Japanese government should abandon its restrictive and discriminatory policies towards foreign business. MITI, however, fought a strong rearguard action against capital liberalisation. It was not until 1973 that the government could announce that Japan was '100 per cent liberalized'.[70] In practice, the Japanese government remained hostile to foreign business in the country. One area of blatant anti-foreign discrimination was in government procurement policies. Characteristically the April 1986 report of the Maekawa Commission, established to investigate the structural reasons for Japan's large trade surplus with the rest of the world, avoided all mention of procurement policy, thus doing little to allay continuing allegations of 'trickery'. There was 'a pervasive Western hunch', the *Financial Times* observed in April 1986, that there was 'something intrinsically unfair about Japan as a trading partner'.[71]

British shipping companies in the early 1950s complained bitterly about 'intrinsically unfair' Japanese government policies in the shipping industry. In order to rebuild its merchant navy, for whose loss it was prevented from issuing outright compensation, the Japanese government subsidised the interest on loans raised by shipping companies or compensated banks when shipping companies failed to repay such loans. Japanese banks, supported by the Bank of Japan, provided easy credit to Japanese shipping companies competing with British companies, although the latter also benefited from the support of their own government. In January 1954 the head of Butterfield & Swire in Japan complained bitterly to the British Ambassador in Tokyo about the 'unfairness' of this system:

> What is really needed is that the banks should stop making advances to the shipping companies, and that the shipping companies should be obliged to lay up ships as other shipping companies do in times of slump ... Japanese companies did not appear to behave by normal commercial standards at all.[72]

The British government sympathised with British shipping companies' complaints that the Japanese government pursued discriminating policies in the sector, but redress in this area was hard to secure. When the Japanese Prime Minister visited Britain in November 1954, British ministers complained about the level of subsidy given to Japanese shipping companies in competition with Japanese firms. The Prime Minister's replies to the complaints, one official later observed, 'were not easy to follow'.[73] After British representations the Japanese government promised to modify regulations which induced importers into Japan to use Japanese vessels. But Japanese government promises seemed – and this was a complaint to be repeated time and time again over the following thirty years – not worth the paper they were written on. The Ministry of Transport in Britain observed bitterly in December 1954:

> The Bank of Japan are deliberately conniving at the breach of the regulations amended by the Japanese at the beginning of this year in order to 'reassure' HMG, and it is inconceivable that the Japanese import licensing and financial authorities do not realise and hence permit what is happening, contrary to the binding obligations upon the Japanese Government under the Peace Treaty and to the principles subscribed to in the memorandum of intention on shipping.[74]

To British eyes, the Japanese did not behave like 'gentlemen'.

The upshot of this discussion is that British business was not alone in

240 R. P. T. Davenport-Hines and Geoffrey Jones

finding it very hard to operate in post-war Japan. Nevertheless British business also laboured under particular handicaps. The first point is that, despite the apparent enthusiasm of some British multinationals to return to Japan, there was a strong pessimism in British government and business circles about Japan's post-war prospects, which meant that the Japanese market was given little consideration in the late 1940s and early 1950s. There was some justification for such pessimism, for the period of fast economic growth we call the 'Japanese miracle' did not begin until the late 1950s: yet the degree of pessimism was excessive. After the war G. C. Allen worked in a section of the Foreign Office concerned with formulating policies towards Japan. He later recalled that 'a deep pessimism about both her short-run and her long-run economic prospects permeated the circles in which British policy towards her was being shaped'.[75] There was also fatalism from the outset about British business prospects, which must have been partly self-fulfilling. 'About the fate of the Japanese economy as a whole', an official British report noted in 1947, 'one can say with certainty that it is bound to be closely linked in future to the economy of the United States.'[76] Undoubtedly, too, many British businessmen held the deepest dislike of the Japanese after the Second World War, and were disinclined to become involved in that country. When two high-ranking Japanese officials visited Hong Kong in 1952, the Chief Manager of the Hongkong Bank noted that:

> When the Japanese call they will receive every courtesy. However, I am afraid I have not completely forgotten the past and it is at times hard not to remember some of our friends who suffered so much.[77]

His predecessor as Chief Manager, 62-year-old Sir Vandeleur Grayburn, had died in extremely unpleasant circumstances in a Japanese prison in Hong Kong in 1943.

A second problem for British business in post-war Japan was a comparative lack of support from the British government. The Supreme Command for the Allied Powers (SCAP) was American-dominated, and British business interests did not have the opportunities of their American counterparts. SCAP officials, for example, looked to Citibank and Chase for facilities rather than to the Hongkong Bank. The security pact of 1952 between the USA and Japan proved to be a funnel of technology from America. However, the British government does not seem to have been a dynamic champion of British business, against either the Americans or the Japanese. G. C. Allen later recalled that after the war the Foreign Office 'had little interest' in Japan's economic affairs:

> one official, in the course of a discussion of some technical economic problem, complained of the sordid subjects that we were being forced to occupy ourselves with. Even on the Cabinet Committee some strange attitudes were

British business in Japan since 1868   241

revealed. One of the members was a Parliamentary Secretary whose firm before the war had had extensive dealings with the great Japanese trading companies. When he began to enlighten his colleagues about the nature of the Zaibatsu, the Chairman cut him short by saying; 'My God, N..., what company you keep'![78]

When a British business pressure group, the China Association, complained in 1950 that it was not receiving 'adequate information on commercial and industrial developments in Japan', it was discovered that the Foreign Office had banned the issue of commercial intelligence reports 'because it was felt that confidential information was being disclosed'.[79] The British Foreign Office and MITI epitomise the different approaches to industrial policies taken by the British and Japanese governments after 1945.

Curiously, it was the ostensibly laissez-faire and non-interventionist Thatcher government which adopted the most aggressive policies designed to 'open' the Japanese market to British business. During the spring of 1987, when Cable & Wireless' attempts to enter the Japanese telecommunications market appeared to be blocked by Japanese obfuscation, the British government threatened direct retaliation against Japanese banks in London. However, this policy was less a sign of changed government attitudes than a reflection of the Conservative Party's special concern for the newly 'privatised' Cable & Wireless Company, combined with slavish subservience to United States foreign policy, which had also found Japanese 'unfair' practices a convenient excuse for poor American industrial performance.

The crucial explanation of the failure of British business in post-war Japan lies in a point we have already made about the inter-war years. Japanese government and business sought from foreigners new technologies and skills which were oriented towards mass demand, and the middle market. Britain had little to offer. This is not the place to retell the depressing story of slow British economic growth after 1945, nor to discuss the problems of the apparent 'de-industrialisation' of Britain after 1973. It is clear, however, that large sections of British manufacturing industry became progressively uncompetitive in world markets after 1950, and offered few if any technologies or other skills wanted by the Japanese. British research, development and technical prowess in the 1950s and 1960s were particularly strong in the nuclear industry and in military hardware – two areas in which the Japanese were not interested.[80] There were also political tensions in the mid-1950s, such as the British attempt to exclude the Japanese from the General Agreement on Tariffs and Trade (GATT). 'There has been scarcely a single occasion when I have seen a Japanese official formally other than to say something unpalatable', a British diplomat reported in 1954:

242 *R. P. T. Davenport-Hines and Geoffrey Jones*

they have been badly spoilt by the Americans who turn the other cheek to the petulant child they have reared ... we ourselves have really done very little to help them since the Occupation ended ... On the trade side we have made concessions, but they were [only] at bottom dictated by our own trade interests.[81]

An exception however was the pharmaceutical sector, where in the early 1950s Japanese business pursued a policy of technical collaboration with European and American manufacturers to import new products. As a result of the war in the Pacific, and consequent shortages of personnel and equipment, the indigenous sector suffered from a technical lag which British industry helped to bridge. Typically, a marketing agreement of 1954 between the small firm of Shin Nihon Jitsugyo and Glaxo Laboratories covering one product, Dionosil (a contrast medium for bronchography) led to an exclusive agency agreement for all Glaxo products in 1955. Following the liberalisation of trade in 1965, Shin Nihon formed its first joint venture company, Glaxo-Fuji Pharmaceutical Laboratories (with the British owning 40%) in 1968. This was followed in 1973 by the formation of Nippon Glaxo Ltd, a 50/50 joint venture company to promote and market Glaxo products in Japan. Under further adjustments in 1975–6 Glaxo raised its stake in Glaxo-Fuji to 50% and in Shin Nihon to 44%. These arrangements resulted in considerable profit to both participants (total sales in 1986 apparently amounted to £70 million, compared with £15 million in 1976),[82] and demonstrated the possibilities for British manufacturing sectors which had remained technologically advanced and competitive in marketing.

Generally, however, where British industry had desirable technologies, it seemed – in the age-old complaint – poor at marketing them. The President of Sumitomo Rubber reflected in 1986 on what had gone wrong with his erstwhile British parent company, Dunlop:

The Birmingham Tyre Technical Centre was the leader of tyre technology in the world. But their splendid results were not connected to the user-oriented products. They made good products and told users to use them. We think it was completely upside-down.[83]

Poor marketing was frequently matched by low-quality goods. This was particularly unfortunate as in post-war Japan quality standards for products, packaging and service were considerably higher than in Britain, or even often in the United States. 'The Japanese have an extremely highly developed sense of quality', the Chief Executive of Dunhill Holdings, a British luxury consumer goods manufacturer which developed a large Japanese market in the 1980s, observed. 'You've simply got to meet their quality aspirations, or you're not going to do business.'[84] Dunhill itself ran into difficulties when it attempted to market in Japan shirts manufac-

British business in Japan since 1868 243

tured in Hong Kong: Japanese consumers wanted the prestige and assumed quality of European-made shirts. Dunhill had to revert to making the same shirts in Europe.

It is clear that, leaving aside barriers to trade, a number of factors contrived to make Japan a 'difficult' market. These factors ranged from the high saving propensities of the Japanese to the difficulties for a foreign venture in becoming a sub-contractor in Japan, and to penetrate the *keiretsu* system of 'mutually supporting groups' of Japanese companies. Given these problems, the lacklustre marketing performance of many British companies was a particular handicap in Japan. If the British literature was full of complaints about Japan's ever-moving invisible trade barriers, Japanese sources in the 1960s and 1970s were full of complaints that British exporters failed to meet delivery dates or provide adequate after-sales service, and were inadequately represented in Japan.[85] The story of a major British confectionery company which tried in the mid-1980s to sell sweets to the Japanese in packages made up by its Hong Kong agent with some of the script in characters unconverted from Chinese to Japanese was all too familiar.[86] In addition to such general problems there was a persistent failure in British business circles to understand Japanese cultural characteristics, such as the importance given to continuity in business relationships and the need to demonstrate a commitment to the market. For many British businessmen the Japanese remained an inscrutable mystery: the chief negotiator for Cable & Wireless in its attempts in 1987 to penetrate the Japanese market concluded of his possible future Japanese business partners: 'We are as different as *sake* and hot water. You just can never tell what they are thinking.'[87]

Japan was for too long regarded as a peripheral market, or was the subject of attitudes scarcely adapted from the time of the Meiji restoration. It was natural that an industrial latecomer such as Japan should have an international competitive advantage based on labour costs and productivity: what was remarkable was that Britain failed to develop compensating managerial advantages, based on longer organisational experience.

8.5 Conclusion

In the early Meiji period British merchants, banks and shipping companies played key roles in developing Japanese foreign trade. By the end of the nineteenth century, however, all these enterprises had undergone 'marginalisation', as Japanese-owned ventures secured dominant positions. In twentieth-century Japan British business activity has been limited. Few British multinationals established factories in Japan: those of

Dunlop and Vickers alone held sustained importance for the Japanese economy. After 1945 Japanese companies made substantial use of international licensing agreements, but little technology was purchased from British sources. The last decade has seen the arrival of Japanese multinationals in Britain, and transfers of capital, technology and management from Japan to Britain.

There are two complementary explanations of the changing nature of British and Japanese business relations. The first explanation focusses on Japan. From the beginning of the Meiji era the Japanese government limited the direct role of foreign business in Japan in order to protect its nascent industrialisation, as adjured by German theoretical writers such as Friedrich List. Foreigners were imported to teach techniques to the Japanese, and then sent home. The Japanese government promoted indigenous business activity, and for various reasons Japanese entrepreneurs proved dynamic. In the twentieth century Japanese governments and business have used a wide range of devices to discriminate against foreign companies, to promote Japanese enterprise, and generally to use foreigners rather than be used by them. The consistency and continuity of purpose of the Japanese have, in a long-term historical perspective, been remarkable. They have also earned Japan a reputation in Britain, dating from the late nineteenth century, for 'trickery', and unfair and unscrupulous practices. British business, it could be argued, has never stood a chance in such an environment.

However, the fact that American business fared better in Japan than British suggests a British dimension to the problem. The concept of 'advantage', used by economists to explain why multinational companies establish factories in foreign countries, holds the key. In the 1870s and 1880s British merchants, banks and shipping companies had skills and technologies absent from Japan. By 1900, however, their 'advantages' had dwindled, and in the twentieth century few British businesses had products or technologies the Japanese needed or wanted. British companies which had marketable assets – such as Dunlop until the 1970s, and Glaxo since the 1970s – have not found operating in Japan a hopeless task. To a very large extent, the causes of British business failure in Japan are to be found in Britain, rather than in Japan.

Notes

1 British business in Asia since 1860

1 Yu-Kwei Cheng, *Foreign Trade and Industrial Development of China* (Washington, 1956); Chi-ming Hou, *Foreign Investment and Economic Development in China 1840–1937* (Cambridge, Mass., 1965); N. Imlah, *Foreign Capital and Economic Development: Japan, India and Canada* (Rutland, Vermont, 1960); M. Kidron, *Foreign Investments in India* (Oxford, 1965); W. Galenson (ed.), *Foreign Trade and Investment: Economic Development in the Newly Industrialising Asian Countries* (Wisconsin, 1985). There are valuable studies of the role of British business in individual countries: G. C. Allen and A. G. Donnithorne, *Western Enterprise in Far Eastern Economic Development: China and Japan* (London, 1954); G. C. Allen and A. G. Donnithorne, *Western Enterprise in Indonesia and Malaya: A Study in Economic Development* (London, 1957).

2 W. Woodruff, *Impact of Western Man* (London, 1966), Table VII/14.

3 D. A. Farnie, 'The Structure of the British Cotton Industry, 1846–1914', in A. Okochi and S. Yonekawa (eds.), *The Textile Industry and its Business Climate* (Tokyo, 1982), p. 51.

4 A. J. H. Latham, *The International Economy and the Underdeveloped World* (London, 1978), p. 68; B. R. Tomlinson, *The Political Economy of the Raj* (London, 1979), pp. 5–6.

5 Tomlinson, *Political Economy*, pp. 2–3.

6 Latham, *International Economy*, pp. 88–90. These figures are particularly fragile given the dubious nature of the trade statistics as a whole, and ignorance about the sources and destination of Chinese trade which passed through Hong Kong. Hong Kong's share of Chinese exports increased from 13% to 29% between 1868 and 1914, and its share of Chinese imports increased from 21% to 29%.

7 See especially D. C. St M. Platt, *Britain's Investment Overseas on the Eve of the First World War* (London, 1986), chapter 4; L. Davis and R. A. Huttenback, 'The Export of British Finance, 1865–1914', *Journal of Imperial and Commonwealth History*, 13 (1985), pp. 28–76; L. E. Davis and R. A. Huttenback, *Mammon and the Pursuit of Empire: The Political Economy of British Imperialism 1860–1912* (Cambridge, 1986).

8 For one estimate of Britain's share of foreign investment in Asia in 1913, see W. Woodruff, *Impact of Western Man*, pp. 154–5.

9 Platt, *Britain's Investment Overseas*, chapter 5.

246 *Notes to pages 5–10*

10 L. G. Sandberg, *Lancashire in Decline: A Study in Entrepreneurship, Technology and International Trade* (Columbus, 1974).

11 Latham, *International Economy*, pp. 98–9. There are problems with India's trade figures in this period which need to be recalled when interpreting their implications. Latham's source for the import figures, for example, makes no allowance for the fact that Burma was separated from the Indian trade statistics after 1935, so that some of India's imports after 1935 came from Burma. The Burma problem partly explains the apparent decline in Britain's share in the 1930s.

12 Ibid., pp. 106–8, 112, 118.

13 Woodruff, *Impact of Western Man*, pp. 156–7, gives an estimate of the British share of foreign investment in Asia in 1938, but his figures for individual countries are unreliable.

14 C. H. Lee, *The British Economy since 1700* (Cambridge, 1986), pp. 220–1, 223–4.

15 E. Kleiman, 'Trade and the Decline of Colonialism', *Economic Journal*, 86 (1976), p. 471.

16 J. Stopford and L. Turner, *Britain and the Multinationals* (Chichester, 1985), p. 81.

17 See B. R. Tomlinson, chapter 4 below, p. 264, note 16.

18 P. Svedberg, 'The Portfolio Direct Composition of Private Foreign Investments in 1914 Revisited', *Economic Journal*, 88 (1978), pp. 763–77.

19 J. H. Dunning, 'Changes in the Level and Structure of International Production: the Last One Hundred Years', in M. Casson (ed.), *The Growth of International Business* (London, 1983), p. 90.

20 For references to concession-hunters in China, see generally S. F. Wright, *Hart and the Chinese Customs* (Belfast, 1950); J. K. Fairbank, K. F. Bruner and E. M. Matheson (eds.), *The IG in Peking*, 2 vols. (London, 1975); and Lo Hui Min, *The Correspondence of G. E. Morrison 1895–1920*, 2 vols. (Cambridge, 1976–8). For references to Algernon Moreing and Sir Edmund Davis of the Chinese Engineering & Mining Company, see Ellsworth Carlson, *The Kaiping Mines 1877–1912* (Cambridge, Mass., 1971); John Hamill, *The Strange Career of Mr Hoover under Two Flags* (New York, 1931), pp. 59–88; H. Hoover, *Years of Adventure* (London, 1952), pp. 65–90; G. H. Nash, *The Life of Herbert Hoover: the Engineer 1874–1914* (New York, 1983), pp. 125–222.

21 O. Checkland, 'The Scots in Meiji Japan 1868–1912', in R. A. Cage (ed.), *The Scots Abroad: Labour, Capital and Enterprise 1750–1914* (London, 1985).

22 Mira Wilkins, 'Defining a Firm: History and Theory', in P. Hertner and G. Jones (eds.), *Multinationals: Theory and History* (Aldershot, 1986), pp. 84–6; M. Wilkins, 'The Free-standing Company, 1870–1914: An Important Type of British Foreign Direct Investment', *Economic History Review*, 41 (1988).

23 S. D. Chapman, 'British-based Investment Groups before 1914', *Economic History Review*, 38 (1985), pp. 230–51; R. Vicat Turrell and J.-J. van Helten, 'The Investment Group: the Missing Link in British Overseas Expansion before 1914', ibid., 40 (1987), pp. 267–74; S. D. Chapman, 'Investment

Notes to pages 11–16 247

Groups in India and South Africa', ibid., 40 (1987), pp. 275–80; Stephanie Jones, *Two Centuries of Overseas Trading: The Origins and Growth of the Inchcape Group* (London, 1986); M. Keswick (ed.), *The Thistle and the Jade: A Celebration of Jardine Matheson & Company* (London, 1982).

24 G. Jones, *The State and the Emergence of the British Oil Industry* (London, 1981), pp. 19–23, 61, 77–9. A history of the Shell Group before 1914, largely from the Dutch perspective, is F. C. Gerretson, *History of the Royal Dutch*, 4 vols. (Leiden, 1958).

25 Jones, *State and Emergence*, pp. 93–5, 151–5.

26 A. Fenichel and G. Huff, 'Colonialism and the Economic System of an Independent Burma', *Modern Asian Studies*, 9 (1975), pp. 321–35; H. E. W. Braund, *Calling to Mind: the First Hundred Years (1870–1970) of Steel Brothers and Company* (Oxford, 1975); A. C. Pointon, *The Bombay Burmah Trading Corporation 1863–1963* (London, 1964); A. McCrae and A. Prentice, *Irrawaddy Flotilla* (Paisley, 1978); A. McCrae, 'The Irrawaddy Flotilla Company', *Business History*, 22 (1978); T. A. B. Corley, *A History of the Burmah Oil Company 1886–1924* (London, 1983).

27 Peter Richardson, *Chinese Mine Labour in the Transvaal* (London, 1982); W. N. Willis, *Western Men with Eastern Morals* (London, 1913).

28 A. S. J. Baster, *The Imperial Banks* (London, 1929); A. S. J. Baster, *The International Banks* (London, 1935).

29 See p. 175 of this volume, and Sir C. Mackenzie, *Realms of Silver* (London, 1954), pp. 215–16.

30 Baster, *International Banks*, p. 176; G. Jones, *Banking and Empire in Iran* (Cambridge, 1986), pp. 56–71.

31 See Jones, *Banking and Empire*. Differences of opinion between London-based boards of British overseas banks and their local managers were not confined to banks operating in Asia: for similar conflicts in British banks in Latin America, see D. Joslin, *A Century of Banking in Latin America* (London, 1963); in Australia, D. J. Merrett, *ANZ Bank* (Sydney, 1985); and in Africa, R. Fry, *Bankers in West Africa* (London, 1976), pp. 63–4. A short popular history of the Hongkong Bank is Maurice Collis, *Wayfoong* (London, 1965). A four-volume academic history of the Bank by F. H. H. King is published by the Cambridge University Press. Volume I is *The Hongkong Bank in Late Imperial China, 1864–1902: On an Even Keel* (Cambridge, 1987).

32 The failure of the Hongkong Bank's bid for the Royal Bank of Scotland is discussed in Stephen Fay, *Portrait of an Old Lady* (London, 1987), pp. 122–6. The international characteristics of British overseas business, especially merchants, in the nineteenth century is treated in Charles A. Jones, *International Business in the Nineteenth Century: The Rise and Fall of a Cosmopolitan Bourgeoisie* (Brighton, 1987).

33 Jones, *Banking and Empire*, p. 28.

34 A. K. Bagchi, 'Anglo-Indian Banking in British India: From the Paper Pound to the Gold Standard', *Journal of Imperial and Commonwealth History*, 13 (1985), p. 96.

35 G. Jones, 'Origins, Management and Performance', in G. Jones (ed.), *British Multinationals: Origins, Management and Performance* (Aldershot, 1986),

248 *Notes to pages 16–24*

pp. 4–6; S. J. Nicholas, 'British Multinational Investment before 1939', *Journal of European Economic History*, 11 (1982), pp. 605–30.

36 Jones, 'Origins', pp. 6–10.

37 Stopford and Turner, *Britain*, p. 82.

38 Tomlinson, p. 265, note 24, of this volume.

39 The British experience has to be seen in the context of the increasing use of joint ventures by all Western multinationals active in the Third World. See Rhys Jenkins, *Transnational Corporations and Uneven Development* (London, 1987), pp. 146–7.

40 The Hongkong Bank's growth after 1945 is surveyed in Collis, *Wayfoong*. The edition reprinted in 1978 has a valuable 'Postscript' by F. H. H. King covering the period 1965–77. See also *Financial Times*, 30 April 1984, p. 11. For the post-1945 growth of the British Bank of the Middle East, and its acquisition by the Hongkong Bank, see G. Jones, *Banking and Oil* (Cambridge, 1987), chapters 1–3.

41 'Hongkong Bank's Dominance Undercut', *Asian Wall Street Journal*, 7 May 1987.

42 See Tomlinson, p. 98 of this volume.

43 See Jones, *Banking and Empire*.

44 Galenson (ed.), *Foreign Trade and Investment*, pp. 228, 278.

45 P. Joseph, *Foreign Diplomacy in China 1894–1900: A Study in Political and Economic Relations* (London, 1928, repr. New York, 1971); N. Pelcovits, *Old China Hands and the Foreign Office* (New York, 1948); D. McLean, 'The Foreign Office and the First Chinese Indemnity Loan, 1895', *Historical Journal*, 16 (1973), pp. 303–21; D. McLean, *Britain and her Buffer State* (London, 1979); D. McLean, 'International Banking and its Political Implications: the Hongkong and Shanghai Banking Corporation and the Imperial Bank of Persia 1889–1914', in F. H. H. King (ed.), *Eastern Banking* (London, 1983); R. P. T. Davenport-Hines (ed.), *Markets and Bagmen* (Aldershot, 1986), pp. 102–30; A. Trotter, *Britain and East Asia 1933–37* (Cambridge, 1975); R. A. Dayer, *Bankers and Diplomats in China 1917–1925* (London, 1981).

46 K. Sinclair, 'Hobson and Lenin in Lahore: Colonial Office Policy towards British Concessionaires and Investors 1878–1907', *Modern Asian Studies*, 1 (1967), pp. 335–52; E. Chew, 'Sir Frank Swettenham and the Federation of Malay States', *Modern Asian Studies*, 2 (1968), pp. 51–96; C. Jeshurun, 'The British Foreign Office and the Siamese Malay States', *Modern Asian Studies*, 5 (1971), pp. 143–60.

47 See for example D. C. St M. Platt, *Finance, Trade and Politics: British Foreign Policy 1815–1914* (Oxford, 1968), pp. 209–48, 262–307; McLean, 'International Banking', pp. 2–3; Davenport-Hines, *Markets and Bagmen*, pp. 169–76; R. P. T. Davenport-Hines, 'The Ottoman Empire in Decline: the Business Imperialism of Sir Vincent Caillard 1883–98', in R. V. Turrell and J.-J. van Helten (eds.), *The City and the Empire* (London, 1985), pp. 118–34.

48 Lord Mersey, *A Picture of Life* (London, 1941), p. 133; Sir Penderel Moon, *Wavell, the Viceroy's Journal* (London, 1973), p. 420; Sir William Ramsay, quoted in David Ayerst, *The Guardian* (London, 1971), p. 362.

49 Information from Sir Anthony Jephcott, March 1984.

Notes to pages 24–33 249

50 For a recent comparison of British, German and American attitudes to business and national policy in another continent, see H. H. Herwig, *Germany's Vision of Empire in Venezuela 1871–1914* (Princeton, 1986).

51 There is a helpful introduction to the general issues in N. Hood and S. Young, *The Economics of Multinational Enterprise* (London, 1979), chapter 8.

52 Sir Humphrey Mynors (ed.), *Thomas Sivewright Catto, Baron Catto of Cairncatto* (Edinburgh, 1962), pp. 70–4; *The Times*, 4 July 1928; cf. *Vickers News*, August 1928.

53 See Tomlinson, pp. 106–12 of this volume.

54 L. G. Reynolds, *Economic Growth in the Third World: an Introduction* (New Haven, 1985), pp. 106–7.

55 S. C. Tsaing and Rong-I Wu, 'Foreign Trade and Investment as Boost for Take-Off', in Galenson (ed.), *Foreign Trade and Investment*, pp. 328–9.

56 A. D. Chandavarkar, 'Money and Credit, 1858–1947', in D. Kumar (ed.), *The Cambridge Economic History of India* (Cambridge, 1983), p. 775.

57 Y. C. Yao, 'Financing Hong Kong's Early Postwar Industrialisation', in King, *Eastern Banking*, pp. 545–67.

58 Tsaing and Wu, 'Foreign Investment', pp. 328–9.

59 Reynolds, *Economic Growth in the Third World*, pp. 45–7.

60 C. A. Fisher, 'The Britain of the East? A Study in the Geography of Imitation', *Modern Asian Studies*, 2 (1968), pp. 343–76.

61 'Far East Imports Account for Half Clothing Market', *Financial Times*, 12 January 1987.

62 For an account of the growth of Japanese investment in Britain see John H. Dunning, *Japanese Participation in British Industry* (London, 1986), chapters 1 and 2.

63 'The Road to Britain', *Far Eastern Economic Review*, 26 November 1987.

64 Marquess of Dufferin and Ava, *Speeches delivered in India 1884–8* (London, 1890), pp. 282–4; George N. Curzon, *Problems of the Far East* (London, 1984), p. 421.

65 'Questions after the Great Escape', *Financial Times*, 19 February 1987.

2 British business in Iran, 1860s–1970s

* We would like to thank Peter Avery, Richard Davenport-Hines, Fred Halliday, Paul Luft and Sir Denis Wright for their assistance in the preparation of this chapter.

1 The best source on the economic history of nineteenth-century Iran is C. Issawi (ed.), *The Economic History of Iran 1800–1914* (Chicago, 1971). The only general study of the twentieth-century economy is J. Bharier, *Economic Development in Iran 1900–1970* (London, 1971). There are surveys of Iran's political and social history in P. Avery, *Modern Iran* (London, 1965) and N. Keddie, *Roots of Revolution* (New Haven, 1981).

2 R. W. Ferrier, *The History of the British Petroleum Company*, vol. I (Cambridge, 1982); Geoffrey Jones, *Banking and Empire in Iran: The History of the British Bank of the Middle East*, vol. I (Cambridge, 1986); Stephanie

250 *Notes to pages 34–40*

Jones, *Two Centuries of Overseas Trading: The Origins and Growth of the Inchcape Group* (London, 1986).

3 R. A. McDaniel, *The Shuster Mission and the Persian Constitutional Revolution* (Minneapolis, 1974), pp. 12–13; W. Floor, *Industrialization in Iran 1900–1941* (Centre for Middle Eastern and Islamic Studies, Durham, Occasional Paper Series, No. 23, 1984), p. 10.

4 D. Wright, *The English Amongst the Persians* (London, 1977), pp. 94ff.

5 A. Seyf, 'Some Aspects of the Economic Development in Iran 1806–1906' (unpublished PhD thesis, Reading University, 1982), p. 101.

6 S. Jones, *Two Centuries*, pp. 79–101.

7 'The Story of the Euphrates Company', *The Near East and India*, 24 November 1932.

8 S. Jones, *Two Centuries*, p. 102.

9 J. D. Scott, *Siemens Brothers 1858–1958* (London, 1958), pp. 36–7, 53, supplemented by information on the Indo-European Telegraph Company in BT 31/30769/3953, PRO. See also Wright, *The English*, pp. 129–33.

10 G. Jones, *Banking and Empire*, pp. 9–15.

11 N. Keddie, *Religion and Rebellion in Iran: The Tobacco Protest 1891–1892* (London, 1966); Wright, *The English*, pp. 158–9.

12 G. Jones, *Banking and Empire*, p. 22.

13 R. L. Greaves, *Persia and the Defence of India 1884–1892* (London, 1959), p. 122; there is a survey of early railway projects in Iran in R. I. Lawless (ed.), *The Gulf in the Early 20th Century: foreign institutions and local responses* (University of Durham, Centre for Middle Eastern and Islamic Studies, Occasional Papers Series, No. 31, 1986).

14 D. McLean, *Britain and Her Buffer State* (London, 1979), pp. 64–70; G. Jones, *Banking and Empire*, pp. 93–4.

15 Ferrier, *History*, pp. 15–201; Geoffrey Jones, *The State and the Emergence of the British Oil Industry* (London, 1981), pp. 128–76.

16 'The New Oriental Bank Corporation: A Lesson in Bad Banking', *Banker's Magazine* (1894); G. Jones, *Banking and Empire*, pp. 21–2.

17 G. Jones, *Banking and Empire*, pp. 23, 35–6, 341–9.

18 There is an excellent account of the impact of the world-wide depreciation of silver on Iran in P. Avery and J. Simmons, 'Persia on a Cross of Silver 1880–1890', *Middle Eastern Studies* (1974).

19 G. Jones, *Banking and Empire*, pp. 53–4, 85.

20 H. J. Whigham, *The Persian Problem* (London, 1903), pp. 290–303; Avery, *Modern Iran*, pp. 95–6, 325–6; Wright, *The English*, pp. 99–100; Issawi (ed.), *Economic History*, pp. 301–5.

21 G. Jones, *Banking and Empire*, pp. 11–12.

22 S. Chapman, *The Rise of Merchant Banking* (London, 1984), pp. 114, 132. A history of the Hongkong Bank by F. H. H. King is being published by the Cambridge University Press: see n. 31 to chapter 1, above. For an account of the Sassoon family, see C. Roth, *The Sassoon Dynasty* (London, 1942), and S. Jackson, *The Sassoons* (London, 1968).

23 T. A. B. Corley, *A History of the Burmah Oil Company 1886–1924* (London, 1983), pp. 95–111, 181–98, 238–9.

Notes to pages 40–9 251

24 B. V. Anan'ich, *Rossikoe Samoderzhavii Vyvaz Kapitalov* (Leningrad, 1975); G. Jones, *Banking and Empire*, pp. 54–6, 86–7, 98–9.

25 W. H. Floor, 'The Bankers (sarraf) in Qajar Iran', *Zeitschrift der Deutschen Morganlandischen Gesellschaft* (1979); Bharier, *Economic Development*, pp. 239–40.

26 S. Jones, *Two Centuries*, p. 103; Ferrier, *History*, pp. 306–12, 316–19, 333–41.

27 Ferrier, *History*, pp. 185–91.

28 Ferrier, *History*, pp. 74–8; G. Jones, *State*, p. 136.

29 Ferrier, *History*, p. 280; G. Jones, *Banking and Empire*, p. 171.

30 In McLean, *Britain*, p. 64.

31 Keddie, *Roots*, pp. 82–3; M. E. Yapp, '1900–21: The Last Years of the Qajar Dynasty', in H. Amirsadeghi (ed.), *Twentieth Century Iran* (London, 1977), pp. 20–1.

32 For the brief revival of the Persian Transport Company, see Caesar Hawkins to Sir Hugh Barnes, 10 November 1919, R27, British Bank of the Middle East (hereafter BBME) Archives. We are grateful to the Hongkong Bank Group for permission to consult these archives. For the postwar revival of the Persian Railways Syndicate, and the brief flurry of interest in it from Vickers and Armstrong Whitworth, see Report of the Directors, PRS, 27 February 1920, HO 28A, and correspondence in Files R39/7, R39/10 and R40, BBME.

33 Ferrier, *History*, chapter 5; G. Jones, *State*, chapter 5.

34 G. Jones, *Banking and Empire*, p. 91.

35 G. Jones, *Banking and Empire*, p. 195.

36 The political and economic history of this period is surveyed in A. Banani, *The Modernisation of Iran 1921–1941* (Stanford, 1961); H. Katouzian, *The Political Economy of Modern Iran* (London, 1981); G. Lenczowski (ed.), *Iran under the Pahlavis* (Stanford, 1978); Floor, *Industrialization*, pp. 15–44.

37 Ferrier, *History*, pp. 591–631; P. J. Beck, 'The Anglo-Persian Oil Dispute 1932–33', *Journal of Contemporary History* (1974); R. B. Stobaugh, 'The Evolution of an Iranian Oil Policy, 1925–1975', in Lenczowski (ed.), *Iran*.

38 Bharier, *Economic Development*, p. 156; Keddie, *Roots of Revolution*, pp. 109–10.

39 Statement by Anglo-Iranian's Chairman, *Financial Times*, 1 July 1948.

40 A. Sampson, *The Seven Sisters* (London, 1975), pp. 124–5.

41 Sampson, *Seven Sisters*, pp. 131–2. For an account of Mossadeq's views on the oil industry see Farhad Diba, *Mossadegh. A Political Biography* (London, 1986), pp. 84ff, 115ff.

42 Sepehr Zabih, *The Mossadegh Era* (Chicago, 1982), p. 7.

43 Sampson, *Seven Sisters*, pp. 133–6, 140–1; Kermit Roosevelt, *Countercoup: The Struggle for the Control of Iran* (New York, 1979); B. Rubin, *Paved with Good Intentions: The American Experience and Iran* (New York, 1980), pp. 54–90; C. M. Woodhouse, *Something Ventured* (London, 1982). Zabih, *Mossadegh Era*, argues that internal Iranian factors were more important in Mossadeq's overthrow than the British and American governments.

44 Sir Roger Stevens to Rt Hon. Anthony Eden, 4 January 1955, Political Review

252 *Notes to pages 49–56*

for Persia, 1954, FO 371/114805, PRO; Sampson, *Seven Sisters*, pp. 144–7; see also Fred Halliday, *Iran: Dictatorship and Development* (London, 1979), chapter 6.

45 G. Jones, *Banking and Empire*, pp. 215–17.

46 G. Jones, *Banking and Empire*, pp. 301, 309–11.

47 G. Jones, *Banking and Empire*, pp. 283–6, 305–9; Frances Bostock and Geoffrey Jones, *Planning and Power in Iran* (London, 1988), chapters 1 and 4.

48 G. Jones, *Banking and Empire*, pp. 317–31.

49 Geoffrey Jones, *Banking and Oil. The History of the British Bank of the Middle East*, vol. II (Cambridge, 1987), chapter 1.

50 G. Jones, *Banking and Empire*, pp. 332–7.

51 S. Jones, *Two Centuries*, pp. 102–5.

52 Avery, *Modern Iran*, pp. 325–6.

53 Annual Economic Report for 1937, FO 371/21894.

54 Information from Richard Davenport-Hines.

55 Banani, *Modernisation*, pp. 133–41; Richard Costain's contract to build eleven miles of single-track railway, incorporating seven tunnels and two large span bridges, was worth £1 million in 1936: we are grateful to Richard Costain Ltd for this information.

56 Report by Sir George Binney on the Persian Rail Negotiations, August–October 1950, in Binney to Lord Leathers, 8 January 1952, FO 371/98670.

57 G. Middleton to A. D. M. Ross, 31 March 1952, FO 371/110028.

58 Commercial Secretary's Report on Economic Conditions in Persia, October 1944, FO 371/40167.

59 Telegram from Sir Reader Bullard, 21 March 1945, FO 371/45441.

60 Sir John le Rougetel to Foreign Office, 9 November 1946, FO 371/52734; Memorandum by Sir Alexander Gibb and Partners, enclosed in A. M. Gibb to L. F. L. Pyman, 20 September 1945, FO 371/45442.

61 G. B. Baldwin, *Planning and Development in Iran* (Baltimore, 1967).

62 R. Couldrey to L. F. L. Pyman, 17 September 1948, FO 371/68713; Minutes by R. A. Clinton Thomas, 14 and 21 January 1949; Telegram from Sir Oliver Franks, 21 January 1949, FO 371/75482.

63 Tehran Confidential Letter to London, 4 January 1950, BBME.

64 A Summary of the progress made on various capital development projects in Persia, 19 February 1947, BT 11/3368, PRO.

65 London Confidential Letter, 8 February 1928, X27, BBME.

66 Letter from Kenneth Brooke, 18 August 1948: information from Charlie Wilkinson, from researches on Glaxo.

67 W. R. Louis, *The British Empire in the Middle East 1945–51* (Oxford, 1984), pp. 642–89.

68 Report on Trade with Persia by Commercial Secretary, Tehran, 1 May 1946, FO 371/52763.

69 Miss E. P. D. Hill to Miss Ashe, 19 September 1950, FO 371/82342.

70 Sir George Binney to Lord Leathers, 9 January 1952, FO 371/98670.

71 G. Jones, *Banking and Empire*, pp. 157–8, 284–5.

72 G. Jones, *Banking and Empire*, p. 218.

73 Sampson, *Seven Sisters*, pp. 134–5. The Minister in question was Sir Kenneth

Notes to pages 56–63   253

Younger, Minister of State at the Foreign Office. See also Louis, *British Empire*, p. 648.

74 G. Jones, *Banking and Empire*, pp. 317–18; Louis, *British Empire*, pp. 651–3.

75 Minute by D. L. Stewart, 12 May 1954, FO 371/110024.

76 R. G. Couldrey to D. A. Logan, 17 August 1950, FO 371/82334.

77 Board of Trade Circular, 10 March 1924, X29, BBME; Note on Trade with Persia, 1 May 1946, FO 371/52763; Titchener's Speech to Board of Trade, 27 September 1954; and Draft Article for Board of Trade Journal, FO 371/110028.

78 *Financial Times*, 5 December 1957. In 1957 Britain's exports to Iran were running at the annual rate of some £33 millions, which was higher than the pre-oil dispute peak: see R. Stevens to J. Selwyn Lloyd, 1 August 1957, FO 371/127073.

79 Bharier, *Economic Development*, p. 193.

80 J. Amouzegar, *Iran: An Economic Profile* (Washington D.C., 1977), p. 156.

81 J. L. B. Titchener to L. A. C. Fry, 29 May 1954, FO 371/110027.

82 Memorandum by Board of Trade, 10 March 1955, FO 371/110026.

83 Minute by P. L. Stewart, 27 October 1954, FO 371/110014.

84 H. Razavi and F. Vakil, *The Political Environment of Economic Planning in Iran, 1971–1983* (Boulder, Colorado, 1984), p. 28; W. H. Forbis, *Fall of the Peacock Throne* (New York, 1980), pp. 242–4; for information on the car kits operation, see also *Financial Times*, 26 August 1987, on the closure by Peugeot Talbot, successor to the Rootes Group, of its Coventry plant.

85 L. Turner and J. M. Bedore, *Middle East Industrialisation. A Study of Saudi and Iranian Downstream Investments* (London, 1979), pp. 46–7, 53.

86 R. Wilson, *The Economies of the Middle East* (London, 1979), pp. 17–18. Additional information from Sir Denis Wright, British Ambassador to Iran in the 1960s and subsequently a director of Mitchell Cotts.

87 Telegram from Sir Roger Stevens, 10 May 1955, FO 371/114847.

88 Robert Graham, *Iran. The Illusion of Power* (London, 1978), p. 110.

89 Ewbanks to W. E. F. Crawford, British Embassy, Beirut, 30 December 1954, FO 371/110086.

90 Minute by R. Belgrave, 7 January 1955, FO 371/110086.

91 Sir Lepel Griffin to G. Newell, 31 October 1890, X74/2, BBME.

92 G. Jones, *Banking and Empire*, p. 165.

93 G. F. Hiller to L. E. M. Taylor, 20 April 1955, FO 371/114823.

94 M. H. Pesaran, 'Economic Development and Revolutionary Upheavals in Iran', in H. Afshar (ed.), *Iran: A Revolution in Turmoil* (London, 1985), pp. 26–7.

95 Halliday, *Iran: Dictatorship*, p. 156.

96 See Thomas Ricks, 'Background to the Iranian Revolution: Imperialism, Dictatorship and Nationalism, 1872 to 1979', in A. Jabbari and R. Olson (eds.), *Iran: Essays on a Revolution in the Making* (Lexington, Kentucky, 1980), p. 19; and, generally, Wright, *The English*, pp. 129–33.

97 D. N. Wilber, *Iran. Past, Present and Future* (Princeton, 1967), p. 131.

98 Floor, *Industrialization*, pp. 29–30.

254 *Notes to pages 63–71*

99 C. Issawi, 'The Economy: An Assessment of Performance', in E. Yar-Shater (ed.), *Iran Faces the Seventies* (New York, 1971).

100 For the pre-1932 period, see Ferrier, *History*, chapter 10.

101 Ibid., p. 398.

102 Bharier, *Economic Development*, p. 162.

103 P. Asheghian, 'Technology Transfer by Foreign Firms to Iran', *Middle Eastern Studies* (1985), p. 27; V. F. Nowshirvani and R. Bildner, 'Direct Foreign Investment in the Non-oil Sectors of the Iranian Economy', *Iranian Studies* (1973), pp. 89–94.

104 J. Bharier, 'Banking and Economic Development in Iran', *Banker's Magazine* (1967), p. 295; G. Jones, *Banking and Empire*, p. 45.

105 Floor, *Industrialization*, p. 29.

106 Ferrier, *History*, pp. 276, 401; L. P. Elwell-Sutton, *Modern Iran* (London, 1941), pp. 106–7, 159.

107 G. Jones, *Banking and Empire*, p. 283.

108 Floor, *Industrialization*, p. 29.

109 Ferrier, *History*, pp. 432–3; Elwell-Sutton, *Modern Iran*, pp. 107, 159.

110 C. Issawi, *An Economic History of the Middle East and North Africa* (London, 1982), p. 204.

111 Persian Industries and Products, Branch Reports, November 1926, V7, BBME.

112 D. A. H. Wright to A. Eden, 13 February 1954, FO 371/109998.

3 British business in Russian Asia since the 1860s

1 T. S. Willan, *The Early History of the Russia Company. 1553–1603* (Manchester, 1956), pp. 1–2.

2 It is interesting to note that along with the Company's commitment to the development of trade with the interior of Russia, the first instances of British capital investment in Russia can be found. According to Vaughn, simultaneously with the development of a considerable trade between the two countries, 'factories were established in various parts of Russia – Kholmogory, Novogorod, Vologda, and Moscow ...' See Ernest V. Vaughn, 'English Trading Expeditions Into Asia Under the Authority of the Muscovy Company (1557–1581)', in *Studies in the History of English Commerce in the Tudor Period* (New York, 1912), p. 129.

3 The grant of exclusive rights by Queen Mary in 1555 was matched with a similar grant of privileges from Ivan IV. In addition to monopoly rights on trade with all Russian territories, the grant from Ivan gave the Company the sole right to any transit trade through Russia 'into Media, Persia, Bogharia and other Eastern countries'. See Vaughn, 'English Trading Expeditions', pp. 192–3; and Willan, *The Early History of the Russia Company*, pp. 12–13, 67, 76.

4 The commodities exchanged varied little as well. See Willan, *The Early History of the Russia Company*, pp. 185–7, 274–5, 280–1; Howard P. Kennard (ed.), *The Russian Year Book, 1911* (London, n.d.); and *Obzor vneshnei torgovli rossii po evropeiskoi i aziatskoi grantisam* [Survey of Russian Foreign Trade through Europe and Asia] (Petrograd, 1916).

5 Vaughn, 'English Trading Expeditions', p. 129.

Notes to pages 71–2 255

6 Ibid., p. 178.

7 Rumours of the vast riches of Siberia had long excited many foreign adventurers and merchants. So jealous was the Muscovite government of any foreign encroachment in Siberia that foreigners were forbidden under pain of death to visit Siberian shores. The later Imperial Russian government likewise attempted to dissuade foreign exploratory or commercial expeditions venturing into Siberian waters or indeed, into Siberia itself. See Centrosoyus (England) Ltd, *Siberian Co-operation and the Commercial Exploitation of the Northern Route from Europe to Siberia* (London, 1920), p. 3; and Konstantine Krypton, *The Northern Sea Route. Its Place in Russian Economic History Before 1917* (New York, 1953).

8 The majority of pre-war British investments in Russia took the form of portfolio investments which are outside the scope of this work. Other works on foreign investment in Russia include J. P. McKay, *Pioneers for Profit. Foreign Entrepreneurship and Russian Industrialization, 1885–1913* (Chicago, 1970); Olga Crisp, *Studies in the Russian Economy before 1914* (London, 1976); P. V. Ol', *Inostrannye kapitaly v rossii* [Foreign Capital in Russia] (Petrograd, 1922); L. Ia. Eventov, *Inostrannye kapitaly v rossii* [Foreign Capital in Russia] (Moscow, 1931). Paul Gregory's study, *Russian National Income, 1885–1913* (Cambridge, 1982), takes issue with the commonly held notion that Russian industrial and economic development was largely dependent on foreign investments and provides an interesting contrast to the above-mentioned works.

9 Since these companies were capitalised in roubles it is far more accurate to give the values in roubles rather than convert them to sterling. Where conversions have been done the pre-war par exchange rate of 9.46 roubles to the pound sterling has been used.

There exist several excellent studies on the role of foreign capital in the development of the Russian petroleum industry. See the section on Russian oilfields in Geoffrey Jones, *The State and the Emergence of the British Oil Industry* (London, 1981), pp. 50–62; Geoffrey Jones and Clive Trebilcock, 'Russian Industry and British Business 1910–1930: Oil and Armaments', in *The Journal of European Economic History*, 11 (1982); W. A. Otis, *The Petroleum Industry of Russia*, US Department of Commerce, Trade Information Bulletin No. 263; Robert Tolf, *The Russian Rockefellers. The Saga of the Nobel Family and the Russian Oil Industry* (Stanford, 1976).

10 Jones, *The State and the Emergence of the British Oil Industry*, pp. 50, 61–2. Jones draws his statistics from P. V. Ol', *Inostrannye kapitaly*, pp. 44–54.

11 'Report on the Mineral and Metallurgical Industries of Russia', Parliamentary Papers. Miscellaneous Series. Diplomatic and Consular Reports. Russia. No. 555 (1901).

12 These companies were: the Russian Petroleum Company (Ltd), the Baku Russian Petroleum Company, 1909 (Ltd), the Russian United Petroleum Company (Ltd), the European Oilfields Corporation (Ltd), the New Schibaeff Petroleum Company (Ltd), and the Bibi-Eibat Oil Company. See Leonard J. Lewery, *Foreign Capital Investments in Russian Industries and Commerce*, Department of Commerce. Bureau of Foreign and Domestic Commerce.

256 *Notes to pages 72–6*

Miscellaneous Series, No. 18 (Washington D.C., 1923), p. 15, as from the summary of the investigation published by the Soviet Institute of Economic Research.

13 The three wholly British-owned companies were: the Russian Petroleum Company (Ltd), the Baku Russian Petroleum Company, 1909 (Ltd), the Russian United Petroleum Company (Ltd).

14 Lewery, *Foreign Capital Investments*, p. 16.

15 Findings published by the Soviet Institute of Economic Research indicated that the British share probably exceeded this estimate by a considerable amount. See Lewery, *Foreign Capital Investments*, p. 16.

16 Ibid., p. 17.

17 Ibid., p. 18. The West Ural Petroleum Company and the Ural-Emba Oil Fields (Ltd), were wholly British-owned, while the Emba-Caspian Oil Company and the Ural-Caspian Oil Company operated through Russian holding companies by the same name.

18 The three British companies were Spies Petroleum Company, North Caucasian Oil Fields Company, and Anglo-Terek Petroleum Company. The fourth, the Gleboff-Grozny Petroleum Company, operated through the Russian-registered Cheleken Daghestan Petroleum Company. (Ibid., p. 19.)

19 Ibid., p. 21.

20 Ibid., p. 22; and Ol', *Inostrannye kapitaly*, p. 43.

21 Violet Conolly, *Beyond the Urals. Economic Developments in Soviet Asia* (London, 1967). Despite its notoriously low returns, British capital accounted for 70% of the total in the Russian gold and platinum industry immediately prior to the war. 'Report on the Mineral and Metallurgical Industries of Russia', Parliamentary Papers. Miscellaneous Series. Diplomatic and Consular Reports. Russia. No. 555 (1901). CMD 430–10, p. 26; Conolly, *Beyond the Urals*, p. 46.

22 Lewery, *Foreign Capital Investments*, p. 22; and Conolly, *Beyond the Urals*, pp. 49–50.

23 Conolly, *Beyond the Urals*, p. 46.

24 Lewery, *Foreign Capital Investments*, p. 22.

25 Ibid., pp. 22–3.

26 Conolly, *Beyond the Urals*, pp. 50–1.

27 Lewery, *Foreign Capital Investments*, pp. 22–3.

28 Parliamentary Papers. Miscellaneous Series. Diplomatic and Consular Reports. Russia. No 555 (1901).

29 By the eve of the war, Siberian butter was meeting some 19% of Britain's total butter requirements. According to the Soviet historian Lyashchenko, 'the import of butter from Russia was the result of considerable investment by British importing firms in Siberian co-operatives, supplying them with credit, separators, packing materials, and organising refrigerating and warehousing facilities' (my translation). The data, however, tends to suggest the reverse – that is, that the growing volume of Siberian butter imported into Britain prompted increased investment in the allied businesses. P. I. Lyashchenko, *Istoriia narodnogo khoziastva za revoliutsiia 1917 g* [History of the National Economy before the 1917 Revolution] (Moscow, 1949), pp. 591–2; Kennard,

The Russian Year Book. 1913; N. A. Kryokov, *Russko-angliskaya torgovlaya plata. Anglia. Kak rinok' selskokhozyastvennikh productov'* [Anglo-Russian Trade Payments. England. A Market for Agricultural Produce] (St Petersburg, 1910). For references to British investments in a meat canning factory near Petropavlosk and two cheese manufacturing concerns in the Altai and Kurgan Districts of Siberia, see 'Report of the Trade and Commerce of the Consular District of Omsk', Parliamentary Papers. Accounts and Papers. Consular Reports. Russia. 1913, pp. 48, 49.

30 British Consul, Ekaterinburg, to Preston, 18 January 1918, No. 3/18. Foreign Office Commercial Intelligence Files, FO 368/1965.

31 'Report on the Trade and Commerce of the Consular District of Omsk', 1913.

32 'Report Received from Mr. H. Cooke, the Special Commissioner appointed by the Commercial Intelligence Committee of the Board of Trade, on the Conditions and Prospects of British Trade in Siberia', Accounts and Papers. Consular Reports. Russia. 1904, p. xi.

33 *Torgovlo-promyshlennaya gazetta* [Trade and Industry Gazette], as cited in Accounts and Papers, 1914–16. Vol. LXXIV, No. 5414. Russia, 1913.

34 Increased foreign interest in the development of the trade and industry of the region sparked a new wave of Russian protectionism, however, and in 1885 a special imperial commission appointed to investigate the question reported that it believed the development of foreign trade and industry in Siberia 'to be more harmful than helpful to the interests of the Russian Government'. It was recognised that Russian manufactured goods could not compete successfully with those of foreign manufacture, and the prohibitions on trade were seen as a means of 'sealing off local trade from the flood of foreign duty goods in the interests of native industry'. Consequently, restrictions on foreign ownership and prohibitive duties were imposed to prevent foreign penetration of the region. See A. L. Kulomzin (ed.), *Istoricheski obzor deyatel'nosti komiteta ministrov* [Historical Survey of the Work of the Council of Ministers], vol. IV (St Petersburg, 1902), p. 173; and Krasnoyarsk Territory Historical Archives, *Doklad Yeniseiskovo gubernskovo sekretarya. Delo o razvitii torgovykh snoshenii s Sibir'yu morskim putyom po reke Yeniseyu* [Report of the Secretary of the Yenisei Province]. Statistical Committee of Yeniseisk Province, Collection 31, Archival No. 18/23, pp. 9–10; both as cited in Krypton, *The Northern Sea Route*, pp. 38–9.

35 Cooke's report, p. ix.

36 Two avid supporters of Siberian trade via the Kara Sea were Alfred Derry – of the Kensington emporium of Derry and Toms – and the Norwegian business-man Jonas Lied. In 1909 Lied put up £13,000 capital to establish the Lied Joint Stock Company in London for the purpose of undertaking a 'careful study of all the conditions of possible trade with central Siberia through the Kara Sea'. It was not until 1912, after much investigation, that the first steamship was despatched by this company. See Conolly, *Beyond the Urals*, p. 16; and Krypton, *The Northern Sea Route*, pp. 138–9.

37 Cooke's commercial mission never made it beyond the Lake Baikal region, however, and British business in the Far East remained unrepresented until 1908, when Vice-Consul Hodgson filed his first report on the District of

258 *Notes to pages 78–80*

Vladivostok. See 'Report for the Years 1908–1909 on the Trade of Vladivostok'. Accounts and Papers, Annual Series. Diplomatic and Consular Reports. Russia. No. 4452.

38 Cooke's report, pp. 38, 39, 43.

39 Kennard, *The Russian Year Book. 1912*, p. 183; and Cooke's report, p. 38.

40 Cooke's report, p. 11.

41 Cooke's report, pp. 87, 88. Curiously, the one area in which Britain did have an advantage in Siberian trade was that of shipping. In the case of the Kara Sea route, British shipping exercised a virtual monopoly, and in Vladivostok British vessels accounted for roughly half of all the tonnage entering and clearing that port prior to the War. See 'Report of the Trade of Siberia', Accounts and Papers, Miscellaneous Series. Diplomatic and Consular Reports. Russia. 1902, vol. CIII. CMD 787–21.

42 'Report on the Trade of Vladivostok and District for the Year 1911', Accounts and Papers. Miscellaneous Series. No. 5041. Diplomatic and Consular Reports. 1913, p. 7.

43 Cooke's report, p. 8.

44 A debate over the quality and effectiveness of British marketing abroad has developed among business historians. While it has been argued that there is evidence that British merchants and businessmen abroad were neither negligent, incompetent nor ignorant in their considerations of local market conditions, reports filed from Siberia especially reflect an all-round dissatisfaction with British performance. Indeed, the failure of the British to capture any significant proportion of the Siberian market, despite the fact that their goods were often preferred over the more common, cheaper German goods, stands tribute to the assessments made by Cooke and his colleagues. See Stephen J. Nicholas, 'The Overseas Marketing Performance of British Industry, 1870–1914', *The Economic History Review* (November 1984); and R. P. T. Davenport-Hines (ed.), *Markets and Bagmen* (Aldershot, 1986), pp. 5–14.

45 This is rather ironic since it was the British themselves who had initiated the practice at the turn of the eighteenth century. Concentrating on the development of the Russian market after the conclusion of the trade treaty of 1754, the British were the first to make the practice of granting long-term credit an established custom in the Muscovite trade. Once introduced, this practice took root and it became very rare to find Russian merchants paying cash for any purchases whatsoever. I. M. Kulisher, *Ocherk istorii russkoi torgovli* [An Essay on Russian Trade History] (Petrograd, 1923), p. 194.

46 *Annual Statement of the Trade of the United Kingdom*, Accounts and Papers, vol. LXXXVIII, 1914.

47 While the first full year of the War saw Britain providing the majority of Russian imports, by 1916 the bulk of this trade had been lost to the United States. The increase in the value of American exports to Russia even before the US entered the War is staggering: compared to the $31.1 million worth of goods it sold to Russia in 1914, American exports had increased nearly tenfold by 1916 to over $309.8 million. The future value of such trade was not lost on American businessmen or, indeed, on the US government. See G. K. Seleznev,

Notes to pages 80–4 259

Ten dollara nad rossiye. Iz istorii amerikano-russkikh otnoshenniyi [Ten Dollars over Russia. From the History of American–Russian Relations] (Moscow, 1957), p. 24.

48 Cecil's Minutes on Résumé from Vice-Consul Nash, Ekatrinburg, n.d. (circa May/June 1918). FO 371/3292.

49 The Russia Committee. 'Notes on Allied Policy in Siberia', 23 April 1918. FO 371/3292.

50 Sir J. Jordan, Peking, to the Foreign Office, 28 January 1918. FO 371/3291.

51 Vice-Consul Nash, Irkutsk, to the Foreign Office, 28 January 1918. FO 371/3291.

52 Ambassador Francis, Vologda, to Secretary of State. Despatch 1118, 11 July 1918. National Archives Record Group 59, State Department Decimal File 861.00/2575; and British response in Balfour to Reading, Washington. Tel. 4316, 11 July 1918. Wiseman MSS Collection (Yale University), as cited in Richard K. Ullman, *Anglo–Soviet Relations*, vol. I (Princeton, N.J., 1961), p. 233.

53 See: 'Memorandum on the Tzaritsyn Works', n.d. (circa February 1924). Vickers Ltd, Archives, Cambridge University Library. Envelope b-40, 'War Work. Vickers Ltd. and the Imperial Russian Government'.

54 M. Romanoff, Kyshtim, to Russo–Asiatic Consolidated Ltd, London. Sent via Lindley, Petrograd. No. 131, RussTrade. 15 January 1918. FO 368/1965.

55 Lindley, Petrograd, to the Foreign Office. No. 131(R). Russian Trade and Treaty. 15 January 1918. FO 371/3294; and Lindley to Department Overseas Trade. No. 130(R). 15 January 1918. FO 368/1965.

56 Knox, Vladivostok, to War Office. Tel. 9005, 1 August 1919; and War Office to BritMiss (Vladivostok), for Knox. Tel. 80251, 5 August 1919. WO 33/967.

57 Remark concerning Baku made by Lord Robert Cecil, at the 40th meeting of the Eastern Committee, 2 December 1919. Cab. 27/24.

58 H. Fountain, Board of Trade, to George Tweedy. Commercial Relations and Treaties Series (CRT 7657), 20 November 1918. FO 368/1974; J. Cadman for W. Long, Petroleum Executive to the Comptroller, Foreign Trade Department of the Foreign Office, 10 December 1918. FO 368/1974.

59 The Urquhart concession was to include '12 developed metal mines, coal mines, four non-ferrous smelters, a refinery, iron and steel mills, twenty saw mills, the Ridder lead–zinc mines, and other mines and smelting properties in the Altai and Urals region', *Le Petit Parisien*, 27 October 1922, as cited in Anthony C. Sutton, *Western Technology and Soviet Economic Development*, vol. I: *1917–1930* (Stanford, 1968), p. 77, n. 3.

60 The Lena concession included the Sissert Copper Mines; the Altai District Mining Company; Nikolopavdinsky platinum mines; copper, lead and zinc deposits in the Irtish River District; North Kuznetsk Coal Mines; anthracite mines at Yegoskoi in the Urals; gold mines on the Lena–Vitim Rivers in Siberia; the Zivianovsky, Zmeynogorsky and Pryittishky Districts; copper and iron smelters at Sissert and Revdinsky; Degtiarinsky Copper Mines; Gumeshevsky copper smelter; wire- and nail-making factories in the Urals; a railroad in the Lena–Vitim area; and a shipping system on the Lena River. Sutton, vol. I, p. 95.

260 *Notes to pages 84–7*

61 US State Department Decimal File 861.5017 – Living Conditions/163; and the *Times*, 20 November 1928, both as cited in Sutton, *Western Technology and Soviet Economic Development*, vol. II: *1930–1945* (Stanford, 1971), pp. 19, 24. For the Soviet explanation of the attack upon and ultimate expulsion of the Lena Goldfields Company Ltd, see S. A. Bernstein, *The Financial and Economic Results of the Working of the Lena Goldfields Company Limited* (London, 1931).

The Lena Goldfields Company took the Soviet government to an international court of arbitration in an attempt to win damages against their losses. While the court did award the company the right to collect nearly £13 million, protracted negotiations resulted in that government settling the claim by paying only £3 million over twenty years.

62 Sutton, *Western Technology*, vol. II, pp. 71, 77, 79, 95–100.

63 Sutton, *Western Technology*, vol. I, p. 32.

64 Sale and Company of London and Shell had both successfully negotiated an agreement for the export and sale of Soviet oil abroad, though Shell chose to sell through exclusive dealerships only. Further, in 1925 that company expanded its interests to include equal participation in the £1.25 million programme to modernise and expand the capacity of the Baku–Batum pipeline. See Sutton, *Western Technology*, vol. I, pp. 32–3, 41–2.

65 Sutton, *Western Technology*, vol. I, p. 21.

66 Sutton, *Western Technology*, vol. I. pp. 26–7. This was no doubt due to the fact that General Electric bought the Metropolitan-Vickers Company in 1927. A similar shift from Metropolitan-Vickers equipment to that manufactured by GE occurred in China as well. See R. P. T. Davenport-Hines, *Dudley Docker* (Cambridge, 1984), pp. 180–1.

67 Sutton, *Western Technology*, vol. II, p. 170. Despite the breakdown in diplomatic relations in 1927 over the so-called 'Arcos Affair', the company continued to have uninterrupted business with the Soviet Union from 1921 until 1933, when six of its engineers were arrested and expelled from the country on charges of espionage. Under the strict interpretation of Soviet law, the engineers were indeed spies, as they had been transmitting certain economic information concerning Russia back to Britain.

68 Sutton, *Western Technology*, vol. II, pp. 159, 173.

69 Sutton, *Western Technology*, vol. I, p. 199.

70 *New York Times*, 16 March 1928.

71 A good example of this is the dogged Soviet loyalty to the Fordson tractor throughout the 1920s. See Christine White, 'Ford in Russia. In Pursuit of the Chimeral Market', *Business History*, 28 (1986).

Further, it is significant to note that the Soviets recognised the United States as being the most valuable source of technology. Commenting on Soviet industrial achievements prior to 1933, *Za Industrializatsiiu* noted that it was 'a combination of American business and science with Bolshevik wisdom' that had resulted in the success of the First Five Year Plan. See Sutton, *Western Technology*, vol. II, p. 1.

72 Alan Monkhouse, Vickers' chief engineer in the USSR, pointed out that at the same plant where Vickers turbines were being constructed under license, a

Notes to pages 87–90 261

'great American company' had also contracted to render technical assistance, and in this way American designs were introduced. Sutton, *Western Technology*, vol. I, pp. 165, 187.

73 Sutton, *Western Technology*, vol. I, p. 100.

74 A number of important technical trade agreements in such fields as aviation and petroleum and chemical engineering were concluded with American firms between 1936 and 1941. Sutton, *Western Technology*, vol. II, p. 2.

75 While there were certainly vast infusions of Western goods and technology of all sorts into the USSR during the course of the War, these can only be considered to be a part of the Allied war effort – that is, aid as opposed to trade. Even so, the War provided an added impetus to the industrial development of Soviet Asia through the government's efforts to secure key industries against the advancing German armies. The relocation of existing plants and the construction of numerous new factories beyond the Ural mountains provided a substantial foundation for the post-war drive to industrialise the remote regions.

76 A 1960 agreement provided for the delivery and erection of machinery for a new synthetic rubber complex in Siberia. Sutton, *Western Technology and Soviet Economic Development*, vol. III: *1945–1965* (Stanford, 1978), p. 156.

77 Sutton, *Western Technology*, vol. III, p. 183. There is some question as to the reliability of some of Sutton's information on the recent British contracts with Russia. The location of the polyester fibre plant provided by Polyspinners Ltd, for example, is given by Sutton as Irkutsk, Siberia. A list of John Brown Company's contracts with the Soviet Union gave the location of the huge polyester fibre plant which used ICI technology (like the Polyspinners contract) as Mogilev, Belorussia; there is no mention of John Brown participating in the construction of a vast polyester combine in Irkutsk. The list was made available to me by Mr A. G. Bruce at John Brown plc in London, 5 December 1986.

78 A. G. Bruce, 'The John Brown Group's Historical and Continuing Commitment to Trade with the Soviet Union', *Messemagazin* (April 1985).

79 The first contract, worth £175 million, was concluded with a subsidiary of Davy International for the construction of two methanol plants, one of which was projected as being the 'biggest in the world'. The other contract, signed in December 1976 with the Coberro consortium, was a £100 million deal for lightweight compressor units for pumping gas from Western Siberia. *The Times* Special Report, 'Siberia', 20 September 1978.

80 Sutton, *Western Technology*, vol. III, p. 56.

81 *The Times*, 20 September 1978; 26 September 1978.

82 *The Times*, 20 September 1978.

83 *The Times*, 13 October 1970.

84 *The Times*, 26 March 1970; 18 May 1977; 20 September 1978; 4 December 1978; 31 January 1980; 15 November 1980.

85 While Britain's position as a hard-line NATO member may have contributed to this reluctance, it is more likely due to the traditionally conservative nature of British financial institutions.

86 On average, about 80% of all present British imports from the USSR consist of

262 Notes to pages 91–4

raw materials, of which 40% are industrial diamonds, 30% oil of a type not available from North Sea reserves, and 12% timber and cork. *The Times*, 20 September 1978; 7 January 1980.

87 *The Times*, 11 January 1974.

88 It was this contract, providing 21 of the 125 gas turbines for the controversial Urengoy pipeline, that alleviated an earlier threat to jobs at John Brown's Clydeside works where the turbines were manufactured. See *The Times*, 9 January 1982; 1 July 1982; 2 August 1982; 3 August 1982; 30 August 1982; and *British–Soviet Trade*, a 1986 Briefing Paper supplied by the Department of Trade and Industry.

89 The agreement provides that 'Both Parties will promote the realisation ... of specific co-operation projects ... [and] provide patents, licenses, know-how, technical information and new technology, deliveries of machinery and equipment and provision of specialists and means of financing'. It was further specified that both countries would 'proceed on the basis that the equipment and technological processes supplied will accord with the latest achievements of advanced technology'. See 'UK/USSR Economic and Industrial Co-operation Programme, 1986–1990', OT3/5, Department of Trade and Industry.

4 British business in India, 1860–1970

1 The geographical spread of this chapter is deliberately vague, but strictly limited. 'India' here means mainland South Asia, excluding Burma, before 1947, and the Republic of India afterwards. As will be clear from the text, a careful categorisation of regional diversities is not part of my purpose here. The research on which this chapter is based was supported, in part, by a project grant from the Economic and Social Research Council and assistance from the Masters and Fellows of Trinity College, Cambridge, and the Leverhulme Trust.

2 For a summary of recent research, see D. A. Washbrook, 'Progress and Problems: South Asian Economic and Social History c. 1720–1860', *Modern Asian Studies* (forthcoming); also, C. J. Bayly, *Rulers, Townsmen and Bazaars: North Indian Society in the Age of British Expansion, 1770–1870* (Cambridge, 1983).

3 On the monetary and banking history of the *Raj* in the late nineteenth century, and its implications for private capitalists, see B. R. Ambedkar, *The Problem of the Rupee* (Bombay, 1923); S. Ambirajan, *Political Economy and Monetary Management, India 1766–1914* (New Delhi, 1984); A. K. Bagchi, 'Transition from Indian to British-Indian Systems of Money and Banking, 1800–1850', *Modern Asian Studies*, 19 (1985), and 'Anglo-Indian Banking in British India: From the Paper Pound to the Gold Standard', *Journal of Imperial and Commonwealth History*, 13 (1985).

4 A. K. Banerji, *Aspects of Indo-British Economic Relations, 1858–1898* (Bombay, 1982). One crore = ten millions (usually written 1,00,00,000). The exchange rate of the rupee steadily declined from around Rs10 = £1 in the 1870s to Rs17 = £1 in the early 1890s. The exchange then hardened to Rs15

Notes to pages 96–7   263

= £1 from the mid-1890s to 1916. From 1916 to 1926 the exchange rose and fell sharply once more, stabilising at Rs13 = £1 from 1927 to the 1950s. For account purposes the exchange rate is conventionally taken as Rs13 = £1 for the whole of the inter-war period. From the late 1950s on the rate ran at around Rs18 = £1.

5 Within the 'organised' banking sector, the foreign Exchange Banks held 34% of total deposits made in India in 1914, the largely expatriate Presidency Banks a further 45%, and the Indian joint-stock banks a further 21%. By 1937 the Exchange Banks held 27%, the Imperial Bank (successor to the Presidency Banks) 30%, and the Indian joint-stock Banks 43%. See Gokhale Institute of Politics and Economics, *Notes on the Rise of the Business Communities in India* (Institute of Pacific Relations, New York, 1951), pp. 9, 14. Indian indigenous banks were entirely responsible for the financing of agricultural production and cottage industry in 1914; by the 1930s some of this role had been taken over by cooperative societies and the downward spread of Indian joint-stock banks. For individual histories of the Exchange Banks, see G. Tyson, *A Hundred Years of Banking in Asia and Africa: A History of National and Grindlays Bank Limited 1853–1963* (London, 1963), and Compton Mackenzie, *Realms of Silver: One Hundred Years of Banking in the East* [Chartered Bank] (London, 1954).

6 There are surprisingly few modern scholarly accounts of the history of the expatriate agency houses, either individually or in the aggregate. Those that are available include R. S. Rungta, *Rise of Business Corporations in India, 1851–1900* (Cambridge, 1970); the same author's 'Bowreah Cotton and Fort Gloster Jute Mills, 1872–1900', *Indian Economic & Social History Review*, 22 (1985); B. R. Tomlinson, 'Colonial Firms and the Decline of Colonialism in Eastern India, 1914–1947', *Modern Asian Studies*, 15 (1981); Omkar Goswami, 'Then Came the Marwaris; Some Aspects of the Changes in the Pattern of Industrial Control in Eastern India', *Indian Economic & Social History Review*, 22 (1985); and Henner Papendieck, *Britische Managing Agencies im Indischen Kohlenbergbau 1893–1918* (New York, 1981). Useful information and sources on these firms will also be found in a number of broader works on the industrial history of the period, such as D. H. Buchanan, *The Development of Capitalistic Enterprise in India* (New York, 1934); C. P. Simmons, 'Indigenous Enterprise in the Indian Coal-Mining Industry c1835–1939', *Indian Economic & Social History Review*, 13 (1976); R. K. Ray, *Industrialisation in India: Growth and Conflict in the Private Corporate Sector 1914–1947* (Delhi, 1979); Aditya Mukherjee, 'Indian Capitalist Class and Foreign Capital', *Studies in History 1* (1979); C. Markovits, *Indian Business and Nationalist Politics, 1931–39* (Cambridge, 1985); A. K. Bagchi, *Private Investment in India 1900–1939* (Cambridge, 1972). Professor Bagchi's book also contains a useful bibliography, including listings of a number of privately printed old-style company histories. On the managing agency system, see also P. Lokanathan, *Industrial Organisation of India* (London, 1935), and R. K. Nigam, *Managing Agencies in India: First Round: Basic Facts* (New Delhi, 1957). The evidence collected by a number of commissions of enquiry is another valuable source. Most useful are the Indian

264 Notes to pages 97–101

government's currency committees (1893 and 1898), the Royal Commissions on Indian Currency (1913 and 1926), the Indian Industrial Commission (1916–18), the Indian Fiscal Commissions (1921 and 1949), the Central Banking Enquiry Committee (1931) and the various Indian Tariff Board enquiries of the 1920s, 1930s, 1940s and 1950s.

7 Gokhale Institute, *Notes on the Rise of the Business Communities in India*, pp. 4–5.

8 Ibid., pp. 10 & 57–8.

9 Calculated from data in Government of India, *Report of the Monopolies Inquiry Commission 1965* (New Delhi, 1965), vol. II, Appendix D.

10 See M. Kidron, *Foreign Investments in India* (Oxford, 1965), chapter 2.

11 See Tomlinson, 'Colonial Firms'.

12 M. D. Morris, 'South Asian Entrepreneurship and the Rashomon Effect', *Explorations in Economic History*, 16 (1979).

13 For an introduction to the history of these Indian entrepreneurs, see Ray, *Industrialisation in India*, pp. 276–91.

14 B. R. Tomlinson, 'Foreign Private Investment in India, 1920–1950', *Modern Asian Studies*, 12 (1978), pp. 64–5.

15 Calculated from data in Government of India, Department of Company Affairs, *Directory of Joint-Stock Companies in India, 1975* (New Delhi, 1975).

16 In 1958 the percentage of British DFI in India was only slightly lower than in the whole of Europe (7.4% to India, 8.4% to Europe), while by 1971 the proportion was much smaller (4.5% to India, 17.6% to Europe). In terms of the numbers of manufacturing affiliates established by British MNEs, India was host to about 4% of the total in the 1920s, about 8% from 1930 to 1945, up to a peak of 11% in the early 1950s, falling back to around 5% for the years down to 1965, and then tailing away to less than 2% by 1970. See T. Houston and J. Dunning, *U.K. Industry Abroad* (London, 1976), Table 5:2; M. Lipton and J. Firn, *Erosion of a Relationship: India and Britain since 1960* (London, 1975), Table 6:6.

17 See P. Chaudhuri, *The Indian Economy* (London, 1978), p. 165, and Sanjaya Lall, 'India', in J. Dunning (ed.), *Multinational Enterprises, Economic Structure and Internal Competitiveness* (Chichester, 1985), p. 316. General studies of the activities of MNEs in India include Kidron, *Foreign Investments*; K. M. Kurian, *The Impact of Foreign Capital in the Indian Economy* (New Delhi, 1966); P. Patnaik, 'Imperialism and the growth of Indian capitalism', in R. Owen and B. Sutcliffe (eds.), *Studies in the Theory of Imperialism* (London, 1972).

18 Calculated from data in Government of India, *Report of the Industrial Licensing Policy Inquiry Committee* [Dutt Committee], Appendix III; and Lall, 'India', pp. 316–18.

19 The following examples are drawn from B. R. Tomlinson, 'Continuities & Discontinuities in Indo-British Economic Relations: British Multinational Corporations in India, 1920–1970', in W. J. Mommsen and J. Osterhammel (eds.), *Imperialism and After: Continuities and Discontinuities* (London, 1986). Useful published studies of individual multinational firms in India will

Notes to pages 104–7 265

be found in D. K. Fieldhouse, *Unilever Overseas: the Anatomy of a Multi-national 1895–1965* (London, 1978); W. J. Reader, *Metal Box: A History* (London, 1976), chapter 2; M. Modig, *Swedish Match Interests in British India during the Inter-War Years* (Stockholm, 1979).

20 Comparative data on major British MNEs between 1953 and 1973 reveals that a number of the companies heavily involved in India failed to grow as fast as the norm – Brooke Bond, ICI, Vickers, Turner Newall, Tube Investments, Hawker Siddeley, and Babcock & Wilcox among them. Other companies with major Indian interests, such as GKN, BOC, Metal Box, and Dunlop, did no more than hold their own in relative growth in this period. Of the MNEs that grew fastest in the 1950s and 1960s, those that increased their capital by a factor of nine or more, only Glaxo and GEC had had major investments in India at the start of the period. See Houston and Dunning, *U.K. Industry Abroad*, pp. 158–9.

21 See *Directory of Joint-Stock Companies in India, 1975*.

22 See A. Das Gupta and N. Sengupta, *Government and Business in India* (revised edn., Calcutta, 1981), chapter 9.

23 Data on the size and characteristics of recent foreign investment in India is provided by regular surveys in the monthly *Bulletin* of the Reserve Bank of India. See, in particular, 'India's International Investment Position 1973–4', in vol. 32, 3 (March 1978); and 'India's International Investment Position, 1974–5 to 1976–7', in vol. 38, 12 (Dec. 1984).

24 There is evidence to suggest that India was an inhospitable environment for many British manufacturers for other reasons as well. The use of joint ventures with local capital in the 1960s often signified a lack of commitment to an overseas operation. The proportion of British subsidiaries in India set up in this form in India was unusually large. The overwhelming majority of such companies cited the need for a local partner to provide facilities and resources, rather than implicit or explicit host-government pressure, as their most important motive. This suggests that particular conditions in India made her a less suitable base for 'pure' MNE activity and presented problems that internalisation could not overcome. See Howard Davies, 'Technology Transfer through Commercial Transactions', *Journal of Industrial Economics*, 26 (1977); J. W. C. Tomlinson, *The Joint-Venture Process in International Business: India and Pakistan* (London, 1970), pp. 26–7.

25 In the remittance crisis of the First World War the government of India and India Office gave special facilities to these five banks, plus that of Cox and Company. In September 1931, when the Imperial Bank of India set up a system of licensing foreign exchange dealers to help cope with the monetary crisis caused by sterling leaving the gold standard, the approved list had been expanded to include a number of other banks run by Britons (Allahabad Bank, Lloyds Bank, P & O Banking Corporation, Grindlay & Company, and Thomas Cook & Son); by Indians (Bank of India, Central Bank of India, and Bank of Baroda); by Japanese (Bank of Taiwan, Sumitomo Bank, Yokohama Specie Bank, and Mitsui Bank); and by other foreign nationals (Banco Nationale Ulta Marine, Comptoir Nationale d'Escompte de Paris, National City Bank of New York, Netherlands Trading Society, and Netherlands Indies Commercial Bank).

266 *Notes to pages 107–14*

26 On stores policy, see S. K. Sen, *Studies in Economic Policy and Development of India (1848–1939)* (Calcutta, 1972), chapter 10; on the founding of the Reserve Bank of India, see S. L. N. Simha, *History of the Reserve Bank of India, 1935–1951* (Bombay, 1970), and B. R. Tomlinson, *The Political Economy of the Raj, 1914–1947: the Economics of Decolonization in India* (London, 1979), pp. 79–81, 128–31.

27 There has been a great deal of recent research on the agrarian economy of Bengal in the first half of the twentieth century. For an accessible starting point in this, see Omkar Goswami, 'Agriculture in Slump: the Peasant Economy of East and North Bengal in the 1930s', *Indian Economic and Social History Review*, 21 (1984).

28 There is a great deal of information about the investment and operating decisions of British businessmen in India during the 1880s and 1890s in the evidence presented to the three major currency commissions of the period: *Royal Commission on Recent Changes in the Relative Value of the Precious Metals* (1888) [Gold & Silver Commission]; *Report of the Indian Currency Committee* (1893) [Herschell Committee]; *Report of the Indian Currency Committee, 1898* [Fowler Committee].

29 For evidence on this, see the annual reports of the United Kingdom Trade Commissioner in India in the 1920s and 1930s. An interesting review of the First World War years, and preceding decades, will be found in *Report on the Condition and Prospects of British Trade in India at the Close of the War* (Cmd 442 of 1919).

30 The Colonial Development Fund is rightly thought to have been grossly inadequate to meet British Africa's needs for public capital investment, but no such scheme existed at all for India. Indeed, India made net repayments of public sterling capital in the 1930s. On Africa, see J. Forbes Munro, *Africa and the International Economy, 1800–1960* (London, 1976), pp. 154–5. On China, see S. L. Endicott, *Diplomacy and Enterprise: British China Policy 1933–37* (Manchester, 1975), chapters 5 and 6. Most of these British initiatives in China were never put into effect, of course. For a more sceptical view of their importance, see William C. Kirby, *Germany and Republican China* (Stanford, 1984), pp. 226–9.

31 For a useful introduction to the literature on British aid to India, see Lipton and Firn, *Erosion of a Relationship*, chapter 7.

32 On the sterling balances question, see B. R. Tomlinson, 'Indo-British Relations in the Post-Colonial Era: The Sterling Balances Negotiations, 1947–49', *Journal of Imperial & Commonwealth History*, 13 (1985).

33 Recent work on the links between business and politics includes Ray, *Industrialisation*, chapter 6; Markovits, *Indian Business and Nationalist Politics*; Mukherjee, 'Indian Capitalist Class'; and A. D. D. Gordon, *Businessmen and Politics: Rising Nationalism and a Modernising Economy in Bombay, 1918–1933* (New Delhi, 1978).

34 A. K. Banerji, *India's Balance of Payments: Estimates of Current and Capital Account from 1921–22 to 1938–39* (London, 1963), chapter 6. For a critical review of earlier estimates, see ibid., pp. 149–68, and Reserve Bank of India, *Census of India's Foreign Liabilities and Assets as on 30th June 1948* (Bombay, 1950), Appendix I.

Notes to pages 114–20 267

35 Banerji, *India's Balance of Payments*, chapter 6, and his *Aspects of Indo-British Economic Relations, 1858–98* (Delhi, 1982), pp. 240–1. Davis and Huttenback's recent calculation of the volume of British finance called up by London-based companies operating in India in the period from 1865 to 1914 suggests that, on varying assumptions, finance for the private sector was between 45% and 49% of the total (see Lance Davis and Robert A. Huttenback, 'The Export of British Finance, 1865–1914', *Journal of Imperial & Commonwealth History*, 13 (1985), Table 1).

36 For more details of these calculations, see B. R. Tomlinson, 'Foreign Investment in India and Indonesia, 1920–1960', *Itinerario*, 1986–1 (forthcoming), Appendix B.

37 See Banerji, *India's Balance of Payments*, pp. 171, 178, 210–23; for other statistical data on the structural shift in expatriate investment in the inter-war period, see M. M. Mehta, *Structure of Indian Industries* (Bombay, 1961), pp. 333, 346–7.

5 Early British business in Thailand

* I am grateful to the editors and to Dr Ian Brown for helpful comments on an earlier version of this paper.

1 In June 1939 the name Thailand was officially adopted in place of Siam, but the former name has been used in this chapter. Similarly certain former names for towns and provinces have been used here.

2 The figures are based on calculations presented in this paper and in H. G. Callis, *Foreign Capital in Southeast Asia* (Institute of Pacific Relations, New York, 1942).

3 The best account of the role of the Chinese in Thailand is G. W. Skinner, *Chinese Society in Thailand: An Analytical History* (New York, 1957). See also J. P. Jiang, 'The Chinese in Thailand, Past and Present', *Journal of Southeast Asian History*, March 1966, pp. 39–65.

4 J. L. S. Girling, *Thailand: Society and Politics* (London, 1981), p. 74; US Dept of Commerce, Consular Reports, *Report for Siam for the Year 1868*, p. 641. J. M. McCarthy, *Surveying and Exploring in Siam* (Ithaca, N.Y., 1900), p. 3.

5 British Consular Reports: *Siam for the Year 1889*, Annual Series 771, pp. 18–19. Skinner, *Chinese Society*, pp. 61, 172. Net arrivals were, of course, considerably less.

6 C. M. Wilson, *Thailand, A Handbook of Historical Statistics* (Boston, Mass., 1983), pp. 25–6.

7 Callis, *Foreign Capital in Southeast Asia*, pp. 59–70.

8 P. Sithi-Amnuai, *Finance and Banking in Thailand: A Study of the Commercial System, 1888–1963* (Bangkok, 1964), pp. 35–6. *Compradores* were intermediaries between the Western and Chinese business sectors. They were responsible for the hiring, dismissal and conduct of local staff and negotiated and secured the business of the Western firm with local customers.

9 H. Warington Smyth, *Five Years in Siam* (London, 1898), vol. I, pp. 319–20;

268 *Notes to pages 120–4*

also the same author's 'Notes on a Journey to some of the South-Western Provinces of Siam', *The Geographical Journal* (November 1895), pp. 527–8.

10 M. Laugesen, P. Westphall and R. Dannhorn, *Scandinavians in Siam* (Bangkok, 1980), pp. 48–57.

11 Ibid., pp. 55–6.

12 There are no collected data on British enterprises in pre-1914 Siam. The examples here are drawn mainly from the very useful consular reports furnished by British and American officials. See for example British Consular Reports: *Siam for the Year 1889*, pp. 20–5; US Consular Reports: *Siam, Bangkok for the year 1872* (1873), p. 992.

13 British Consular Reports, *Siam for the Year 1889*, p. 20.

14 J. S. Girling, *Thailand: Society and Politics* (Cornell, 1981), p. 57. The role of the British Financial Advisers should not be exaggerated. See Ian Brown, 'British Financial Advisers in the Reign of King Chulalongkorn' *Modern Asian Studies*, (April 1978), pp. 193–215.

15 P. Sithi-Amnuai, *Finance and Banking*, pp. 31–8, 49; on the role of the Hongkong and Shanghai Bank see Thiravet Pramuanratkarn, 'The Hongkong Bank in Thailand: A Case of the Pioneering Bank', in F. H. H. King (ed.), *Eastern Banking: Essays in the History of the Hongkong and Shanghai Banking Corporation* (London, 1983), pp. 421–34. Insurance was also dominated by foreign, largely British firms before 1941. No Siamese insurance company was started until 1929. P. Sithi-Amnuai, *Finance and Banking*, p. 38. Of seven promoters named in the charter of the Siam Commercial Bank in 1906, four were Siamese subjects, two German, and one Danish (PRO, FO 422/61/83, No. 19. Mr Paget to Sir Edward Grey, 8 March 1907).

16 'Review of the Teak Market', *The Record*, 22 October 1926, p. 379 (Ministry of Commerce and Communications, Bangkok).

17 Balance sheets of the Borneo Company Ltd and the Siam Forest Company show that working capital (largely advances on timber already felled and on the rivers) was about 60–75% of total assets (Inchcape Archives, Records of the Siam Forest Company and Borneo Company Ltd). I am grateful to the Inchcape Company archivist, Dr Stephanie Jones, for permission to use these archives.

18 There were, for example, substantial Asian holdings in Australian tin mining companies. It was claimed in 1928 that about 40% of the capital of Australian-registered tin mining companies in Siam came from Chinese and Siamese investors. (*The Mining Magazine*, October 1928, p. 14).

19 James Ingram, *Economic Change in Thailand, 1850–1970* (Stanford, 1971), p. 101.

20 *Report on the Teak Trade in Siam*, Foreign Office, Miscellaneous Series, No. 357, 1895, pp. 7–8; W. A. Graham, *Siam* (London, 1924), vol. II, p. 68.

21 An attitude of suspicion towards Western capital was prevalent in much of the period before 1940. See Callis, *Foreign Capital in Southeast Asia*, p. 60; Tej Bunnag, *The Provincial Administration of Siam, 1892–1915* (Kuala Lumpur, 1977), p. 167; J. W. Cushman, 'The Khaw Group: Chinese Business in Early Twentieth-century Penang', *Journal of Southeast Asian Studies*, March 1986, p. 63.

22 On the development of the railway system see Ingram, *Economic Change in*

Notes to pages 124–30 269

Thailand, pp. 85–7; *Importers and Exporters Directory for Siam, 1924* (2nd ed.), Ministry of Commerce Bangkok, 1924, pp. 24–30; D. F. Holm, 'The Role of the State Railways in Thai History, 1892–1932' (unpublished PhD thesis, Yale University, 1977).

23 Holm, 'The Role of the State Railways', pp. 63–86.

24 Letter dated March 12 1896, PRO, FO 17/1294, p. 155.

25 Callis, *Foreign Capital in Southeast Asia*, p. 59.

26 The best account of the development of the Thai economy is Ingram, *Economic Change in Thailand*. See also Akin Rabibhadana, *The Organization of Thai Society in the Early Bangkok Period, 1782–1873* (Cornell Data Paper, 74, Southeast Asia Program, New York, 1969). For a Thai view see Suthy Prasartset and Chattip Nartsupha, 'The Rise of Dependent Commodity Production in Siam, 1855–1910', *The Review of Thai Social Science*, 3 (1977), pp. 144–68.

27 Ingram, *Economic Change in Thailand*, p. 52.

28 A. W. Graham, *Siam: A Handbook of Practical, Commercial, and Political Information* (London, 1912), p. 413.

29 C. M. Wilson, *Thailand, A Handbook of Historical Statistics*, pp. 159–60. In 1903 no less than 97% of rice exports reached Bangkok by boat and 93% of other exports. A. C. Carter (ed.), *The Kingdom of Siam* (New York and London, 1904), p. 230.

30 *Siam Statistical Yearbook for 1916* (Bangkok), p. 114.

31 *Commercial Directory for Thailand for B.E. 2484 (1941)*, 5th ed. (Dept of Commerce, Bangkok), gives details of the nationality of principal foreign enterprises.

32 Ingram, *Economic Change in Thailand*, p. 35.

33 Hong Lysa, *Thailand in the Nineteenth Century: Evolution of the Economy and Society* (Singapore, 1984), pp. 75–110; 'The Tax Farming System in the Early Bangkok Period', *Journal of Southeast Asian Studies*, September 1983, pp. 382–3; Akin Rabibhadana, *Organization of Thai Society*, pp. 140–2.

34 F. E. Hyde, *Far Eastern Trade, 1860–1914* (London, 1973), p. 18.

35 W. F. Vella, *Siam Under Rama III, 1824–51* (New York, 1957); Likhit Dhiravegin, *The Meiji Restoration (1868–1912) and the Chakkri Reformation (1868–1910): A Comparative Perspective*, vol. I (Thammasat University, Bangkok, 1984), pp. 417–29.

36 Likhit Dhiravegin, *Meiji Restoration*, pp. 417–29. N. Tarling, 'Siam and Sir James Brooke', *Journal of the Siam Society*, November 1960, pp. 45–54.

37 Borneo Company Ltd, *Seventy Years Trading in Bangkok, 1856–1926* (Bangkok, 1926), pp. 2–3.

38 Ibid., p. 3.

39 Ingram, *Economic Change in Thailand*, pp. 45–6.

40 *Bangkok Calendar for 1863*, p. 110.

41 In the late 1880s the British Consul reported that 'the tical (baht) is seldom seen above Raheng. North of that town the rupee is the customary medium', Consular Reports, *Siam for the Year 1889*, p. 14. By 1909 the import of rupees for the area 'used by teak companies for employees' was declining rapidly, *Report of the Financial Adviser on the Budget for 128 (1909–10)* [1909], p. 12.

270 *Notes to pages 131–8*

42 J. G. Campbell, *Siam in the Twentieth Century* (London, 1902), p. 25; W. A. Graham, *Siam*, vol. II, pp. 100–1.

43 The fact that so many of Siam's imports and exports passed through the entrepôts of Hong Kong and Singapore makes classification by country of origin and destination impossible. It is safe to say, though, that Britain was easily the leading country supplying Siam's imports.

44 Borneo Company Ltd, *Seventy Years Trading in Bangkok*, pp. 1–4.

45 Pramuanratkarn, 'The Hongkong Bank in Thailand', p. 421; *Bangkok Calendar for 1867*.

46 Borneo Company Ltd, *Seventy Years Trading in Bangkok*, p. 3; Inchcape Archives, Borneo Co. Minute Books, 20 May 1869.

47 Borneo Company Ltd, *Seventy Years Trading in Bangkok*, p. 4; Inchcape Archives, Borneo Company Balance Sheet for 1870 (in manuscript).

48 Ingram, *Economic Change in Thailand*, pp. 70–1.

49 J. A. Ramsay, 'Modernization and Centralization in Northern Thailand, 1875–1910', *Journal of Southeast Asian Studies*, March 1976, pp. 22–3.

50 R. H. Macaulay, *History of the Bombay Burmah Trading Corporation Ltd, 1864–1910* (London, 1934), pp. 3–5.

51 Good accounts of the workings of teak forests are given in Macaulay, *History* and the W. A. Elder manuscript (Inchcape Archives, 158-page unpublished manuscript). See also *Report on the Teak Trade in Siam*, and R. Campbell, *Teak-Wallah: The Adventures of a Young Englishman in Siam in the 1920's* (London, 1935).

52 Consular Reports, *Report on the Trade and Commerce of Chieng Mai for 1903*, Annual Series 3291, p. 4; ibid., for 1907, Annual Series 4105, p. 5. Elephants involved considerable outlays for the teak companies. In 1910 the Bombay Burmah Trading Corporation had around 1,040 elephants and the Borneo Company over 600 elephants in Siam (Inchcape Archives, Borneo Company minutes).

53 W. S. Bristowe, *Louis and the King of Siam* (London, 1976), p. 55.

54 PRO FO 69/42, letters from T. G. Knox; especially Report by T. G. Knox on the Burn case, 27 June 1865. W. S. Bristowe, *Louis and the King of Siam*, pp. 61–2.

55 Inchcape Archives, Borneo Company Minute Books.

56 Macaulay, *History*, p. 21.

57 Laugesen, Westphall and Dannhorn, *Scandinavians in Siam*, p. 38; Bristowe, *Louis and the King of Siam*, p. 69.

58 Consular Reports, *Commercial Report by Her Majesty's Agent and Consul-General in Siam for the year 1882*, pp. 1–2. In 1884 and 1885 the provisions of the treaty were extended to Nan and Phrae, and in 1896 to six more provinces including Raheng. See Luang Nathabanja, *Extra-Territoriality in Siam* (Bangkok, 1924), pp. 247–50.

59 Inchcape Archives, Borneo Company Minute Books, 11 March 1885; Graham, *Siam, A Handbook*, p. 391.

60 On Cheek and Leonowens see Bristowe, *Louis and the King of Siam*; Inchcape Archives, 'The Borneo Co. Ltd since 1856' (unpublished manuscript); Macaulay, *History*, pp. 53–4.

Notes to pages 138–47 271

61 Inchcape Archives, Correspondence between King Chulalongkorn and John Harvey.

62 Inchcape Archives, Borneo Company Minute Books, 11 March 1885.

63 There are several manuscript histories of the Siam Forest Company (Anglo-Thai Corporation) in the Inchcape Archives, on which this section is largely based.

64 Inchcape Archives, *Concession of Forest Rights in Siam*, signed C. H. Dennis, dated 10 November 1885.

65 Inchcape Archives, *The Siam Forest Co. Ltd, Prospectus*, 1892, pp. 2–3.

66 Inchcape Archives, 'History of the Anglo-Thai Corporation Ltd' (unpublished manuscript), p. 13.

67 Inchcape Archives, *The Siam Forest Co. Ltd, Prospectus*, 1892, p. 3.

68 Inchcape Archives, Siam Forest Company, Report of the Directors for 1897.

69 Inchcape Archives, letter from Frederic Clarke to J. M. Ryrie, 9 May 1899.

70 Macaulay, *History*, pp. 51–4.

71 Ibid., pp. 55–6.

72 Bristowe, *Louis and the King of Siam*, p. 79.

73 Inchcape Archives, Borneo Company Minute Books, 22 April 1897.

74 J. A. Ramsay, 'The Development of Bureaucratic Policy: The Case of Northern Siam' (unpublished PhD thesis, Cornell University, 1971), pp. 131–2.

75 Herbert Slade was an influential figure in the establishment of effective control over Siam's forest resources. He issued an important report to the Bangkok government in 1896. On the changes he introduced see A. C. Carter (ed.), *The Kingdom of Siam*, pp. 173–6; Macaulay, *History*, pp. 60–7.

76 Macaulay, *History*, p. 65: Slade estimated that 20–30% of trees were wasted under the existing methods of exploitation (Thai National Archives, R.5., Ministry of the Interior, Report of Herbert Slade, 16/9, p. 24).

77 *Commercial Directory for Siam, 1929*, 3rd ed. (Ministry of Commerce and Communications), pp. 47–8. For a discussion of the teak leases from a British point of view see Macaulay, *History*, pp. 75–8.

78 Ingram, *Economic Change in Thailand*, p. 106.

79 H. Warington Smyth, *Five Years in Siam*, vol. I, pp. 316–20; vol. II, pp. 1–33. On the growth of Siam's tin exports after 1855 see Malcolm Falkus, 'Aspects of the Development of Tin Output in Siam and Malaya, 1870–1914', Paper presented at the International Mining History Conference, Melbourne University, August 1985.

80 In Burma, too, British trading companies controlled teak production; the leading firms in 1914 were the Bombay Burmah Trading Corporation, Steel Brothers, Macgregor and Company, Darwood and Company, and Foucar and Company (Macaulay, *History*, pp. 39–40).

81 H. Warington Smyth, *Five Years in Siam*, vol. I, pp. 315–20.

82 On the business enterprise of the Khaw family see J. W. Cushman, 'The Khaw Group: Chinese Business in Early Twentieth-century Penang', *Journal of Southeast Asian Studies*, March 1986, pp. 58–79; F. D. Birch, 'Tropical Milestones: Australian Gold and Tin Mining Investments in Malaya and Thailand, 1880–1930' (unpublished MA thesis, Melbourne University, 1976).

272 *Notes to pages 148–52*

83 See, for example, PRO FO 422/68, No. 21, memorandum from Mr Beckett to Sir Edward Grey, 30 April 1913: 'The policy of economic development hitherto pursued by the king and the government has been one tending, as far as possible, towards the exclusion of foreign commercial interests, and the acquisition by the Royal Family and courtiers of all material points of vantage.' Also 'strong representations' to Prince Damrong from the British Consul for the Siamese Malay States in Penang, 2 July 1907 (National Archives, R.5., Ministry of Interior, 53/5).

84 H. Warington Smyth, *Five Years in Siam*, vol. II, p. 297.

85 Tej Bunnag, 'Thesapiban Form of Government: A Revolution or an Evolution?', *Journal of Social Science Review*, I, March 1976, pp. 231–6.

86 National Archives, R.5., Ministry of Agriculture, 1–6.

87 In 1928 there were only four Western rubber plantations in Siam, two of which belonged to the Siamese Tin Syndicate (*Siam Directory for 1928*, Bangkok, pp. 211–18).

88 Memorandum of Mr Westengard, General Adviser to the Siamese government, 30 May 1908. National Archives R.5. Ministry of Foreign Affairs 8/4.

89 See Memorandum from Mr Westengard to Prince Devawongse, April 27 1906 (National Archives, R.5., Ministry of Interior, 1–56).

90 Prince Damrong to King Chulalongkorn, 4 June 1903, National Archives R.5. Ministry of Interior, 1–56. Also Consul-General Sir John Anderson to Mr Beckett, PRO FO 422/61/61, enclosure 2.

91 Cushman, 'The Khaw Group', and J. W. Cushman, 'A Marriage of Convenience: Australian Mining Investment and its Thai Sponsors in Early Twentieth-century Siam', International Conference on Thai Studies, August 1984; F. D. Birch, 'Tropical Milestones'. See also T. A. Miles, 'The Life Story of Capitan Edward Thomas Miles, Master Mariner and Pioneer of Tin Dredging' (Typescript, Australian National University Library, 1969); T. A. Miles, 'Diamond Jubilee of Tin Dredging', Parts 1–3, *Tin International*, January 1967, pp. 3–7; February 1967, pp. 31–8; March 1967, pp. 70–3. And see E. T. Miles, 'History of the Tongkah Harbour Dredging Enterprise', *The Mining Magazine*, March 1919, pp. 182–4.

92 Cushman, 'The Khaw Group', p. 75; K. G. Tregonning, *Home Port Singapore: A History of Straits Steamship Company Limited, 1890–1965* (1967), pp. 56–8.

93 T. A. Miles, 'Diamond Jubilee of Tin Dredging', Part 1, p. 4.

94 *Australian Mining Standard*, 11 January 1911, p. 183. For details of the scheme drawn up between Miles and the Siamese government see the letter from Phya Rasada to Prince Damrong, July 23 1906 (National Archives, R.5., Ministry of Agriculture, 1–6).

95 Birch, 'Tropical Milestones', p. 145.

96 T. A. Miles, 'Diamond Jubilee of Tin Dredging', Part 3, pp. 70–3; S. Cunningham-Brown, *The Traders: A Story of Britain's South-east Asia Commercial Adventure* (London, 1971), pp. 207–9.

97 T. A. Miles, 'Diamond Jubilee of Tin Dredging', Part 3, pp. 72–3.

98 Ibid., pp. 72–3.

Notes to pages 153–61 273

99 Thus PRO FO 422/61/6 enclosure 3, Mr C. McArthur to Sir J. Anderson (12 September 1906): 'British interests in Tongkah will not prosper unless they are represented by the immediate clique of relations of Mr Kaw Sin [*sic*] Bee.'
100 Cushman, 'A Marriage of Convenience', p. 12.
101 *Australian Mining Standard*, 11 January 1911, p. 159.
102 *Commercial Directory for Siam, 1929*, pp. 118–29.
103 Birch, 'Tropical Milestones', p. 220.
104 Ibid., pp. 241–2.
105 Figures in this and the subsequent paragraph from *Siam Statistical Yearbook*, various dates.
106 The Borneo Company Ltd, *Seventy Years Trading in Bangkok*, p. 4.
107 Laugesen, Westphall and Dannhorn, *Scandinavians in Siam*, p. 48. Loftus was also involved in the first Bangkok tramway company, formed in 1887 (Consular Reports, *Report for Siam for the Year 1889*, p. 20).

6 British business in Malaysia and Singapore since the 1870s

* A first draft of this article was prepared by Jean-Jacques van Helten. He was prevented from completing the article on accepting a non-academic appointment in Australia late in 1986, whereupon the article was re-written in its present form by Geoffrey Jones. Both authors would like to thank Ian Brown, Gill Burke, Malcolm Falkus and Stuart Muirhead as well as Richard Davenport-Hines for their comments on the various drafts, while stressing that they hold no responsibility for the statements expressed in this final version.

1 L. J. Zimmerman, 'The Distribution of World Income 1860–1960', in Egbert de Vries (ed.), *Essays on Unbalanced Growth* (The Hague, 1962), pp. 52–3.
2 *Financial Times*, Supplement on Malaysia, 20 July 1987.
3 Wong Lin Ken, 'Singapore: Its Growth as an Entrepot Port, 1819–1941', *Journal of Southeast Asian Studies*, 9 (1978).
4 There is a valuable study of the British agency houses by J. H. Drabble and P. J. Drake, 'The British Agency Houses in Malaysia: Survival in a Changing World', *Journal of Southeast Asian Studies*, 12 (1981); see especially pp. 297–306 for their nineteenth-century growth. The best overall study of the history of British business in Singapore and Malaya remains G. C. Allen and A. G. Donnithorne, *Western Enterprise in Indonesia and Malaya* (London, 1957). None of the agency houses has a first-rate business history, but see S. Cunyngham-Brown, *The Traders* (London, 1971) for Guthries; and Boustead and Company, *East India Merchants Established 1828* (n.d.). See also J. J. Puthucheary, *Ownership and Control in the Malayan Economy* (Singapore, 1960).
5 Stephanie Jones, *Two Centuries of Overseas Trading. The Origins and Growth of the Inchcape Group* (London, 1986), pp. 19–21, 195–215.
6 Compton Mackenzie, *Realms of Silver* (London, 1954), pp. 104–15, 215–16; Chee Peng Lim, Phang Siew Nooi and Margaret Boh, 'The History and Development of The Hong Kong and Shanghai Banking Corporation in Peninsular Malaysia', in F. H. H. King (ed.), *Eastern Banking* (London, 1983),

274 *Notes to pages 161–4*

pp. 350–5; and F. H. H. King, *The History of the Hongkong and Shanghai Banking Corporation*, vol. I: *The Hongkong Bank in Late Imperial China, 1864–1902: On an Even Keel* (Cambridge, 1987), esp. pp. 264, 347–50.

7 Wong Lin Ken, 'Singapore', p. 84; Allen and Donnithorne, *Western Enterprise*, pp. 54–60; Chiang Hai Ding, 'Sino-British Mercantile Relations in Singapore's Entrepot Trade, 1870–1915', in J. Ch'en and N. Tarling (eds.), *Studies in the Social History of China and Southeast Asia* (Cambridge, 1970).

8 P. J. Drake, 'The Economic Development of British Malaya to 1914', *Journal of Southeast Asian Studies*, 10 (1979), pp. 272–8. Lim Chong Yah, *Economic Development of Modern Malaya* (Kuala Lumpur, 1967) provides a basic account of the country's modern economic history. See also D. Lim, *Economic Growth and Development in West Malaysia* (Kuala Lumpur, 1973). Arnold Wright (ed.), *Twentieth Century Impressions of British Malaya* (London, 1908) provides a richly illustrated contemporary account of the economic and social conditions in early twentieth-century Malaya, and contains a great store of information about British enterprise in this period. The book gives accounts of each of the British tin and rubber companies active in Malaya, and also discusses sectors which historians have little researched. W. Makepeace on 'The Press', for example, examines the British-managed but usually locally registered companies which published the English-language newspapers such as the *Straits Times*. These companies were often linked with other British interests. The *Times of Malaya* Press Ltd, for example, was established in Ipoh in 1904 'in furtherance of the mining, planting and mercantile interests of the Federated Malay States and Straits Settlements . . . The capital was subscribed in Malaya by British subjects' (p. 261). These were mainly individual British expatriates, but included the Straits Trading Company (see later in this article) and a British subject of Chinese descent.

9 Yip Yat Hoong, *The Development of the Tin Mining Industry of Malaya* (Kuala Lumpur, 1969), p. 62.

10 W. Woodruff, *The Rise of the British Rubber Industry* (Liverpool, 1958); Angus McLaren, *Birth Control in Nineteenth-Century England* (London, 1978), pp. 22, 225.

11 Junid Saham, *British Industrial Investment in Malaysia 1963–1971* (Kuala Lumpur, 1980), pp. 18–19, citing data from a Royal Institute of International Affairs survey in 1937. In 1910 around half of total British investments in the Malay States and Straits Settlements were in tin and rubber. See G. Paish, 'Great Britain's Capital Investments in Individual Colonial and Foreign Countries', *Journal of the Royal Statistical Society*, 74 (1911), p. 180.

12 Wong Lin Ken, *The Malayan Tin Industry to 1914* (Tucson, 1965), pp. 26–8; R. N. Jackson, *Immigrant Labour and the Economic Development of Malaya, 1786–1920* (Kuala Lumpur, 1961), pp. 30–6.

13 Allen and Donnithorne, *Western Enterprise*, p. 156; Yip Yat Hoong, *Development*, pp. 95–109.

14 These figures are taken from Edward Ashmead's annual returns, published in the late January issues of the *Mining Journal*, and E. Ashmead, *Twenty-Five Years of Mining, 1880–1904* (London, 1909).

Notes to pages 165–9 275

15 See J.-J. van Helten, 'Mining Share Manias and Speculation: British Investment in Overseas Mining, 1880–1913', *Business History Review* (forthcoming).

16 J. F. Hennart, 'Internalization in Practice: Early Foreign Direct Investments in Malaysian Tin Mining', *Journal of International Business Studies* (1986), p. 133. For a helpful long-term historical survey of vertical integration in the world tin industry by the same author, see Hennart, 'The Tin Industry', in M. Casson (ed.), *Multinationals and World Trade* (London, 1986).

17 Wong Lin Ken, 'Western Enterprise and the Development of the Malayan Tin Industry to 1914', in C. D. Cowan (ed.), *Economic Development of South-East Asia* (London, 1964), pp. 138–9, 149.

18 F. A. Swettenham, *About Perak* (Singapore, 1893), p. 341.

19 Yip Yat Hoong, *Development*, pp. 133–4.

20 Song Ong Siang, *One Hundred Years' History of the Chinese in Singapore* (London, 1923), pp. 110–16.

21 Yip Yat Hoong, *Development*, pp. 139–43; F. D. Birch, 'Tropical Milestones: Australian Gold and Tin Mining Investments in Malaya and Thailand, 1880–1930' (unpublished MA thesis, Melbourne University, 1976), pp. 10–162. Birch notes that 'Australian companies were more successful than most other European companies mining in Malaya' and were among the 'most profitable of the early companies' (pp. 40–1). In 1919 Australian-registered companies accounted for 20% of total 'sterling' capital invested in tin (p. 161).

22 *A History of the Pahang Consolidated Company Limited 1906–1966* (London, 1966).

23 For a discussion of the international mining market around the turn of the century, see R. V. Turrell with J.-J. van Helten, 'The Rothschilds, the Exploration Company and Mining Finance', *Business History*, 28 (1986), pp. 181–205.

24 Wong Lin Ken, 'Western Enterprise', pp. 148–9; Federated Malay States, *Mines Department Report*, 1913, pp. 20–2. For the abolition of tax farming, see John G. Butcher, 'The demise of the Revenue Farm System in the Federated Malay States', *Modern Asian Studies*, 17 (1983).

25 K. G. Tregonning, *Straits Tin. A Brief Account of the First Seventy-five Years of The Straits Trading Company, Ltd 1887–1962* (Singapore, n.d.).

26 J. W. Cushman, 'The Khaw Group: Chinese Business in Early Twentieth Century Penang', *Journal of Southeast Asian Studies*, 17 (1986); Allen and Donnithorne, *Western Enterprise*, pp. 158–60. See also chapter 5 in this volume.

27 Yip Yat Hoong, 'Malaya under the Pre-War International Tin Agreement', *Malayan Economic Review*, 5 (1960), pp. 59–65.

28 Yip Yat Hoong, *Development*, pp. 153, 158–9.

29 Allen and Donnithorne, *Western Enterprise*, p. 157; William L. Baldwin, *The World Tin Market* (Durham, NC, 1983), p. 245.

30 *Statist*, 11 February 1935; *Economist*, 2 March and 13 July 1935.

31 Committee of Treasury Minutes, 23 October 1935, 4 December 1935, 17 June 1936, 10 February 1937, Bank of England Archives, File G 14/244.

32 Allen and Donnithorne, *Western Enterprise*, pp. 158–60; J. Thoburn, *Multi-*

276 *Notes to pages 169–73*

nationals, Mining and Development (Aldershot, 1981), pp. 64–5; Bill Freund, *Capital and Labour in the Nigerian Tin Mines* (London, 1981), pp. 116–17.

33 London Metal Exchange to Secretary of State for the Colonies, 7 August 1935, Colonial Office Files, Public Record Office (PRO), CO 852/4/4. See also the views of Frank Mair, Chairman of Gopeng Consolidated, expressed in the *Financial Times*, 28 March 1931.

34 Freund, *Capital and Labour*, pp. 121–2.

35 Memorandum by J. A. Calder, 2 September 1935, PRO CO 852/4/4.

36 Yip Yat Hoong, *Development*, pp. 283–4; Allen and Donnithorne, *Western Enterprise*, p. 162; P. P. Courtenay, *A Geography of Trade and Development in Malaya* (London, 1972), pp. 120–1; J. Campbell, *International Tin Control and Buffer Stocks* (London, 1944); Freund, *Capital and Labour*, pp. 125–6.

37 James C. Jackson, *Sarawak. A Geographical Survey of a Developing State* (London, 1968), pp. 138–51; F. C. Gerretson, *History of the Royal Dutch* (Leiden, 1958), vol. IV, pp. 86–8. In the early 1950s there was some criticism from American sources of Shell's 'wasteful' exploitation methods at Miri. Colonial Office officials dismissed such criticisms as an example of a 'parochial refusal to acknowledge the success of British enterprise or see anything good in British administration of backward areas', Memorandam of September 1952 on article by Ashton Greene, PRO CO 1022/363. For a contemporary account of Sarawak's early oil industry, see T. G. Cochrane, 'Empire Oil: The Progress of Sarawak', *Journal of the Royal Society of Arts*, 72 (1924). B. A. St J. Hepburn, *The Handbook of Sarawak* (Singapore, 1949), especially pp. 124–8, is also useful.

38 Allen and Donnithorne, *Western Enterprise*, p. 106; for an interesting account of the social impact of the plantations upon local people and upon Singapore, see W. N. Willis, *Western Men with Eastern Morals* (London, 1913). The Malayan experience can be seen in comparative perspective in Voon Phin Keong, *Western Rubber Planting Enterprise in Southeast Asia, 1876–1921* (Kuala Lumpur, 1976).

39 C. Barlow, *The Natural Rubber Industry. Its Development, Technology and Economy in Malaysia* (Kuala Lumpur, 1978); J. C. Jackson, *Planters and Speculators: Chinese and European Agricultural Enterprise in Malaya 1780–1921* (Kuala Lumpur, 1968).

40 J. H. Drabble, *Rubber in Malaya 1876–1922. The Genesis of the Industry* (Kuala Lumpur, 1973), pp. 22, 66–7. This is the standard work on the early Malayan rubber industry. On the finance of the industry, see R. Stillson, 'The Financing of Malayan Rubber 1905–1923', *Economic History Review*, 24 (1971) and J. H. Drabble and P. J. Drake, 'More on the Financing of Malayan Rubber, 1905–1923', *Economic History Review*, 27 (1974).

41 Drabble and Drake, 'British Agency Houses', pp. 306–11; Jones, *Two Centuries*, pp. 214–15.

42 P. T. Bauer, 'Malayan Rubber Policy', in T. H. Silcock (ed.), *Readings in Malayan Economics* (Singapore, 1961); a first-rate survey of more recent research on the smallholding sector is J. H. Drabble, 'Peasant Smallholdings in the Malayan Economy: An Historical Study with Special Reference to the Rubber Industry', in James C. Jackson and Martin Rudner (eds.), *Issues in*

Notes to pages 173–81 277

Malaysian Development (Singapore, 1979). The studies by Lim Teck Ghee, *Origins of a Colonial Economy: Land and Agriculture in Perak 1874–1897* (Penang, 1976) and *Peasants and their Agricultural Economy in Colonial Malaya 1874–1941* (Kuala Lumpur, 1977) provide essential data on British colonial policy towards agriculture in Malaya.

43 Jackson, *Sarawak*, pp. 89–92, 98–9. British North Borneo saw a further variation of plantation agriculture. In the late nineteenth century Dutch, German and – later – British planters established a large tobacco industry which, however, gave way to rubber from the 1900s. See David W. John and James C. Jackson, 'The Tobacco Industry of North Borneo: A Distinctive Form of Plantation Agriculture', in *Journal of Southeast Asian Studies*, 4 (1973).

44 Drabble, *Rubber in Malaya*, p. 199.

45 For an analysis of the IRRA see P. Bauer, *The Rubber Industry. A Study in Competition and Monopoly* (London, 1948); U.E. Knorr, *World Rubber and its Regulation* (Stanford, 1945); and A. McFadyean (ed.), *The History of Rubber Regulation, 1934–43* (London, 1944).

46 See the critical assessment of 'The Working of Rubber Regulation' in PRO CO 852/607/2 98894, as well as the sources previously cited.

47 Courtenay, *Geography*, p. 124; Barlow, *Natural Rubber Industry*, pp. 62–73.

48 Lim Chong Yah, *Economic Development*, pp. 128–43, Appendices 5.1 and 5.2; Allen and Donnithorne, *Western Enterprise*, pp. 142–5; Courtenay, *Geography*, p. 125.

49 MacKenzie, *Realms of Silver*, pp. 215–16.

50 Chee Peng Lim, *et al.*, 'History and Development', pp. 366–7.

51 S. W. Muirhead, 'The Mercantile Bank of India on the East Coast of Malaya', in King (ed.), *Eastern Banking*.

52 J. B. Ross to J. Crichton, 5 May 1941, MB1002:5, Mercantile Bank Archives, Hongkong Bank Group Archives.

53 C. R. Wardle to R. Cromartie, 1 August 1927, MB1190.

54 Muirhead, 'Mercantile Bank of India', p. 668.

55 Chee Peng Lim, *et al.*, 'History and Development', pp. 358–62.

56 R. N. Drake to J. B. Crichton, 11 September 1946, MB1001:5.

57 Allen and Donnithorne, *Western Enterprise*, pp. 206–7; Lim Chong Yah, *Economic Development*, pp. 233–6.

58 C. R. Wardle to R. N. Drake, 10 February 1949, MB970.

59 R. N. Drake to C. F. Pow, 1 February 1952, MB1000:10.

60 Chief Manager to R. D. Cromartie, 6 October 1927, MB1190.

61 Thoburn, *Multinationals*, p. 66; D.K. Fieldhouse, *Unilever Overseas* (London, 1978), pp. 546–52.

62 Yip Yat Hoong, *Development*, pp. 346–70.

63 'Battle for Sime Darby', *Far Eastern Economic Review*, 3 December 1976.

64 Saham, *British Industrial Investment*, p. 26.

65 Ibid., chapter 5, provides a detailed account of these developments; Drabble and Drake, 'British Agency Houses', pp. 311–12.

66 Martin Rudner, 'Malayan Rubber Policy: Development and Anti-Development during the 1950s', *Journal of Southeast Asian Studies*, 7 (1976).

278 *Notes to pages 181–6*

67 For Britain's post-war sterling problems, see S. Strange, *Sterling and British Policy* (London, 1971); L. S. Pressnell, 'The End of the Sterling Area', *The Three Banks Review*, March 1979; and A. Cairncross, *Years of Recovery* (London, 1985).

68 International Bank for Reconstruction and Development, *The Economic Development of Malaya* (Singapore, 1955), p. 499. This book provides a comprehensive contemporary account of the Malayan economy in the early 1950s and is an invaluable source.

69 'Brief by the Malayan Rubber Industry', 1951, PRO CO 852/1161/1.

70 Memorandum on the United Kingdom's Economic Interests in the Far East, South-East Asia and South Asia, 1955, 23 November 1956, Foreign Office Files, PRO, FO 371/123251.

71 Saham, *British Industrial Investment*, p. 49. Lutz Hoffman and Tan Siew Lee, *Industrial Growth, Employment and Foreign Investment in Peninsular Malaysia* (Kuala Lumpur, 1980) examines in detail the impact of Malaysian government policies on foreign investment. The authors suggest that tax incentives had little impact on foreign investment levels, pointing instead to the moderate tariff protection policies pursued in the 1960s.

72 Hafiz Mirza, *Multinationals and the Growth of the Singapore Economy*, (London, 1986), especially chapter 3; Chia Siow Yue, 'The Role of Foreign Trade and Investment in the Development of Singapore', in W. Galenson (ed.), *Foreign Trade and Investment* (Madison, 1985), pp. 259–91.

73 Chia Siow Yue, 'Role', pp. 292–3; K. Yoshihara, in *Foreign Investment and Domestic Response* (Singapore, 1976), pp. 111–13, noted a lack of enthusiasm by British companies in the early 1970s for investing in Singapore, especially compared to their American and Japanese competitors. There is a study of British investment in Singapore in the immediate post-independence period in Gethyn Davies, 'United Kingdom Investment', in Helen Hughes and You Poh Seng (eds.), *Foreign Investment and Industrialisation in Singapore* (Canberra, 1969).

74 Mirza, *Multinationals*, p. 95.

75 Mirza, *Multinationals*, pp. 134–5; see also Tan Chwee Huat, *Financial Institutions in Singapore* (Singapore, 1984).

76 Mercantile Bank Manager Penang to C. R. Wardle, 19 March 1962, MB2140.

77 C. R. Wardle to Sir Michael Turner, 29 December 1961, MB1325.

78 C. R. Wardle to T. J. McG. Wilkie, 23 December 1960, MB2131.

79 Letters to Managers of Ipoh, Singapore, Kuala Lumpur and Penang, 4 March 1960, MB2129; C. R. Wardle to Sir Michael Turner, 29 December 1961, MB1325.

80 C. R. Wardle to T. J. McG. Wilkie, 5 June 1962, MB2137.

81 Chee Peng Lim, *et al.*, 'History and Development', pp. 369–91.

82 Thoburn, *Multinationals*, pp. 82–3; Baldwin, *World Tin*, p. 40; *Far Eastern Economic Review*, 3 December 1976. On Slater Walker and Haw Paw, see Charles Raw, *A Financial Phenomenon* (New York, 1977), pp. 317–20, 340, 343–4.

83 *Far Eastern Economic Review*, 3 December 1976, 24 December 1976, 3 October 1980; Drabble and Drake, 'British Agency Houses', pp. 324–5.

Notes to pages 186–91 279

84 *Far Eastern Economic Review*, 16 February 1979, 20 March 1980, 13 September 1981. In 1988 PNB sold the nonplantation activities of Guthrie back to British interests.

85 *Far Eastern Economic Review*, 1–7 October 1982.

86 *Financial Times*, Supplement on Malaysia, 20 July 1987; Far Eastern Economic Review, *Asia 1987 Yearbook*, p. 191.

7 British business in China, 1860s–1950s

1 For a discussion of the 'level of analysis' problem in the context of theories of theories of imperialism, see J. Osterhammel, 'Semi-colonialism and Informal Empire in Twentieth-century China: Towards a Framework of Analysis', in W. J. Mommsen and J. Osterhammel (eds.), *Imperialism and After: Continuities and Discontinuities* (London, 1986), pp. 290–314.

2 See G. W. Gong, *The Standard of 'Civilization' in International Society* (Oxford, 1984), and his 'China's Entry into International Society', in H. Bull and A. Watson (eds.), *The Expansion of International Society* (London, 1984), pp. 171–83.

3 L. Dermigny, *La Chine et l'Occident: le commerce à Canton au XVIIIe siècle, 1719–1833* (Paris, 1964), vol. I, p. 91; O. H. K. Spate, *The Pacific since Magellan*, vol. II: *Monopolists and Freebooters* (London and Canberra, 1983), p. 98.

4 On the one exception – the Dutch presence in Japan – see G. K. Goodman, *Japan: The Dutch Experience* (London, 1986).

5 E. H. Pritchard, *Anglo-Chinese Relations during the Seventeenth and Eighteenth Centuries* (Urbana, Ill., 1929), p. 80. For a comprehensive description of these mechanisms see Dermigny, *La Chine*, especially vol. I, pp. 274ff, and C. J. A. Jörg, *Porcelain and the Dutch China Trade* (The Hague, 1982), pp. 46–90.

6 M. Mancall, *China at the Center: 300 Years of Foreign Policy* (New York and London, 1984), p. 55.

7 K. N. Chaudhuri, 'The English East India Company in the 17th and 18th Centuries: A Pre-modern Multinational Organization', in L. Blussé and F. Gaastra (eds.), *Companies and Trade* (Leiden, 1981), pp. 29–46. See also Chaudhuri's *The Trading World of Asia and the English East India Company, 1660–1760* (Cambridge, 1978), especially pp. 19ff.

8 On this final phase see Hoh-cheung Mui and L. H. Mui, *The Management of Monopoly: A Study of the English East India Company's Conduct of Its Tea Trade, 1784–1833* (Vancouver, 1984).

9 M. H. Hunt, *The Making of a Special Relationship: The United States and China to 1914* (New York, 1983), pp. 8–12.

10 Dermigny, *La Chine*, vol. III, pp. 1197ff. For a concise account of the China trade in the early nineteenth century see F. Wakeman, Jr, 'The Canton Trade and the Opium War', in J. K. Fairbank (ed.), *The Cambridge History of China*, vol. X (Cambridge, 1978), pp. 166–71.

11 On these crises see W. E. Cheong, 'The Crisis of the East India Houses 1830–1834', *Revue internationale de l'histoire de la banque*, 9 (1974), pp. 107–33; Cheong, *Mandarins and Merchants: Jardine Matheson & Co., a*

280 *Notes to pages 191–2*

China Agency of the Early Nineteenth Century (London and Malmö, 1978), pp. 32–43, 87ff; T. Hamashita, 'Foreign Trade Finance in China, 1810–50', in L. Grove and C. Daniels (eds.), *State and Society in China: Japanese Perspectives on Ming-Qing Social and Economic History* (Tokyo, 1984), pp. 387–435.

12 See Hao Yen-p'ing, *The Commercial Revolution in Nineteenth-Century China: The Rise of Sino-Western Mercantile Capitalism* (Berkeley, Los Angeles and London, 1986).

13 D. A. Farnie, *The English Cotton Industry and the World Market, 1815–1896* (Oxford, 1979), p. 91, Table 5. For broader discussions of China's resistance to foreign goods see R. Murphey, *The Outsiders: The Western Experience in India and China* (Ann Arbor, Mich., 1977), p. 99ff; S. R. Brown, 'The Partially Opened Door: Limitations on Economic Changes in China in the 1860s', *Modern Asian Studies*, 12 (1978), pp. 177–92; and, in particular, G. G. Hamilton, 'Chinese Consumption of Foreign Commodities: A Comparative Perspective', *American Sociological Review*, 42 (1977), pp. 877–91.

14 On the opium trade of the 1850s and 1860s see E. LeFevour, *Western Enterprise in Late Ch'ing China: A Selective Survey of Jardine, Matheson and Company's Operations, 1842–1862* (Cambridge, Mass., 1971), pp. 22–30. The imports of opium, as registered by the Imperial Maritime Customs, peaked in 1879, and then slowly declined until the First World War. See Hsiao Liang-lin, *China's Foreign Trade Statistics, 1864–1949* (Cambridge, Mass., 1974), pp. 52–3, Table 2. The opium trade had been legalised in 1858.

15 LeFevour, *Western Enterprise*, p. 48.

16 J. Ahvenainen, *The Far Eastern Telegraphs* (Helsinki, 1981), pp. 44–5; Wang Shu-huai, 'China's Modernization in Communications, 1860–1916: A Regional Comparison', in Hou Chi-ming and Yu Tzong-shian (eds.), *Modern Chinese Economic History* (Taipeh, 1979), pp. 335–6. On the 'communications revolution' in general see D. R. Headrick, *The Tools of Empire: Technology and European Imperialism in the Nineteenth Century* (New York and Oxford, 1981), pp. 129ff.

17 On the Hongkong Bank as a 'local' bank see F. H. H. King, 'Establishing the Hongkong Bank: The Role of the Directors and their Managers', in King (ed.), *Eastern Banking: Essays in the History of the Hongkong and Shanghai Banking Corporation* (London, 1983), pp. 32, 39–42, 57.

18 Wu Chengming, *Diguozhuyi zai jiu Zhongguo de touzi* [Imperialist Investment in Pre-revolutionary China] (Beijing, 1958), p. 41.

19 A. Feuerwerker, 'Economic Trends in the Late Ch'ing Empire, 1870–1911', in J. K. Fairbank and Liu Kwang-ching (eds.), *The Cambridge History of China*, vol. XI (Cambridge, 1980), pp. 50–3. The same is true for the early twentieth century, see J. Osterhammel, *Britischer Imperialismus im Fernen Osten. Strukturen der Durchdringung und einheimischer Widerstand auf dem chinesischen Markt 1932–1937* (Bochum, 1983), pp. 133–7.

20 On tea, see R. P. Gardella, 'The Boom Years of the Fukien Tea Trade', in E. R. May and J. K. Fairbank (eds.), *America's China Trade in Historical Perspective: The Chinese and American Performance* (Cambridge, Mass. and London, 1986), pp. 37–49; W. T. Rowe, *Hankow: Commerce and Society in*

Notes to pages 192–5 281

a Chinese City, 1796–1889 (Stanford, 1984), pp. 131–6. Among Europeans, only the Russians managed to penetrate the Chinese countryside and to establish tea factories in the interior. On the organisation of silk exports see L. M. Li, *China's Silk Trade: Traditional Industry in the Modern World, 1842–1937* (Cambridge, Mass., 1981), pp. 154–62.

21 See T. G. Rawski, 'Chinese Dominance of Treaty Port Commerce and its Implications, 1860–1864', *Explorations in Economic History*, 7 (1970), pp. 451–73; Hao Yen-p'ing, *The Comprador in Nineteenth-century China: Bridge between East and West* (Cambridge, Mass., 1970), pp. 154–62. The seminal research on this question was done by the eminent economic historian Wang Jingyu and was first published in 1965, now republished in his book *Shijiu shiji xifang zibenzhuyi dui Zhongguo de jingji qinlüe* [The Economic Invasion of China by Western Capitalism in the Nineteenth Century] (Beijing, 1983), pp. 483–537.

22 Li, *China's Silk Trade*, p. 165. On this early factory see also S. R. Brown, 'The Ewo Filature: A Study of the Transfer of Technology to China in the 19th Century', *Technology and Culture*, 20 (1979), pp. 550–68.

23 For a summary of foreign direct investment in China before 1895 see S. R. Brown, 'The Transfer of Technology to China in the Nineteenth Century: The Role of Foreign Direct Investment', *Journal of Economic History*, 39 (1979), pp. 181–98. For a more comprehensive survey see O. E. Nepomnin, *Ekonomicheskaya istoriya Kitaya 1864–1894 gg.* (Moscow, 1974), pp. 204–29, and, above all, Wang Jingyu, *Shijiu shiji*, especially pp. 114ff.

24 For an overview of these enterprises, see S. C. Thomas, *Foreign Intervention and China's Industrial Development, 1870–1911* (Boulder, Col. and London, 1984), pp. 59–108.

25 On the role of Western technical advisers see the case-studies in T. L. Kennedy, *The Arms of Kiangnan: Modernization in the Chinese Ordnance Industry, 1860–1895* (Boulder, Col. and London, 1978).

26 LeFevour, *Western Enterprise*, pp. 73–93.

27 The organisational type 'investment group' is defined and described in S. D. Chapman, 'British-based Investment Groups before 1914', *Economic History Review*, 2nd ser., 38 (1985), pp. 230–47, and the same author's *The Rise of Merchant Banking* (London, 1984), pp. 140–4.

28 See S. F. Wright, *Hart and the Chinese Customs* (Belfast, 1950); L. K. Little, 'Introduction', in J. K. Fairbank, K. F. Bruner and E. M. Matheson (eds.), *The I.G. in Peking: Letters of Robert Hart. Chinese Maritime Customs, 1868–1907*, vol. I (Cambridge, Mass., 1975), pp. 7–30.

29 On early British steamship business in China see Liu Kwang-ching, *Anglo-American Steamship Rivalry in China, 1862–1874* (Cambridge, Mass., 1962); and his 'British-Chinese Steamship Rivalry in China, 1873–85', in C. D. Cowan (ed.), *The Economic Development of China and Japan: Studies in Economic History and Political Economy* (London, 1964), pp. 49–78.

30 J.-P. Lehmann, *The Image of Japan: From Feudal Isolation to World Power, 1850–1905* (London, 1978), pp. 163–7.

31 C. F. Remer, *Foreign Investments in China* (New York, 1933), p. 361, Table 4. Remer's criterion for 'direct' investment is that 'the property remains under

282 *Notes to pages 195–7*

foreign control and management' and that 'the business risk and, usually, the legal ownership remain with the investor' (ibid., pp. 65 and 66, n. 14). Remer includes investments made by *residents* in China possessing foreign nationality. Since the legal and ethnic position of foreigners in China was clearly demarcated, this convention has some justification in the case of China.

32 A. Fishlow, 'Lessons from the Past: Capital Markets during the 19th Century and the Interwar Period', *International Organization*, 39 (1985), p. 394, Table 2.

33 Remer, *Foreign Investments*, p. 360.

34 R. Y. Eng, 'Chinese Entrepreneurs, the Government and the Foreign Sector: The Canton and Shanghai Silk-reeling Enterprises', *Modern Asian Studies*, 18 (1964), pp. 363–4.

35 A. D. Chandler, Jr, *The Visible Hand: The Managerial Revolution in American Business* (Cambridge, Mass. and London, 1977), p. 382.

36 S. G. Cochran, *Big Business in China: Sino-Foreign Rivalry in the Cigarette Industry, 1890–1930* (Cambridge, Mass. and London, 1980), p. 16.

37 Ibid., p. 13. According to Mira Wilkins, 'BAT remained under the control of U.S. stockholders until the mid-1920s.' M. Wilkins, 'The Impacts of American Multinational Enterprise on American-Chinese Economic Relations, 1786–1949', in May and Fairbank (eds.), *America's China Trade*, p. 270.

38 So far, there are no complete histories of these groups; their development in the twentieth century especially has not yet been thoroughly studied. Preliminary accounts are M. Keswick (ed.), *The Thistle and the Jade: A Celebration of 150 Years of Jardine, Matheson and Co.* (London, 1982); and C. Drage, *Taikoo* (London, 1970).

39 S. Marriner and F. E. Hyde, *The Senior: John Samuel Swire, 1825–1898: Management in Far Eastern Shipping Trades* (Liverpool, 1967), pp. 103–4.

40 China's first modern cotton mill started operation in 1890. Chao Kang, *The Development of Cotton Textile Production in China* (Cambridge, Mass., 1977), p. 106.

41 Ibid., p. 117.

42 T. Wright, *Coal Mining in China's Economy and Society, 1895–1937*, (Cambridge, 1984), p. 120.

43 W. F. Collins, *Mineral Enterprise in China*, revised ed. (Tianjin, 1922), pp. 54–60.

44 Lee En-han, 'China's Response to Foreign Investment in her Mining Industry (1902–1911)', *Journal of Asian Studies*, 28 (1968), pp. 66, 69–71.

45 Wang Jingyu (ed.), *Zhongguo jindai gongye shi ziliao, dier ji (1895–1911)* [Materials on the History of Industry in China, Second Collection, 1895–1911], vol. I (Beijing, 1957), p. 92.

46 For brief histories of the Pekin Syndicate, see Hou Chi-ming, *Foreign Investment and Economic Development in China, 1840–1937* (Cambridge, Mass., 1965), pp. 71–3; Osterhammel, *Britischer Imperialismus*, pp. 51–3, 367–82.

47 E. C. Carlson, *The Kaiping Mines, 1877–1912*, 2nd ed. (Cambridge, Mass., 1971), p. 24.

48 Ibid., p. 55.

Notes to pages 198–200 283

49 Ibid., pp. 57–69, 71–4; V. Schmidt, *Aufgabe und Einfluss der europäischen Berater in China: Gustav Detring (1842–1913) im Dienste Li Hung-changs* (Wiesbaden, 1985), pp. 99–108; G. N. Nash, *The Life of Herbert Hoover: The Engineer, 1874–1914* (New York and London, 1983), pp. 117–59; G. Kurgan-Van Hentenryk, *Léopold II et les groupes financiers belges en Chine* (Brussels, 1972), pp. 672–716. The Belgian share of the capital declined subsequently, and the crucial position of General Manager of the Kaiping mines and later of the Kailuan Mining Administration was in British hands from 1904. However, Belgians continued to be represented on the senior engineering staff until they were 'purged' in early 1935. See Public Record Office (Kew), FO 371/19284/F2568, E. Teichman, minute, 9 March 1935.

50 Wright, *Coal Mining*, p. 123; Osterhammel, *Britischer Imperialismus*, p. 54.

51 Sir Eric Teichman, *Affairs of China: A Survey of the Recent History and Present Circumstances of the Republic of China* (London, 1938), p. 275.

52 Xu Gengsheng, *Zhong-wai heban meikuangye shihua* [History of Sino-Foreign Joint Ventures in Chinese Coal Mining] (Shanghai, 1947), pp. 14–20.

53 Remer, *Foreign Investments*, pp. 359–60.

54 For a lucid analysis of the coal market in China, see Wright, *Coal Mining*, chapter 4.

55 R. W. Huenemann, *The Dragon and the Iron Horse: The Economics of Railroads in China, 1876–1937* (Cambridge, Mass. and London, 1984), p. 113.

56 A. P. Winston, 'Does Trade Follow the Dollar?', *American Economic Review*, 17 (1927), cited in J. Foreman-Peck, *A History of the World Economy: International Economic Relations since 1850* (Brighton, Sussex, 1983), p. 142. See also Huenemann, *The Dragon*, pp. 108, and 290 n. 23.

57 See Hsu Cheng-kuang, 'Foreign Interests, State and Gentry-Merchant Class: Railway Development in Early Modern China, 1895–1911' (unpublished Ph.D. thesis, Brown University, 1984), chapters 4–6.

58 On various aspects see E-tu Zen Sun, *Chinese Railways and British Interests 1898–1911* (New York, 1954); Lee En-han, *China's Quest for Railway Autonomy, 1904–1911: A Study of the Chinese Railway-Rights Recovery Movement* (Singapore, 1977); E. W. Edwards, 'Great Britain and China, 1905–1911', in F. H. Hinsley (ed.), *British Foreign Policy under Sir Edward Grey* (Cambridge, 1977), pp. 351–61; D. McLean, 'Finance and "Informal Empire" before the First World War', *Economic History Review*, 2nd ser., 29 (1976), pp. 291–305. Much information will be found in chapters 5, 6 and 7 of Professor F. H. H. King's *History of the Hongkong and Shanghai Banking Corporation*, vol. II: *The Hongkong Bank in the Period of Imperialism and War, 1895–1918: Wayfoong, the Focus of Wealth* (Cambridge, 1988).

59 Huenemann, *The Dragon*, p. 78, Table 4; p. 98, Table 5.

60 Chang Kia-ngua, *China's Struggle for Railroad Development* (New York, 1943), p. 153.

61 For details see Osterhammel, *Britischer Imperialismus*, pp. 415–17.

62 C. T. Andree *et al.*, *Geographie des Welthandels*, vol. III (Vienna, 1930), pp. 291, 309.

63 E. M. Gull, *British Economic Interests in the Far East* (London, 1943), p. 50.

284 *Notes to pages 200–4*

64 Ibid., p. 105.
65 Hou Chi-ming, *Foreign Investment*, p. 17, Table 4.
66 Ibid., p. 14.
67 Ibid., p. 225, Table 45.
68 For data on these and other firms see Osterhammel, *Britischer Imperialismus*, pp. 129–31, 369. On Dodwell & Company see S. Jones, *Two Centuries of Overseas Trading: The Origins and Growth of the Inchcape Group* (London, 1986), p. 183. On the Hongkong Bank, see F. H. H. King, *The History of the Hongkong and Shanghai Banking Corporation*, vol. III. *The Hongkong Bank Between the Wars and the Bank Interned, 1919–1941: Return from Grandeur* (Cambridge, 1988).
69 On this concept see Osterhammel, 'Semi-colonialism', pp. 300–3.
70 Teichman, *Affairs of China*, p. 138.
71 A. L. McElderry, *Shanghai Old-Style Banks (Ch'ien-chuang), 1800–1935* (Ann Arbor, Mich., 1976), p. 171.
72 Lan Tianzhao, 'Diguozhuyi zai jiu Zhongguo "touzi" de tezheng' ['Special Features of Imperialist "Investments" in Pre-revolutionary China'], *Xueshu yuekan*, 1958, no. 3, p. 45.
73 Remer, *Foreign Investments*, p. 94.
74 *Report of the Hon. Richard Feetham, C.M.G., to the Shanghai Municipal Council* (Shanghai, 1931), vol. I, p. 323 (my calculation).
75 For the evidence on which these estimates are based, see Osterhammel, *Britischer Imperialismus*, pp. 222–6.
76 Remer, *Foreign Investments*, p. 94.
77 See Osterhammel, *Britischer Imperialismus*, pp. 131–40.
78 A. F. Baker, in *China Press. Coronation and Sino-British Trade Supplement*, 12 May 1937, p. 47; C. K. Moser, *Where China Buys and Sells* (Washington, D.C., 1935), p. 12.
79 On the organisation of engineering imports see G. C. Allen and A. G. Donnithorne, *Western Enterprise in Far Eastern Economic Development* (London, 1954), pp. 93–7.
80 Ibid., pp. 69ff; Osterhammel, *Britischer Imperialismus*, pp. 182ff.
81 J. Arnold, *Commercial Handbook of China*, vol. II (Washington, D.C., 1920), p. 322; also A. S. Pearse, 'The Cotton Industry of Japan, China and India and its Effects on Lancashire', *International Affairs*, 11 (1933), p. 646.
82 Osterhammel, *Britischer Imperialismus*, p. 41, Table 5.
83 Chen Zhen (ed.), *Zhongguo jindai gongye shi ziliao* [Materials on the History of Modern Industry in China], 2nd collection, vol. I (Beijing, 1958), p. 161; *North China Herald*, 29 November 1933, p. 336; *Finance & Commerce*, 17 July 1937, p. 63.
84 For a brief summary see J. H. Dunning, 'Changes in the Level and Structure of International Production: The Last One Hundred Years', in M. Casson (ed.), *The Growth of International Business* (London, 1983), p. 93. See also G. Jones (ed.), *British Multinationals: Origins, Management and Performance* (Aldershot, 1986).
85 Wilkins, 'The Impacts of American Multinational Enterprise', p. 227.
86 Chen Zhen (ed.), *Zhongguo jindai gongye shi ziliao*, 2nd collection, vol. I,

Notes to pages 204–8 285

pp. 155–7; Yang Dajin, *Xiandai Zhongguo shiye zhi* [Gazetteer of Contemporary Chinese Industry] (Changsha, 1938), vol. I, pp. 473–95; C. Wilson, *The History of Unilever*, vol. II (London, 1954), p. 364.

87 ICI Archives (London), Central Registry Papers 2/2–117.

88 Tsang Chih, *China's Postwar Markets* (New York, 1945), p. 67; J. J. Beer, *The Emergence of the German Dye Industry* (Urbana, Ill., 1959), p. 95.

89 Imperial Chemical Industries (China) Ltd., 'Notes prepared...for Information of the Mission', 15 September 1930, Public Record Office (PRO), BT 59/1; ICI Archives, Sir William Coates Papers, file 'Foreign Merchanting Companies'.

90 Cheng Chu-yuan, 'The United States Petroleum Trade with China', in May and Fairbank (eds.), *America's China Trade*, pp. 216–17.

91 PRO FO 371/53597/F12898, 'Memorandum of Meeting at Petroleum Division on 30 August 1946'.

92 Osterhammel, *Britischer Imperialismus*, pp. 42–3.

93 Apart from Sherman Cochran's first-rate monograph (*Big Business in China*) which does not cover the period after 1930, there is now a vast collection of documents, mainly from the archives left behind by BAT in China: Shanghai shehui kexueyuan jingji yangjiusuo [Economic Research Institute at the Shanghai Academy of Social Science] (ed.), *Ying-Mei Yan Gongsi zai Hua qiye ziliao huibian* [Documents on the Enterprises of BAT in China], 4 vols. (1652 pages!) (Beijing, 1983).

94 A. Macmillan, *Seaports of the Far East: Historical and Descriptive Commercial and Industrial Facts, Figures and Resources*, 2nd ed. (London, 1925), p. 100.

95 Ibid., p. 89.

96 P. Mielmann, *Deutsch-chinesische Handelsbeziehungen am Beispiel der Elektroindustrie, 1870–1949* (Bern, 1984), pp. 176ff.

97 Cheng Chu-yuan, 'United States Petroleum Trade', pp. 221, 223; *ICI Annual Reports* (1933–6); *Chamber of Commerce Journal*, 67, no. 8 (August 1935), p. 22; *Finance and Commerce*, 11 September 1935, p. 272; PRO FO 371/17069/F4909, Chungking Intelligence Report, April–September 1933; ICI Archives, Central Registry Papers, files 857/1/1 and 17A/22/25. In contrast to many other British companies, ICI supported a strong *political* stand against Japan's encroachment on China.

98 Osterhammel, *Britischer Imperialismus*, pp. 225–6.

99 PRO T 188/136 Beale to Crowe, 5 March 1937.

100 King, *The History of the Hongkong and Shanghai Banking Corporation*, vol. I: *The Hongkong Bank in Late Imperial China, 1864–1902: On an Even Keel* (Cambridge, 1987), pp. 77, 510–8; C. T. Smith, 'Compradores of the Hongkong Bank', in King (ed.), *Eastern Banking*, p. 111.

101 See Kuo Ting-yee and Liu Kwang-ching, 'Self-strengthening: The Pursuit of Western Technology', in Fairbank (ed.), *The Cambridge History of China*, vol. X, pp. 537–41.

102 Thomas, *Foreign Intervention*, p. 104.

103 See the recent masterly study by M.-C. Bergère, *L'âge d'or de la bourgeoisie chinoise 1911–1937* (Paris, 1986), especially pp. 105ff.

286 *Notes to pages 209–11*

104 G. A. Haley, 'The Chemical and Dye Trades of China', *Chinese Economic Journal*, 9 (1931), p. 984.

105 ICI Archives, Central Registry Papers, file 2/1–2 B/4; PRO FO 371/20257/F6591, Tsingtao/Tsinan Intelligence Report, April–September 1936.

106 See Cochran, *Big Business*, pp. 61–77, 145–50, 176–95.

107 See Xiong Fu, 'Shilun Minsheng gongsi de fazhan' ['On the Development of the Minsheng Company'], *Sichuan daxue xuebao*, 1981, no. 4, pp. 34–9.

108 T. G. Rawski, *China's Transition to Industrialism: Producer Goods and Economic Development in the Twentieth Century* (Ann Arbor, Mich., 1980), pp. 7–15.

109 Remer, *Foreign Investments*, pp. 401–2; W. K. K. Chan, 'The Organizational Structure of the Traditional Chinese Firm and its Modern Reform', *Business History Review*, 46 (1982), pp. 229–32.

110 Ibid., p. 233; Bergère, *L'âge d'or*, pp. 159–71.

111 See P. M. Coble, *The Shanghai Capitalists and the Nationalist Government, 1927–1937* (Cambridge, Mass., 1980), especially chapter 8; W. C. Kirby, *Germany and Republican China* (Stanford, 1984), chapters 4 and 7; A. V. Meliksetov, *Byurokraticheskyi kapital v Kitae* (Moscow, 1971); Bergère, *L'âge d'or*, pp. 208ff, and her 'The Chinese bourgeoisie, 1911–37', in J. K. Fairbank (ed.), *The Cambridge History of China*, vol. XII (Cambridge, 1983), pp. 809–25.

112 For an elaboration of this argument see J. Osterhammel, 'Imperialism in Transition: British Business and the Chinese Authorities, 1931–37', *China Quarterly*, 98 (June 1984), pp. 260–86. On the differences of opinion among British businessmen in China see S. L. Endicott, *Diplomacy and Enterprise: British China Policy, 1933–1937* (Manchester, 1975), pp. 26ff.

113 See R. A. Dayer, *Bankers and Diplomats in China 1917–1925: The Anglo-American Relationship* (London, 1981).

114 See E. S. K. Fung, 'The Sino-British Rapprochement, 1927–1931', *Modern Asian Studies*, 17 (1983), pp. 79–105; W. R. Louis, *British Strategy in the Far East, 1919–1939* (Oxford, 1971), pp. 109–70; P. Lowe, *Britain in the Far East* (London and New York, 1981), pp. 128–35.

115 On Beale, see Osterhammel, *Britischer Imperialismus*, pp. 97–9. Beale's ideas were not entirely novel, their ancestry reaching far back into the nineteenth century. But they gained new urgency in the 1930s.

116 Gull, *British Economic Interests*, p. 190.

117 H. Abend, *My Years in China, 1926–1941* (London, 1944), p. 267.

118 R. W. Barnett, *Economic Shanghai: Hostage to Politics, 1937–1941* (New York, 1941), p. 39; *British Chamber of Commerce Journal* (Shanghai), 25 (1940), p. 74.

119 Wang Yizhong, 'Ba nian lai Shanghai gongye de zong qingsuan' ['A Summary Account of Industry in Shanghai during the Past Eight Years'], *Jingji zhoubao*, 1, no. 6 (6 December 1945), p. 13. On the concept of 'forelands' see G. G. Weigend, 'Some Elements in the Study of Port Geography', *Geographical Review*, 48 (1958), p. 195.

120 Hongkong and Shanghai Banking Corporation, *124th Report of Directors to the Ordinary General Meeting of Shareholders* (Hong Kong, 1940), p. 12.

Notes to pages 211–13 287

121 Wilson, *History of Unilever*, vol. II, p. 365; ICI, *Annual Report for 1938*, pp. 4, 19, and *Annual Report for 1939*, p. 18.
122 See the statistical materials in Chen Zhen (ed.), *Zhongguo jindai gongye shi ziliao*, 2nd collection, vol. II, pp. 850–1, 856–7, 862, 874–5; for BAT, in particular, see *Ying-Mei Yan Gongsi* (as in note 93 above), vol. IV, p. 1527.
123 Wright, *Coal Mining*, p. 127; Osterhammel, *Britischer Imperialismus*, p. 293.
124 Gull, *British Economic Interests*, pp. 198–9.
125 See G. B. Endacott, *Hong Kong Eclipse* (Hong Kong, 1978), especially pp. 69ff. For an account of the experiences of a member of staff of Jardine Matheson & Co. in Japanese internment see G. H. Gomperz, *China in Turmoil, 1924–1948* (London, 1967).
126 A. Shai, *Britain and China 1941–47: Imperial Momentum* (London, 1984), pp. 106–24.
127 PRO FO 371/63282/F846, G. V. Kitson, memo 'The British Position in China', 21 January 1947; PRO FO 371/63413/F585 Foreign Office Industrial and Economic Planning Staff, memo 'British Business Investments in China' (n.d. [January 1947]).
128 PRO FO 371/53595/F6952, British Embassy Chungking, memo, 18 April 1946.
129 School of Oriental and African Studies (London), John Swire & Sons Papers, II 2/20 (box 407), memo 'China and Japan 1946' (n.d.).
130 Shai, *Britain and China*, pp. 151–2.
131 On diplomatic assessments see D. C. Wolf, ' "To Secure a Convenience": Britain Recognizes China – 1950', *Journal of Contemporary History*, 18 (1983), pp. 302–4. See also R. Ovendale, 'Britain, the United States, and the Recognition of Communist China', *Historical Journal*, 26 (1983), pp. 139–58.
132 PRO FO 371/69545/F17436, Urquhart, 'Note on Prospects in a Communistic China', 29 November 1948. On the views among Britons in Shanghai at this time see also N. Barber, *The Fall of Shanghai: The Communist Takeover of 1949* (London, 1979), pp. 59ff. See also the eye-witness account, L. Taire, *Shanghai Episode: The End of Western Commerce*, 2nd ed. (Hong Kong, 1958).
133 PRO FO 371/69550/F18520, Urquhart to Stevenson, 17 December 1948.
134 V. H. Li, 'State Control of Foreign Trade after Liberation', in V. H. Li (ed.), *Law and Politics in China's Foreign Trade* (Seattle and London, 1977), p. 339; B. Grossmann, *Die wirtschaftliche Entwicklung der Volksrepublik China* (Stuttgart, 1960), p. 52. For a detailed account of Western business in China after 1949, see B. Hooper, *China Stands Up: Ending the Western Presence 1948–1950* (Sydney, 1986), pp. 85ff.
135 PRO FO 371/92259/FC1103/2, British Chamber of Commerce (Shanghai), 'Memorandum on British Trading Conditions in China', 15 October 1950. One example is given in *The House of Dodwell: A Century of Achievement, 1858–1958* (London, 1958), pp. 51–2.
136 T. N. Thompson, *China's Nationalization of Foreign Firms: The Politics of Hostage Capitalism, 1949–1957* (Baltimore, 1979), p. 53.

288 *Notes to pages 213–17*

137 Ibid., p. 60; China Association, *Annual Report 1954/55* (London, 1955), p. 2.

138 PRO FO 371/83352/FC1106/210, John Kenyon (Patons & Baldwins), 'General Report on China' (n.d., [August 1950]).

139 PRO FO 371/75864/F1472, P. D. Coates, Minute, 29 January 1949.

140 J. Gallagher and Ronald Robinson, 'The Imperialism of Free Trade', *Economic History Review*, 2nd ser., 6 (1953), pp. 1–15.

141 See, for example, R. P. T. Davenport-Hines, 'The British Engineers' Association and Markets in China 1900–1930', in R. P. T. Davenport-Hines (ed.), *Markets and Bagmen* (Aldershot, 1986), pp. 102–30. The broader issues are discussed in C. A. Wurm, 'Britische Aussenwirtschaft 1919–1939: Exportverfall, Aussenhandelsorganisation und Unternehmerverhalten', *Scripta Mercaturae*, 17 (1983), pp. 1–40, especially pp. 15–29.

142 Bureau International du Travail, *L'Industrie textile dans le monde*, vol. I (Geneva, 1937), p. 148: *Manchester Chamber of Commerce Annual Report for 1937*, p. xxxvi.

143 Calculated on the basis of Hsiao Liang-lin, *China's Foreign Trade Statistics*, pp. 22–4, 148–50.

144 According to estimates by Remer and Hou Chi-ming, during the period from 1902 to 1930, 60% of profits derived from (all-foreign) direct investments were reinvested in China. Hou Chi-ming, *Foreign Investment*, p. 103. Perhaps more conclusive is the qualitative evidence we have, such as the statement by a knowledgeable observer that before 1937 most of the profits of British shipping lines in China were reinvested. PRO FO 371/75864/F2240, Money (Ministry of Transport) to Coates, memo 'British Shipping Interests in China Trade' (January 1949).

145 Remer, *Foreign Investments*, p. 364.

146 Osterhammel, *Britischer Imperialismus*, p. 60, Table 8.

147 King, *The History of the Hongkong and Shanghai Banking Corporation*, vol. I, pp. 54–5, 143–4, 466–7.

148 I have elsewhere called this 'symbiotic penetration': Osterhammel, 'Semi-colonialism', p. 304.

149 In March 1937, the government-controlled China Merchants Steam Navigation Company opened regular traffic to Manila – its first venture beyond Chinese coastal waters. John Swire & Sons Papers, III/1/17 Butterfield & Swire (Shanghai) to John Swire & Sons, 3 April 1937.

150 See Wu Yugan, *Zhongguo guoji maoyi gailun* [Outline of China's Foreign Trade] (Shanghai, 1930), pp. 490–9; F. E. Hyde, 'British Shipping Companies and East and South-East Asia, 1860–1939', in C. D. Cowan (ed.), *The Economic Development of South-East Asia* (London, 1964), pp. 39ff.

8 British business in Japan since 1868

* We are grateful to participants at the Anglo-Japanese Business History Conference held at the London School of Economics on 20 August 1986, to Malcolm Falkus, Howard Gospel, Frank H. H. King, Ian Nish, Kaoru Sugihara, Steven Tolliday, Kazuo Wada and Takeshi Yuzawa for helpful comments on this

Notes to pages 219–21 289

chapter, and to the Department of Trade and Industry for supplying statistics on British foreign direct investment. We were privileged to see a draft of a pioneering paper by Mark Mason, 'The Door Ajar: Japanese Government Policy and Inward Direct Investment, 1899–1931', which was delivered at the 1987 American Business History Conference in Wilmington, Delaware. Other emendations were suggested to Davenport-Hines at a seminar on 10 January 1987 organised by Yoshitaka Suzuki at the Faculty of Economics, Tohoku University, Sendai, whose financial generosity is also acknowledged.

1 G. C. Allen and A. G. Donnithorne, *Western Enterprise in Far Eastern Economic Development, China and Japan* (London, 1954), p. 194.
2 Ian H. Nish, *The Anglo-Japanese Alliance* (London, 1966), pp. 7, 10; S. Gwynn, *The Letters and Friendships of Sir Cecil Spring Rice*, vol. I (London, 1929), p. 145; Lord Neidpath, *The Singapore Naval Base and the Defence of Britain's Eastern Empire 1919–1941* (Oxford, 1981), pp. 31, 37–41.
3 H. J. Jones, *Live Machines: Hired Foreigners and Meiji Japan* (Tenterden, 1980), p. 7. See also R. S. Schwontes, 'Foreign Employees in the Development of Japan', in A. W. Burks (ed.), *The Modernizers. Overseas Students, Foreign Employees and Meiji Japan* (Boulder and London, 1985). On the Scots in Japan, see Olive Checkland, 'The Scots in Meiji Japan, 1868–1912', in R. A. Cage (ed.), *The Scots Abroad: Labour, Capital, Enterprise, 1750–1914* (London, 1985).
4 Allen and Donnithorne, *Western Enterprise*, p. 193; S. W. Roskill, *Naval Policy Between the Wars*, vol. I (London, 1968), pp. 245, 529–30; M. D. Kennedy, *Some Aspects of Japan and her Defence Forces* (London and Kobe, 1928), pp. 31–47; Harald Penrose, *British Aviation: the Adventuring Years 1920–29* (London, 1973), pp. 96–7; Desmond Young, *Rutland of Jutland* (London, 1963), pp. 80–3 and *passim*. Squadron Leader F. J. Rutland was employed as an expert by Mitsubishi and acted as a Japanese spy in California before his internment by the British in 1941. Another aviation expert in Japan was the Master of Sempill (later 19th Baron Sempill), against whom MI5 found 'grave and substantiated' evidence in 1926. See Foreign Office Despatch 9 of 24 January 1927 to Sir Beilby Alston, FO 371/11964, Public Record Office (PRO).
5 Jones, *Live Machines*, p. 131.
6 See G. Saxonhouse, 'A Tale of Japanese Technological Diffusion in the Meiji Period', *Journal of Economic History*, 34 (1974), pp. 149–65.
7 Allen and Donnithorne, *Western Enterprise*, pp. 202–3.
8 On the activities in Japan of such merchant houses as Jardine Matheson, Butterfield & Swire, Glover and Company, and Samuel Samuel & Company, see, especially, S. Marriner and F. E. Hyde, *The Senior John Samuel Swire 1825–98. Management in Far Eastern Shipping Trades* (Liverpool, 1967); R. Henriques, *Marcus Samuel* (London, 1960); S. Sugiyama, 'Thomas B. Glover: A British Merchant in Japan, 1861–70', *Business History*, 26 (1984); Grace Fox, *Britain and Japan 1858–1883* (Oxford, 1969), chapter 12; J. McMaster, *Jardines in Japan, 1859–1967* (Groningen, 1967); Kanji Ishii,

290 *Notes to pages 222–5*

Kindai Nippon to Igirisu Shihon [Modern Japan and British Merchants] (Tokyo, 1984) is an outstanding study of the activities of Jardine Matheson in Japan between 1859 and 1888.

9 Allen and Donnithorne, *Western Enterprise*, pp. 204–5. For an introduction to the substantial literature on the growth of Mitsui Bussan Kaisha and other general trading companies, see Shin-ichi Yonekawa, 'The Formation of General Trading Companies: A Comparative Study', *Japanese Yearbook on Business History*, 2 (1985) and Hiroaki Yamazaki, 'The Logic of the Formation of General Trading Companies in Japan', in Shin'ichi Yonekawa and Hideki Yoshihara (eds.), *Business History of General Trading Companies* (Tokyo, 1987).

10 F. E. Hyde, *Far Eastern Trade 1860–1914* (London, 1973), p. 158.

11 For a detailed study of the growth of the Japanese shipbuilding industry, see William D. Wray, *Mitsubishi and the N.Y.K., 1870–1914, Business Strategy in the Japanese Shipbuilding Industry* (Cambridge, Mass., 1984).

12 T. Hamashita, 'A History of the Japanese Silver Yen and the Hongkong and Shanghai Banking Corporation, 1871–1913', in F. H. H. King (ed.), *Eastern Banking* (London, 1983), p. 323. See, generally, Hugh T. Patrick, 'Japan 1864–1914', in Rondo Cameron (ed.), *Banking in the Early Stages of Industrialization* (London, 1967), pp. 239–89; and F. H. H. King, *The History of the Hongkong and Shanghai Banking Corporation*, vol. 1: *The Hongkong Bank in Late Imperial China, 1861–1902: On an Even Keel* (Cambridge, 1987), pp. 44, 157–8, 288.

13 BT 31/11517/88771, PRO.

14 Allen and Donnithorne, *Western Enterprise*, pp. 214–15.

15 Hamashita, 'A History of the Japanese Silver Yen', p. 337.

16 The authors are grateful for information on the Hongkong Bank and Japanese loans supplied by Professor F. H. H. King. See also Compton Mackenzie, *Realms of Silver* (London, 1954), p. 204, for mention of Chartered Bank's role in foreign loans. For the importance of this capital inflow, see B. R. Tomlinson, 'Writing History Sideways: Lessons for Indian Economic Historians From Meiji Japan', *Modern Asian Studies*, 19 (1985), pp. 686–7. There is an alternative view in E. Reubens, 'Foreign Capital and Domestic Development in Japan', in S. S. Kuznets *et al.* (eds.), *Economic Growth: Brazil, India, Japan* (Chapel Hill, 1955), chapter 6.

17 Colin M. Lewis, *British Railways in Argentina, 1857–1914: A Case Study of Foreign Investment* (London, 1983).

18 S. Sugiyama, 'Thomas B. Glover: A British Merchant in Japan, 1861–70', and Olive and Sydney Checkland, 'British and Japanese Economic Interaction under the Early Meiji: the Takashima Coal Mine 1868–88', *Business History*, 26 (1984). See also J. McMaster, 'The Takashima Mine: British Capital and Japanese Industrialisation', *Business History Review*, 37 (1963).

19 See M. Wilkins, *The Emergence of Multinational Enterprise* (Cambridge, Mass., 1970); P. Hertner, 'German Multinational Enterprise before 1914: Some Case Studies', in Peter Hertner and Geoffrey Jones (eds.), *Multinationals: Theory and History* (Aldershot, 1986); Geoffrey Jones, 'The Expansion of British Multinational Manufacturing', in T. Inoue and A. Okochi (eds.),

Notes to pages 225–7 291

Overseas Business Activities: Proceedings of the Ninth Fuji Conference (Tokyo, 1984); Geoffrey Jones (ed.), *British Multinationals: Origins, Growth and Performance* (Aldershot, 1986).

20 J. Hirschmeier and T. Yui, *The Development of Japanese Business* (London, 1981), p. 148. For a detailed study of early German multinational activity in Japan see H. Watanabe, 'A History of the Process Leading to the Foundation of Fuji Electric', *Japanese Yearbook on Business History*, vol. I.

21 Allen and Donnithorne, *Western Enterprise*, p. 231; Geoffrey Jones, 'The Growth and Performance of British Multinational Firms before 1939: The Case of Dunlop', *Economic History Review*, 37 (1984), p. 39.

22 W. J. Reader, *Imperial Chemical Industries: A History* (London, 1970), vol. I, p. 148.

23 Clive Trebilcock, *The Vickers Brothers: Armaments and Enterprise 1854–1914* (London, 1977), p. 134; R. P. T. Davenport-Hines, 'Vickers as a Multinational before 1945', in Geoffrey Jones (ed.), *British Multinationals*, pp. 52–4.

24 We are grateful to S. J. Nicholas for this information on Babcock & Wilcox.

25 Y. Tsurumi, *Technology Transfer and Foreign Trade. The Case of Japan, 1950–1966* (New York, 1980), p. 95. Some early British multinationals also had marketing operations in Japan before 1914. For the case of the Gramophone Company see Geoffrey Jones, 'The Gramophone Company: an Anglo-American Multinational, 1898–1931', *Business History Review*, 59 (1985), pp. 84–5, and P. Gronow, 'The Record Industry Comes to the Orient', *Ethnomusicology*, 25 (1981), pp. 272–3.

26 Allen and Donnithorne, *Western Enterprise*, p. 225.

27 Geoffrey Searle, *The Quest for National Efficiency* (Oxford, 1971), pp. 57–8; R. P. T. Davenport-Hines, *Dudley Docker* (Cambridge, 1984), p. 45. Gell's letter is cited in Searle. For counter-arguments against 'a stunted, lymphatic, yellow-faced heathen, with a mouthful of teeth three sizes too big for him, bulging slits where his eyes ought to be, blacking-brush hair, a foolish giggle, a cruel heart and the conceit of the devil', see Thomas Crosland, *The Truth about Japan* (London, 1904) and W. Sorley Brown, *The Life and Genius of T. W. H. Crosland* (London, 1928), pp. 141–5.

28 Vicary Gibbs to Herbert Gibbs, 31 July 1905, re: Tokyo harbours loan, Guildhall Library, London, ms. 11040/5. Lord Revelstoke's remark is also quoted in his letter.

29 Geoffrey Jones, 'The Performance of British Multinational Enterprise, 1890–1945', in Hertner and Jones (eds.), *Multinationals: Theory and History*, pp. 105–6.

30 J. H. B. Noble, memorandum of 1909, box 165, Armstrong papers, Tyne & Wear County Record Office.

31 Sir Douglas Brownrigg to David Fraser, 20 December 1911, George Ernest Morrison papers, vol. 62, State Library of New South Wales, Sydney (hereafter NSWSL).

32 Stafford Ransome, *Japan in Transition* (London, 1899), p. 7.

33 Patrick Chance of Shanghai, in Lo Hui-Min (ed.), *The Correspondence of*

292 *Notes to pages 227–32*

G. E. Morrison 1895–1912 (Cambridge, 1976), p. 104. The papers at the Thomas Fisher Library of the University of Toronto of a British journalist at Shanghai, J. O. P. Bland, exemplify Westerners' embittered xenophobia. For a fascinating survey of British attitudes to Japanese and treaty-port life, see Sir Hugh Cortazzi, *Victorians in Japan: In and Around the Treaty Ports* (London, 1987).

34 *The Guardian*, 22 May 1986, p. 11.

35 Morrison Diary, 31 May 1907, NSWSL.

36 Minute by Llewelyn, 11 March 1925, of conversation with Sir George Hadcock, ADM 1/8676/42, Public Record Office.

37 In Christopher Hawtree (ed.), *Night and Day* (London, 1985), p. 24.

38 See Saxonhouse, 'A Tale of Japanese Technological Diffusion', p. 150; G. Saxonhouse, 'Country Girls and Communication among Competitors in the Japanese Cotton Spinning Industry', in H. Patrick (ed.), *Japanese Industrialisation and its Social Consequences* (Berkeley, Calif., 1976), p. 116.

39 Saxonhouse, 'A Tale of Japanese Technological Diffusion', pp. 163–4.

40 Cf. R. P. T. Davenport-Hines, 'The British Engineers' Association and Markets in China, 1900–1930', in R. P. T. Davenport-Hines (ed.), *Markets and Bagmen* (Aldershot, 1986), pp. 102–23.

41 Robert Young, 'Commercial Morality in Japan', *Nineteenth Century*, 40 (1896), p. 124.

42 A. R. Paget, memorandum of 25 August 1923, Hadfield papers, Sheffield City Library. We owe this reference to Geoffrey Tweedale.

43 Allen and Donnithorne, *Western Enterprise*, p. 204.

44 Foreign Office minute by J. A. Dilcher, 21 November 1953, FO 371/105412, PRO.

45 Mira Wilkins, *The Maturing of Multinational Enterprise* (Cambridge, Mass., 1974), p. 58.

46 For a detailed study of the Japanese car industry before the Second World War, see M. Udagawa, 'The Pre-War Japanese Automobile Industry and American Manufacturers', in *Japanese Yearbook on Business History* (1985), vol. 2.

47 Jones, 'The Gramophone Company', p. 97; Davenport-Hines, 'Vickers as a Multinational before 1945', pp. 53–4.

48 Memorandum by UK Representative on the Far Eastern Commission, 15 December 1947, FO 371/63669, No. F16880/1/23, PRO.

49 Federation of British Industries, Report of Mission to the Far East, August–November 1934, p. 38.

50 D. C. Coleman, *Courtaulds*, (Oxford, 1969), vol. 2, pp. 380–1; R. A. Church, *Kenricks in Hardware* (Newton Abbot, 1969), p. 149. Japan was described by the British Admiralty in 1921 as the 'Germany of the Far East' whose commercial penetration of India was 'very embarrassing' and of China 'notorious'. Quoted by Lord Neidpath, in *Singapore Naval Base*, pp. 39–40.

51 Board of Trade Memorandum on Japanese Textile Competition, enclosed in Foreign Office to British Ambassador, Washington, 22 December 1948, FO 371/69815E, No. F/17376/60/23, PRO. Very similar sentiments were expressed by MPs, especially those representing constituencies where the

Notes to pages 232–9 293

textile and pottery industries were strong, during a House of Commons debate in November 1951 on the ratification of the Peace Treaty with Japan. See *Parliamentary Debates, House of Commons*, 494 H.C. Deb. 5s, 26 November 1951.

52 N. S. Roberts, memorandum on Japanese competition, 9 November 1951, FO 371/92640, No. FJ112101, PRO.

53 Wilkins, *Maturing*, pp. 230–3.

54 Tsurumi, *Technology Transfer*, p. 130.

55 Sir Victor Wellesley, quoted R. d'O. Butler, D. Dakin and M. E. Lambert (eds.), *Documents on British Foreign Policy*, second series, vol. IX (London, 1965), p. 27.

56 Jones, 'The Growth and Performance of British Multinational Firms before 1939: The Case of Dunlop', pp. 49–50. Dunlop Board Minute of 23 June 1939, Dunlop Archives.

57 Minutes of Directors Conferences, 6 January 1925 and 8 July 1925, Rowntree Archives. For a survey of Rowntree's development as a multinational in the inter-war years see Geoffrey Jones, 'The Chocolate Multinationals: Cadbury, Fry and Rowntree 1918–1939', in Jones (ed.), *British Multinationals*.

58 Jones, 'The Growth and Performance of British Multinational Firms before 1939: The Case of Dunlop', p. 50.

59 Wilkins, *Maturing*, p. 159.

60 Sir Alvary Gascoigne to Foreign Office, 9 October 1947, FO 371/63664, No. F 13696/1/23, PRO. See also R. Buckley, *Occupational Diplomacy. Britain, the United States and Japan 1945–1952* (Cambridge, 1982), p. 131.

61 Vickers archives, Cambridge University Library, memorandum of 14 July 1952; Kenzo Yutani to Vickers Armstrong, 19 December 1952, VA 892.

62 'A Forecast of the Future Development of the Japanese Economy and of Future Opportunities of British Trade with Japan', memorandum by M. Macrae, November 1947, FO 371/63669, No. F 16880/1/23, PRO.

63 A. Goodman to Board of Trade, 15 November 1948, FO 371/69815E, No. F17433/4/23, PRO. See also Buckley, *Occupation Diplomacy*, pp. 197, 273.

64 British Embassy, Tokyo to Foreign Office, 12 May 1953, FO 371/105409, PRO.

65 D. G. Rhys, *The Motor Industry: An Economic Survey* (London, 1972), p. 192; M. A. Cusumano, *The Japanese Automobile Industry: Technology and Management at Nissan and Toyota* (Cambridge, Mass. and London, 1985), pp. 88–112.

66 'Breaking the Mould of Old Practices', *Financial Times*, 7 March 1986, p. 16.

67 Tsurumi, *Technology Transfer*, p. 136.

68 Wilkins, *Maturing*, p. 349.

69 Tsurumi, *Technology Transfer*, pp. 137–9.

70 Chalmers Johnson, *MITI and the Japanese Miracle* (Stanford, 1982), pp. 276–9, 285–8, 302.

71 *Financial Times*, 8 April 1986, p. 20.

72 British Embassy, Tokyo to Foreign Office, 6 January 1954, FO 371/110469, No. FJ1392/2, PRO.

73 Draft letter from Minister of Transport and Civil Aviation to Chairman,

294 *Notes to pages 239–43*

British Council of British Shipping, 11 November 1954, FO 371/110469, No. FJ1392/32A, PRO.

74 Ministry of Transport to Foreign Office, 24 December 1954, FO 371/110469, No. FJ1392/37, PRO.

75 G. C. Allen, 'Britain's Perspective of Japan's Post-War Economic Prospects', *Proceedings of the British Association for Japanese Studies*, 2 (University of Sheffield, 1977), p. 162.

76 'A Forecast of the Future Development of the Japanese Economy and of Future Opportunities for British Trade with Japan', by Mr Minster Macrae, November 1947, FO 371/63669, No. F16880/1/23, PRO.

77 We thank Professor F. H. H. King for this quotation, and the Hongkong Bank for permission to use it. See J. C. MacDermott, memorandum on first impressions upon return to Japan, 23 September 1945, FO 371/40430, PRO: 'It is very pleasing to see the enemy capital brought so low, but at the same time it is depressing to live entirely surrounded by rubble ... the "stunned" and "dazed" reactions of the Japanese people to defeat ... [are] of course their natural dumbness ... As we all know, they don't think politically for themselves ... they are now a fourth-class nation, but they have not yet got round to understanding what the loss of their Empire will really mean, how poor they are going to be, nor do they realise how cordially the rest of the world hates them.'

78 Allen, 'Britain's Perception of Japan's Post-War Economic Prospects', p. 155.

79 Board of Trade to Foreign Office, 28 February 1950, FO 371/83860, No. FJ1121/48, PRO.

80 See, generally, K. B. Clark, R. H. Hayes and C. Lorenz, *The Uneasy Alliance: Managing the Productivity–Technology Dilemma* (Cambridge, Mass., 1985). Japan did buy the British-designed Calder Hall reactor for its civilian nuclear energy programme, but this was a technical and commercial failure and from the mid-1960s the Japanese opted for American light water reactors. See Richard J. Samuels, *The Business of the Japanese State* (Ithaca, 1987), pp. 238–40.

81 Sir Norman Brain to Denis Allen, 28 July 1954, FO 371/110436, No. FJ1152, PRO.

82 Figures circulated from research on Glaxo by Charlie Wilkinson.

83 'Breaking the Mould of Old Practices', *Financial Times*, 7 March 1986.

84 'Breaching a Cultural Barrier', *Financial Times*, 25 June 1987.

85 *British Trade with Japan* (Embassy of Japan, 1977).

86 'A UK Bridge with Japan', *Financial Times*, 17 February 1986.

87 'Try Hard to Take the Terror out of that Kamikaze Trip to Tokyo', *The Guardian*, 17 August 1987.

Index

A. M. Odman & Company, 132
Afghanistan, 91
agency houses, 10, 19–21, 41, 96–100, 103, 105, 108, 113, 115, 160, 168, 171–6, 180, 185–7, 191–2
Agra Bank, 11
agribusiness, 60, 86, 125
aircraft industry, 224
Alkali and Chemical Corporation, 102
All-Union Electrical Trust, 86
Alliance Bank of Simla, 11
Amalgamated Russian Petroleum, 73
Amalgamated Tin Mines of Nigeria, 170
American Motor Corporation, 230
American Steam Mill of Bangkok, 133
Anderson, H. N., 136–7, 156
Anderson, Sir John, 145, 149, 152
Anglo-American Corporation, 185
Anglo-Iranian Oil Company, *see* British Petroleum
Anglo-Iranian Pharmaceutical Company, 51, 55
Anglo-Japanese Bank, 223
Anglo-Maikop Corporation, 83
Anglo-Oriental Company, 154, 168
Anglo-Persian Oil Company, *see* British Petroleum
Aramco, 60, 65
Argentina, 195
armaments industry, 230, 234
Armenians, 40, 42
Armitage-Smith, Sir Sydney, 46
Armstrong, Whitworth & Company, 43, 225, 227–8
Arnhold & Company, 203
Asbestos Cement, 102
Ashok Leyland, 102
Asiatic Petroleum Company, 202, 205, 207–8, (*see also* Shell Group)
Associated Biscuits, 102
Austin Motor Company, 235–6
Australia, 4, 12, 16, 127–8, 146, 149, 150, 152–3, 154, 156, 164, 166, 168, 205, 232–3

Babcock & Wilcox, 225–6, 231, 233–4
Baku Petroleum Company, 73
Bandoeng Pool, 168
Bangnon Valley Dredging Company, 152
Bangkok Dock Company, 121, 156
Bangkok Rice Mill, 132
Bank Melli Iran, 49–50, 53
Bank of Bombay, 94
Bank of England, 169
Bank of Japan, 239
Bank of Rotterdam, 132–3
banking, 9, 12–15, 18, 26, 33, 94, 96, 106–7, 108, 121, 127, 131, 133, 156, 160–1, 175–8, 182–4, 206, 222–4, 237
Banque de l'Indochine, 121
Banque Franco-Japonaise, 223
Barings, 224, 226
Beale, Sir Louis, 210
Belgium, 199
Bibi-Eibat Oil Company, 72–3
Bird-Heilgers, 98
Binney, Sir George, 53, 56
Blue Funnel Steamship Company, 131, 222
BMW, 238
Board of Trade, 54, 56, 57, 77–8, 83
Bolivia, 166, 169
Bombay Burmah Trading Company, 11, 123, 134, 136, 139, 142–3, 145
Boots Pure Drug Company, 51, 55
Borneo Company, 10, 123, 129, 131–2, 136, 138, 141, 143, 145, 156, 160, 170
Boustead & Company, 160, 172
Bowring, Sir John, 128, 137, 148
Brazil, 164, 171, 195
Britannia Biscuits, 102
British American Tobacco, 16, 195–6, 201–2, 205–6, 208–9, 211–15, 235
British and Chinese Corporation, 199
British Bank of the Middle East, 18, 58, 59
British Drug Houses, 51
British Indian Steam Navigation Company, 10, 34, 39

296 Index

British Leyland Motor Corporation (now Rover), 30, 89, 102, 238
British Motor Corporation, 236
British Oxygen (BOC), 102, 237
British Petroleum (formerly Anglo-Persian Oil Company, previously Anglo-Iranian Oil), 24, 33, 36, 39, 41, 42, 45, 46–8, 55, 56, 60, 63, 64, 65, 89
Brooke Bond, 102
Brooke family, Rajahs of Sarawak, 159, 160, 170, 173
Brown, John & Company, 89, 91
Brunei, 30, 171
Brunner Mond, 229
Burma, 2, 168–9, 190
Burmah Oil Company, 11, 36, 44, 102
Burn, Captain R. C., 136
Butterfield & Swire, 10, 18, 30, 193, 196, 202–3, 213, 239

Cable & Wireless, 241, 243
Campbell, George Murray, 124
Canada, 104
Canton-Kowloon Railway, 198–9
Capel, James, 30
Capital Exports, 4, 186
carpet industry, 38–9, 41, 45, 51, 65, 180
Case, Jack, 206
Caspian and Black Sea Oil & Trading Company, 72
Cassel, Sir Ernest, 42
Cathay Pacific Airways, 30
Cecil of Chelwood, 1st Viscount, 80
Central Bank of Western India, 223
Ceylon, 7, 13, 172, 174, 195
Chambers of Commerce, 15
Charter Consolidated, 184–5
Chartered Bank of India, Australia & China (see also Standard Chartered Bank), 12, 13, 30, 59, 106, 121, 161, 176, 201, 223
Chartered Mercantile Bank of India, London & China, see Mercantile Bank of India
Chase Manhattan Bank, 59, 240
Chater, C. P., 152
Cheek, Dr Marian A., 138–9, 141, 142
chemical industry, 101, 180
Chemicals and Fibre Company, 102
Chiang Kai-Shek, 204, 209
China, 3–4, 157, 189–216, 229
China General Omnibus Company, 201
China Navigation Company, 203
China Printing and Finishing Company, 204
China Soap Company, 204

China Trust, 39–40
Chinese indigenous competition, 4, 27, 31, 119–20, 127, 130, 133, 146–8, 161, 164–7, 177, 182, 188
Chloride Company, 102
Chulalongkorn, King of Siam, 125, 127, 138
Citibank, 240
Clark, Sir William, 80
Clarke, F. S. and Company, 141
coal, 99, 101, 109, 141, 170, 197–8, 206, 208, 214, 221, 225
coffee, 13, 171
Colonial Office, 169–70, 188
Columbia Graphophone Company, 230
Commercial Bank Corporation of India and the East, 223
Commercial Bank of London, 223
Commercial Union Insurance, 141
compradores, 119, 161, 176, 183, 208
Consolidated Tin Smelters, 168–9
Consortia, 51, 53, 88
Cooke, Henry Arthur, 77
Cornish capital and migrants, 9, 164
corruption, 44, 57, 61–2, 67, 229
Costain, Richard, 52–3
Courtaulds, 89, 232
Cowdray, 1st Viscount, 43
Crédit Lyonnais, 182
Curzon of Kedleston, 1st Marquess, 23, 30, 43, 45, 46
Czechoslovakia, 53

D. M. Horne & Company, 141
Damrong, Prince, 148–9, 153–4
D'Arcy, W. K., 36, 44
Datsun, 236
Davenport's joke shop, 228
David Colville & Sons, 53
Davy International, 89
dawn raids, 186, 188
Deebok Dredging Company, 152
Denmark, 14, 53, 77, 120–1, 123, 128, 136–7, 143, 155
Dennis, C. H., 139–40
Dent & Company, 192
Department of Overseas Trade, 80
dependency model, 25
Des Voeux, Sir William, 14
Detring, Gustav, 198
Deutsch-Asiatische Bank, 223
direct foreign investment, 7–9, 16, 26, 28, 29, 46, 63, 71–2, 74, 84, 85, 90, 91, 101–5, 155, 163–4, 195, 215, 217, 219, 226, 232–3, 236, 237
Dodwells, 10
Dorman Diesel Company, 59–60

Index 297

Dorman Long, 53
Dufferin and Ava, 1st Marquess of, 2, 30, 139
Duke, James, 196
Dunhill Holdings, 242–3
Dunlop Rubber Company, 16, 102, 172–3, 225–6, 231, 233–4, 237, 242, 244
Dutch East Indies, 166–70, 173–4, 216

East Asiatic Company, 136–7, 143
East India Company, 1, 3, 93, 114, 129, 159, 191
East India Ocean Steamship Company, 131
Eastern Bank, 106
Eastern Shipping Company, 150
Eastern Smelting Company, 150, 167, 169
Eastern Trading Company, 154
Ebtehaj, Abol Hassan, 50, 56, 61–2
Elder, W. A., 141
electrical engineering, 85–7, 120–1, 225
elephants, 123, 134–5, 143
Emba Petroleum & Trading Company, 73
Euphrates and Tigris Steam Navigation Company, 34
European Oil Fields Corporation, 73
Evans, Sons, Lescher & Webb, 51
Ewart Latham & Company, 139
Ewbanks electrical consultancy, 61
Ewo Cotton Mills, 197, 201, 204, 211, 215
Export Credit Guarantee Department, 59, 112
export platform investment, 28, 111
exports, British to Asia, 3–6, 34, 53, 70–1, 77–9, 155, 191–2, 218
Exxon, 186

Fairfield Shipbuilding Company, 227
Fairmile Construction Company, 57
Ford, Henry, 204, 230, 233
Foreign Office, 15, 22–4, 43, 44, 53–9, 61, 66, 70, 80, 124, 181, 212, 235, 240–1
France, 4, 53, 104, 124, 128, 130, 174, 198
Frankau, Adolph, 206
free-standing firms, 9–10, 19, 123, 155, 166

Gell, Philip Lyttelton, 226
General Electric (of USA), 85, 87, 225
General Motors, 230, 233
Germany, 14, 22, 28, 53, 55, 57, 58, 70, 77–9, 87, 88, 90, 104, 105, 124, 130, 156, 199, 221, 222, 225
Gibb, Sir Alexander, 54, 55, 64

Gibbs, Livingstone & Company, 203
Gibbs, Vicary, 226
Glaxo-Fuji Pharmaceutical Laboratories, 242
Glaxo Laboratories Ltd, 51, 102, 242, 244
Glover, Thomas, 9, 225
Godfrey Philips 9, 102
gold, 69, 74–5, 126, 148, 152, 170, 184–5
Gopeng Consolidated Company, 164
Gouria Petroleum Corporation, 85
Gout, William, 53
Gray Dawes, 34, 39
Gray Mackenzie, 10, 34, 39, 41
Grayburn, Sir Vandeleur, 240
Green Island Cement Company, 201
Grey, Hamilton, 130
Guest Keen Nettlefolds (GKN), 53, 60, 102
Guest Keen Williams, 102
Gull, E. Manico, 200
Guthrie & Company, 145, 152, 160, 172, 175–6, 179, 186

Hadfield, Sir Robert, 229
Hansa Line, 57
Harrison & Crosfield, 172, 179–80, 186
Hart, Sir Robert, 193
Harvey, John, 138
Haw Paw, 184
Hay, Sir John, 176
Heard & Company, 129
Hindustan Lever, 102
Honda, 30
Hong Kong, 2, 3, 7, 8, 19, 21, 26, 28, 129, 191–3, 215–16, 240, 243
Hongkong & Shanghai Banking Corporation (Hongkong Bank), 12, 14–15, 18, 26, 30, 39–40, 106–7, 121, 132, 160–1, 176, 177–8, 182–4, 192, 199, 201, 208, 211, 215, 223–4, 230, 234, 240
Hongkong & Whampoa Dock Company, 196
Hoover, Herbert, 198
Hotz, I. C. P. & Company, 34, 39
Howeson, John, 168–9
Hutchinson Whampoa, 19

I. C. P. Hotz & Company, 34, 39
Imperial Bank of India, 107
Imperial Bank of Persia, 13, 20, 35–6, 38–45, 49–50, 55–6, 61, 63, 65, 223, 234, (see also British Bank of the Middle East)
Imperial Chemical Industries (ICI), 89, 102–3, 204–5, 207–9, 211
Inchape Group, 33

298 Index

India, 3, 5, 7, 8, 25, 92–116, 174, 195, 229
India Office, 94, 159
Indian Explosives Company, 102
Indian Oxygen Company, 102
Indo-China Steam Navigation Company, 203
Indo-European Telegraph Company, 35, 51, 62
Indonesia, 8
insurance, 7, 51, 131, 156, 230
International Banking Corporation, 223
International Business Machines (IBM), 230, 238
International Telephone & Telegraph Corporation (ITT), 24, 230
Iran, 5–6, 31–67, 229
Iran National Vehicle Manufacturing Company, 59
Iran Shellcott Company, 60
Irano-British Bank, 59
Irrawaddy Flotilla and Burmese Steam Navigation Company, 11
Italy, 53, 70, 197

J. & P. Coats and Company, 16, 225–6, 231, 234
J. S. Parker & Company, 129
Japan, 3–4, 5, 7, 21, 29, 58, 63, 90, 99, 111, 155, 157, 182, 186, 190, 195, 211, 217–44
Japanese Shipping Company, 222
Japanese Steelworks, 225
Jardine Matheson, 10, 15, 18, 124, 192, 196, 199, 202–3, 213
joint ventures, 16, 18, 104, 225–6, 230, 233, 236, 238
Jones, Henry, 149, 151
jute, 20, 97, 99, 100, 101, 108, 109, 115

Kailaun Mining Administration, 198, 201, 211
Kaiping collieries, 197–8
Kenricks, 231
Keswick, William, 39
Khatoo Deebok Dredging Company, 152
Khaw Sin Bee, 148–54, 167
Kirghiz Corporation, 75
Knox, T. G., 136
Koh Guan Company, 149–50
Krasin, Leonid, 84
Kyshtin Corporation, 75, 82

labour, 11, 64–5, 97, 204
languages, British ineptitude for, 57, 78–9
Lebanon, 18
Leith-Ross, Sir Frederick, 110

Lena Gold Mining Corporation, 75
Lena Goldfields Company, 75, 84–7
Leonowens, Louis, 138, 141–6, 152, 156
Leyland Motors, 59
Li Ka-shing, toy manufacturer, 19
licensing, 104, 226, 234, 235, 237
Lindley, Sir Francis, 80
Livesey, Son & Henderson, 124
Loftus, Captain A., 156
London Bank of Mexico and South America, 223
London Tin Corporation, 168–70, 179, 184–5
Longman, publishers, 28
Lonrho, 24
Luanzho Mining Company Ltd, 198
Lucas Industries, 102
Lynch Brothers, 34, 36, 39, 41

Macao, 28
MacArthur, Douglas, 234
McCarthy, E. T., 152
McGilvary, Daniel, 136, 138
McLean, David, 39
Macmillan, publishers, 28
Maekawa Commission, 238–9
Malaya, 5, 7, 8, 147, 157–88
Malayan Banking Berhad, 182
Malaysian Mining Corporation, 185
managing agents, see agency houses
Marine Midland Bank, 18
Markwald, A., 130, 132
Marwari community, 19, 27
Mason, D. K., 129
Matchbox toys, 30
Matheson, Hugh, 39
Mercantile Bank of India (until 1892 Chartered Mercantile Bank of India, London & China; after 1958 Mercantile Bank Ltd), 12–13, 18, 95, 106, 110, 132, 160–1, 176–8, 183, 223
Mercedes Benz, 238
Mersey, 2nd Viscount, 23
Mesopotamia Persia Company (Mespers), 34, 41, 43, 51
Metal Box, 102, 234
Metropolitan Vickers Electrical Company, 54, 85–6
Mexico, 130, 195
Midland Bank, 30
Miles, Edward, 149–54
Ministry of International Trade and Industry (Japan) (MITI), 235–6, 238, 241
Ministry of Transport (Britain), 239
Minsheng Company, 209

Index 299

Mitchell Cotts, 60
Mitsubishi, 222, 224
Mitsui, 141, 221–2, 224–5, 233, 234
Mobil Oil, 6
Morrison of Lambeth, Lord, 55
Moscow Narodny Bank, 83
Mossadeq, Mohammed, 24, 46–7, 56, 58
motor car industry, 172, 230, 233, 235–6, 238
Mowlem civil engineers, 53, 60
multinationals, 1, 16, 18, 21, 33, 46, 96, 100–5, 111, 113–14, 204, 216, 225–7, 230–4, 237–8, 240, 243, 244
Myddleton Investments, 102

Nanyang Brothers, 209
National Bank of China, 141
National Bank of India, 106
nationalisation, 18, 33, 51
Netherlands, 104, 128, 174
New Economic Policy (Malaysia), 184
New Oriental Bank Corporation, see Oriental Bank Corporation
New Zealand, 150, 165, 205
Newly Industrialising Countries (NICs), 7, 26, 28, 157
Nigeria, 169
Nihon Electric Company, 225
Nippon Glaxo Ltd, 242
Nippophone Company, 230
Nissan Motor Company, 233, 235–6
Nisshin Kisen Kaisha, 206
Nobel's Explosives Company, 225–6
North German Lloyd Steamship Company, 131
Northern Bank of Scotland, 132
Nuttall Mowlem, 53

Oil Fields Finance Corporation, 73
oil industry, 6, 10–11, 15, 24, 25, 31, 36–7, 46–9, 55–6, 62, 68, 72–4, 82–5, 116, 126, 170–1, 182, 186, 222, 232, 238
Okura, Baron, 235
Okura, Kiachiro, 223
opium, 3, 39, 129, 141, 147, 165, 168, 191, 192, 193
Oriental Bank Corporation (reconstructed in 1884 as New Oriental Bank Corporation), 12, 13, 36, 132, 160, 223–4
Oriental Carpet Manufacturers Company, 38–9, 65
Oriental Hotel (Bangkok), 156
Osaka Oxygen Company, 237
Osaka Spinning Company, 221
Ottoman Bank, 50

Overend and Gurney Bank, 223
Overseas Chinese Banking Corporation, 177
Overseas Consultants Inc., 54
oyatoi (hired menials), 220–1, 224

Pahang Consolidated Company, 166
Pahlavi Foundation, 62
Paish, Sir George, 4
Pakistan, 7, 8, 112
Palfreyman, A. W. 151, 153
palm industry, 5, 174–5, 179
Panama, 104
Pao, Sir Y. K., 19
Parr's Bank, 224
Parry & Company, 102
Parson Turbine Company, 226
Patiño, Simon, 169
Patons & Baldwin, 204, 213
Pekin Syndicate, 197–8, 201
Peninsula & Oriental Steamship Company, 10
pepper, 141, 156, 169, 173, 179
Pernas, 184–6
Perry, Commodore Matthew, 129
Persian Railways Syndicate, 39, 43
Persian Transport Company, 36, 39, 43
Petroleum & Trading Company, 73
pharmaceuticals industry, 51, 101, 169, 182, 236–7, 242
Philippines, 8, 190
Pickenpack Thies, 130, 132
Platt Brothers of Oldham, 221
Poland, 91
Polyspinners Ltd, 88–9
portfolio investment, 7, 9, 101, 155
Portugal, 70, 128

Queensberry, 9th Marquess of, 59

Raffles, Sir Stamford, 3, 129, 159–60
railways, 4, 5, 35–6, 39, 53, 77, 94, 96, 106, 114–15, 124–7, 134, 136, 148, 154, 156, 198–200, 225, 230
Ralli and Angelestou, 34
Rama IV (Mongkut), King of Siam, 129, 138
Ramsay, Sir William, 23
Razaleigh, Tunku, 184
Reagan, Ronald, 91
Renong Dredging Company, 152
Reserve Bank of India, 107, 114
Reuter, Baron Julius de, 35, 44
Revelstoke, 2nd Baron, 226
Reza Khan, 23, 33, 45, 49, 51, 53, 57
Ridder Mining Corporation, 75
Rising Sun Petroleum Company, 222

300 *Index*

Ronpibon Extended Company, 152
Rootes, 1st Baron, 59
Rothschild, N. M., 224
Rowntree, 233
Royal Bank of Scotland, 15, 30
Royal Dutch Shell, *see* Shell Group
rubber industry, 5, 24, 26, 31, 122, 149, 163–4, 171–5, 177, 179, 225
Russell & Company, 130
Russia, 2, 4, 23, 31, 33–4, 40, 44–5, 68–91, 192, 195, 226
Russia Company, 70
Russian General Oil Corporation, 72
Russian Petroleum Company, 73
Russian United Petroleum Company, 73
Russo-Asiatic Corporation, 75–6, 82, 84
Russo-Chinese Bank, 223
Ryrie, John, 140

S. Moutrie & Company, 206
S. P. Goodale & Company, 129
Sale & Company, 85
Salisbury, 3rd Marquess of, 124
Samuel and Company, 42–3
sapphires, 120
Sarawak, 159–60, 170–1, 173
Sassoon, David & Company, 15, 34, 39
Saudi Arabia, 47
Schmidt, Remi, 130
Scott, Herbert George, 152
Scott, Thomas, 152
Scottish capital and migrants, 9, 120, 219
Selangor Rubber Company, 172
Sempill, 19th Baron, 220, 289
Shell Group (officially the Royal Dutch Petroleum and Shell Transport and Trading Company), 10–11, 24, 48, 60, 72–3, 85, 170–1, 182, 186, 205, 236
Shibaura Electric Company, 225
Shin Nihon Jitsugyo, 242
Shinwell, Lord, 55
shipping companies, 33, 34, 51, 57, 106, 111, 126, 131, 155, 160, 203, 207, 216, 222, 224, 234, 239, 244
Siam Commercial Bank, 121
Siam Forest Company (Anglo-Siam Corporation after 1917), 135, 139–43, 145–6
Siamese Tin Syndicate, 152, 156
Siberian Supply Company, 82
Siemens, 35, 206
Siemssen & Company, 206
silk, 221–2
silver, 13, 38, 75, 108
Sime Darby, 172, 176, 179–80, 185–6
Simon Carves & Company, 89

Simons, Williams & Company, 151
Singapore, 7, 8, 21, 26, 129, 157, 159–61, 181–2, 216
Sissert Company, 75
Slade, Herbert, 144
Slater Walker, 184
Socfin, 174
Société des Mines d'Etain de Perak, 164
South Korea, 8, 26, 28
South Manchuria Railway, 198
South Russia Banking Agency, 12
Spies Petroleum Company, 74
Standard Chartered Bank, 30, 182
Standard Oil Company, 205, 214
Steel Brothers & Company, 11
Stevenson, 1st Baron, 173–4
Straits Steamship Company, 150
Straits Trading Company, 150, 167, 169
Suez Canal, 109, 160
sugar, 115, 121, 130, 141, 196, 214
Sumatra, 174
Sumitomo Bank, 224
Sumitomo Rubber Industries, 237, 242
Sweden, 104
Swettenham, Sir Frank, 161–3
Switzerland, 53, 104
Sze Hai Tong Bank, 121

Taikoo Sugar Refinery, 196, 215
Taiwan, 8, 26, 28, 190
Tanalyk Corporation, 75
tariffs, 20, 28, 62, 101, 107, 116, 128, 191, 204
Tate & Lyle Sugar Company, 62
tea, 4, 20, 99, 109, 115, 191, 192
teak industry, 26, 121–2, 126, 128, 132–46, 160
technology transfer, 1, 19, 26–7, 30, 63–4, 85–6, 89, 150, 154, 165, 187, 217, 221, 226, 234, 235–6, 238, 244
telegraphs, 34–5, 62
Texaco Oil, 205
textiles, 3, 5, 28, 39, 70, 97, 100, 115, 191, 203–4, 215, 225–6, 228, 232
Thailand, 8, 28, 1217–56, 170, 174
Thatcher, Margaret, 241
tin, 5, 31, 120–2, 127–30, 146–54, 161–71, 17–8, 184–5
Tinplate Company of India, 102
tobacco, 180, 195–6, 205–6, 235
Tobacco Corporation, 42
Tongkah Harbour Dredging Company, 154
Toyota Motors, 230, 233, 236
Transvaal, 11, 164
Treasury, 56, 210
Tribeni Tissues, 102

Index 301

Tronoh group, 185
Tube Investments, 102
Turkey, 70
Turner Newall, 102

Unilever, 101–2, 179, 204, 211
Union Bank of Australia, 223
Union Cold Storage Company, 86
United Malayan Banking Corporation, 182
United States of America, 5, 7, 14, 58, 60, 63, 70, 77–8, 83, 85, 104, 105, 120, 128, 129, 163, 168–9, 174, 180, 182, 199, 222, 225, 240–1
United Steel Companies, 53
Ural-Caucasus Corporation, 73
Urquhart, Leslie, 81–2, 84
Urquhart, Sir Robert, 212–13

Venezuela, 47
Vestey, 1st Baron, 86
Vickers Ltd, 43, 81–2, 85, 87, 225, 234, 244
Vossuq od-Douleh, 44

War Office, 82–3
Wavell, 1st Earl, 23
Wellcome Foundation, 51
Wellesley, Sir Victor, 23–4
Western Electric Company, 225
Westminster Bank, 224, 230
Wheelock Marden, 19
Whiteaway Laidlaw, 207
Wilkins, Mira, 9, 234, 238
Williams, Harvey & Company, 169
Wonckhaus & Company, 57
Wycon Services, 88–9

Yarrow Shipbuilding Company, 54
Yokohama Specie Bank, 111, 224, 230
Yongli Company, 208–9
Yuan Shikai, 198
Yule, Sir David, 24
Yunnan Railway, 198

zaibatsu, 222
Ziegler & Company, 34, 38–9
Zimbabwe, 24

For EU product safety concerns, contact us at Calle de José Abascal, 56–1°, 28003 Madrid, Spain or eugpsr@cambridge.org.

www.ingramcontent.com/pod-product-compliance
Ingram Content Group UK Ltd.
Pitfield, Milton Keynes, MK11 3LW, UK
UKHW010859060825
461487UK00012B/1225